Court Interpreters and Fair Trials

John Henry Dingfelder Stone

Court Interpreters and Fair Trials

palgrave
macmillan

John Henry Dingfelder Stone
Hochschule Rhein-Waal
Rhine-Waal University of Applied Science
Kleve, Germany

ISBN 978-3-030-09210-8 ISBN 978-3-319-75355-3 (eBook)
https://doi.org/10.1007/978-3-319-75355-3

Softcover re-print of the Hardcover 1st edition 2018

Cover credit: Laura Catlin / EyeEm

Printed on acid-free paper

This Palgrave Macmillan imprint is published by the registered company Springer International Publishing AG part of Springer Nature.
The registered company address is: Gewerbestrasse 11, 6330 Cham, Switzerland

This book is dedicated to MDS, Juju and the Dude, for changing my life.

Preface

I worked as a trial prosecutor in Victoria, Texas for a few years when I was fresh out of law school. The location of the town meant that a number of our defendants (and witnesses) spoke only Spanish and were reliant on court-appointed interpreters throughout the judicial process. In practice, this meant that we used bilingual defense attorneys, court clerks, or even one of our own legal assistants from the District Attorney's Office. It never occurred to me at the time that any of these defendants received anything less than a fair proceeding using one of our "interpreters".

After a few more years working as an appellate prosecutor, I got married, moved to Germany and began teaching part-time at the Johannes Gutenberg-Universität Mainz's Faculty of Translation Studies, Linguistics and Cultural Studies in Germersheim. As coincidence would have it, this was one of the preeminent training facilities for interpreters in the world and my interactions with the academic staff there fatally undermined every assumption I had made as a prosecutor about courtroom interpreting. In my experience, most attorneys (myself included) and judges were blithely unaware of the impact that court interpreters can have on criminal trials. Likewise, the court interpreters I'd met, despite some research in the area by interpreting studies scholars, largely failed to understand how their standard practices often undermined the actual legal proceedings they were employed to enable. The more I learned about the interpreting process, the more I began to reflect on its fair trial implications.

When I later took a Research Fellow position at the Max Planck Institute for Comparative Public Law and International Law in Heidelberg, I started to dig into these issues. Granted access to a world-class library and surrounded by some of the brightest legal minds in Europe, what started as a simple research project in my spare time turned into a doctoral dissertation which has now spawned a book. I suffer no illusions that it will solve any of the issues that arise from using court interpreters in criminal proceedings. However, I hope that in its own small way it can bridge the gap between the legal profession and interpreters and open their eyes to an issue they have both been content to ignore for far too long.

Along the way I have been helped by a number of people whom I can never truly thank properly. Prof. Dr. Dr. h.c. Rüdiger Wolfrum was the ideal doctoral supervisor, allowing me the freedom to work at my own pace and in my own manner. Thanks as well to the members of my doctoral committee at the University of Hamburg, Prof. Dr. Dr. h.c. Jürgen Basedow and Prof. Dr. Peter Mankowski, for their support. My former colleagues in Germersheim at the Faculty of Translation Studies, Linguistics and Cultural Studies provided continual guidance and material above and beyond what was strictly necessary. I am similarly indebted to my former co-workers at both the Max Planck Institute for Comparative Public Law and International Law and the Max Planck Foundation for International Peace and the Rule of Law. Ali Zakouri and the great staff at the Max Planck Library deserve specific mention here for their assistance with my research. Dr. Dominik Zimmerman, Dr. Sigrid Mehring, and Dr. Daniel Heilmann each lived through the ups and downs of my research, reading drafts and offering insightful comments without which this book would be much the poorer. Dr. Kathrin Scherr was the best boss I could have had, equal parts understanding and demanding, and her contribution to this book is beyond measure. Special thanks goes as well to Dr. Johann-Christoph Woltag, who was always there when I needed him, whether that meant reading a chapter or commiserating over a beer.

On a more personal note, I am deeply thankful to my Mom and Dad for loving me enough to let me find my own path in the world, even if that took me across the Atlantic. It is a sacrifice I never truly appreciated until I became a parent myself. Finally, this book would not have been possible without the unwavering support and encouragement of my wife. As an interpreter and scholar herself, she has been a constant resource as to her profession and a necessary foil relentlessly challenging my misguided prosecutorial arrogance. That she does not agree with everything I've written about her profession not only makes her continued support even more incredible, but also absolves her of any mistakes I have made throughout this book.

Kleve, Germany John Henry Dingfelder Stone

Contents

1 Introduction 1
1 An Unchallenged Assumption 1
2 Objectives of the Book 2
3 Structure of the Study 4
4 Conclusion 5
Bibliography 6

2 The Right to an Interpreter 9
1 Introduction 9
2 The Source of a Right to an Interpreter Under International Law 10
3 The Purpose of the Right to an Interpreter 11
4 The Appointment of a Court Interpreter 14
4.1 Identity of Legitimate Claimants 14
4.2 The Timing of the Appointment 16
4.3 Language Competence 17
5 The Competence of the Interpreter 20
5.1 Defining the "Competence" of a Court Interpreter 21
5.2 The Difficulties in Enforcing Competency Standards 24
6 Practical Considerations 25
6.1 Multiple Interpreters 25

6.2 The Extent of the Interpretation 28
6.3 Translation 29
6.4 A "Free" Interpreter 32
7 Appellate Oversight of the Right to a Court Interpreter 33
7.1 Allegedly Inadequate Interpretation 34
7.2 Failure to Appoint a Court Interpreter 35
7.3 Practical Considerations in the Appellate Sphere 39
7.4 The End Outcome 42
8 Conclusion 42
Bibliography 44

3 Courtroom Interpreting 53
1 Introduction 53
2 General Overview of Courtroom Interpreting 55
2.1 Introduction 55
2.2 The Different Interpreting Techniques Used in the Courtroom 56
2.3 How the Different Techniques Are Used in the Courtroom 59
2.4 Basic Expectations of the Court Interpreter 64
3 A Theoretical Overview of Courtroom Interpreting: The Effort Model 76
3.1 Introduction 76
3.2 Cognitive Capacity and the Tightrope Theory 77
3.3 The Efforts 79
3.4 The Effort Models of Interpreting 84
3.5 Improving or Managing Cognitive Capacity 89
4 Conclusion 98
Bibliography 99

4 The Right to a Fair Trial 103
1 Introduction 103
2 General Overview of the Right to a Fair Trial Under International Law 105
3 Analysis of the Individual Rights 108
3.1 Equality Before the Court (Article 14 [1]) 108
3.2 Right to Adversarial Proceedings (Article 14 [1]) 112

3.3 Right to an Oral Hearing (Article 14 Generally) 114
3.4 Right to Be Informed of the Charge (Article 14 [3] [a]) 116
3.5 Right to Adequate Time and Facilities to Prepare a Defense (Article 14 [3] [b]) 118
3.6 Right to Be Tried Without Undue Delay (Article 14 [3] [c]) 123
3.7 Right to Be Present at Trial (Article 14 [3] [d]) 131
3.8 Right to Counsel (Article 14 [3] [d]) 133
3.9 Right to Examine Witnesses (Article 14 [3] [e]) 139
3.10 Right to Appeal (Article 14 [5]) 145
3.11 Right to Overall Fairness in the Proceedings (Article 14 Generally) 149
4 Conclusion 151
Bibliography 153

5 Interpreter Error and Its Implications 159
1 Introduction 159
2 Interpreter-Based Problems 160
2.1 Introduction 160
2.2 Pragmatic Versus Verbatim Debate from the Legal Perspective 161
2.3 Stepping Outside the Neutral Role 167
2.4 Issues of Control 180
2.5 Coping Strategies 184
2.6 Conclusion 190
3 Language-Based Problems 190
3.1 Introduction 190
3.2 Content Problems 191
3.3 Style Problems 215
3.4 Conclusion 240
Bibliography 241

6 Systemic Issues 247
1 Introduction 247
2 Fatigue 247
2.1 Overview 247
2.2 Implications of Fatigue 249

3 Lack of Preparation Time and Documents 249
3.1 Overview 249
3.2 Implications of the Lack of Preparation Time and Documents 250
4 Poor Working Conditions 252
4.1 Overview 252
4.2 Implications of Poor Working Conditions 254
5 The Overall Level of Court Interpreters 255
5.1 Introduction 255
5.2 The Reality of the Interpreting Market 257
5.3 Implications of the Overall Level of Court Interpreters 261
5.4 Conclusion 263
6 Lack of Impartiality 264
6.1 Overview 264
6.2 Actual and Perceived Bias 264
6.3 Implications of Actual and Perceived Bias 266
7 Conclusion 268
Bibliography 269

7 **Analysis** 275
1 Introduction 275
2 Rights Related to the Production of Evidence 276
2.1 Introduction 276
2.2 The Common Occurrence of Interpreter Error 276
2.3 The Legal Implications of Interpreter Error on the Production of Evidence 280
2.4 Conclusion 284
3 Rights Related to the Understanding of Evidence 284
3.1 Introduction 284
3.2 The Common Occurrence of Interpreter Error 285
3.3 The Legal Implications of Interpreter Error on the Understanding of Evidence 286
3.4 Conclusion 288
4 Rights Unrelated to Evidence 289
4.1 Introduction 289
4.2 Equality Before the Court 289

4.3 Right to Be Tried Without Undue Delay 292
4.4 Right to Counsel 294
4.5 Right to an Interpreter 296
4.6 Right to Appeal 297
4.7 Conclusion 299
5 Conclusion and Reflections on Overall Fairness 299
5.1 The Individual Fair Trial Rights 299
5.2 The Right to Overall Fairness 302
5.3 Conclusion 303
Bibliography 304

8 Conclusions and Proposals 309
1 Introduction 309
2 Better Informed Courtroom Actors 311
2.1 Overview 311
2.2 Better Working Conditions 311
2.3 Reduction in Problematic Actions 312
2.4 Revised Judicial Control Over Problematic Actions 312
2.5 Combating Fatigue 314
2.6 Better Appointment Procedures 315
2.7 Conclusion 315
3 Better Court Interpreters 315
3.1 Increased Quantity and Quality of Court Interpreter Training 316
3.2 Increase in the Remuneration of Court Interpreters 317
3.3 Mandatory Certification Standards 319
3.4 Remote Video Interpreting 320
3.5 Conclusion 322
4 Better Oversight 323
4.1 Team Interpreting 323
4.2 Foreign Language Record 324
4.3 Conclusion 326
5 Final Thoughts 326
Bibliography 328

Index 333

1

Introduction

1 An Unchallenged Assumption

In the past few decades, the increased rates of international trade, travel and migration have led to a rising number of criminal defendants and courtroom participants who do not speak the language of the court in which they find themselves. Such individuals present numerous problems for courts, mainly because criminal justice systems, with some notable exceptions, are monolingual in nature and ill-equipped to handle multilingual proceedings. The traditional solution to any courtroom linguistic problems has been the appointment of a court interpreter, or, more aptly described, the appointment of a multilingual individual to interpret, as it is not uncommon for unqualified and untrained individuals to be drafted into service by the court (Stern 2011, p. 339; see also Chap. 6). This is even more true when the language in question is itself uncommon in the area. Once appointed, court interpreters have usually been left alone by courts to do their job with little oversight. Courtroom participants primarily desire to communicate across any language barriers and they are generally pleased when the interpreter allows them to do so. Removal of the language barrier permits the court to revert back to its

J. H. Dingfelder Stone, *Court Interpreters and Fair Trials*,
https://doi.org/10.1007/978-3-319-75355-3_1

innate monolingual nature under the assumption that a comparable fair trial can be achieved through the simple addition of an interpreter. But what if this narrative is an illusion, an overestimation of the corrective capacity of court interpreters?

The difficulty with this narrative is that the utilization of a court interpreter comes at a price. Not all interpreters are created equal, and even the best interpreters are not automatic machines capable of flawless performance at all times. Interpreters exercise judgment, alter information, transform speech styles, and generally make a multitude of undetected alterations that can and do influence the trustworthiness of a criminal trial. Even something so apparently trivial as the accent of the interpreter can have an impact on the proceedings: French Canadian jurors view witnesses who testify through a European French interpreter more favorably than those who are interpreted by one who speaks Canadian French (Berk-Seligson 1990, p. 146). The shortcomings of court interpretation have long been known to the interpreting community, but have received little acknowledgement from legal scholars. This lack of awareness has led to a scarcity of scholarly attention concerning the legal effects of court interpretation within the criminal justice system, which in turn has allowed courts to operate under the assumption that the mere appointment of an interpreter is a sufficiently corrective measure.

2 Objectives of the Book

This book tests this assumption by assessing the impact of court interpreters on the integrity of the right to a fair trial under international law. Specifically, it analyzes a broad range of examples showing the various different manners by which an interpreter can influence a criminal proceeding. Alterations of both information content and speech style are considered, as are the numerous systemic issues that arise from the appointment of a court interpreter. These factors are evaluated to determine the extent to which they may negatively affect an accused's right to a fair trial. Based upon this analysis, suggestions as to how to further safeguard the right to a fair trial in this particular context are presented.

With respect to fair trial rights, the focus of the study is on the fairness of criminal proceedings at the national level, as measured against international standards. Given that Article 14 of the International Covenant on Civil and Political Rights ('ICCPR') is generally accepted as customary international law (if not *jus cogens*) (Boas et al. 2011, p. 12; Boas 2010, pp. 329–330; Robinson 2009, pp. 6–7, 11; Orakhelashvili 2006, p. 60; Turner 2005, p. 22), the fair trial rights contained therein are used as benchmark standards. In order to gain a fuller understanding of the intricacies of these rights, it is occasionally necessary to consult alternate sources of international law that contain similar wording. In particular, Article 6 European Convention for the Protection of Human Rights and Fundamental Freedoms ('ECHR') proves useful, since it contains language that is nearly identical to Article 14 ICCPR. As such, although certainly not conclusive, interpretations by the European Court of Human Rights ('ECtHR') of the ECHR fair trial rights are at worst persuasive authority as to the meaning of the ICCPR rights (Nowak 2005, p. 307; McGoldrick 1994, p. 438).

While such cross-fertilization of legal standards is a normal and useful occurrence, (de Zayas 1997, p. 696), only minimal consideration is given to the caselaw of the international criminal tribunals (the International Criminal Court ['ICC']; the International Criminal Tribunal for the Former Yugoslavia ['ICTY']; the International Criminal Tribunal for Rwanda ['ICTR']), specifically because the interpretation procedures exhibited in these courts are very different from those used in domestic proceedings and are not sufficiently analogous to allow useful comparatives. Furthermore, while it is true that national courts contribute considerably to the interpretation of international treaties such as the ICCPR, the sheer volume of material arising from these courts makes their consultation well-beyond the scope of this book. As such, even though the focus is on fair trial standards as applied in domestic criminal proceedings, no particular jurisdiction is specifically targeted or discussed, though the English-language nature of the work naturally leads to a healthy inclusion of considerations familiar to common law jurisdictions.

3 Structure of the Study

Following upon this introduction, Chap. 2 discusses the legal right to an interpreter under international law, since one cannot fully understand how courtroom interpreters affect an accused's right to a fair trial without first understanding the circumstances which mandate the appointment of an interpreter. Furthermore, many of the legal and practical issues that arise from interpreter performance are well-illustrated by a detailed examination of an accused's right to an interpreter. Thus, a thorough treatment of the subject serves as an excellent introduction to the overall topic. Chapter 3 provides a general introduction to the mechanics of courtroom interpreting. Legal practitioners often fail to appreciate the complexity and ambiguity of the task that interpreters perform. However, by focusing on the theoretical and practical aspects of courtroom interpreting, this Chapter seeks to demystify the interpreting process for a legal audience. This facilitates a better understanding of the unseen complications that interpreters cause throughout legal proceedings.

Chapter 4 focuses on explaining the different components of the right to a fair trial as set out in Article 14 ICCPR. The discussion is not comprehensive, though, as the use of interpreters does not impact every aspect of every fair trial right. Rather, only those rights (and the specific facets of those rights) that are affected are examined. Included in this Chapter is a short explanation as to the relationship between court interpreters and the specific rights discussed. Having clarified the role of interpreters in the courtroom, and the particular fair trial rights at stake, Chap. 5 presents and analyzes the multitude of problems created by the usage of court interpreters in criminal proceedings, as well as their possible impacts on the right to a fair trial. These complications are divided into two groups: those related to conscious decisions on the part of the interpreter and those that arise as an unintentional side-effect from the inherent difficulty of the interpreting process itself. Following upon this discussion, Chap. 6 examines the numerous systemic issues associated with court interpreters, such as fatigue, that likewise complicate criminal proceedings. These aspects are analyzed for their possible effects on an accused's right to a fair trial.

The role of Chap. 7 within the study is to bring all of these disparate strands of information together in one final analysis in order to assess the overall impact of court interpreters on the right to a fair trial. Emphasis is not only placed upon the individual fair trial rights as discussed in Chap. 4, but also on the overall fairness of the proceeding. A final conclusion sets out a series of proposals meant to decrease the impact court interpreters have on criminal proceedings.

4 Conclusion

Any academic work concerning interpreting necessarily involves the usage of examples in multiple languages. Some care has been taken, where such instances occur, to render these into English for the casual reader. However, the fact that this study is written in English, and is primarily concerned with English language examples, also necessarily means that some of the interpreter errors and linguistic distortions that it highlights may appear specific to that language and not easily transportable to other linguistic contexts. An example is the common usage of so-called false friends by interpreters (de Jongh 1992, p. 77). However, while the specific false friends discussed in the text may be particular to a certain language combination (such as "actually"-"*aktuell*" in English-German), the practice of mistakenly using such apparently (but falsely) equivalent terms is common to interpreters working in nearly every language combination. As such, even though the discussion may appear bound to the particularities of English, the practice is, in most instances, applicable to interpreters who work in other languages as well. Regardless, the intent of the study is not to detail every possible interpreter error in every language combination in the world; this is an obviously absurd task. Rather, it is to assess the myriad ways that court interpreters may have an impact on the right to a fair trial by analyzing those interpreter actions and errors that appear most consequential and most prevalent. For this task, it is sufficient to confine the study to a single "home" language.

In addition, some explanation must be given with respect to certain choices of phrasing and vocabulary that have been made throughout the book. To increase the readability of the text and to reduce unnecessary repetition, the terms "court interpreter" and "courtroom interpreter" have been used interchangeably. Likewise, although "to translate" is normally restricted to the context of written texts, while "to interpret" generally involves spoken words, here each of these has also been used, unless otherwise specifically noted, as generic terms meaning the alteration of words from one language to another. However, the designations "translator" and "interpreter" are not used interchangeably, but rather remain restricted to their specific contexts (written and oral, respectively). Another linguistic choice concerns the gender of certain courtroom participants: an accused is always referred to as a male, while a court interpreter is continually referred to as a female. Neither of these assumptions is meant as a slight to either sex, but rather the choice reflects the common reality of criminal proceedings and reduces unnecessary linguistic confusion arising from an overabundance of identical pronouns. The other, less-mentioned, courtroom participants are generally identified in the plural ("they").

Bibliography

Berk-Seligson, S. (1990). *The Bilingual Courtroom: Court Interpreters in the Judicial Process*. Chicago: University of Chicago Press.

Boas, G. (2010). War Crimes Prosecution in Australia and Other Common Law Countries: Some Observations. *Criminal Law Forum, 21*(2), 313–330.

Boas, G., Bischoff, J. L., Reid, N. L., & Taylor, B. D., III. (2011). *International Criminal Procedure*. Cambridge: Cambridge University Press.

de Jongh, E. (1992). *An Introduction to Court Interpreting: Theory & Practice*. Lanham: University Press of America.

de Zayas, A. (1997). The United Nations and the Guarantees of a Fair Trial in the International Covenant on Civil and Political Rights and the Convention Against Torture and Other Cruel, Inhuman or Degrading Treatment or Punishment. In D. Weissbrodt & R. Wolfrum (Eds.), *The Right to a Fair Trial* (pp. 669–696). Berlin: Springer.

McGoldrick, D. (1994). *The Human Rights Committee: Its Role in the Development of the International Covenant on Civil and Political Rights*. Oxford: Clarendon Press.

Nowak, M. (2005). *U.N. Covenant on Civil and Political Rights: CCPR Commentary* (2nd ed.). Kehl: Engel.
Orakhelashvili, A. (2006). *Peremptory Norms in International Law*. Oxford: Oxford University Press.
Robinson, P. (2009). The Right to a Fair Trial in International Law, with Specific Reference to the Work of the ICTY. *Berkeley Journal of International Law Publicist, 3*, 1–11.
Stern, L. (2011). Courtroom Interpreting. In K. Malmkjær & K. Windle (Eds.), *The Oxford Handbook of Translation Studies* (pp. 325–342). Oxford: Oxford University Press.
Turner, J. I. (2005). Nationalizing International Criminal Law. *Stanford Journal of International Law, 41*, 1–51.

2

The Right to an Interpreter

1 Introduction

When analyzing the possible impact of court interpreters on the right to a fair trial under international law, the logical starting point is an examination of the accused's right to an interpreter. While not every court interpreter is assigned to a criminal proceeding pursuant to this right, as will be seen in the following Chapters, many of the general standards to which court interpreters are held originate from the cases and scholarly discussions associated with this right. Additionally, many of the complications presented by the use of court interpreters in criminal proceedings are likewise foreshadowed by a detailed examination of this right. As such, gaining a greater understanding of the right to an interpreter at this early stage will pay dividends in subsequent Chapters.

J. H. Dingfelder Stone, *Court Interpreters and Fair Trials*,
https://doi.org/10.1007/978-3-319-75355-3_2

2 The Source of a Right to an Interpreter Under International Law

The explicit right to an interpreter is found in Article 14 (3) (f) ICCPR, which states that a criminal defendant shall be entitled to "have the free assistance of an interpreter if he cannot understand or speak the language used in court." The fair trial rights guaranteed in Article 14 ICCPR are considered to be customary international law (Boas et al. 2011, p. 12; Boas 2010, pp. 329–330; Robinson 2009, pp. 6–7, 11; Orakhelashvili 2006, p. 60; Turner 2005, p. 22). Unfortunately, accepting Article 14 (3) (f) ICCPR as the definitive statement of the right to an interpreter isn't overly helpful when it comes to understanding what exactly the right entails. Despite its overwhelming acceptance by the international community, Article 14 (3) (f) has yet to be fleshed out by the Human Rights Committee ('HRC'). Thus, it is helpful in many instances to refer to the more developed caselaw of the ECtHR concerning its interpretation of the Article 6 (3) (e) ECHR right to an interpreter, which uses language identical to that employed in Article 14 (3) (f) ICCPR (see also Nowak 2005, p. 343). Within reason, reference can also be made to the meanings ascribed to these provisions by selected domestic courts, given that national level courts play a key role in the interpretation and implementation of international treaties and norms (Trechsel 2005, p. 6).

Furthermore, in addition to the explicit Article 14 (3) (f) right, there also arguably exists a secondary right to an interpreter arising from the various specific fair trial guarantees set out in Article 14. In this context, it must be remembered that the subsections of Article 14 (3) are explicitly minimum guarantees; as such, higher levels of protection may occasionally be necessary to ensure a fair trial (HRC General Comment No. 13). Moreover, since the right to an interpreter is, at its core, a part of the right to a fair trial and is meant to achieve that overarching purpose, there may exist situations where Article 14 (3) (f) ICCPR does not automatically grant an interpreter, but an interpreter is nonetheless necessary to fully realize the right to a fair trial. For instance, where an accused wishes to call a foreign-language witness to testify on his behalf, his right to call and examine that witness under Article 14 (3) (e) may require the appointment of a court interpreter.

Likewise, fulfillment of the overall general right to a fair trial may also necessitate the use of a court interpreter (Trechsel 2005, p. 335). As such, in determining the right to an interpreter under international law, one must look beyond the specific textual grant appearing in Article 14 (3) (f) ICCPR, and evaluate the overall necessities of a fair trial as well. In this instance, fair trial rights under customary international law may be more expansive than those protected by Article 14 ICCPR, and the Article 14 fair trial rights do not act as a limitation on that customary right.

3 The Purpose of the Right to an Interpreter

In order to determine the actual boundaries and protections provided by the right to a court interpreter under the ICCPR, it is helpful to understand what purpose the right serves within the fair trial framework. It is a given that, as a formal part of the right to a fair trial, the right to an interpreter is meant to ensure the fulfillment of that overall goal. However, the concept of a fair trial is rather broad and encompasses a variety of different underlying rights, not all of which are effectively advanced by the right to an interpreter. There are specific guarantees within the framework that are enabled by the right to an interpreter: namely, those rights comprising the so-called "right of defense" and considerations of equality.

In General Comment No. 13, the HRC stated that the right to an interpreter is meant to alleviate language difficulties which "may constitute a major obstacle to the right of defence" (§13). As such, it can be said that the right to an interpreter, itself, is meant to ensure that the right of defense is effectively exercised. This right can be seen as encompassing various different guarantees (Nowak 2005 pp. 337–338). Of these, from the standpoint of interpreting at least, it is perhaps the right to be present at, and participate in, one's own trial that is most obviously implicated. As Nowak has asserted, under the right to defense (Article 14 [3] [d] ICCPR), "all persons charged with a criminal offense have a primary, unrestricted right to be present at the trial and to defend themselves" (2005, p. 339). To be present at one's own trial is not satisfied simply by the physical presence of the defendant, rather the defendant must be able to understand the proceedings (Schabas 2007, p. 288). This necessity has been affirmed by the ECtHR in the *Kamasinski* case (*Kamasinski v. Austria* [ECtHR 1989] §§82–83). In this respect, scholars often speak of a defendant's "linguistic presence" (de Jongh 2008, p. 21; Pantoga 1999, p. 619; Mikkelson 1998b; González et al. 1991, pp. 49–50). But the presence of the defendant, linguistically and physically, is not enough to ensure a fair trial; the defendant must be able to participate in his own defense (Nowak 2005, p. 339; *Kamasinski v. Austria* [ECtHR 1989] §§82–83; *Lagerblom v. Sweden* [ECtHR 2003] §49). In this regard, where the defendant is not able to effectively communicate with the court or his counsel, the court interpreter is essential as a means of allowing the defendant to participate in his own defense (Trechsel 2005, p. 328). Thus, it can be asserted that the right to an interpreter is also essential in guaranteeing the fulfillment of the rights to both have (Article 14 [3] [d]) and communicate (Article 14 [3] [b]) with legal counsel as well.

The second purpose of the right to an interpreter is to uphold the notion of equality: Article 14 (1) ICCPR specifically guarantees that "all persons shall be equal before the courts and tribunals." This has been interpreted to guarantee the linguistic equality of a defendant vis-à-vis any other defendant before the court on similar charges (HRC General Comment No. 13, §14). The ECtHR has certainly interpreted the ECHR's nearly identical right to an interpreter provision in this manner, stating that the purpose of the right was to attenuate the "disadvantages that an accused who does not understand or speak the language used in court suffers as compared with an accused who is familiar with that language" (*Luedicke, Belkacem and Koç v. Germany* [ECtHR 1978] §42). The concept of equality also extends to the defendant's linguistic equality vis-à-vis the prosecutor, thus bringing the principle of the equality of arms into consideration.[1] Merrills and Robertson (2001) have actually advanced the notion of equality (both of arms and in the sense of dis-

[1] The equality of arms, while not specifically guaranteed in the ICCPR, has been recognized by the HRC as a part of the ICCPR fair trial framework (*Guesdon v. France* [HRC 1990] §10.2; *Barzhig v. France* [HRC 1991] §5.5).

crimination with respect to other defendants) as the principle purpose behind the design of the right to a court interpreter (p. 131).

However, viewing the right to an interpreter as a solution to inequality is not without its critics. Trechsel (2005) has argued that the right is meant to "constitute the key which opens the door of communication between the accused and the judge" and any elimination of inequality is only a secondary effect (p. 329). This criticism, while perhaps accurate with respect to civil law jurisdictions that center heavily on the actions of the judge as an investigating and inquisitorial authority at trial, is not convincing with respect to common law jurisdictions, which adhere to an adversarial principle and place little emphasis on communication between the judge and defendant (Spencer 2005, pp. 25–26). Moreover, even if one assumes that the primary purpose of the provision is indeed to establish communication between the court and the defendant, then one must ask why such communication is necessary. One possible answer is that otherwise the defendant's position before the court would not be equal vis-à-vis the prosecutor or other similarly situated defendants. Thus, even if Trechsel is correct, his assertion does little to undermine the concept of equality as a driving purpose behind the right to an interpreter.

When seeking to determine the actual legal boundaries of the right to an interpreter, as will be done shortly, awareness of these underlying purposes behind the right is of paramount importance. Knowing what the right is meant to accomplish, and more specifically, the particular aspects of the right to a fair trial that it is intended to buttress, allows one to more accurately determine what its provisions actually mean (or should mean). However, just as the right to an interpreter is meant to have a positive impact on various aspects of the right to a fair trial, it can also have negative ramifications on those very same aspects (and others as well), as will be seen in Chap. 5. Unfortunately, since courts and scholars have so far failed to acknowledge these negative aspects of the use of an interpreter, they as yet do not factor into the current state of the right under international law. As such, they will not be considered in the current analysis of the right.

4 The Appointment of a Court Interpreter

The obvious place to begin the analysis of the right to an interpreter is with the appointment of the interpreter herself. Article 14 (3) (f) ICCPR states that:

> 3. In the determination of any criminal charge against him, everyone shall be entitled to the following minimum guarantees, in full equality:
>
> ...
>
> (f) To have the free assistance of an interpreter if he cannot understand or speak the language used in court

This language raises three initial issues concerning the appointment of an interpreter. First, what individuals within the criminal justice system are entitled to a court interpreter? Second, at what stage in the criminal process are these individuals entitled to an interpreter? Third, what level of language inability triggers the right to an interpreter? These questions will be analyzed in order.

4.1 Identity of Legitimate Claimants

The explicit language of Article 14 (3) (f), which grants the right to an interpreter to "everyone" "in the determination of any criminal charges against him", leads to the interpretation that only the criminal defendant himself is entitled to an interpreter as a matter of law. This reading has been advanced in several domestic jurisdictions as well (Brown-Blake 2006, p. 411; Laster and Taylor 1994, pp. 78–79). However, the necessities of a fair trial may require the right to broaden further.

For instance, Article 14 (3) (e) guarantees a defendant the right "to obtain the attendance and examination of witnesses on his behalf under the same conditions as witnesses against him." Where a defense witness does not speak the language used in court, it is incumbent that a court interpreter be available in order to ensure the defendant access to that evidence on his behalf. As such, the right to an interpreter would appear to extend beyond the criminal defendant's personal use and outside of the defendant's language abilities as well.

The HRC, for its part, seems to have confirmed this interpretation in *Guesdon v. France*. In *Guesdon* (1990), a Breton-speaking defendant asserted that Article 14 (3) (e) and (f) granted him the right to an interpreter for both himself and his witnesses, even though both he and his witnesses were admittedly capable of expressing themselves in the native language of the court (French, in this case). In holding that the defendant was not entitled to a court interpreter, the HRC noted that "[o]nly if the accused or the defence witnesses have difficulties in understanding, or in expressing themselves in the court language, must the services of an interpreter be made available" (*Guesdon v. France* [HRC 1990] §10.2). Although the HRC's statement is largely dicta, its implication is clear: the right to an interpreter is not necessarily limited to a criminal defendant, but may extend to any non-conversant defense witnesses as well where the right to a fair trial so requires.

Likewise, the right to a fair trial may also necessitate the appointment of an interpreter to alleviate any communication problems between the defendant and his attorney (Trechsel 2005, pp. 338–339). Article 14 (3) (b) ICCPR states that a defendant is entitled to "have adequate time and facilities for the preparation of his defence and to communicate with counsel of his own choosing." Where the language barrier prevents communication between the defendant and his chosen counsel, the necessity of that communication to the realization of a fair trial would seem to mandate the use of an interpreter. From a logic standpoint, this would appear to be the case even where the defendant is conversant in the language of the court and it is the chosen attorney who is deficient (though, from a practical standpoint, it is difficult to imagine that a court would voluntarily appoint counsel with insufficient language skills). It must be noted, however, that the choice of such an attorney may have ramifications as to who pays for the court interpreter (Trechsel 2005, pp. 338–339; see also *X. v. Germany* [ECtHR 1983]).

4.2 The Timing of the Appointment

A second facet of the appointment analysis involves determining at what point in the criminal justice process an individual becomes entitled to an interpreter. Unfortunately, Article 14 (3) ICCPR is less than explicit in this regard, though the exact alignment of the text with that of the ECHR allows the caselaw of the ECtHR to be of some indirect guidance on the issue (Nowak 2005, p. 318).

What is clear from Article 14 (3) ICCPR is that the right to an interpreter only adheres when an individual is the target of a "criminal charge". This term, however, is far from clear. Nowak has argued that it must be autonomously interpreted, meaning that its definition must be independent from any "formal classification under national law", since to do otherwise would allow domestic jurisdictions to avoid the limitations imposed under Article 14 ICCPR by simply classifying criminal actions as administrative matters (Nowak 2005, pp. 314, 318). Such an interpretation would align Article 14 with the much-criticized Article 6 jurisprudence of the ECtHR (see also Nowak 2005, p. 318; van Dijk 2003, p. 361; Leigh 1997, p. 646). Under this approach, whether or not a criminal charge exists is dependent upon the type of sanctioned offense, as well as the nature and severity of the possible punishment (Nowak 2005, p. 318). Nor is the formal lodging of a criminal complaint determinative as to when a "criminal charge" officially exists, rather it is "the date on which State activities substantially affect the situation of the person concerned" that plays the decisive role (Nowak 2005, pp. 318–319). An individual's arrest may serve this purpose, but usually the initial "notification of a specific accusation" starts the process (Nowak 2005, p. 318).

Within the specific context of the right to an interpreter, however, linking the attachment of the right to the official establishment of a "criminal charge" under Article 14 (3) might not serve the overarching necessities of a fair trial. Although Harris et al. (2009) confidently asserts that the analogous ECHR right to an interpreter doesn't "benefit suspects being questioned by the police prior to their being 'charged'", it is far from clear that allowing the police to gather evidence from such a suspect without an interpreter would satisfy the underlying requirements of a fair trial (p. 327). Where the suspect is later found to require an interpreter for court hearings, such a finding would likely cast doubt on any evidence gathered in this manner. As such, the "autonomous" interpretation of "criminal charge" in the broader context of Article 14 (3) ICCPR may not function as well within the specific context of subsection (f) and the use of interpreters.

Another possible drawback to the "autonomous" approach lies in its lack of guidance to States concerning the actual application of Article 14 ICCPR. Given the minimal HRC practice in this area, States are generally left to their own devices when deciding whether a "criminal charge" exists within their system or not (Nowak 2005, p. 318; McGoldrick 1994, pp. 397–398). Within the context of appointing an interpreter, this can have substantial negative effects. Anecdotal evidence shows that judges tend to be reluctant to appoint interpreters in general (Aliverti and Seoighe 2017, p. 143 [with respect to the United Kingdom]; Laster and Taylor 1994, pp. 96–97 [with respect to Australia]; Chang and Araujo 1975, p. 802 [with respect to the United States]), and the lack of a clear mandate as to when the right to an interpreter attaches is unlikely to alleviate this pattern. For the time being, however, the "autonomous" approach, due to its scholarly backing and ECtHR roots, as well as the absence of any contradictory HRC practice, would appear to be the likely winner as to the definition of "criminal charge". Thus, the right to an interpreter can be seen to attach from the initiation of such a charge, and remain applicable until the end of any criminal proceedings, including any appellate procedures (Nowak 2005, p. 319).

4.3 Language Competence

The third and final facet concerning the appointment of an interpreter revolves around the language ability of the defendant. Specifically, under Article 14 (3) (f) ICCPR, the charged individual is only entitled to an interpreter where "he cannot understand or speak the language used in court." This phrasing creates an obvious language threshold, and given the inclusion of the right to an interpreter under the fair trial rubric, the interpretation of that threshold must ultimately revolve around the ability of the defendant to receive a fair trial given his respective language abilities (see for example *R. v. Johnson* [1987] [Australia] p. 440).[2] The difficulty, of course, is in determining what level of language is adequate to allow a defendant to participate sufficiently in his criminal proceedings that a fair trial can be had.

This has yet to be satisfactorily addressed through caselaw at the international level. The leading HRC case is the previously-discussed *Guesdon v. France*, wherein the HRC was confronted with a Breton-speaking defendant who asserted a right to an interpreter even though he admitted being capable in the native language of the court. The HRC held that the defendant was only entitled to an interpreter where he had "difficulties in understanding, or in expressing [himself] in the court" (*Guesdon v. France* [HRC 1990] §10.2; see also *Barzhig v. France* [HRC 1991]). In the HRC's view, the right to an interpreter was one of necessity, not preference. This is a view that has found favor in other international fora as well (see for example *Prosecutor v. Zejnil Delalić* [ICTY 1997]). However, in so holding, the HRC unfortunately failed to define what exactly constituted sufficient linguistic "difficulty" in a court setting. As such, establishing the threshold of linguistic inability that triggers the right to an interpreter has largely been left to existing domestic legislation or caselaw.

Naturally, the threshold differs from jurisdiction to jurisdiction. This is entirely logical, given that the domestic legal basis for the right to an interpreter in many jurisdictions pre-dates the ICCPR, and thus owes its origin to purely domestic sources ranging from express statutory or constitutional provisions to common law decisions (Brown-Blake 2006, pp. 392–393). In the United States of America ('U.S.'), for instance, the determination of whether or not a defendant is entitled to an interpreter hinges on whether he can "comprehend the proceedings and communicate effectively with counsel" (*United States v. Febus* [7th Cir. 2000] p. 791). In making this decision, the trial judge is given wide discretion to consider the "defendant's knowledge of English and the complexity of

[2] "Ultimately the decision whether or not a witness should have an interpreter will be answered in the light of the fundamental proposition that the accused must have a fair trial" (*R. v. Johnson* [1987] [Australia] p. 440).

the proceedings and testimony" (*United States v. Febus* [7th Cir. 2000] p. 791; see also Pettys 2009, p. 256; Hench 1999, p. 253; Shulman 1993, p. 179). In Australian and British courts as well, the ultimate decision on language competence is left to judicial discretion (Aliverti and Seoighe 2017, p. 142; Mikkelson 2000, p. 6; Laster and Taylor 1994, pp. 95–97). This reliance on judicial discretion unsurprisingly leads to the result that each individual judge follows his or her own standard and makes each decision on a case-by-case basis (Trechsel 2005, p. 334).

The individual determination of language competence by judges creates numerous problems. For one, judges do not always understand the significance of a court interpreter to the realization of a fair trial, nor are they generally aware of the "unique needs of the linguistic minority in the courtroom" (Davis and Hewitt 1994, p. 121). Likewise, they frequently underestimate the possible contribution that a defendant can make to his own defense (Grabau 1996, p. 6), and just as frequently overestimate a defendant's ability to understand a sophisticated legal process with which they, as judges, are intimately familiar (Laster and Taylor 1994, pp. 89–90). As a result, judges are apt to turn to court interpreters not as a matter of right for the defendant, but rather as a last resort when all other forms of communication have failed (Laster and Taylor 1994, pp. 89–90; Chang and Araujo 1975, p. 802; *R. v. Tran* [Supreme Court 1994] [Canada] §15).[3] This natural reluctance to appoint an interpreter tends to hide itself behind a series of poor assumptions that judges make regarding language abilities in the courtroom. For example, longtime residents of a country are assumed to speak that country's language at a competent level (Phelan 2011, p. 83; Trechsel 2005, pp. 334–335; Chang and Araujo 1975, pp. 802–803). Furthermore, individuals who are conversant in normal circumstances on everyday topics are presumed to be capable of understanding complex legal language in a stress-filled situation (*Interpreters in the Courtroom* 2008 [Foley Statement]; Shepard 2007, p. 643; McCaffrey 2000, p. 374;

[3] "Historically, the common law has not always been consistently supportive of an accused's need for the assistance of an interpreter, even in serious criminal trials" (*R. v. Tran* [Supreme Court 1994] [Canada] §15).

Laster and Taylor 1994, pp. 89–90). These assumptions ultimately serve to reinforce the judge's natural reluctance, and lead to a subjective determination of language competence taken by an individual who is not trained to assess language ability.

However, criticizing judges in this context seems overly harsh given that a viable alternative to such decisions is not altogether apparent. As Trechsel (2005) has noted, objectively measuring the language abilities of a defendant is problematic at best, and impossible at worst (p. 334). Even assuming that the defendant cooperates in such an assessment (which is a sizeable assumption in some instances), any linguistic test would need to be specifically tailored not only to legal language in general, but perhaps even to the particular complexity of the charged crime itself (Trechsel 2005, p. 334; Laster and Taylor 1994, p. 90). Furthermore, it is difficult to imagine an objective test being able to assess whether an individual's language ability would withstand the increased stress inherent in a legal proceeding (Laster and Taylor 1994, p. 90).[4]

As can be seen from the above discussion, not only is there little guidance as to what level of language a defendant should possess in order to "understand or speak the language used in court", there is little scholarly agreement on what such guidance would even entail. The end result is that the current definition of language incompetence ultimately relies on the discretion of national level judges and results in the appointment of fewer court interpreters than many advocates (and even judges) would prefer (Laster and Taylor 1994, p. 96; Schweda-Nicholson 1989, p. 711).

5 The Competence of the Interpreter

Even where a linguistically incapable defendant is granted a court interpreter, this doesn't immediately ensure a fair trial (Lindie 1993, p. 409). The right to an interpreter implies a certain minimum level of quality with respect to the court interpretation (Nowak 2005, p. 344). Where

[4]Noting that the "language proficiency of a victim giving evidence in a rape case ... can easily give way under the pressure of cross-examination" (Laster & Taylor 1994, p. 90).

this minimum level is not met, it is unlikely that the defendant involved will have "understood … the language used in court" adequately enough to have received a fair trial. Indeed, some scholars have argued that the appointment of a bad interpreter is worse than not having an interpreter appointed at all; as such, the right might be better understood as one to a *competent* interpreter (LaVigne and Vernon 2003, p. 889).

5.1 Defining the "Competence" of a Court Interpreter

As with the definition of language incompetence, the difficulty in this context is that there exists little or no guidance at the international level as to how to assess whether or not an interpreter is competent (Trechsel 2005, p. 339). Indeed, international caselaw on the issue is generally uninterested in the qualifications or abilities of the interpreter, but is rather solely interested in the quality of the resulting interpretation. The ECtHR's *Kamasinski v. Austria* is a good example. In *Kamasinski* the defendant was interrogated by police on several occasions using a variety of different interpreters, including an unregistered interpreter and a fellow prisoner of limited English-speaking skills. The ECtHR held that the defendant's right to an interpreter was not violated because an "interpreter was present on each occasion" (*Kamasinski v. Austria* [ECtHR 1989] §77). The court emphasized that it was unconvinced that the interpretation "led to results compromising [the defendant's] entitlement to a fair trial or his ability to defend himself" (*Kamasinski v. Austria* [ECtHR 1989] §77). Thus, it can be assumed from *Kamasinski* that the identity and training of the interpreter is less important to fair trial considerations than the actual end result of the interpretation. This is an entirely logical approach, given that the interpretation of the proceedings is what ensures a fair trial, not the mere presence of a well-qualified interpreter. However, as will be discussed in more detail below, it must be questioned whether an appellate court is in any position to judge the adequacy of an interpreter's work, especially considering that most appellate records consist of only the native language of the court (Kahaner 2008–2009, p. 226; Shepard 2007, p. 645).

The veritable absence of international caselaw and guidance on this issue means that the domestic jurisdictions have largely been left to create and enforce their own competency standards (Trechsel 2005, p. 339). Unfortunately, even at the national level, there are often "no universally acceptable standards for assessing competency" (Steele 1991–1992, p. 238; see also Heller 1994–1995, p. 368). For the most part, national courts and legislation focus as much on the qualifications and abilities of the interpreter as they do on the actual work product in any one given trial. In U.S. federal courts, for example, the competency of a court interpreter is linked to certification or accreditation (Court Interpreter's Act of 1978, §1827 [b] [2]). The federal court system currently administers a certification regime only for Spanish language interpreters (though in the past it has also offered certification in both Haitian Creole and Navajo) (de Jongh 2008, p. 25). Under the Court Interpreter's Act of 1978, federal judges are required to use only federally certified court interpreters when they are reasonably available (§1827 [b] [2]). Where such certified interpreters are not reasonably available (which, given that certification only exists in 3 languages, is often), the judge may use "otherwise qualified" interpreters (Court Interpreter's Act of 1978, §1827 [b] [2]; see also Kahaner 2008–2009).[5] The U.S. state court systems each use their own organization and standards, some involving certification programs in various languages, and some that do not (see generally Griffin and Cole 2007).

Denmark also employs a certification system; §149 Danish Administration of Justice Act requires that all court interpreters "should be authorized" (Hertog and Vanden Bosch 2001, p. 13; Schweda-Nicholson and Martinsen 1995 p. 262). In addition to meeting certain technical requirements (such as possessing Danish nationality and being over 25 years of age), an aspiring interpreter must either: (for English, Spanish, French, German, or Italian) undertake training and pass a language examination administered by a part of the Danish Ministry of Industry; or (for every other language) pass an oral examination from the

[5] Noting that in order to be considered an "otherwise qualified" interpreter, generally membership in a professional interpreting association is necessary, or the individual must have some previous employment affiliation as an interpreter with either the United Nations, a U.S. governmental department or another similar entity (Kahaner 2008–2009, p. 228).

National Commission of the Danish Police (Hertog and Vanden Bosch 2001, p. 13; Schweda-Nicholson and Martinsen 1995, p. 262). Belgium, on the other hand, is less regulated. Each Court of First Instance, in conjunction with the public prosecutor's office, creates a list of approved "sworn interpreters" for that court to use (Hertog and Vanden Bosch 2001, p. 11). However, in practice, the qualifications and competence of these interpreters is rarely checked, and there currently exists neither a national registration or certification system, nor any law mandating any particular quality prerequisites (Hertog and Vanden Bosch 2001, p. 11). Canada is even less regulated. Under Canadian law, interpreters must be competent and impartial, but the determination of competence is left to the individual judges, and the caselaw on the issue has not been entirely conclusive (see for example *R. v. Tran* [Supreme Court 1994] §§56–68).[6] At the end of the day, according to one Canadian scholar, the only necessity is that the interpreter takes an oath to interpret to the best of his or her ability (Heller 1994–1995, p. 368). No nationally accepted standard for determining the competence of court interpreters exists (Heller 1994–1995, p. 368; *R. v. Tran* [Supreme Court 1994] §64).

As can be seen in the examples above, there is no common standard for determining the competence of court interpreters (see for example ed. Hertog and van Gucht 2008). Some jurisdictions employ relatively strict certification regimes, others require professional or community accreditation, while others require nothing at all outside of an oath (Michael 2016, pp. 228, 230 [with respect to Nigeria]; Martin and Ortega Herráez 2011 [no enforceable accreditation in Spain] p. 14; Hayes and Hale 2010 [voluntary accreditation in Australia] p. 123; O'Brien 2010 [no accreditation in Ireland]; Tursun 2010 ["no specific test or minimum standard of expertise" in China] p. 562; Kolb and Pöchhacker 2008 [no accreditation in Austria] p. 28; *Court Interpreter's Job Is No Easy Task* 2002 [no accreditation in Japan]; Morris 1998 ["no quality assurance standards" in Israel] p. 7; see also Spronken and Attinger 2005 [with respect to the varying

[6] Setting out a set of criteria (continuity, precision, impartiality, competency and contemporaneousness) in order to determine the competence of an interpretation, but providing little as to the necessary qualifications of the interpreter herself (*R. v. Tran* [Supreme Court 1994] [Canada] §§56–68).

E.U. standards]). Indeed, some jurisdictions employ a flexible combination of all three, depending upon the comparative availability of interpreters in a particular language. The result is that there is no agreed upon international law standard for what constitutes a "competent" court interpreter. Unhelpful and uninformative as it may be, all that can be said is that the likely standard almost certainly revolves around the defendant's ability to receive a fair trial, since this is the overarching reason for the right to an interpreter in the first place.

5.2 The Difficulties in Enforcing Competency Standards

In spite of the flexible standards, or even complete absence of standards in some jurisdictions, many courts still experience significant difficulties both finding and keeping competent court interpreters. These difficulties can, in part, be traced back to the natural complexity of court interpreting itself, which requires a specific educational, cultural, and training background (as will be discussed in the next Chapter). Understandably, not many individuals in society possess these attributes. The relative scarcity of capable individuals can be most obviously seen in the extremely low pass rates on certification exams in the U.S. federal system: the overall certification rate invariably hovers below 10%, which is astonishing given that generally only the most experienced court interpreters even attempt to gain certification (de Jongh 2008, p. 25; Hewitt and Lee 1996, p. 26). The exotic nature of the language required often also contributes to the lack of skilled interpreters (Mikkelson 1998b, pp. 5–6; Hammond 1993). Regardless of the objective reason for the shortage of competent court interpreters, the existence of this shortage has real effects on the actual enforcement of domestic competency standards. While these effects will be more closely examined in Chap. 6, it is helpful to quickly visit them in this context.

The shortage of obviously qualified court interpreters can lead attorneys and judges to settle for "good enough" (Shepard 2007, p. 646). In some instances, this involves accepting bailiffs, building janitors, the arresting officer, the judge's secretary, the prosecuting attorney, or even a co-defendant as an acceptable court interpreter in a criminal proceeding (Shepard 2007, p. 646; Heller 1994–1995, p. 368). Judges sometimes merely administer the requisite interpreter oath and commence the proceeding without questioning the court interpreter's capabilities or possible conflicts of interest (Davis and Hewitt 1994, p. 132). Often, simply being bilingual in the requisite language is enough to attain an appointment (Hale 2011, p. 15; Moeketsi 1999, p. 7; Grabau 1996, p. 6; Laster and Taylor 1994, p. 91; Benmaman 1992, p. 448; González et al. 1991, p. 51). Naturally, such flexible standards can create a wide variance in the competence of practicing court interpreters. And while one must be tolerant of the fact that "interpreter error is inevitable" (McCaffrey 2000, p. 393), it is not difficult to see how the appointment of random bilingual individuals (even one without an obvious conflict of interest) can undermine the concept of a "competent" court interpreter, regardless of how stringent the competency standards are in a particular jurisdiction.

6 Practical Considerations

The eventual appointment of a competent individual as interpreter does not, by itself, fulfill a defendant's right to an interpreter. Since the overarching purpose animating the right is the necessity of a fair trial, it is logical that this necessity places certain demands on the practical aspects of the right to an interpreter. In other words, simply having a competent interpreter is not always enough to ensure a fair trial; there are other practical considerations in the implementation of the right to an interpreter that need to be considered.

6.1 Multiple Interpreters

Although most of the discussion, and existing legal standards, concerning competency and the right to an interpreter revolve around the competence of the appointed interpreter, it must be remembered that the general abilities of the interpreter are only a more easily verifiable substitute for the actual adequateness of the proceedings themselves. This distinction is important, because the necessity of a satisfactory interpretation may require more than one interpreter be appointed.

The general practice in national courts is to appoint a single court interpreter for a defendant (or witness) (Stern 2011, p. 332; Mason 2008, p. 8; see also Heller 1994–1995, pp. 381–382; Shulman 1993, p. 193; Steele 1991–1992, pp. 243–44). This interpreter's job is to make the oral proceedings of the courtroom understandable for the defendant (or to eliminate the language barrier with respect to a testifying witness) (Steytler 1993, p. 206; Steele 1991–1992, pp. 223–224; González et al. 1991, pp. 17–18). However, court interpreting is an inherently stressful and difficult task, more so even than other forms of interpreting (such as conference interpreting) (Davis and Hewitt 1994, p. 135; Craney 1989–1990, p. 27). It requires an intensity of concentration so demanding that studies have noted a significant diminishment in both accuracy and efficiency after only 30 minutes of continuous court interpreting (Mason 2008, p. 9; Davis and Hewitt 1994, p. 135). Chapter 6 will discuss in more depth the possible impact of interpreter fatigue on accuracy and its ramifications on the right to a fair trial; it is enough here to simply note that ensuring a competent interpretation (and thus a fair trial) in some instances may require either the imposition of frequent breaks for a solitary interpreter or the appointment of multiple interpreters to share the workload (Heller 1994–1995, p. 381).

There are also logistical situations that may necessitate the use of two or more interpreters. For instance, where both the accused and a testifying witness do not speak the language of the court, employing a single interpreter for the proceedings may be insufficient (Heller 1994–1995, p. 381; Chang and Araujo 1975, pp. 821–822). Assuming that the accused and the witness both speak the same language (the simplest form of this problem), the interpreter would likely be used to interpret the witness's testimony for the court. Obviously, in this situation, the defendant would be able to understand both the court's questions and the testimony from the witness's original language, but he would not be in a position to understand the entire proceedings (any discussions between the judge and the attorneys, for instance) unless the interpreter interpreted these interactions for the witness, which is not assured. And even where this is done, it is likely done simultaneously, and quietly enough so as not to disturb the entire courtroom, which naturally makes it unlikely that the accused would be able to hear the interpretation. Furthermore, using the single interpreter for the witness makes it impossible for the accused to communicate with his attorney during the proceedings, which is an obvious impediment to an adequate defense (Chang and Araujo 1975, pp. 821–822). Finally, allowing a single interpreter to handle both the defendant and any subsequent witnesses is to invite the risk of bias. Since the interpreter has likely been involved in sensitive attorney-defendant discussions, as well as the overall preparation of the defense, her eventual interpretation of the witness's testimony may be subconsciously influenced by the privileged information she possesses about the case (González et al. 1991, p. 496; Chang and Araujo 1975, pp. 821–822).

These elements, taken together with the obvious benefit of having an extra interpreter in the courtroom checking the accuracy of the interpretation (Heller 1994–1995, p. 381; Chang and Araujo 1975, pp. 821–822), counsel in favor of using multiple interpreters in such situations. However, that is seldom the case in national courtrooms, for a variety of understandable reasons. First, judges are rarely educated as to the drawbacks of using only a single interpreter in these situations. Second, employing multiple interpreters increases costs, an outcome most courts seek to avoid (Heller 1994–1995, p. 381; Chang and Araujo 1975, pp. 821–822). Third, as previously mentioned, the scarcity of competent court interpreters makes it difficult in some instances for courts to find one adequate interpreter, let alone two or more. Thus, even though using multiple, alternating interpreters is the norm at international criminal tribunals, (Stern 2011, p. 332; Karton 2008, pp. 22–23; Stern 2001, p. 21) the practical impediments to such a policy make it quite rare at the national level. The question, though, is whether multiple interpreters are required in order to ensure a fair trial. There is little doubt that multiple interpreters may be helpful in order to render a complete and accurate word-for-word interpretation of the proceedings, but it is not clear that such a complete interpretation is necessary to a fair trial. Something less than word-for-word may be sufficient, and if this is in fact true, then the arguments mandating the use of multiple interpreters are correspondingly weakened.

6.2 The Extent of the Interpretation

The question, then, becomes to what extent must a criminal proceeding be interpreted in order to ensure a fair trial. Regrettably, Article 14 (3) (f) ICCPR is not specific in this regard, stating only that a defendant is entitled to an interpreter "if he cannot understand or speak the language used in court." Nowak (2005) has interpreted the reference to the "language used in court" as implying that "the entire *oral hearing* must be translated" (p. 343 [emphasis in the original]). Trechsel (2005) is in accord, arguing that the entire trial must be interpreted "from start to finish" and that the accused must "be able to understand every sentence that is uttered" (p. 337). If these interpretations of Article 14 (3) (f) ICCPR are correct, then a complete interpretation of the proceedings would be necessary, thus raising the minimum level of interpreter competence required while simultaneously bolstering the arguments in favor of multiple interpreters.

However, it is difficult to see this necessity in the language of Article 14 (3) (f) ICCPR. Subsection (f) sets a limit on when an interpreter is given to a defendant; it doesn't appear to imply or mandate any particular level of interpretation. Rather, as previously argued, the requirement of an adequate interpretation would appear to come from the overall purpose of ensuring a fair trial. *Kamasinski* supports this analysis. In *Kamasinski*, the court interpreters failed to interpret the entire proceedings for the defendant, instead simply summarizing the events (§27). The ECtHR held that this fact alone was insufficient to find a violation of the right to a court interpreter, placing great worth in the fact that the defendant was not "unable because of deficient interpretation either to understand the evidence being given against him or to have witnesses examined or cross-examined on his behalf" (*Kamasinski v. Austria* [ECtHR 1989] §83). In other words, the attributes of a fair trial existed, even where the interpretation left something to be desired.

Kamasinski, of course, involved the ECHR, and as such, is not a definitive interpretation of the identical ICCPR provision. It is still unsettled whether the ICCPR requires more or less precision with respect to the interpretation of criminal proceedings. Scholars, as noted, find fault with the *Kamasinski* decision, and argue that fair trial standards require a complete, non-summarized interpretation (a "comprehensive" interpretation) (Nowak 2005, p. 343; Trechsel 2005, p. 337). International criminal courts (the ICC, ICTY, and ICTR most prominently) employ this standard as well, utilizing multiple interpreters and producing comprehensive simultaneous interpretations of court proceedings (Elias-Bursać 2015, pp. 74, 89–92; Namakula 2014, pp. 131, 136; Stern 2011, p. 330). Several prominent national jurisdictions, such as the U.S. (*United States v. Joshi* [11th Cir. 1990] p. 1309; *United States ex rel. Negron v. New York* [2nd Cir. 1970] pp. 389–390), Canada (*R. v. Tran* [Supreme Court 1994] §§61–62) and Australia (*De La Espriella-Velasco v. The Queen* [Court of Appeal Western Australia 2006] pp. 144–145), also require non-summarized interpretations as the baseline standard. However, national courts naturally follow a variety of different procedures, which is entirely logical given the various levels of emphasis that national jurisdictions place on oral proceedings (Stern 2011, p. 329; Trechsel 2005, p. 338). As such, it is nearly impossible to distill any absolute guidance as to the level of comprehensiveness required in this area. What is clear, though, is that enough of the proceedings must be interpreted so as to allow the defendant not only to understand what is occurring in the courtroom, but also to allow him to participate in his own defense. On this principle, at least, scholars, national jurisdictions, and *Kamasinski* all seem to agree.

6.3 Translation

To this point, the entire discussion concerning the right to an interpreter for linguistically incapable defendants has revolved around the interpretation of the oral portions of any criminal proceedings. Given that, in the linguistic field, "to interpret" involves the transfer of *oral* content from one language to another, as opposed to "translation" which concerns the same process in relation to *written* documents (Benmaman 1992, p. 445), this limitation is entirely appropriate (Harris 1967, p. 368). There is, however, more to criminal proceedings than oral hearings. And it is questionable whether an accused can receive a fair trial where he is unable to understand or read any documentary evidence submitted against him at trial (Nowak 2005, p. 343). This is especially true in jurisdictions that rely more heavily on written documentary evidence (Trechsel 2005, p. 338). For this reason, the "right to an interpreter" has expanded to include a limited right to the translation of written documents as well (Nowak 2005, p. 343).

The ECtHR, in its jurisprudence, has explicitly extended a defendant's right to a court interpreter to include the translation of any documents "which it is necessary for him to understand … in order to have the benefit of a fair trial" (*Kamasinski v. Austria* [ECtHR 1989] §74; see also *Luedicke, Belkacem and Koç v. Germany* [ECtHR 1978] §48). The "necessary for a fair trial" language, however, precludes the necessity of translating each and every document for the defendant, since not every prosecutorial document is essential to a defendant's understanding of the proceedings (*Kamasinski v. Austria* [ECtHR 1989] §74). Furthermore, indulging in such an extensive translation program for defendants would not only likely delay trials to an extent that could "jeopardize the right of the accused to an expeditious trial" (de Meester 2010, p. 472), but would also likely be cost-prohibitive (Merrills and Robertson 2001, p. 131).[7] Article 67 (1) (f) of the Rome Statute of the International Criminal Court is in accord with the ECtHR practice in this respect, requiring "translations as are necessary to meet the requirements of fairness." In its Decision on the Requests of the Defence of 3 and 4 July 2006 in the *Lubanga* case, the ICC took great pains to emphasize the ECtHR caselaw when interpreting Article 67 (1) (f), going so far as to declare that their interpretation was "fully consistent with the case law of the ECHR on this matter" (*Prosecutor v. Thomas Lubanga Dyilo* [Pre-Trial Chamber I ICC 2006] p. 466). The practice of the *ad hoc* criminal tribunals, however, appears to broaden this entitlement in the name of equality, allowing defendants access to translated documents well beyond what the ECtHR would consider "necessary" (Dingfelder Stone, J. 2012, p. 172).

[7] Cost alone, however, cannot and should not be an absolute barrier to the translation of necessary documents. As U.S. District Court Judge Weinstein held in the context of "due process" (the equivalent term for American fair trial standards): "If the government cannot afford to provide due process to those it prosecutes, it must forego prosecution" (*United States v. Mosquera* [EDNY 1993] [United States] p. 176).

The HRC, though, has been less clear in its approach. In *Harward v. Norway* (1994), the applicant asserted that he was not provided with adequate translations of the documents used against him at trial, and that he was therefore denied the right to have adequate time and facilities to prepare his defense (§3.3). The HRC held that the right to a fair trial required that the defense be given the "opportunity to familiarize itself with the documentary evidence against an accused", but that this did not necessarily require the translation of relevant documents, so long as they were furnished to the accused's counsel, who presumably would be linguistically capable of reading and understanding their contents (*Harward v. Norway* [HRC 1994] §9.5). Although this case would seem to preclude the necessity to translate any relevant documents for the defendant as a fair trial requirement (which is, after all, the general basis for the extension of the right in this regard), the decision must be read with some element of caution. In its opinion, the HRC placed some emphasis on the "particular circumstances of the case", one of which was the fact that the defendant in *Harward* had been assigned a competent court interpreter who was capable of translating any necessary documents for the defendant at the request of defense counsel (§9.5). Thus, while the decision may seem to categorically deny any right to the translation of relevant documents, this denial rests substantially upon the fact that the accused, in fact, was given the opportunity to have the documents translated by his interpreter, and chose not to avail himself of that opportunity.

Furthermore, the HRC was careful to stress in its opinion that the defendant's right to have adequate facilities to prepare his defense, specifically, was not violated (*Harward v. Norway* [HRC 1994] §9.5). Thus, it might be argued that the decision has little applicability as to the necessity of translations as part of the right to a court interpreter, which protects a different facet of the right to a fair trial. As in *Harward*, translations may not be necessary in order to prepare a defense, especially where the defendant has access to a court interpreter and is represented by linguistically capable counsel. Yet, the right to a court interpreter is not meant to ensure the preparation of a defensive strategy, rather it is primarily intended to guarantee that the defendant understands the oral proceedings and is able to participate in his defense (*Guesdon v. France* [HRC 1990] §10.2). As Nowak (2005) has asserted, where non-translated documents are entered into evidence during the oral proceedings, it may not be possible for the defendant to fully comprehend the oral proceedings without simultaneously understanding the written documents as well (p. 343). In this manner, the lack of translated materials, where those materials are necessary to the oral proceeding, can not only render that proceeding incomprehensible, but also impair the defendant's ability to participate effectively in his own defense. As such, it may be that, even though the right to have adequate time and facilities to prepare a defense does not entitle a defendant to the translation of necessary documents, the right to a court interpreter does. The cautious and specific language employed by the HRC in the *Harward* case leaves this as a legitimate possibility; one that would bring the HRC's interpretation of the right to a court interpreter in line with that of the ECtHR, scholars, and the various international criminal tribunals.

6.4 A "Free" Interpreter

A final practical consideration related to the right to a court interpreter concerns the eventual payment of the interpreter. Article 14 (3) (f) ICCPR entitles a linguistically incapable defendant to "the free assistance of an interpreter." HRC General Comment No. 13 has interpreted this phrasing as granting every such defendant an interpreter "free of any charge" (§13). Thus, it would seem quite clear that the cost of the court interpreter must be borne by the State, and not the accused. This interpretation, straightforward though it may appear, has actually produced a significant portion of the ECtHR's limited caselaw in the area.

The practice of some European States prior to 1978 was to grant language incapable defendants a court interpreter, but then to force those defendants who were ultimately convicted to pay any interpreting expenses as a cost of court (Harris et al. 2009, p. 327; Trechsel 2005, pp. 330–331). In *Luedicke, Belkacem and Koç v. Germany* (1978), the ECtHR ruled that this behavior was incompatible with the common sense meaning of the word "free", and would unacceptably place linguistically incompetent defendant's at a possible disadvantage (§§40–42). A defendant with borderline language capabilities might choose to forego his right to an interpreter in order to minimize any later costs, thereby possibly tainting the fairness of his eventual trial (*Luedicke, Belkacem and Koç v. Germany* [ECtHR 1978] §42). In the view of the ECtHR, the right to a court interpreter was specifically meant to eliminate any such disadvantage *Luedicke, Belkacem and Koç v. Germany* ([ECtHR 1978] §42). Scholars have soundly endorsed the ECtHR's decisions in this area, reasoning that any interpreting costs should be paid by the State since the interpreter assists the court as much as it does the defendant (Trechsel 2005, pp. 330–331) and is also technically part of the State's facilities (like clerks and the courtroom itself) (Harris et al. 2009, p. 327). Although the HRC has yet to establish any caselaw on this issue, its consideration of State Reports has intimated an alignment with the ECtHR's understanding as to the ultimate payment of interpreting costs (see among others HRC Concluding Observations: Canada [1985] §206; HRC Concluding Observations: Bulgaria [1979] §124; HRC Concluding Observations: Federal Republic of Germany [1978] §345).

7 Appellate Oversight of the Right to a Court Interpreter

The primary focus to this point has been on the defendant's right to have a court interpreter appointed and on the standard of adequacy applicable to that interpreter's work. These are the substantive provisions of the right to an interpreter. There remains, however, a procedural element to the right, which can be just as important to the actual, practical enjoyment of that right. The implementation of the right to an interpreter at the trial court level is only effective where appellate oversight exists to remedy any lapses in trial court judgment (Laster and Taylor 1994, p. 101). Where a defendant has no redress at the appellate level, then the right is no longer an entitlement, but rather a discretionary "statement of principle" (Laster and Taylor 1994, p. 101). While every convicted defendant is entitled to appeal his conviction under Article 14 (5) ICCPR, it is rather the standards that apply during that appeal and their practical application that are of interest in this context. Concerning the right to a court interpreter, appellate oversight generally arises in two distinct circumstances: first, where the court appointed a court interpreter but the defendant later claims that the interpretation was not adequate; and second, where the court fails to appoint an interpreter and the defendant later claims that it should have. Each of these situations will be considered in turn, followed by a discussion involving the practical application of appellate standards to court interpreting generally.

7.1 Allegedly Inadequate Interpretation

Where the defendant claims that his court-appointed interpreter provided an inadequate interpretation of the proceedings, the initial question that must be addressed is whether the defendant raised the issue at trial. In *Griffin v. Spain* (1995), the HRC was confronted with a case in which the defendant's interpreter was wholly inadequate (Nowak 2005, p. 344). However, since the defendant's attorney did not complain to the court during the trial concerning the quality of the interpretation, the HRC refused to consider his claim (*Griffin v. Spain* [HRC 1995] §9.5). As such, failure to bring the court's attention to the inadequacy of the interpretation qualifies as a waiver of that claim.

Perhaps the more daunting question, though, revolves around the determination as to whether or not the interpretation was indeed inadequate. As previously discussed, although no consensus international law standard exists on this point, at a minimum, the interpretation provided must allow the defendant to "understand the evidence" against him and to defend himself. In essence, this approach amounts to an appellate harm standard. Where the accused can understand and participate in the proceedings, then he has received a fair trial specifically because the quality of the interpretation did not harm him. Thus, the adequacy of the interpretation is assessed by its result (whether or not the trial was ultimately fair) and not by its objective "correctness". Presumably, where an interpreter's work has failed to allow the defendant to understand the proceedings, the appellate court would overturn the original conviction. However, as of yet, there is no international level case in which this has occurred. Even at the national level, it appears that the "vast majority" of cases are affirmed (Davis et al. 2004, pp. 5–6). Though, as will be seen, these results may have as much to do with how appellate courts practically apply adequacy standards, as with the standards themselves.

7.2 Failure to Appoint a Court Interpreter

The second situation that gives rise to appellate litigation involves the court's failure to appoint a court interpreter for a defendant who later claims that he was unable to comprehend the proceedings. In making such a claim, the defendant must prove that he was originally entitled to an interpreter, which is by no means straightforward (see for example *Juma v. Australia* [HRC 2003][8]; *Domukovsky and others v. Georgia* [HRC 1998][9]; see also Harris et al. 1995, p. 272). However, the key factor in such situations is whether the defendant asserted his right to a court interpreter at the time of the original proceedings. Where the defendant requested an interpreter and was denied, the appellate court will largely defer to the trial court's determination as to the defendant's language competence. As has been previously discussed, in making this determination, the courts have been given little guidance outside of Article 14's general language that the defendant be unable to "understand or speak the language used in court."

A trickier question is presented when the defendant failed to request an interpreter at trial, but then on appeal claims that he did not receive a fair trial specifically because he lacked an interpreter. In this instance, the issue becomes whether the defendant can effectively waive his right to an interpreter. The HRC, for its part, has been silent on the idea of waiver in this context, and since the international criminal tribunals automatically interpret their proceedings, they have never been presented with the issue. The closest thing to actual jurisprudence on the issue arises from the ECtHR.

---

[8]Where the HRC found the author "could express himself adequately in English", did not apply for an interpreter at his trial and refused one during his appeal, it was held that he had "failed to substantiate his claim sufficiently" (*Juma v. Australia* [HRC 2003] §7.3).

[9]Where the author did not show that he had insufficient knowledge of Georgian, he failed to meet his burden (*Domukovsky and others v. Georgia* [HRC 1998] §18.7).

In *Kamasinski*, the defendant complained that the court had failed to provide him with a translated indictment, and as such he had been unable to adequately defend himself (*Kamasinski v. Austria* [ECtHR 1989] §§78–81). The ECtHR held that, as a result of the oral explanations that he had received concerning the indictment, he had been sufficiently informed of the charges against him and was not prevented from defending himself (*Kamasinski v. Austria* [ECtHR 1989] §81). The Court also noted that the defendant and his counsel had "waived interpretation of the indictment" (*Kamasinski v. Austria* [ECtHR 1989] §80). This emphasis on the waiver of interpretation by the ECtHR has been interpreted by scholars as an indication that the right to an interpreter may be waived (Harris et al. 1995, p. 271). This, however, appears to be a bit of a stretch. That the applicant in *Kamasinski* was allowed to forego the interpretation of a single document, the contents of which he was already well-informed, is not necessarily an indication that a defendant could choose to effectively forego any understanding of an entire criminal proceeding.

The most recent ECtHR case in this area is the *Cuscani v. United Kingdom* case, though it too fails to provide any easy answers. In *Cuscani*, the Italian-speaking applicant agreed to plead guilty to criminal charges in an English court, however because he had some difficulty communicating, the judge assigned him a court interpreter at his counsel's request and reset the case for a later hearing (*Cuscani v. United Kingdom* [ECtHR 2002] §§13–16). At the subsequent hearing, the court interpreter failed to show up, yet the applicant's counsel (without consulting the applicant) agreed to "make do" without the professional interpreter; the plea hearing proceeded and the applicant was convicted and sentenced (*Cuscani v. United Kingdom* [ECtHR 2002] §§17–19). The ECtHR overturned the conviction, holding that the applicant had been denied his right to a court interpreter, and thus his right to a fair trial (*Cuscani v. United Kingdom* [ECtHR 2002] §40). The Court reasoned that the judge, having become aware of the applicant's communication difficulties, should have consulted with the applicant as to his understanding and comprehension before allowing applicant's counsel to waive the right to an interpreter (*Cuscani v. United Kingdom* [ECtHR 2002] §§38–39).

At first glance, the *Cuscani* opinion seems to essentially hold that the right to an interpreter cannot be waived without the accused's consent.

However, a deeper look at the language in *Cuscani* reveals that it isn't really a waiver case at all. The ECtHR was less interested in whether the applicant consented to the waiver, and more interested in whether or not the applicant actually needed an interpreter to have "full involvement in a matter of crucial importance" (*Cuscani v. United Kingdom* [ECtHR 2002] §38). *Cuscani*, under this view, does nothing more than require a judge to assess, in conjunction with the accused, whether the accused has sufficient language skills to be engaged in the proceedings, which sounds suspiciously similar to the threshold standard that would entitle the accused to a court interpreter in the first place. Thus, *Cuscani* leaves open whether the applicant could have waived his right to an interpreter even where his linguistic inability entitled him to such an interpreter. Naturally, where the accused has sufficient language skills to have "full involvement" in the proceedings, he is likely not entitled to a court interpreter, and thus has no right that he can waive. But where he lacks these language skills, his ability to waive his right to an interpreter would equate to an ability to effectively choose not to understand the proceedings. This is a far sight from the *Kamasinski* applicant's waiver of the interpretation of a single document. Since this more aggressive waiver ultimately implicates the right to a fair trial, it is questionable whether the defendant would have the discretion to waive his right to an interpreter, since the issue of whether or not a defendant understands the criminal proceedings against him is as much for the protection of society as it is for the individual defendant (Loucaides 2003, pp. 48–50; Ferguson 2002, pp. 560–561).

Unfortunately, the practice in national jurisdictions does little to settle the debate concerning waiver. While most jurisdictions appear to allow defendants to waive their right to an interpreter, there is little agreement as to the form that waiver may ultimately take. Nigeria, for instance, takes the stance that a defendant who has failed to assert his right to an interpreter at trial has effectively waived that right (Michael 2016, p. 224; Brown-Blake 2006, pp. 402–403). U.S. courts, however, do not allow a tacit waiver where the judge was aware of the defendant's linguistic issues, rather any waiver of the right must be made by the defendant personally in the language of the court (*United States v. Tapia* [5th Cir. 1980] p. 1209; *United States ex rel. Negron v. New York* [2nd Cir. 1970] p. 390). Canada also requires an affirmative waiver on the record by the defendant in the language of the court, yet the Supreme Court of Canada has strongly indicated that such a waiver would not be accepted where the defendant genuinely does not understand the proceedings from a linguistic perspective (*R. v. Tran* [Supreme Court 1994] §77). Thus, for Canada at least, there is an indication that the right may not, where actually necessary, be subject to waiver. For its part, Australia requires an explicit and informed waiver of the right either by, or on behalf of, the defendant (Brown-Blake 2006, p. 403; Laster and Taylor 1994, pp. 100–101). As can be seen from this admittedly brief survey of various jurisdictions, there is no set practice as to the circumstances under which the right to an interpreter may be waived, or even if it may be waived.

Nor does mere logic and common sense solve the dilemma, as even the extreme approaches have some logical backing. For instance, there is much to be said for the Canadian Supreme Court's approach, wherein the fair trial is as much for society as for the defendant himself, and as such, a defendant may not simply choose to be absent from his trial (Loucaides 2003, pp. 48–50; Ferguson 2002, pp. 560–561). This, however, would seem to fly in the face of the HRC's *Griffin* decision, where, because the defendant failed to alert the trial court as to the inadequacy of his interpreter, the HRC refused to hear that defendant's claim that he was effectively "absent" from his trial. In addition, with respect to common law jurisdictions, it makes little sense to not allow a defendant to waive his interpreter and therefore his right to understand his trial, when that same defendant can plead guilty and waive the entire trial.

The opposite end of the spectrum, the Nigerian approach of tacit waiver that places the burden on the defendant to assert his right to an interpreter, also has some internal logic. Since the defendant (or at least his attorney) is in the best position to know whether or not he understands the proceedings, it makes sense to require him to inform the court where he does not understand (Brown-Blake 2006, pp. 402–403). Moreover, some form of tacit waiver must exist, otherwise every judge would be required to enquire into every defendant's language abilities and procure an on-the-record waiver before any trial, simply to remove any possible grounds for appeal (Stavros 1993, p. 257). This is a rather expensive and time-consuming requirement. The downside of the Nigerian approach, of course, is that it places the burden of positive assertion on a defendant who, by definition, will not understand what is occurring in the courtroom due to language deficiencies (Bergenfield 1977–1978, p. 560). In other words, an individual with probably no knowledge of the court system, who is unable to speak the language, and who doesn't understand the proceedings is required to assert a positive right that he likely has no idea even exists. Fair trial standards almost certainly merit more protection than this approach affords. But with little guidance from the international level in this respect, and the extreme divergence of national jurisdictions, there is little agreement as to the appropriate level of protection concerning the waiver issue.

7.3 Practical Considerations in the Appellate Sphere

Regardless of the technical standards being employed by appellate courts concerning the right to an interpreter, there are several practical problems with the actual application of these standards at both the trial and appellate level. Generally, these problems concern the adequacy of trial records and the competence of judges in language-related matters. In short, it is wasteful to argue too much over the finer details of the various legal standards where linguistically untrained judges are applying those standards using inadequate records.

Trial records in national jurisdictions are invariably monolingual print records, preserving only the language of the court, and not that of linguistically incapable defendants or witnesses (Stern 2011, p. 336; Shlesinger 1989, p. 31; Safford 1977, p. 26). As a result, the court interpreter's words are the only permanent record of any language incapable individual's statements (Koo 2009, p. 218; Mikkelson 1998b, p. 2; González et al. 1991, p. 17). In many instances, it is the adequacy of this interpreter's performance that is being assessed. From a distance, the trial record may not contain any errors, however, not all interpreter error is immediately noticeable or blatant enough to be obvious (Hayes and Hale 2010, p. 130; LaVigne and Vernon 2003, p. 920). Since only one side of the discussion is preserved in the record, court interpreters are free to modify or augment an individual's answers in order to produce statements that "make sense in relation to the questions being asked" (Heller

1994–1995, p. 373). Moreover, court interpreters have an incentive to take such actions and to smooth over any misunderstandings or communication problems they might have with defendants or witnesses, as judges tend to blame the interpreter for any miscommunications (Hale 2007, p. 200; Hale 2004, p. 1; Morris 1995, p. 31; see also Stern 2001, p. 24 [noting the same as to parties to the case]). None of these actions would be discernible from the record, yet each would be instrumental to an appellate court's decision as to the adequacy of an interpretation.

Even where an interpreter is not involved, trial records can be problematic. For instance, where a defendant later claims that he should have been given an interpreter, the trial record may not accurately reflect that defendant's language abilities. Where the defendant chooses to testify on the record and answer questions, and thus provide ample evidence of his linguistic ability, that evidence may well be unrepresentative of his general linguistic competence (Bergenfield 1977–1978, p. 558). For example, an unresponsive or incomprehensible answer, normal evidence of linguistic difficulty, might also be taken as evasiveness or a lack of truthfulness (Heller 1994–1995, pp. 369–370). In addition, language deficient individuals will likely have acquired coping mechanisms, allowing them to "appear as if they understand, when in fact they do not" (LaVigne and Vernon 2003, p. 920). There is also the possibility that the defendant chooses not to testify or to speak, thus leaving the record completely devoid of any evidence as to his linguistic ability (Bergenfield 1977–1978, p. 558). And yet, on such a record must the appellate court base its decision.

However, an accurate and representative trial record is only part of the problem. Even assuming that appellate judges were given a bilingual trial record, and thus could provide oversight of the interpreter's work, this is not a function for which judges are trained. Asking an appellate judge to assess the accuracy of a court interpreter's work after the fact is akin to asking a court interpreter to evaluate the appropriateness of the judge's legal rulings (LaVigne and Vernon 2003, p. 915). Each profession requires job-specific skills and training. Furthermore, it is illogical for a jurisdiction, as some do, to maintain that court interpreters need such specialty training and certification in order to interpret in court, and then allow an untrained, uncertified individual to determine whether their work is up to standard.

Appellate courts, in many national jurisdictions (see above) and at the international level (see Harris et al. 1995, p. 272), are aware of these shortcomings, and thus defer to the trial judge's discretion concerning matters of language and interpretation. It is believed that "the trial court's proximity to the defendant and its ability to observe problems at first hand" endow it with an advantage when assessing such matters (Bergenfield 1977–1978, p. 559). However, in many circumstances, the trial judge is in no better position than the appellate court. For example, trial judges generally suffer from the same lack of linguistic training as appellate judges (Tuck 2010, p. 940; Mikkelson 2000, p. 16). Nor does proximity to the defendant make the trial judge any more able to assess the defendant's ability to comprehend the proceedings without an interpreter: judges rarely determine an individual's mental competence to stand trial absent expert opinion and there is an argument to be made that linguistic competence should be treated in the same manner (McCaffrey 2000, p. 388). In addition, even the simple task of relying on the defendant's assertions of linguistic competence is fraught with practical danger, since the defendant himself is often not able to self-assess his own level of understanding (LaVigne and Vernon 2003, p. 920). Moreover, "no one wants to appear ignorant or unintelligent", and thus the defendant simply may not be willing to admit to the court that he doesn't understand (LaVigne and Vernon 2003, p. 920).

Being able to observe the proceedings in person also doesn't cure a trial judge's inability to assess the accuracy of an interpreter's work. Trial courts simply have "no systematic means of recognizing poor interpretation" (Heller 1994–1995, p. 381). Judges, for the most part, must take on blind faith that the interpreter is performing adequately (Lore 2010, p. 2). In fact, it is virtually impossible for a trial judge to determine whether the interpretation of a particular statement is accurate or not, let alone a full trial (Hovland 1992–1993, p. 479). Even where the judge possesses some facility with the defendant's language, the practical necessities of being a trial judge limit their ability to monitor the interpreter's work since they cannot be expected to provide exhaustive oversight of both the legal and linguistic aspects of the trial simultaneously (Tuck 2010, p. 940). Nor, again, are they trained to even perform such a task.

7.4 The End Outcome

At the end of the day, appellate courts are left consulting unclear trial records in order to enforce uncertain standards revolving around determinations for which they are invariably untrained and with which they are, thus, uncomfortable. One approach to such a situation would be to overcompensate by erring on the side of caution and rule in favor of linguistically incapable individuals wherever there is doubt as to whether or not they received a fair trial. The reality, however, is quite the opposite. The practice of deferring to the discretion of the trial judge in these matters means that most appellate challenges are denied (Phelan 2011, p. 93; Hayes and Hale 2010, pp. 119, 126; Davis et al. 2004, pp. 5–6; Heller 1994–1995, pp. 369–370). Making matters worse is the fact that very few cases involving the adequacy of an interpreter's work are ever even discovered, since there is generally no one in the courtroom capable of noticing any inadequacies (Hayes and Hale 2010, p. 130; Heller 1994–1995, pp. 369–370; Shulman 1993, p. 176). Such a case comes to light only on those rare instances where, by chance, a bilingual individual is at the trial, "close enough to the interpreter to hear both versions, alert enough to compare them," and then confident enough to inform someone of the noticed problems (Heller 1994–1995, p. 369; Shlesinger 1989, p. 32). Naturally, these circumstances do not lead to an overabundance of cases or appellate decisions, which may, in part, be to blame for the lack of clear appellate standards at both the national and international level. Unfortunately, this combination of ambiguous appellate standards and practical application problems creates a lethal mixture resulting in very real dangers for the enforcement of the right to an interpreter at the appellate level.

8 Conclusion

The reasons for the existence of the right to an interpreter, and what it is meant to accomplish, appear fairly clear. However, the legal standards created to achieve these goals have been rather less than clear. In the end, though, there are some firm statements that can be made about the right to an interpreter under international law. First, it applies in relation to defendants whose linguistic inability (as determined by the trial court) does not allow them to understand or participate in the proceedings at issue. Second, the right likely applies in any proceedings arising after "the date on which State activities substantially affect the situation of the person concerned" (Nowak 2005, pp. 318–319). Finally, the right entitles the particular defendant to a competent interpretation of the proceedings free of charge, such that he can actually understand and participate in those proceedings. What can also be said is that the practical implementation of these standards leaves a great deal to be desired. The ambiguous standards are unevenly applied by trial judges who are given wide discretion by appellate courts to make decisions concerning language abilities for which they are largely not trained. In addition, appellate court oversight is hindered by the distance of the appellate judges from the decisions being made and the inadequacy of the trial records concerning linguistic rulings. The combination of relatively uncertain legal standards and limited appellate enforcement of those standards has served to restrict the practical effectiveness of the right to an interpreter.

All things considered, however, it should not be too surprising that the legal norms in this area are unsettled. In effect, the right to an interpreter is not actually a stand-alone right, but rather the means to effectively accomplish a larger right: the right to a fair trial. Thus, the right to an interpreter only exists in so far as necessary to achieve a fair trial (Brown-Blake 2006, p. 394). Following upon that, any interpretation of what the right actually entails is therefore necessarily linked with understanding what the right to a fair trial requires of it. If this is assumed to be true, then in order to establish the actual limitations of the right to an interpreter, one must dissect and understand the fair trial provisions and how the work and actions of interpreters effect those provisions.

Court interpreters, though, are not simply a benign addition to the courtroom, working tirelessly to help the court alleviate whatever language issues hinder its provision of a fair trial. The entire situation is more complex than that, and almost certainly more complicated than most courts fully understand. The utilization of court interpreters in the pursuit of a fair trial can have both positive and negative ramifications. Unfortunately, this is true irrespective of the competence of the interpreter's actual performance. The addition of a court interpreter into the complicated ecosystem of a criminal proceeding necessarily changes that proceeding. In order to understand these changes, and how they can undermine the very fair trial provisions the right to an interpreter is meant to buttress, a more thorough discussion of the work of court interpreters is necessary.

Bibliography

Aliverti, A., & Seoighe, R. (2017). Lost in Translation? Examining the Role of Court Interpreters in Cases Involving Foreign National Defendants in England and Wales. *New Criminal Law Review, 20*(1), 130–156.

Benmaman, V. (1992). Legal Interpreting: An Emerging Profession. *Modern Language Journal, 76*, 445–454.

Bergenfield, G. (1977–78). Trying Non-English Conversant Defendants: The Use of an Interpreter. *Oregon Law Review*, *57*, 549–565.

Boas, G. (2010). War Crimes Prosecution in Australia and Other Common Law Countries: Some Observations. *Criminal Law Forum, 21*(2), 313–330.

Boas, G., Bischoff, J. L., Reid, N. L., & Taylor, B. D., III. (2011). *International Criminal Procedure*. Cambridge: Cambridge University Press.

Brown-Blake, C. (2006). Fair Trial, Language and the Right to Interpretation. *International Journal on Minority and Group Rights, 13*, 391–412.

Chang, W. B. C., & Araujo, M. U. (1975). Interpreters for the Defense: Due Process for the Non-English-Speaking Defendant. *California Law Review, 63*, 801–823.

Court Interpreter's Job Is No Easy Task. (2002, August 26). Japan Policy & Politics.

Craney, G. (1989–90). Language v. the Law. *Barrister,* 16, 20–23, 27, 42.

Davis, L. W., & Hewitt, W. E. (1994). Lessons in Administering Justice: What Judges Need to Know About the Requirements, Role, and Professional Responsibilities of the Court Interpreter. *Harvard Latino Law Review, 1*, 121–176.

Davis, L. W., McKell, M. N., Oldroyd, J. R., & Steed, B. C. (2004). The Changing Face of Justice: A Survey of Recent Cases Involving Courtroom Interpretation. *Harvard Latino Law Review, 7*, 1–25.

de Jongh, E. (2008, July/August). Linguistic Presence v. Linguistic Absence. *Florida Bar Journal, 82*, 20–32.

de Meester, K. (2010). Commentary: Decision on the Requests of the Defence of 3 and 4 July 2006: Situation in the Democratic Republic of the Congo, in the Case of the Prosecutor v. Thomas Lubanga Dyilo (Case no. ICC-01/04-01/06). In A. Klip & G. Sluiter (Eds.), *Annotated Leading Cases of International Criminal Tribunals: The International Criminal Court (2005–2007)* (Vol. 23, pp. 470–478). Antwerp: Intersentia.

Dingfelder Stone, J. H. (2012). Assessing the Existence of the Right to Translation Under the International Covenant on Civil and Political Rights. *Max Planck Yearbook of United Nations Law, 16*, 159–181.

Elias-Bursać, E. (2015). *Translating Evidence and Interpreting Testimony at a War Crimes Tribunal*. London: Palgrave Macmillan.

Ferguson, P. W. (2002, July). Trial in Absence and Waiver of Human Rights. *Criminal Law Review*, 554–565.

González, R., Vásquez, V. F., & Mikkelson, H. (1991). *Fundamentals of Court Interpretation: Theory, Policy, and Practice*. Durham: Carolina Academic Press.

Grabau, C. M. (1996). Court Interpreting: View from the Bench. *State Court Journal, 20*(1), 6–11.

Griffin, P. W., & Cole, S. J. (2007). *White Paper on Court Interpretation: Fundamental to Access to Justice*. Conference of State Court Administrators.

Hale, S. (2004). *The Discourse of Court Interpreting: Discourse Practices of the Law, the Witness and the Interpreter*. Amsterdam: John Benjamins.

Hale, S. (2007). Challenges of Court Interpreting: Intricacies, Responsibilities and Ramifications. *Alternative Law Journal, 32*, 198–202.

Hale, S. (2011). *Interpreter Policies, Practices and Protocols in Australian Courts and Tribunals: A National Survey*. Melbourne: AIJA.

Hammond, R. (1993, October 24). Lost in Translation; For Immigrants in Court, Bad Interpreters Rig the Jury. *Washington Post*, p. C3.

Harris, D. (1967). The Right to a Fair Trial in Criminal Proceedings as a Human Right. *International and Comparative Law Quarterly, 16*, 352–378.

Harris, D. J., O'Boyle, M., & Warbrick, C. (1995). *Law of the European Convention on Human Rights*. London: Butterworths.

Harris, D. J., O'Boyle, M., Bates, E., & Buckley, C. (2009). *Law of the European Convention on Human Rights* (2nd ed.). Oxford: Oxford University Press.

Hayes, A., & Hale, S. (2010). Appeals on Incompetent Interpreting. *Journal of Judicial Administration, 20*(2), 119–130.

Heller, D. J. (1994–95). The Language Bias in the Criminal Justice System. *Criminal Law Quarterly, 37*, 344–383.

Hench, V. E. (1999). What Kind of Hearing? Some Thoughts on Due Process for the Non-English-Speaking Criminal Defendant. *Thurgood Marshall Law Review, 24*, 251–278.

Hertog, E., & van Gucht, J. (Eds.). (2008). *Status Quaestionis: Questionnaire on the Provision of Legal Interpreting and Translation in the E.U.* Antwerpen: Intersentia.

Hertog, E., & Vanden Bosch, Y. (2001). Access to Justice Across Language and Culture in the E.U. In E. Hertog (Ed.), *Aequitas: Access to Justice across Language and Culture in the E.U.* (pp. 5–21). Antwerpen: Lessius Hogeschool.

Hewitt, W. E., & Lee, R. J. (1996). Behind the Language Barrier, or "You Say You Were Eating an Orange?". *State Court Journal, 20*(1), 23–31.

Hovland, D. L. (1992–93). Errors in Interpretation: Why Plain Error Is Not Plain. *Law and Inequality, 11*, 473–503.

Interpreters in the Courtroom. (2008). [Radio Program] ABC Radio National: Damien Carrick.

Kahaner, S. M. (2008–09). The Administration of Justice in a Multilingual Society – Open to Interpretation or Lost in Translation? *Judicature, 92*, 224–231.

Karton, J. (2008). Lost in Translation: International Criminal Tribunals and the Legal Implications of Interpreted Testimony. *Vanderbilt Journal of Transnational Law, 41*, 1–54.

Kolb, W., & Pöchhacker, F. (2008). Interpreting in Asylum Appeal Hearings: Roles and Norms Revisited. In D. Russell & S. Hale (Eds.), *Interpreting in Legal Settings* (pp. 26–50). Washington, DC: Gallaudet University Press.

Koo, A. (2009). Truth Through Court Interpreters. *International Journal of Evidence & Proof, 13*, 212–224.

Laster, K., & Taylor, V. L. (1994). *Interpreters and the Legal System*. Sydney: The Federation Press.

LaVigne, M., & Vernon, M. (2003). An Interpreter Isn't Enough: Deafness, Language, and Due Process. *Wisconsin Law Review, 2003*, 843–936.

Leigh, L. H. (1997). The Right to a Fair Trial and the European Convention on Human Rights. In D. Weissbrodt & R. Wolfrum (Eds.), *The Right to a Fair Trial* (pp. 645–668). Berlin: Springer.

Lindie, B. (1993). Inadequate Interpreting Services in Courts and the Rules of Admissibility of Testimony on Extrajudicial Interpretations. *University of Miami Law Review, 48*, 399–433.

Lore, M. (2010, March 1). Certified Interpreters in Short Supply Throughout Minnesota Court System. *The Minnesota Lawyer.*

Loucaides, L. G. (2003). Questions of Fair Trial Under the European Convention on Human Rights. *Human Rights Law Review, 3*, 27–51.

Martin, A., & Ortega Herráez, J. M. (2011). Interpreting in the Dock. *The Linguist, 50*(4), 14–15.

Mason, M. (2008). *Courtroom Interpreting*. Lanham: University Press of America.

McCaffrey, A. (2000). Don't Get Lost in Translation: Teaching Law Students to Work with Language Interpreters. *Clinical Law Review, 6*, 347–398.

McGoldrick, D. (1994). *The Human Rights Committee: Its Role in the Development of the International Covenant on Civil and Political Rights*. Oxford: Clarendon Press.

Merrills, J. G., & Robertson, A. H. (2001). *Human Rights in Europe: A Study of the European Convention on Human Rights* (4th ed.). Manchester: Manchester University Press.

Michael, C. O. (2016). Communication of an Interpreter and Fair Trial Under Nigerian Criminal Justice System. *International Journal of Legal Discourse, 1*(1), 213–233.

Mikkelson, H. (1998a). The Court Interpreter as Guarantor of Defendant Rights. In *First European Congress on Court Interpreting and Legal Translation – Graz*. [online]. Available at: http://works.bepress.com/holly_mikkelson/8/. Accessed 21 Nov 2017.

Mikkelson, H. (1998b). Towards a Redefinition of the Role of the Court Interpreter. *Interpreting, 3*(1), 21. [online]. Available at: https://works.bepress.com/holly_mikkelson/17/. Accessed 21 Nov 2017.

Mikkelson, H. (2000). *Introduction to Court Interpreting*. Manchester: St. Jerome Publishing.

Moeketsi, R. H. (1999). Redefining the Role of the South African Court Interpreter. *Proteus, 8*(3–4), 12–15.

Mojuta, K., & Arua, A. (2016). The Lexical Problems of Court Interpreters in a Botswana High Court. *Botswana Note and Records, 48*, 193–204.

Morris, R. (1995). The Moral Dilemmas of Court Interpreting. *The Translator, 1*(1), 25–46.

Morris, R. (1998). Justice in Jerusalem – Interpreting in Israeli Legal Proceedings. *Meta, 43*(1), 110–118.

Namakula, C. (2014). *Language and the Right to a Fair Hearing in International Criminal Trials*. Heidelberg: Springer.

Nartowska, K. (2015). The Role of the Court Interpreter: A Powerless or Powerful Participant in Criminal Proceedings? *The Interpreters Newsletter, 20*, 9–32.

Nowak, M. (2005). *U.N. Covenant on Civil and Political Rights: CCPR Commentary* (2nd ed.). Kehl: Engel.

O'Brien, C. (2010, June 7). No Quality Controls Laid Down for Courts and Garda Translators. *Irish Times*, p. 6.

Orakhelashvili, A. (2006). *Peremptory Norms in International Law*. Oxford: Oxford University Press.

Pantoga, H. (1999). Injustice in Any Language: The Need for Improved Standards Governing Courtroom Interpretation in Wisconsin. *Marquette Law Review, 82*, 601–664.

Pettys, T. E. (2009). Counsel and Confrontation. *Minnesota Law Review, 94*, 201–260.

Phelan, M. (2011). Legal Interpreters in the News in Ireland. *Translation & Interpreting, 3*(1), 76–105.

Robinson, P. (2009). The Right to a Fair Trial in International Law, with Specific Reference to the Work of the ICTY. *Berkeley Journal of International Law Publicist, 3*, 1–11.

Safford, J. B. (1977). No Comprendo: The Non-English-Speaking Defendant and the Criminal Process. *Journal of Criminal Law & Criminology, 68*, 15–30.

Schabas, W. A. (2007). *An Introduction to the International Criminal Court* (3rd ed.). Cambridge: Cambridge University Press.

Schweda-Nicholson, N. (1989). *Ad Hoc* Court Interpreters in the United States: Equality, Inequality, Quality. *Meta, 34*(4), 711–723.

Schweda-Nicholson, N., & Martinsen, B. (1995). Court Interpretation in Denmark. In S. E. Carr, R. P. Roberts, A. Dufour, & D. Steyn (Eds.), *The Critical Link: Interpreters in the Community* (pp. 259–270). Amsterdam: John Benjamins.

Shepard, R. T. (2007). Access to Justice for People Who Do Not Speak English. *Indiana Law Review, 40*, 643–657.

Shlesinger, M. (1989). Monitoring the Courtroom Interpreter. *Parallèles, 11*, 29–36.

Shulman, M. B. (1993). No Hablo Ingles: Court Interpretation as a Major Obstacle to Fairness for Non-English Speaking Defendants. *Vanderbilt Law Review, 46*, 175–196.

Spencer, J. R. (2005). Introduction. In M. Delmas-Marty & J. R. Spencer (Eds.), *European Criminal Procedures* (pp. 1–75). Cambridge: Cambridge University Press.

Spronken, T., & Attinger, M. (2005). *Procedural Rights in Criminal Proceedings: Existing Level of Safeguards in the European Union*. Brussels: European Commission.

Stavros, S. (1993). *The Guarantees for Accused Persons Under Article 6 of the European Convention on Human Rights: An Analysis of the Application of the Convention and a Comparison with Other Instruments*. Dordrecht: Nijhoff.
Steele, G. J. (1991–92). Court Interpreters in Canadian Criminal Law. *Criminal Law Quarterly, 34*, 218–251.
Stern, L. (2001). At the Junction of Cultures: Interpreting at the International Criminal Tribunal for the Former Yugoslavia in the Light of Other International Interpreting Practices. *The Judicial Review, 5*(3), 255–274.
Stern, L. (2011). Courtroom Interpreting. In K. Malmkjær & K. Windle (Eds.), *The Oxford Handbook of Translation Studies* (pp. 325–342). Oxford: Oxford University Press.
Steytler, N. C. (1993). Implementing Language Rights in Court: The Role of the Court Interpreter. *South African Journal on Human Rights, 9*, 205–222.
Trechsel, S. (2005). *Human Rights in Criminal Proceedings*. Oxford: Oxford University Press.
Tuck, B. M. (2010). Comment: Preserving Facts, Form, and Function When a Deaf Witness with Minimal Language Skills Testifies in Court. *University of Pennsylvania Law Review, 158*, 905–955.
Turner, J. I. (2005). Nationalizing International Criminal Law. *Stanford Journal of International Law, 41*, 1–51.
Tursun, G. (2010). The Protection of Minorities in Court Proceedings: A Perspective on Bilingual Justice in China. *Chinese Journal of International Law, 9*, 537–563.
van Dijk, P. (2003). Access to Court. In R. St, J. MacDonald, F. Matscher, & H. Petzold (Eds.), *The European System for the Protection of Human Rights* (pp. 345–379). Dordrecht: Nijhoff.

Other Documents

Convention for the Protection of Human Rights and Fundamental Freedoms (1953). 213 UNTS 221, signed 4 November 1950, entered into force 3 September 1953.
Court Interpreter's Act of 1978 (United States) 28 USC §1827.
Human Rights Committee (1978). Concluding Observations of the Human Rights Committee: Federal Republic of Germany. In: Human Rights Committee (22 November 1978). *Report of the Human Rights Committee*, U.N. Doc. A/33/40.

Human Rights Committee (1979). Concluding Observations of the Human Rights Committee: Bulgaria. In: Human Rights Committee (27 November 1979). *Report of the Human Rights Committee*, U.N. Doc. A/34/40.

Human Rights Committee (1984). General Comment No. 13: Equality before the Courts and the Right to a Fair and Public Hearing by an Independent Court Established by Law (Art. 14) (13 April 1984) U.N. Doc. A/39/40 at 143.

Human Rights Committee (1985). Concluding Observations of the Human Rights Committee: Canada. In: Human Rights Committee (19 September 1985). *Report of the Human Rights Committee*, U.N. Doc. A/40/40.

International Covenant on Civil and Political Rights (1976). 999 UNTS 171, adopted 16 December 1966, entered into force 23 March 1976.

Rome Statute of the International Criminal Court (2002). 2187 UNTS 90, adopted 17 July 1998, entered into force 1 July 2002.

List of Cases

Barry Stephen Harward v. Norway (HRC 1994). Communication No. 451/1991 (15 July 1994) U.N. Doc. CCPR/C/51/D/451/1991.

Cuscani v. United Kingdom (ECtHR 2002). Application No. 32771/96 (24 September 2002) 36 EHRR 2.

De La Espriella-Velasco v. The Queen (Court of Appeal Western Australia 2006) 197 Fed. Law R. 125 (Australia).

Dominique Guesdon v. France (HRC 1990). Communication No. 219/1986 (25 July 1990) U.N. Doc. CCPR/C/39/D/219/1986.

Gerald John Griffin v. Spain (HRC 1995). Communication No. 493/1992 (4 April 1995) U.N. Doc. CCPR/C/53/D/493/1992.

Hervé Barzhig v. France (HRC 1991). Communication No. 327/1988 (11 April 1991) U.N. Doc. CCPR/C/41/D/327/1988.

Kamasinski v. Austria (ECtHR 1989). Application No. 9783/82 (19 December 1989) Series A No. 168.

Lagerblom v. Sweden (ECtHR 2003). Application No. 26891/95 (14 January 2003).

Luedicke, Belkacem and Koç v. Germany (ECtHR 1978). Application Nos. 6210/73, 6877/75 & 7132/75 (28 November 1978) Series A No. 29.

Prosecutor v. Thomas Lubanga Dyilo (ICC 2006) ICC-01/04-01/06 (Pre-Trial Chamber I) Decision on the Requests of the Defence of 3 and 4 July 2006. In: A. Klip and G. Sluiter (Eds.), *Annotated Leading Cases of International*

Criminal Tribunals: The International Criminal Court (2005–2007), Vol. 23. Antwerp: Intersentia, pp. 463–466.
Prosecutor v. Zejnil Delalić (ICTY 1997). Case No. IT-96-21-T (Trial Chamber) Order on Zdravko Mucic's Oral Request for Serbo-Croatian Interpretation (23 June 1997).
R. v. Johnson (1987) 25 A. Crim. R. 433 (Australia).
R. v. Tran (Supreme Court 1994) 2 Supreme Court R. 951 (Canada).
Shukuru Juma v. Australia (HRC 2003). Communication No. 984/2001 (28 July 2002) U.N. Doc. CCPR/C/78/D/984/2001.
United States ex rel. Negron v. New York (2nd Cir. 1970). 434 F.2d. 386 (United States).
United States v. Febus (7th Cir. 2000). 218 F.3d. 784 (United States).
United States v. Joshi (11th Cir. 1990). 896 F.2d. 1303 (United States).
United States v. Mosquera (EDNY 1993). 816 F.Supp. 168 (United States).
United States v. Tapia (5th Cir. 1980). 631 F.2d. 1207 (United States).
Victor P. Domukovsky and others v. Georgia (HRC 1998). Communications Nos. 623/1995, 624/1995, 626/1995, 627/1995 (6 April 1998) U.N. Docs. CCPR/C/62/D/623/1995, CCPR/C/62/D/624/1995, CCPR/C/62/D/626/1995, CCPR/C/62/D/627/1995.
X. v. Germany (E.U. Commission 1983). Application No. 10221/82, 6 EHRR 353.

3

Courtroom Interpreting

1 Introduction

Although interpreters and the act of interpreting have existed for centuries as a means to bridge linguistic and cultural gaps (Stern 2011, p. 325; de Jongh 1991, p. 285), their utilization in the courtroom is a more recent occurrence (Mikkelson 1999, p. 1; Benmaman 1992, p. 447). While it is impossible to pinpoint the precise origins of courtroom interpreting, as the fastest growing branch of the interpreting profession, its relevance to modern judicial systems is clear (González et al. 1991, p. 15). Courtroom interpreting allows the system to function with its normal procedures, and yet still accommodate an individual who under those normal conditions would be unable to either understand or participate in the process (Davis and Hewitt 1994, pp. 144–145).

But this participation comes at a price for everyone involved. Language in a courtroom is more than a means of communication, "it is itself a crucial element of the process" (Hale 2007, p. 199). For attorneys, it is

J. H. Dingfelder Stone, *Court Interpreters and Fair Trials*,
https://doi.org/10.1007/978-3-319-75355-3_3

often a tool used to express a position with absolute precision, or, in adversarial systems, a weapon wielded in a symbolic battle (Hale 2001, p. 68; Morris 1995, p. 31). In common law jurisdictions especially, where the majority of evidence is presented orally and cases are won or lost not only on the strength of evidence but also on its presentation, language is the essential element of the entire process. It is therefore unsurprising that attorneys and judges are uncomfortable delegating control over the language of the courtroom to someone from outside the legal system itself, who performs a task about which they understand very little (see Tuck 2010, p. 906).[1] And yet, as the necessity for court interpreters continues to grow, the legal profession finds itself having to accept this reality more and more.

As such, this Chapter will attempt to clarify the process of courtroom interpreting. The initial section will give a general overview of the practical aspects of court interpreting, including the different types of interpretation used, as well as basic expectations vis-à-vis the courtroom interpreter. Following upon this will be a more theoretical discussion, based upon Gile's Effort Model, as to the actual process that occurs when someone interprets and how this process helps to explain the occurrence of interpreter errors. In this context, it is necessary to point out that, given the complexity of this area, the following discussions will naturally restrict themselves to a general overview aimed at those aspects of interpreting that are most likely to affect the right to a fair trial.[2]

[1] Noting that "[j]udges and trial attorneys spend enormous energy sharpening their use of language, but most consider interpreters too blunt an instrument to accurately convey their exact intent across language barriers" (Tuck 2010, p. 906).

[2] It is also necessary in this context to note that the exact terms and structures of interpreting to which this Chapter will refer do not always align with the terms and structures used in the interpreting studies community. The decision to alter specific terms and occasionally reorganize basic interpreting structures was made with the intent to render the area more understandable to attorneys and members of the legal profession. The author is aware that this reorganization removes occasional complexities that are necessary for a full discussion of interpreting studies. However, the complexities removed are those that have limited application to the concept of a fair trial; and as such, were unnecessary for this work.

2 General Overview of Courtroom Interpreting

2.1 Introduction

As previously defined, interpreting is the "oral transfer of meaning" from one language to another, while translating involves written, not oral, content (Morris 1995, p. 25; González et al. 1991, p. 295). Although often used interchangeably, these are in fact two distinct processes that require different skillsets (de Jongh 2008, p. 26; Benmaman 1992, p. 445). Furthermore, interpreters must produce an immediate result for a waiting audience, and therefore work at much higher speeds than translators (de Jongh 1992, p. 36). As such, neither the descriptive terms, nor the professionals involved in the process, are interchangeable. Within this context, scholars generally refer to a "source language" (the language in which the original message can be found) and a "target language" (the language into which the message will be converted) (González et al. 1991, p. 296). It is universally accepted that an interpreter should ideally have greater linguistic ability in the target language than in the source language (Ramler 2007, p. 11). In other words, as everyone who has learned a second language can confirm, it is easier to understand complex foreign language content than to produce such complex content oneself.

Given the natural complexity and precision of legal language, it is understandable that the task of interpreting in a courtroom is considered to be among the most difficult of the interpreting disciplines. Historically, conference interpreting was considered the "highest standard" in interpreting, yet many conference interpreters today view courtroom interpreting as being "in some respects more demanding" (González et al. 1991, pp. 26–27; see also Laster and Taylor 1994, p. 21). For this reason, otherwise qualified and experienced interpreters, when required to interpret in a courtroom, can quickly become overwhelmed with unfamiliar legal terms and procedural maneuvers (Craney 1989–1990, p. 27). The different types of interpreting that are required of a court interpreter on an everyday basis amplify the difficulty of the task. Courtroom interpreters generally must be capable of engaging in simultaneous and consecutive interpreting, summarization, as well as sight translation.

2.2 The Different Interpreting Techniques Used in the Courtroom

2.2.1 Simultaneous Interpreting

Simultaneous interpreting can be defined as the interpreting technique whereby the interpreter listens to the source speaker while concurrently interpreting what is being said into a different language for a distinct audience (de Jongh 1991, p. 288; González et al. 1991, p. 359). This process involves the interpreter hearing one segment of speech (A), analyzing and mentally translating it into a different language, and then orally conveying that translation (de Jongh 1992, p. 45). While this process is ongoing, the interpreter will begin to hear and analyze a second (B) and even third (C) speech segment. Thus, at any given moment, the interpreter may be listening to one segment (C), analyzing a second segment that was previously spoken (B), and orally producing a third segment (A) that predates the others. Throughout this process, the simultaneous interpreter will listen to and analyze approximately 120–180 words per minute (de Jongh 1991, p. 290). This all happens continuously and for as long as the source language is produced by the speaker, and naturally requires extreme concentration on the part of the interpreter while placing her under a great deal of pressure (González et al. 1991, p. 360).

Noticeable in this process, however, is the fact that the interpretation is not truly "simultaneous": the interpreter may be speaking at the same time as the original speaker, but she is actually lagging behind the speaker in meaning (González et al. 1991, p. 360). This time lag is known as "decalage" and is generally no longer than 7–8 seconds (Mikkelson 2000, p. 73; González et al. 1991, p. 360). Simultaneous interpreters must manage their decalage with precision. They can reduce their decalage, thereby speaking more contemporaneously with the speaker and burdening their memory less, but in doing so they risk not hearing enough of the speech to truly understand its meaning (González et al. 1991, p. 360). Conversely, they can extend their decalage in order to gain a better overview of the speech, but doing so places a larger load on their memory. In addition, there is the ever-present risk of falling too far behind and overburdening their memory to the point of collapse (González et al. 1991, p. 360), like a juggler who mistakenly chooses to juggle too many balls at one time, and they all fall to the ground. Management of the decalage is an unavoidable, ongoing process itself that likewise requires scarce resources and also increases the mental strain on simultaneous interpreters.

2.2.2 Consecutive Interpreting

Consecutive interpreting involves the sequential transfer of meaning from one language to another (de Jongh 1992, p. 37). In other words, the interpreter lets the original speaker finish before she begins giving her translation of that speech (González et al. 1991, p. 379). The segments of speech can vary in length from several minutes to a few seconds, and just as in simultaneous interpretation, the density and difficulty of the language varies from speaker to speaker (González et al. 1991, p. 379). In the courtroom setting, speech segments tend towards shorter length, but more complex language (de Jongh 1992, p. 38). The lengthier the speech segments involved, the more likely that the consecutive interpreter will be required to take notes on the speech in order to accurately interpret its meaning (de Jongh 1992, p. 42). Consecutive note-taking itself is a demanding skill that must be both learned and practiced regularly in order to be effective, but can dramatically improve the quality of the end interpretation (de Jongh 1992, p. 42; see generally Dingfelder Stone 2015). The resulting notes, though, are simply an aid to the interpreter's memory, they are not an end in themselves (González et al. 1991, p. 388).

Despite the obviously daunting complexity of simultaneous interpretation, many interpreters consider consecutive interpretation to be more difficult (González et al. 1991, p. 379). Since consecutive interpretation is generally used in question and answer situations, it requires the interpreter to consistently switch between both languages (de Jongh 1992,

p. 37). Thus, the interpreter must be equally comfortable in both languages, since each functions as both a source and target language depending on the speaker (de Jongh 1992, p. 39). Moreover, while the extended length of the speech segments gives the interpreter a chance to see the overall thrust of the speaker's argument, this advantage is undermined by the increased burden such long segments place on the interpreter's memory (González et al. 1991, p. 379). In addition, the concentration required to both take accurate notes, and produce fluent speech from those notes, is extensive. Finally, consecutive interpretation places the interpreter at the center of attention while performing her task, which can be an exceedingly stressful position in comparison to simultaneous interpretation, where the interpreter is mainly an unseen voice working in the background.

2.2.3 Sight Translation

Sight translation can be defined as the oral interpretation of meaning contained in a written document (Mikkelson 2000, p. 76; de Jongh 1991, p. 288). Put plainly, the interpreter is given a written document in one language and is required to then read aloud that document in a different language. It contains elements of both interpretation and translation, and requires the interpreter to instantaneously read and comprehend the written text while producing a target language version of that text for the audience (González et al. 1991, p. 401). The mental process involved has been compared to that of simultaneous interpretation, though with a less noticeable time pressure and resulting decalage (Mikkelson 2000, p. 76).

From the outside perspective, the work of the sight translator is viewed as simple, akin to reading (González et al. 1991, p. 402). This is, however, far from the case, as there exists an underlying complexity to the task (González et al. 1991, p. 402). In addition to the inherent difficulties associated with simultaneously reading and analyzing one language while speaking another, there is the extra burden of the legal language involved: written legal documents (as opposed to oral legal speech) invariably contain more densely-packed information expressed in more complicated language (González et al. 1991, p. 402). Furthermore, written documents lack the speech cues, such as intonation and intentional pauses, that interpreters normally use to decipher the underlying meaning of overly difficult segments (González et al. 1991, p. 402). Adding to the level of difficulty is the fact that interpreters are rarely trained in the area of sight translations, since this is not a normal part of an interpreter's work (González et al. 1991, p. 403).

2.2.4 Summarization

The final technique employed in a courtroom setting is that of summarization, whereby the interpreter listens to the source language speech and then orally transmits the meaning of that speech in condensed summary form to the audience using the target language (de Jongh 1992, p. 49). In other words, the interpreter is summarizing the general idea of the proceedings for the audience. Here, the exact words and phrases used in the courtroom are not conveyed (a process referred to in this work as a "comprehensive interpretation"), but rather only a broad overview of what has transpired. While this method of interpretation is not normally used in legal proceedings, since it "lacks the accuracy and completeness" of the other methods mentioned above, it has also not been completely abandoned by the court system (Stern 2011, p. 330; de Jongh 1992, p. 49; see also Kadric 2000, p. 157). However, it is frowned upon by interpreting associations (see for example NAJIT 2005) and the modern trend is away from summary interpreting (Mikkelson 2000, p. 73), as can be seen by its lack of usage in the ICC, the ICTY, the ICTR, and numerous national systems.

2.3 How the Different Techniques Are Used in the Courtroom

2.3.1 Overview

Generally speaking, courtroom interpreters are necessary in four distinct situations. First, where one or more witnesses do not speak the language of the court, a courtroom interpreter is called upon to interpret their testimony. Second, where the defendant does not speak or understand the language of the court, an interpreter is necessary to allow him to comprehend the proceedings. This is the "right to an interpreter" as dissected in Chap. 2. Third, the same defendant may require an interpreter to allow him to communicate with his attorney (if that attorney does not speak the same language as the defendant). Finally, where documents must be interpreted for the court or for a defendant on the spot, an interpreter may be necessary as well. Each of these situations involves a slightly different interpreting technique.

2.3.2 Witness Interpreter

In the circumstance where a witness is able to neither understand nor communicate in language of the courtroom, the dominant interpreting technique is consecutive interpreting (Stern 2011, p. 331; Davis and Hewitt 1994, pp. 130–131; González et al. 1991, p. 163). The attorney will ask a question in the main courtroom language, which will be interpreted into the witness's language. The witness will then answer using the foreign language, after which the interpreter will translate this answer back into the dominant language for the courtroom. Since the question-and-answer format lends itself to shorter segments, courtroom interpreters rarely take notes during witness testimony (generally only for numbers or names, if at all) (Mikkelson 2000, p. 72).

A noticeable element in this situation is the fact that every statement is made twice: once in the main courtroom language and once in the witness's language. Thus, the consecutive interpretation of a witness greatly extends the procedure, taking nearly twice as long as a normal witness would (Davis and Hewitt 1994, p. 130). In addition, since courtroom interpreters rarely use notes, any longer answers must be broken up into different segments, requiring the attorney and witness to pause and wait on the interpreter, resulting in uneven testimony (Davis and Hewitt 1994, p. 130). Another difficulty arises where one speaker interrupts the interpreter before she has finished (as occasionally occurs), which can result in not only confusion for everyone involved, but also a muddled and unclear record (González et al. 1991, p. 165).

Even with these disadvantages, however, consecutive interpretation is greatly preferred to simultaneous when dealing with witnesses for several reasons. First, having the interpreter speak at the same time as the witness or attorney results in two overlapping voices, which can be distracting to those involved in the procedure and result in an imprecise record (Davis and Hewitt 1994, p. 130).[3] Second, consecutive is generally considered to be more accurate than simultaneous, which makes it more suitable for witness testimony that will be part of the final court record (Stern 2011, p. 331; González et al. 1991, pp. 164–165). Finally, consecutive interpretation allows the courtroom audience to better "assess the verbal and non-verbal behavior of the witness", since they can focus on the witness when the witness is speaking, and the interpreter when the interpreter is speaking, as these are kept separate (González et al. 1991, p. 165). With simultaneous interpretation, the witness is frequently a forgotten afterthought as all attention is placed on the interpreter and the courtroom language rendition. Of course, as will be seen in Chap. 5, consecutive interpretation does not completely alleviate this problem: research has shown that fact-finders base their perceptions of witnesses on the style and mannerisms of the consecutive interpreter rather than the witness themselves (Berk-Seligson 2002, pp. 288–289).

2.3.3 Proceedings Interpreter

Where the defendant is unable to speak or understand the language of the courtroom, the interpreter will generally simultaneously interpret the proceedings for the defendant (Stern 2011, p. 331; Davis and Hewitt 1994, p. 131; de Jongh 1992, p. 45). Summarization is also available as a technique here, but as previously detailed, its use is largely frowned upon by both interpreters and courts (Mikkelson 2000, p. 73). Since the interpreter's translation for the defendant is not part of the record, there is no

[3]It is also possible for courtroom interpreters to use electronic equipment that allows them to provide their translation only to those individuals using a personal headphone (as is the long existing practice in international courts), but such equipment is largely considered beyond the financial reach of domestic courts (Mikkelson 2000, p. 73).

necessity for anyone other than the defendant to hear it, and thus it can be made quietly and contemporaneously without disturbing the other participants in the courtroom (de Jongh 1992, p. 45). Outside of multi-defendant cases in well-funded jurisdictions capable of utilizing electronic equipment, the standard practice in domestic courtrooms is "whisper technique", where the interpreter simply whispers the translation into the defendant's ear (Stern 2011, p. 331; Pantoga 1999, p. 647; González et al. 1991, p. 465).

The disadvantages to simultaneous interpretation in these circumstances are diverse but important. First, since the interpreter is whispering her translation into the defendant's ear, there is virtually no method of assuring the accuracy of her work-product. Second, because the interpreter is not interpreting for the court, her presence is sometimes forgotten by the courtroom participants, which can result in difficulties for the interpreter (lack of sufficient breaks, two people speaking at the same time, etc…). Third, an interpreter who is whispering into a defendant's ear is forced to maintain a close physical proximity to an individual who may, in some instances, be considered dangerous (or potentially dangerous). Yet, whatever negative drawbacks are presented by the use of simultaneous interpretation for a defendant, the option of consecutively interpreting throughout an entire trial is simply unpalatable for most legal systems. The added time and expense is too great, and the benefits too hidden for the normal courtroom participants, who would experience extensive delay for little or no obvious benefit to themselves.

2.3.4 Defense Interpreter

In some circumstances, an interpreter is needed to allow the defendant and his attorney to consult (Chang and Araujo 1975, p. 802). Logically, in these situations, the attorney speaks the language of the court, but the defendant does not, and thus an interpreter is already present in order to allow the defendant to understand the proceedings. However, the interpreter's role and technique here is different than in both of the previously discussed situations. On the one hand, because the discussion between the defendant and his attorney will be off-the-record, there is no need for formal interpretation for the other courtroom participants. Thus, the interpretation must be quiet and can be informal, similar to elements of the whisper technique used as a proceedings interpreter. Yet, on the other hand, since the conversation will likely follow a question-and-answer format, it will be consecutively interpreted like a witness interpreter. These contrasting techniques present another unique situation to which interpreters must be ready to adapt.

2.3.5 Document Interpreter

The final distinct category of usage involves the necessity of contemporaneous document translation. The technique of choice in these circumstances is sight translation (González et al. 1991, p. 404). Such documents may generally be considered of two types: formal and informal (González et al. 1991, p. 404). Informal documents often consist of witness statements, affidavits, letters or other similar manuscripts; they are sometimes handwritten, often disorganized, and tend to contain lower-level language, complete with grammatical errors (González et al. 1991, p. 404). These elements make their translation extremely difficult (González et al. 1991, p. 405). Formal documents are only slightly better. They largely encompass official court documents from either the court itself (to be translated for the defendant) or from a foreign jurisdiction (to be translated for the court) (González et al. 1991, p. 404). In either case, they normally contain very high-level vocabulary, technical terms, and dense legal language (González et al. 1991, p. 405). Since the prior translation of such documents is not always possible (though recommended), sight translation is frequently necessary.

2.3.6 Conclusion

The end outcome is that no fewer than three different interpreting techniques are generally necessary during each trial: consecutive for witness interpretation and attorney consultations; simultaneous for interpretation of the proceedings; and sight translation for any document interpretation.

Given these requirements, it is obvious that the demands placed upon court interpreters are substantial. Unlike a conference interpreter who may exist solely in the realm of simultaneous interpretation for an entire job, the courtroom interpreter must be capable of switching between each technique as required by the circumstances. This requires a certain technical flexibility and mental agility that not all interpreters possess.

Yet, while interpreters do exist who are capable of such feats, the circumstances of a particular trial may dictate that more than one interpreter is necessary. For instance, the existence of multiple foreign language individuals in the courtroom may require extra interpreters, even where the participants all speak the same foreign language. An interpreter who is consecutively interpreting a witness's testimony for the court is unable to simultaneously interpret any attorney objections or comments from the judge for anyone else in the courtroom, because to do so would require either that she interrupt the courtroom actors (to provide space for a consecutive interpretation) or simply speak over them (for simultaneous). Nor is a foreign language defendant in such circumstances able to consult with his attorney, or ask the interpreter for clarification if he did not understand her interpretation of the witness (Chang and Araujo 1975, p. 821). Thus, while it may be theoretically possible for a single interpreter to technically handle the entirety of a proceeding, this may not be a practical solution (Davis and Hewitt 1994, p. 133). As such, the above-discussed situations not only dictate the technique of interpretation that is appropriate, but they also help determine the number of interpreters that may be necessary.

2.4 Basic Expectations of the Court Interpreter

2.4.1 Introduction

Having established what interpreting techniques are essential in each particular situation that requires a courtroom interpreter, it is still necessary to determine the legal expectations for the court interpreter's performance. In 1977, at least in one country, such legal expectations were "non-existent" (Safford 1977, p. 16). And while court interpreting has come a long way in the intervening 40 years, no single accepted canon of ethics or legal requirements to guide the performance of interpreters currently exists (Stern 2011, p. 334; European Commission 2009, p. 7; González et al. 1991, p. 474). In fact, some countries still impose no ethical obligations on their court interpreters at all (Taibi and Martin 2012 [concerning Spain], p. 79; European Commission 2009 [surveying E.U. national practices], p. 7). However, even in the absence of such an overriding ethical framework, there are some aspects of interpreting that can be considered as common throughout the profession (Stern 2011, pp. 334–335; González et al. 1991, pp. 475–513). In this respect, the discussion will focus on these areas that have produced commonly-accepted standards within the profession: the interpreter's role within the courtroom; the expectation of her level of performance; and the specific ethical considerations applicable to a court interpreter.

2.4.2 The Role of the Courtroom Interpreter and the Scope of Her Activities

The role of the interpreter within the judicial system is not well understood, even among experienced foreign language professionals themselves (de Jongh 1991, p. 285). Judges tend to view courtroom interpreters one way, while attorneys and defendants also each maintain their own individual expectations of the interpreter (Stern 2011, p. 333; Morris 1999, p. 26, 2001, p. 13). As such, in order to understand the courtroom interpreter's place within the system, it is easiest to begin by discussing what roles the interpreter does **not** inhabit.

The Invisible Machine

Judges, and sometimes attorneys as well, often view the courtroom interpreter as a mechanical object which automatically transforms speech from one language into another (Stern 2011, p. 333; Hale 2004, p. 12; Ibrahim and Bell 2003, p. 219; Jacobsen 2003, p. 224; Morris 1995, p. 27). Part of this viewpoint is the assumption by court personnel that "interpreting is a mechanical process requiring automatic responses rather than judgment or discernment" (Mikkelson 2008, p. 82). Or, as a former Judge on the Supreme Court of South Australia noted, "[t]he interpreter should look upon himself rather as an electric transformer, whatever is fed into him is to be fed out again, duly transformed" (quoted in Hale 2004, p. 8). This caricature brings with it the expectation that the interpreter should remain invisible and compliant, performing only those actions that are assigned to her and exercising no independent judgment of her own (Mikkelson 2008, p. 83; Morris 1995, p. 27). The courtroom interpreter in this view is nothing more than a "reluctantly accepted practical necessity" that should not disturb the parties as they conduct their business (Morris 1999, p. 9).

This is an untenable view of courtroom interpreting and the interpreting process. It rests chiefly on the assumption that a message expressed in one language can be easily deconstructed and re-encoded in a different language with little loss of meaning and at minimal effort (Morris 1995, p. 30). In other words, it assumes that the interpretation of language is akin to mathematics, in that a right answer always exists (LaVigne and Vernon 2003, p. 868). Unfortunately, this is an unrealistic expectation. Foreign language professionals have long maintained that exact equivalence only rarely exists between different languages, and as a result, there can be few if any "right" answers, rather only a variety of choices each with their own slightly different connotations that partially overlap with the original word (Gile 2009, p. 52; González et al. 1991, pp. 30–31). It is the peculiar expertise of interpreters that informs their decisions as to which word to choose under the specific circumstances, and it is this expertise that allows them to articulate as closely as possible in one language what was expressed previously in another. These are, however, voluntary choices made between largely equal options based upon the interpreter's subjective understanding of the original message (González et al. 1991, p. 239). As such, interpreting is neither mechanical nor automatic, but instead an "extremely subtle and exacting art" (Heller 1994–1995, p. 379).

Nor is it an art form that can be practiced invisibly. Whether it takes the form of interrupting a witness who fails to speak in manageable segments (Mason 2008, p. 41), asking an attorney to clarify their question

(Berk-Seligson 1990, p. 66), or requesting that the judge speak more loudly (Cardenas 2001, p. 24), interpreters can sometimes only do their job correctly if they are an active participant in the courtroom proceeding. This insertion into, and disruption of, the normal judicial procedures is often tolerated with something less than complete grace: for example, one interpreter who asked the judge to speak more loudly was told "[y]ou don't have to hear, just interpret!" (Cardenas 2001, p. 24). Yet, the process of making these complex choices occasionally requires information that can only be gathered through such interruptions. As such, they occur. Thus, the role of the interpreter in the courtroom is neither mechanical nor invisible, but rather engaged and deliberate.

The Advocate

There is another common misconception, particularly held by interpreters themselves, that the interpreter's role within the courtroom is to help the individual who does not speak the language of the court (Matu et al. 2012, p. 123; Hale 2001, p. 71; González et al. 1991, p. 18). The assumption made in this context is that the individual is disadvantaged by a lack of understanding of both the majority language and the foreign proceedings, and that the interpreter should help them overcome these disadvantages (Stern 2011, p. 333; Hale 2004, p. 8; González et al. 1991, p. 18). In this role, the interpreter is an advocate, entrusted with two separate tasks. First, she is to interpret the language used in the court so as to ensure that the individual does not simply hear what was actually said, but rather understands what was meant (Hale 2004, p. 8; González et al. 1991, p. 18). In other words, she has the license to change the words, phrasing or content of an utterance in order to guarantee that the linguistically disadvantaged person understands the meaning of that utterance. Second, an interpreter is meant to adapt or embellish the individual's responses herself in order to help the case or testimony (Hale 2004, p. 8; González et al. 1991, p. 18). Attorneys as well sometimes view the interpreter's role as that of an advocate, but not necessarily for the linguistically incapable individual, rather for whoever is paying the interpreter for her services (Hale 2004, p. 9). As professionals who work in a client-based system, paying attorneys consider themselves the client of the interpreter, and therefore expect the same advocacy that they give their paying clients (Hale 2004, p. 9).

While the vast majority of attorneys and judges strongly oppose the idea of the interpreter as an advocate, there are some courts that actively endorse it as a means of overcoming the built-in linguistic and cultural disadvantage under which language incompetent individuals suffer (Ibrahim 2007 [with respect to Malaysia], p. 212; see generally González et al. 1991, p. 18). The main difficulty with the utilization of an interpreter as advocate is that it requires the interpreter to actively change information during the interpretation process, not in an attempt to be more accurate, but rather to make the speaker better understood or more positively received. In essence, the audience hears not what the speaker actually said, but either a more simplified version of what the interpreter believes the speaker wanted to say (when speaking to the linguistically incapable individual) or a more favorable version of what the interpreter believes the speaker would have said if they understood the situation completely (when speaking on behalf of the linguistically incapable individual). While this may result in more efficient proceedings and guarantee that the individual understands those proceedings (which, as previously discussed, is the underlying aim of the right to an interpreter), it accomplishes each of these goals by effectively allowing an interpreter, who is rarely trained in the law and often lacks a comprehensive knowledge of the facts in a particular case, to filter the language and content of those proceedings. Naturally, this is not a tolerable outcome for the judicial system. As such, the concept of the interpreter as advocate, even though occasionally embraced by court interpreters themselves, is considered unacceptable and therefore discouraged (González et al. 1991, p. 18).

Facilitator of Communication

The idea that the interpreter's main role is to ensure that the defendant understands the proceedings, as opposed to understanding the language used in the proceedings, leads some interpreters to assume that their job in the courtroom is to facilitate communication between the parties. This conception of court interpretation arises from the experience of interpreters in other branches of interpreting, where the role of "communication facilitator" is well-established (Hale 2004, pp. 11–12; see also Stern 2011, p. 334 [advocating this for court interpreters as well]). In conference interpreting, for instance, it is actually expected that the interpreter will improve the speaker's output, making it less repetitious and more elegant (Hayes and Hale 2010, p. 121; Morris 1995, p. 38; González et al. 1991, p. 27). The main goal, as perceived in this role definition, is not to help one party over the other, but rather to attempt to ensure that both parties effectively understand each other.

While removing the difficulties of communication may, again, produce a more efficient judicial proceeding that the linguistically incapable individual can more easily understand, it is generally agreed upon that it is inappropriate for the interpreter to alter information in order to achieve such communication (Hale 2001, p. 71). Changing, clarifying, or explaining information to either party assumes that the interpreter's subjective understanding of that information is correct. In many instances, this may not be the case. Moreover, acting to ensure communication assumes that the speaker wishes to actually communicate with the other party, which, given that attorneys frequently use language as a weapon or dramatic instrument, also may not be the case (Hale 2004, p. 13; see also Fowler 1995).[4] Therefore, court interpreters are generally instructed to abstain from simplifying language or concepts in order to facilitate communication within the courtroom.

Language Barrier Remover

If the interpreter is neither an invisible machine, a facilitator of communication, nor an advocate, it begs the question as to what exact role the interpreter is supposed to fill in the courtroom. The simple answer

[4] "Lawyers design their questions in order to achieve a number of clearly identifiable ends. Accusations, challenges, justifications, denials, and rebuttals may all be packaged as questions and answers" (Fowler 1995, p. 194).

is that the courtroom interpreter is tasked with removing the language barrier and placing the linguistically incapable individual in a position as similar as possible to that of a comparable individual who does speak the dominant language (Hale 2004, pp. 9–10). If the individual is an illiterate layperson who does not speak the language of the court, then they should be able to understand as much of the proceedings as a dominant-language-speaking illiterate layperson would, no more and no less (Hale 2004, pp. 9–10). In other words, the interpreter's job is to allow the various parties in the courtroom to interact in the exact same manner they would if everyone spoke the language of the court. The easiest way to accomplish this goal is for the interpreter to relinquish her normal responsibility for communication, and to simply interpret the words and phrases that the individuals in the courtroom actually speak (Hale 2004, p. 12).

By focusing on such a "true" interpretation, the interpreter is trusting that the individuals involved in the courtroom will assume responsibility for any miscommunications or misunderstandings themselves, and attempt to solve them on their own (Hale 2001, p. 71). Placing this burden on the courtroom participants mirrors what occurs in any normal proceeding where everyone involved speaks the language of the court. In such situations, many native speakers of the dominant language also fail to understand their own domestic court proceedings and are unable to comprehend the technical language used in that court (Mikkelson 2000, p. 69). They must rely on their attorney or the judge to successfully explain the proceedings or meanings of the language used. Ensuring that interpreters only interpret the language used, and do not actually attempt to clarify or explain the practical meaning or impact of those terms, does nothing more than place the linguistically incapable individual in the exact same position as someone who does in fact speak the language. If that position is one of confusion, then that is a failing of the speakers and the language they choose to employ rather than the interpreter (Hale 2001, p. 71). A question or remark that is unclear in the source language should remain an equally unclear question or remark in the target language.

2.4.3 The Level of Accuracy Required: "True" Interpretation

The Verbatim Requirement

Although it is by and large undisputed that the interpreter should provide an accurate or "true" interpretation of what is said in the courtroom, the definition of what constitutes an "accurate" translation is somewhat less straightforward (Hale 2002, p. 25). It is generally accepted that any interpretation must be "linguistically true and legally appropriate" (González et al. 1991, p. 16) and should, at all times and in all exchanges, "convey the exact meaning and intent of the speaker" (de Jongh 1991, p. 288). This is known as a "legal equivalent" (González et al. 1991, p. 16). In order to achieve such an equivalent, courts generally require interpreters "to render in a **verbatim manner** the form and content of the linguistic and paralinguistic elements of a discourse, including all of the pauses, hedges, self-corrections, hesitations, and emotion as they are conveyed through tone of voice, word choice, and intonation" (González et al. 1991, p. 16 [emphasis in the original]; see also Stern 2011, p. 335). In other words, interpreters must translate the spoken discourse literally word-for-word and emotion-for-emotion, with no allowed deviations, retaining every single element of information present in the original utterance (both spoken and unspoken) (Mikkelson 1998, p. 2; González et al. 1991, p. 16).

This "verbatim requirement" meshes well with the judicial system's view of interpreting as a mathematical process in which a correct answer always exists. There are several advantages to this approach. First, by requiring interpreters to adhere to such a standard of excellence, the court can effectively ignore the language issue and function under the legal fiction that interpreted proceedings are exactly the same as monolingual proceedings (Morris 1995, p. 30). Second, mandating a word-for-word translation protects the record, ensuring that it contains the speaker's exact words rather than an interpreter's explanation or understanding of those words (Mikkelson 1998, p. 2; González et al. 1991, p. 475). Finally, setting such a high standard that protects every single word that is spoken lets the audience (judges, attorneys, juries, etc…) make their own interpretation as to the actual meaning of the original utterance, and thus also their own informed judgment as to the character and nature of the speaker, as opposed to allowing a single interpreter to do so in their stead (González et al. 1991, p. 17).

The Impossibility of the Standard

While the merits of requiring a word-for-word translation are obvious, the verbatim requirement fails to take into consideration the simple fact that a "truly verbatim interpretation is literally impossible" (Mikkelson 1998, p. 4; see also Mikkelson 2010, p. 4). As previously argued, interpretation is not an automatic process where every language possesses an obviously correct equivalent to the original word, but instead, most languages have several suitable options, each with their own slightly different meaning and connotation (Morris 1995, pp. 30–31; González et al. 1991, p. 239). Thus, a word-for-word equivalence simply does not exist often enough to require this as a baseline standard for interpreters.

Nor, in many circumstances, is a verbatim translation even desirable. Take, for instance, the concept of idioms, which are phrases that have a meaning independent of the actual words used (González et al. 1991, p. 243). The meaning of the German idiom "*ich verstehe nur Bahnhof*" is very similar to the English idiom "it's as clear as mud to me". However, were a courtroom interpreter to employ a word-for-word, verbatim translation, an English-language courtroom audience would understand the German speaker to have stated that "I only understand train station." Naturally, this would be nonsense, and would reflect negatively on the speaker. Swear words and insults provide another example. The German insult "*Dummkopf*", for instance, can literally be translated into English as "stupid head". While the courtroom participants would understand the literal meaning of this insult, they cannot gauge its strength and power (or lack thereof), thus making the insult more descriptive than insulting. This is true of any number of swear words in a variety of languages (Hale 2004, p. 16).

Pragmatic Meaning as a Substitute

Since literal word-for-word translations often fail to be completely accurate as to the speaker's meaning and intent, many court interpreters reinterpret the verbatim standard to require not the preservation of every single word, but rather the conservation of "every single element of meaning" (Mikkelson 2000, p. 71). This leads to the practice of "pragmatic translation": court interpreters seek to understand and interpret the real and intended meaning of the spoken words, as opposed to the individual words themselves (Hale 2004, p. 5). Under this standard, "*ich verstehe nur Bahnhof*" would be interpreted as "it's clear as mud to me", and "*Dummkopf*" would be rendered as "idiot", since these translations convey the intended meaning of the speaker's words, even where the actual word-for-word equivalence is lost. The key element in this practice is that the interpreter seeks to produce the same result and impact on the audience with the target language translation as the speaker was hoping to achieve in the source language (Hale 2004, p. 14). Thus, if the speaker was specifically intending to shock or unsettle the audience with his choice of words in the source language, the interpreter will also choose target language words that are likely to shock or unsettle the audience, even where these words are not the direct equivalent of those used by the speaker.

Seeking to reproduce the impact of speech requires not only paying attention to the specific words used by the speaker, but also to "tone, changes of intonation, facial cues, and, especially, gestures, because the full context of an interpreted statement involves verbal as well as nonverbal communication" (de Jongh 1991, p. 290). Also of importance to such an interpretation is the level of formality employed by the speaker, which is known as "register", and can affect how the audience evaluates the speaker (de Jongh 1992, p. 41; Berk-Seligson 1990, pp. 169, 176). Under the pragmatic equivalence practice then, the interpreter must duplicate, as well as possible under the circumstances, the actual meaning of the speaker's words, using both the pragmatically equivalent words as well as the non-verbal elements of communication employed by the speaker. If done correctly, the audience will react to the foreign language speaker as if that person were speaking the language of the court (Mason 2008,

p. 8). Naturally, emphasizing the non-verbal elements of the speaker's utterance in addition to the spoken words adds an extra level of difficulty to what is an already difficult process.

Although well-accepted, the pragmatic standard is not beyond criticism. First, interpreting the verbatim (word-for-word) standard to mean a pragmatic (meaning-for-meaning) standard is less an interpretation of that standard than it is a complete amendment of the process favored by courts. Second, focusing on the meaning of speech requires interpreters to necessarily sacrifice the explicit words used by the speaker in favor of words that the interpreter believes are better suited to the speaker's purpose. This makes the speaker's effectiveness contingent on the skill and intelligence of the interpreter. In specific courtroom situations, such as the cross-examination of a witness, where attorneys carefully choose specific terms and phrases in order to set a trap or establish the grounds for a later legal argument, the court interpreter may not be sufficiently experienced to grasp the actual underlying purpose of the attorney's actions. Third, the sacrificing of words in the name of meaning also creates a slippery slope problem: how many words should be sacrificed and at what point does this sacrifice undermine what the speaker actually said? Finally, just as the pragmatic standard requires interpreters to assess the underlying meaning of speech, it also necessitates that they interpret the original meaning of any non-verbal elements such as gestures, which can vary from culture to culture (de Jongh 1992, p. 58). Although interpreters may be better suited to interpret these elements than the average courtroom participant, this is still not a task for which interpreters are ideally suited, since they are linguistic experts, not cultural experts (González et al. 1991, pp. 502–503). In spite of these reservations, the generally-accepted standard employed in courtrooms today by courtroom interpreters is the pragmatic standard.

2.4.4 The Ethical Standards Applicable to Court Interpreters

The necessity of interpreting accurately is not only a legal standard imposed by the judicial system, it is also an ethical obligation common throughout the profession of courtroom interpreting. That courtroom interpreters are subject to ethical obligations is a fact frequently unknown to the other participants in the courtroom, many of whom bring with them their own expectations as to how the interpreter should behave (Hale 2004, p. 11; Morris 1999, p. 26). Some of these expectations have previously been discussed. In many respects, such as where advocacy is concerned, these expectations will clash with the ethical requirements which govern the interpreter in her particular jurisdiction. As previously mentioned, there exists no uniform canon of ethics applicable to all courtroom interpreters; however, there are some ethical obligations that can be considered as common given their pervasiveness throughout the most important ethical codes (Stern 2011, pp. 334–335; González et al. 1991, pp. 474–513). It goes without saying, of course, that the sitting judge is the final arbiter of the ethical and legal rules applicable in any national courtroom (González et al. 1991, p. 474).

A basic tenet of the profession of courtroom interpreting is that the interpreter must remain neutral in fact (Stern 2011, p. 335; Corsellis and Fernández 2001, p. 79; González et al. 1991, p. 494). The nature of courtroom interpreting requires that interpreters establish a rapport with the individual whom they are interpreting (Mikkelson 2008, p. 83). Likewise, there is an instinctive tendency of the person who does not speak the language of the court to develop a dependency on the interpreter, since she is their only linguistic link to the outside world and to a proceeding which will likely have a significant impact on their life (Mikkelson 2008, p. 83). This natural symbiosis can cause the interpreter to identify with the individual, and in some ways influence the resulting interpretation (Berk-Seligson 1990, p. 109). The previously discussed advocacy role is a normal outgrowth of this organically occurring dynamic (Hale 2004, p. 8). Yet, as sworn officers of the court, interpreters have an ethical obligation to serve the court, not the individual for whom they interpret (Grabau 1996, p. 7; González et al. 1991, p. 494). As such, they are ethically bound to remain neutral towards the linguistically incapable individual, even where this goes against their natural instincts.

In addition, courtroom interpreters are usually required to maintain the appearance of neutrality as well (Corsellis and Fernández 2001, p. 79; González et al. 1991, p. 495). Therefore, interpreters are counseled to avoid unnecessary conversations with the person for whom they are interpreting, as well as generally to avoid any independent conversations with any other individuals involved in the case (Grabau 1996, p. 9; de Jongh 1992, p. 39; González et al. 1991, p. 495). This can be fairly difficult given that the foreign language individual will often feel isolated and therefore naturally attempt to engage the interpreter, the only person with whom they can speak, in casual conversation. Such a conversation, in a language which likely no one else in the courtroom fully understands, is prone to look suspicious and can cause the interpreter to appear biased. This appearance of bias undermines not only the credibility of the interpreter, but also the confidence the other courtroom participants may feel in the overall proceedings.

Aside from issues of neutrality and interpreting accuracy, which account for the most obvious ethical obligations, interpreters are also subject to other, less obvious but equally important, ethical standards. For instance, interpreters are also ethically obligated to keep any and all information that they interpret confidential (Stern 2011, p. 335; González et al. 1991, pp. 498–499). This is especially important when interpreting between a defendant and his attorney, since it helps protect the attorney-client privilege. Likewise, interpreters are bound to stay within their role as interpreters; they may not give the linguistically incapable individual any legal advice or answer any legal questions (Stern 2011, p. 335; González et al. 1991, p. 500). While this may seem rather evident given that the interpreter is not an attorney, it is not always obvious to the foreign language participant; such individuals frequently ask the interpreter for similar advice because they feel a linguistic and personal bond with her. Finally, as an officer of the court, the interpreter is ethically obligated to inform the court of any mistakes in her interpretation (if she notices) or any situation which may compromise her ability to remain neutral (de Jongh 1992, p. 41; González et al. 1991, p. 496).

3 A Theoretical Overview of Courtroom Interpreting: The Effort Model

3.1 Introduction

It is, unfortunately, not enough to simply say that interpreters should interpret accurately. As an aspiration, this is a given; as a reality, it is somewhat more difficult to achieve. Even highly experienced interpreters make "numerous" errors (Gile 2002, p. 163; see also Gile 2009). One can simply accept a certain level of inaccuracy as the cost of court interpreting, or one can attempt to understand why interpreting carries with it such errors. For the present purposes, and in order to gain an enhanced understanding of the specific errors that courtroom interpreters make, it is necessary to investigate what is actually happening when an individual interprets. As such, the theory behind interpreting will be briefly discussed.

In this context, the so-called "effort model" of interpreting created by Gile, which is commonly accepted throughout the interpreting studies community, will be used as the framework for understanding the inner-workings of interpreting (Gile 2009, p. 187; see generally Chabasse and Dingfelder Stone 2015). It is based upon the assumption that interpreting is an inherently complex task that stretches the limited cognitive abilities of the interpreter to the breaking point; thus producing inevitable interpreter error. The details of this theoretical model will be explained, insofar as relevant to courtroom interpreting, as will the various strategies employed by interpreters to deal with situations where their cognitive capacity is overloaded.

3.2 Cognitive Capacity and the Tightrope Theory

As mentioned, the task of interpreting is extremely complex (de Jongh 2008, p. 25). Interpreters simultaneously perform two actions (understanding speech or text and producing speech) that are otherwise almost always executed separately (de Jongh 2008, p. 25). That these two different functions of communication involve two distinct languages only complicates matters. Considering the complexity of the work, it is reasonable to assume that errors could and would be attributed to the shear difficulty of the task. Yet, historically, interpreting error was almost universally attributed to poor working conditions or the inadequate training or knowledge of the interpreter, specifically her insufficient knowledge of the languages used (Gile 2002, pp. 163–164). Naturally, these difficulties were things that supposedly could be overcome through proper planning, training or hard work.

However, studies continuously have shown that even well-regarded interpreters commit errors not only when interpreting highly technical and informationally dense speeches, but also when given clear and relatively simple passages (Gile 2009, p. 157). In response to this evidence, Gile (2002) has postulated that the errors are a result of the inherent difficulty of interpreting itself, rather than the specific complexities of the language to be interpreted (p. 164). Specifically, Gile (2009) argues that the interpreting process requires a certain amount of cognitive resources, and that when the demand on these resources outstrips the brain's cognitive supply, errors result (p. 159).

Cognitive psychology supports Gile's theory: it has long been established that human performance in cognitive tasks depends on a limited supply of processing capacity (Gile 2009, p. 188). Interpreting studies research has also provided evidence that limited cognitive capacity influences interpreting error. In one study, interpreters were given the chance to interpret the exact same speech that they had previously interpreted only a short time before. During the second interpretation, the interpreters consistently made errors on passages of text that they had previously interpreted without problems (Gile 2009, p. 158). Thus, their errors arose not from inadequate knowledge of the language or vocabulary, the usual culprits cited by interpreters, but from an alternate source, most likely the difficulty of the task itself (Gile 2009, p. 158).

Central to Gile's theory that many interpreting errors arise from an overloaded cognitive capacity is the assumption that interpreters consistently work at the so-called "saturation" point (Chabasse and Dingfelder Stone 2015, pp. 76–77; Gile 2009, p. 158). In other words, the task of interpreting routinely requires the absolute maximum of an individual's cognitive capacity, and in the process of interpreting, individuals find themselves consistently at the edge of their mental abilities. While there are no significant studies that directly support this hypothesis of interpreter saturation, it is not difficult to believe that it is true: during a 30-minute segment, interpreters normally will "translate" an average of 3000–3900 words, which is equivalent to 12–15 typewritten, double-spaced pages (de Jongh 2008, p. 26). For the sake of comparison, the output of a normal translator working at an international organization ranges anywhere from 3 to 10 pages in a single day (de Jongh 2008, p. 26).

3.3 The Efforts

To understand how the limited cognitive capabilities of a human can affect interpreting, it is useful to delve further into the characteristics of cognitive capacity itself, particularly as it relates to interpreting. At the outset, one must distinguish between two types of cognitive operations: those that are automatic and those that are non-automatic (Gile 2009, p. 159). Automatic functions are those that the brain performs without conscious effort; as such they are performed relatively quickly and require little to no processing capacity (Gile 2009, p. 159). In contrast, non-automatic functions are those that require the conscious attention of the individual; thus, they are not only more time-consuming, but also require larger amounts of the brain's processing capacity (Gile 2009, p. 159). While there is still some debate as to whether non-automatic functions can ever truly be made fully automatic (compare Gile 2009, pp. 185–186 with González et al. 1991, p. 333), what can be said is that at a minimum they can be made more automatic and therefore less draining on the individual's cognitive capacity. For example, as one first learns to ride a bicycle, it requires considerable attention to simultaneously pedal, balance, and steer. However, after practice, these individual processes can become second-nature and therefore capable of performance with limited conscious effort. In the context of interpreting, several individual processes or so-called "efforts" have been identified through Gile's work, and the interpreting community generally.

3.3.1 The Listening and Analysis Effort ('L')

Naturally, before one can interpret speech or text for the audience, one must first hear/read and understand what has been said or written. At its most basic level, this involves the collection of a continuous stream of sounds and their organization into meaningful units which can then be compared to the listener's previously-acquired vocabulary (González et al. 1991, p. 300). Listening, in this respect, is more than simply hearing; it is a voluntary activity that requires a high level of concentration (de Jongh 1992, pp. 32–33; González et al. 1991, p. 380). Listening to a foreign language requires even higher levels of concentration, because the act of organizing the sounds into words can be complicated by accent and the unavoidable limitation of the listener's vocabulary (González et al. 1991, p. 381). For interpreters, this is even more demanding, because, unlike a normal listener who can tune out occasionally, yet still understand the overall idea of the speech, the interpreter is responsible for every single word (Gile 2009, p. 162). Moreover, a normal listener is more likely to be previously acquainted with the subject matter and the specific technical language involved, whereas the interpreter will be less proficient in these areas (Gile 2009, p. 162).

This process of hearing, evaluating the sounds, organizing them into words, and then determining their ultimate meaning within the context of the other words is defined as the "listening and analysis effort" (Gile 2009, p. 160). It involves elements of listening, understanding, and analysis; as such, it is a non-automatic function that requires part of the brain's cognitive capacity (Gile 2009, pp. 160–161). At the same time, the more comfortable the interpreter can become with a language, and the more easily a speaker can be understood (through, for instance, the elimination of any background noise or the lack of a pronounced accent), the less cognitive capacity will be required to actively listen to and understand that speaker.

3.3.2 The Production Effort ('P')

If the first part of the interpreter's task is to understand what has been said or written, the last part is surely the transformation of that meaning into another language. This is referred to as the "production effort", and consists of not only the obvious element of speaking the eventual words for the audience, but also the planning of what will be said and the monitoring and self-correction of what was actually said (Gile 2009, p. 163). From the outside, speech production by an interpreter can (and perhaps should) appear effortless or automatic, but that is far from the case (Gile 2009, pp. 163, 165). Normally, when an individual speaks, they can choose their own words and grammatical structures, thereby avoiding any uncomfortable situations. For instance, an English speaker who is unsure whether the past tense of "to swim" is "swam" or "swum" can avoid the construction altogether by saying that they "have been swimming". An interpreter, however, being responsible for every word and every nuance of the speech, has a limited ability to avoid uncomfortable usages (Gile 2009, p. 163). Her speech is constrained by what someone else has already said, not by what she wishes to say. This complicates her eventual speech production.

Moreover, the process of production involves more than the relatively simple aspect of just speaking. It also consists of planning that output beforehand, given what has been understood from the source language. This involves taking the understood meaning of the speech segment (or written text when performing sight translation) and deciding how best to express this meaning in the target language. Given the high standard of accuracy required in courtroom interpreting, this involves the conscious analysis of different options and an eventual choice. And since the grammatical structures of languages rarely match up exactly, the interpreter must furthermore choose not only the correct words to express the meaning, but also the most appropriate target language grammatical structure as well (Gile 2009, p. 164). Once these choices have been made and an overall plan developed as to how to accurately integrate each of these choices into a seamless final target language speech segment, the interpreter must consciously pay attention to what she actually says. This is known as "self-monitoring", and is a key aspect of production given that the interpreter is simultaneously listening to (or reading) the next segment in the other language which will often interfere with the interpreter's output (González et al. 1991, p. 367). Where the interpreter recognizes that she has erred in her interpretation, she will as a rule correct herself before proceeding further (González et al. 1991, p. 368). Although the end outcome of the interpreter's work may appear relatively straightforward (simple speech), each of the individual processes (planning the output, producing the speech, and then both monitoring and correcting that speech) comprising that task requires part of the brain's limited cognitive capacity.

3.3.3 The Memory Effort ('M')

Between the understanding of the source language speech and its eventual output in the target language, the interpreter's short-term memory is necessarily engaged. While the production effort actively attempts to formulate an interpretation and speech plan for its eventual output in the target language, the source language segment unavoidably must be kept in memory. In this context, the "memory effort" is understood to consist of only very short-term memory, lasting at most a few seconds (Gile 2009, p. 165). Experiments have shown that such short-term memory has a limited capacity and can only handle approximately seven pieces of information (de Jongh 1992, p. 43).

Given these limitations, the interpreter does not attempt to memorize the words in the speech in the same manner that people memorize poems or song lyrics for later recall, though some memory of the original phrasing is necessary in order to self-monitor the output and ensure that it correctly matches the original speech segment (de Jongh 1992, p. 31). Rather, interpreters remember the "meaning" extracted from the original words (de Jongh 1992, p. 31). As such, without the proper functioning of the listening and analysis effort, and thus the achievement of an actual understanding of the speech segment, the memory effort itself is largely unworkable. Likewise, if the production effort stalls and more and more pieces of information require storage before being translated and spoken to the audience (thus extending the decalage in simultaneous), the memory effort can be quickly overburdened. Also burdensome to the memory effort is the introduction of completely new information: older, more familiar information (such as often-used vocabulary) is easier to handle and more likely to be remembered (González et al. 1991, p. 385). Unfortunately for interpreters, from a cognitive standpoint the usage of short-term memory is non-automatic, and thus these extra burdens impact the overall available cognitive capacity (Gile 2009, p. 166).

3.3.4 The Note-Taking Effort ('N')

In the context of consecutive interpreting, the memory effort is supplemented by note-taking on longer segments of information (Gile 2009, p. 175). As previously mentioned, these notes detail only a representative part of the information received; the rest of the information is stored in the interpreter's long-term memory (this is distinct from the interpreter's short-term memory as represented in the memory effort) (Gile 2009, p. 178). The notes serve to assist the interpreter in recalling the bulk of the information from her long-term memory. In this respect, most interpreters only note the meaning of the text, and do not record the specific non-verbal elements of the speech segment (such as register) for later recall (González et al. 1991, p. 393). These are also entrusted to the interpreter's long-term memory.

There is some debate among interpreters and interpreting studies scholars as to the proper method for taking notes (Gile 2009, p. 179). There is little agreement as to whether notes should be taken using symbols or actual language, and as to whether any language used in the notes should be in the source or target language, or a mixture (Gile 2009, p. 179; but see also Dingfelder Stone 2015, pp. 152–153 [discussing the different approaches]; Andres 2002 [advocating a mixture of symbols, words, abbreviations and arrows], p. 95; de Jongh 1992 [advocating symbols], p. 45). There is also disagreement as to whether interpreters should be taught a set system, or whether they should be left to develop their own system (Gile 2009, p. 179). Unfortunately, there is limited empirical evidence that can be used to solve these debates; but in reality, most interpreters find their own individual solutions to these problems through trial and error (de Jongh 1992, p. 42). What is essential to the interpreting process is that the interpreter be comfortable enough with the task of taking notes that she can do so without drawing away too many cognitive resources from the other efforts involved in interpreting (Gile 2009, p. 178). The "note-taking effort" is different from the other efforts in this sense, because it is non-essential. Its role is to relieve excess burden from the other efforts. If its usage hinders the other efforts by demanding too much concentration, it may actually be detrimental to the process rather than complementary (Gile 2009, p. 178).

3.3.5 Other Efforts

The efforts detailed above constitute the major, independent processes that occur during interpreting. Of course, since there are several different types of interpreting techniques, there likewise exist variations on the different efforts themselves, as well as more minor efforts that exist only in a particular interpreting situation. Each of these lesser efforts, as well as the derivatives of the normal efforts, will be dealt with in their specific context. Finally, there is one overarching effort that is essential to the entire process: the mental capacity exerted by the individual in coordinating each of the other efforts and ensuring that the cognitive resources themselves are distributed in an efficient and productive manner (Gile 2009, pp. 167–168). This entails both the interpreter's conscious technical decisions (such as whether to extend the decalage) as well as the interpreter's instinctual management decisions (such as naturally concentrating more on accented speech). This process is known as the "coordination effort" or simply "C" (Gile 2009, p. 168).

3.4 The Effort Models of Interpreting

3.4.1 Introduction

Having detailed the specific, individual efforts that occur during the interpreting process, it is necessary to discuss how each of these efforts fits together in the different interpreting techniques practiced in a court of law. Gile's work in this area again serves as a basis point, since he has set out several models relating to consecutive and simultaneous interpretation, as well as to sight translation (Gile 2009, pp. 167–180). As with the efforts themselves, these models are based as far as possible on the applicable theories of cognitive psychology, and are well known throughout the interpreting community (Gile 2009, p. 187).

3.4.2 Simultaneous Interpreting

Simultaneous interpreting consists of four specific efforts: L (listening and analysis); M (memory); P (production); and C (coordination) (Gile 2009, pp. 167–168). The interpreter will be listening and attempting to comprehend one segment of speech (the L effort), while orally producing the translated version of an earlier segment of speech (the P effort), all at the same time as remembering a speech segment that has already passed (the

M effort) and still needs to be translated and spoken in the target language. Thus, at any given moment, any or all of the above-mentioned efforts may be working simultaneously, since these individual efforts must be somehow coordinated as well (the C effort) (Gile 2009, p. 168). It is expedient to believe that each of these efforts works in a sequential manner upon speech segments, like an assembly line for interpretation. However, this is not always the case (Gile 2009, p. 168). As will be seen later, sometimes interpreters consciously reorder speech segments as a "coping strategy", orally producing a translation of a later, easier segment while holding an earlier but more difficult segment for continued analysis (Gile 2009, p. 168). Thus, the application of the individual efforts is not always sequential in manner, which can complicate the coordination effort.

In order for this rather complicated set of interactive tasks to run smoothly, and thus for the simultaneous interpreter to work efficiently and well, the interpreter must have the available mental capacity to handle the work required (Gile 2009, p. 170). During simultaneous interpretation, each effort requires a certain variable amount of the brain's available resources. For example, sometimes the L effort needs more than normal (where the speech is heavily accented), sometimes it needs less (where the speech is unusually clear) (González et al. 1991, p. 381). For the simultaneous interpreter to be successful, each individual effort must receive enough of the brain's limited mental resources that it can fulfill its primary task (Gile 2009, p. 170). Naturally, the allocation of this cognitive capacity is a zero-sum game: where one effort receives extra mental resources, the other efforts must necessarily make do with less. Thus, where the simultaneous interpreter must pay extra attention to a heavily-accented speaker, she has less overall ability to produce an elegant translation in the target language (Gile 2009, p. 171). The reverse is true as well; if the speaker is unusually easy to understand, the interpreter can devote more resources to the final output.

3.4.3 Consecutive Interpreting

In the context of courtroom interpreting, Gile's model for consecutive interpreting is helpful, but not definitive. This is because it is based upon consecutive interpreting that involves longer pieces of information and note-taking, neither of which is always present in the courtroom versions of consecutive (Gile 2009, p. 175; Mason 2008, p. 73). As such, adaptations must be made to account for the specific courtroom experience. Gile (2009) divides consecutive interpreting into two different phases: the comprehension phase and the reformulation phase (p. 175). Each of these will be discussed separately.

The Comprehension Phase

The comprehension phase occurs when the interpreter is listening to the speaker (the L effort), storing in memory what was said (the M effort), and taking notes on the speech in order to assist her memory (the N effort) (Gile 2009, p. 175). The coordination of these efforts (the C effort) is also necessary (Gile 2009, p. 175). Since courtroom interpretation rarely involves the taking of notes, an effort model for short-passage consecutive interpreting would likely omit the N effort. Compensating for this omission, the M effort would necessarily be expanded to include not only short-term memory retention (Gile refers to several seconds at most), but also more extended memory (closer to de Jongh's estimation of 15–20 seconds for short-term memory retention) (Gile 2009, pp. 175–176; de Jongh 1992, p. 43).

In any event, not taking notes logically means the M effort will require more cognitive resources (Gile 2009, p. 178). This, in turn, results in less mental capacity being available for the other efforts. As with simultaneous interpreting, the comprehension phase of consecutive interpreting is a zero-sum game. Taking notes itself involves the use of significant mental resources, and also adds an extra variable that must be coordinated (Gile 2009, p. 178). This is not always a solution for an overloaded memory (Gile 2009, p. 178). A consecutive interpreter that is not comfortable using notes may simply be introducing a new N effort into the equation that takes over the resources dedicated to the M effort, but at the end of the day still results in a limited amount of cognitive resources for the other necessary efforts. This is more akin to changing the problem than finding a solution.

The Reformulation Phase

In consecutive interpreting, once the speaker has finished speaking, the interpreter must give an accurate translation of what the speaker said. Gile refers to this as the reformulation phase (Gile 2009, p. 176). In his evaluation, it consists of reading and understanding the notes that have been taken (known as the "Read" effort), the recollection of the original speech based upon these notes (the "Rem" effort), the production of a translated version in the target language (the normal P effort), and the coordination of each of these facets (the C effort) (Gile 2009, p. 176). Since courtroom interpreting rarely involves the taking of notes, an adapted version of this model would likely omit the "Read" effort, but would of course result in the extension of the "Rem" effort to include memory recollection not from notes, but rather from the interpreter's short-term memory.

Naturally, the omission of notes from the reformulation phase results in an increased demand for mental resources in order to buttress the interpreter's memory requirements. However, quite unlike the comprehension stage and simultaneous interpreting, here, the interpreter is not reliant on the speaker for the pace of the speech and instead is in control of the interpreting situation (Gile 2009, p. 176). Thus, the efforts need not necessarily be exercised simultaneously; the interpreter can devote her cognitive resources to the effort of recollection ("Rem"), while consciously choosing not to produce any interpretation yet for the audience (the P effort). Likewise, the interpreter can focus her attention on the correct formulation of a grammatically difficult sentence in the target language without fear of missing any speech from the speaker. As such, the consecutive interpreter is more easily able to manage her cognitive resources (Gile 2009, p. 176). Of course, there is a natural limitation on the amount of mental resources that the interpreter can take away from her memory in these circumstances, since she must still attempt to maintain maximum recollection of the original speech. But the lack of time pressure does significantly expand the maximum amount of resources that can be devoted to any one effort at any one time, while simultaneously reducing the pressure on the coordination effort.

3.4.4 Sight Translation

Sight translation, from the perspective of an interpreting model, is actually fairly similar to simultaneous interpreting. It consists of virtually the exact same efforts: L (listening and analysis); M (memory); P (production); and C (coordination) (Gile 2009, pp. 179–180). In the case of sight translation, however, the L effort is not concerned with organizing sounds into understandable words and meaning, but rather organizing written letters into understandable words and meaning (Gile 2009, p. 180). This is distinct from the previously mentioned "Read" effort which is more about extrapolating the larger story from a small subset of information (notes) than it is about actually reading that information as it is written. By way of contrast, the sight translation L effort is simply a matter of normal everyday reading and understanding of text as it is written.

The M effort of memory is also much less important in sight translation than it is in simultaneous or consecutive (Gile 2009, p. 180). The interpreter need not commit very much information to short-term memory because any information which may be necessary is represented in the text before her. Similarly, because the interpreter controls the pace of the sight translation (as in consecutive's reformulation phase), there is little time pressure (Gile 2009, p. 180). This results in a better ability to manage cognitive capacities; to slow down or even reread difficult sections of the text. Yet, these advantages do not necessarily make sight translation easier than the other interpreting techniques from a cognitive capacity standpoint. The nature of the texts that are normally sight translated (either dense legal texts or grammatically incorrect witness statements) (González et al. 1991, p. 402) make automatic comprehension (the L effort of reading and understanding) very difficult and reformulation of those concepts into the target language (the P effort) likewise troublesome (Gile 2009, p. 180).

3.4.5 Conclusion

What should be apparent from these models is that they all operate under the cognitive psychology assumption that there is a limited amount of mental capacity available to the task of interpreting. Furthermore, they assume a zero-sum game: where one mental effort receives a larger portion of the brain's resources, the other efforts must necessarily make do with a lesser portion. It follows from these statements that any negative variation in an interpreting situation will automatically result in a less-than-optimum interpretation or outright interpreter error. Thus, for example, where there is background noise that makes it more difficult for the interpreter to hear, and she therefore must concentrate harder on the listening effort of the process and is less able to afford capacity to the production phase, an imperfect target language translation will result. Of most importance in this respect is the hypothesis that every negative circumstance affecting a courtroom interpreter will necessarily have a knock-on effect that undermines the eventual interpretation.

In addition, if Gile is correct in his assumption that the task of interpreting is inherently difficult and therefore forces interpreters to work at the edge of their mental capabilities, then it naturally follows that an interpreter can only be as good as her cognitive capacities allow. In other words, just as any negative variation in the circumstances will adversely affect interpreter output, any weakness in the overall capacity of the interpreter will also negatively affect the end product. Since interpreters work at the edge of their cognitive abilities, any limitation in those abilities will result in a less-than-optimum interpretation.

3.5 Improving or Managing Cognitive Capacity

3.5.1 Introduction

If it is a given that an interpreter can only interpret as well as her cognitive capacities allow, then it begs the question whether an interpreter can ever increase her cognitive capacities. It is questionable whether this is possible (Gile 2009, pp. 185–186). Individuals who practice interpreting do improve as interpreters; however, it is unclear whether this is an actual expansion of their cognitive capabilities or simply a reduction in their need for those cognitive capacities to adequately interpret (Gile 2009, pp. 185–186). For example, an interpreter who improves her German skills will have an easier time listening to and understanding German language speech, and thus her L effort will not require as much cognitive capacity to fulfill its role in the interpreting process.

This does not mean, however, that interpreters cannot improve upon their ability to handle situations where their cognitive capacity is overloaded, the so-called "saturation" point. On the one hand, as the example above shows, they can improve the efficiency of their interpreting efforts to avoid reaching the saturation point. In addition, they can also use so-called "coping strategies" to more efficiently handle overload situations when they do occur. Each of these approaches will be outlined in this section, since how interpreters choose to deal with overload issues in an attempt to limit interpreter error also has an effect on the eventual errors that do occur.

3.5.2 Improving Efficiency

Within the context of cognitive capacities and interpreting models, the goal of efficiency simply means that the efforts employed by the interpreter need or demand fewer cognitive resources. In this manner, by improving the efficiency of a particular effort, the interpreter leaves more cognitive resources for the other efforts. There are a variety of different tactics that an interpreter can employ to achieve this result. Providing a comprehensive list here would be neither instructive nor particularly useful given the focus of this work on the legal aspects of courtroom interpreting, however a few representative examples will be given to illustrate the concept.

As a starting point, the interpreter can simply improve her ability in a particular language. Since the listening effort is dependent on the ability to understand and analyze the meaning of speech, becoming more comfortable with the language allows the interpreter to concentrate less on this facet of interpretation. Additionally, the listening effort can be made easier by enhancing the interpreter's extralinguistic knowledge, that is to say, becoming more comfortable with the subject matter and the situation itself (de Jongh 1992, p. 26). For example, an interpreter who is not conversant in the subject matter of the speech will not only need to use mental resources to understand the language, but also to understand the concepts about which the speaker is speaking (de Jongh 1992, pp. 26–28). In contrast, an interpreter who already understands the subject matter of the speech will need fewer mental resources to make sense of the speaker's meaning.

Similarly, the interpreter can become more informed as to the culture of the speaker. Since "[a]ll languages belong in a cultural framework and exist within that framework", the interpreter will have an easier time understanding the language itself if she is familiar with the culture to which it belongs (de Jongh 1992, p. 59). This is true for several reasons. First, familiarity with the culture will allow the interpreter to be more comfortable understanding any specific dialects or accents (de Jongh 1992, p. 53). Second, idioms and cultural references will be more quickly processed and understandable, such as the aforementioned "*ich verstehe nur Bahnhof*" (de Jongh 1992, pp. 27, 61). Third, being culturally aware allows the interpreter to better understand, and later convey, any non-verbal elements of communication, since most of these tend to be specific to a particular cultural (de Jongh 1992, pp. 62–63). Such cultural awareness can go a long way towards lightening the demands of the listening effort.

As far as is possible, interpreters can also work to "automate" parts of the interpreting process in order to reduce the burdens of specific tasks on their cognitive capacities (Gile 2009, p. 159; Riccardi 2005, p. 758). Note-taking, for instance, can be practiced to an extent that it evolves into a nearly automatic process (González et al. 1991, p. 333). In this manner, the "automation" of note-taking can lighten the cognitive demand throughout consecutive interpretation, and allow the interpreter to focus her limited mental resources on other aspects of the process. This appears to be true for a number of different facets of interpreting, including the core process of transforming the meaning expressed in the source language into an accurate target language representation (González et al. 1991, p. 314). The more interpreters practice the actual translation of meaning between languages – the process of recognizing several different word choice possibilities, analyzing their suitability for the particular source word used, and quickly making a decision as to the appropriate target language word – the more automatic and unconscious this process becomes (Riccardi 2005, pp. 758–759; González et al. 1991, p. 314).

Although these examples signify only a very small portion of the possibilities available to interpreters, one can quickly see that, in effect, they all require some sort of pre-interpretation training or practice, either as to language acquisition or technique improvement. In this respect, the interpreting models and the concept of cognitive capacity result in a completely logical outcome that is true of many other professions as well: the individuals who are highly skilled, have excellent knowledge, and have practical experience will be better at their particular job (Morris 1995, p. 42). This is no less true of interpreters.

3.5.3 Coping Strategies

Unfortunately, improving the efficient usage of one's limited cognitive capacities is not a miracle cure for interpreting error. Interpreting, by its very nature, involves situations in which the mental resources available are simply not adequate to perform the required task (Gile 2009, pp. 157, 191). In fact, cognitive overload is so common that interpreters sometimes refer to their work as an exercise in "permanent crisis management" (Gile 2009, p. 191). To manage these ongoing crises, interpreters are taught, and routinely employ, a modest set of "coping strategies" (Gile 2009, p. 191). These techniques allow them to work around or through situations that threaten to overload their cognitive capacities. Though, as will be seen, some of these strategies are simply not appropriate in the realm of courtroom interpreting.

One coping strategy that has already been discussed is the taking of notes. While consecutive interpreting often is benefited by extensive note-taking, simultaneous interpreters also occasionally use note-taking skills to deal with difficult passages of text. Specifically, speeches that contain numbers or names demand extra memory effort, and writing this information down can temporarily relieve the interpreter of having to retain such precise and unfamiliar information (Dingfelder Stone 2015, p. 156; Gile 2009, p. 204). Another strategy that is utilized almost universally is anticipation. Interpreters who are highly familiar with the subject matter or speaker will often be able to "grasp the intent of a message before all of the words that comprise it have been uttered" (González et al. 1991, p. 364). This is also true as to the grammatical structure of a sentence or phrase: the more familiar the interpreter is with the language, the more ability she has to anticipate how the speaker will grammatically continue their speech (González et al. 1991, pp. 364–365). Using this strategy, the consecutive interpreter can pay less attention to the speech (lower listening effort) and more attention to her notes, and simply check back in to confirm that her assumptions were correct (Gile 2009, p. 174). For the simultaneous interpreter, anticipation is even more key, since it allows her to begin interpreting a passage more quickly, thus reducing the lag time between the speaker and her interpretation, the so-called decalage (Gile 2009, p. 204). As discussed, this reduces the burden on the interpreter's memory effort.

A further coping strategy of interest revolves around how interpreters handle a situation where they have missed or misunderstood an important word or phrase. Normally, interpreters are taught to either omit the portion of the speech that they have missed (an alternative that is somewhat heavy-handed) or to attempt to reconstruct the missing speech segment from context (Gile 2009, pp. 201, 210). In essence, when employing the latter strategy, interpreters are reporting, based upon their familiarity with the speaker and subject matter, what they believe the speaker said, rather than what was actually said. In the case of simultaneous interpretation, reconstruction allows the interpreter to continue interpreting without interrupting the speaker for clarification, which is often not possible given the circumstances. With regards to consecutive interpretation, the option exists to ask the speaker for clarification after the fact, but interruption of the speaker to do so is considered highly controversial within the interpreting community (González et al. 1991, pp. 395–396).

Interpreters also must deal with situations where the particular word they need simply does not come to mind. When this occurs, it can quickly threaten the interpreter's cognitive capacity: focusing her mental resources on finding the correct word necessarily deprives the other processes of necessary resources. Such a small problem can trigger what is known as a "failure sequence": the inability to find the correct word can act as a roadblock to the process, limiting the interpreter's ability to move forward with the interpretation (Gile 2009, pp. 171–173). When this occurs in simultaneous interpreting (or during the note-taking process for consecutive interpreting), the interpreter's memory can quickly become overloaded as the speech passages build up and no progress has been made with translation. In such situations, interpreters have several main options to alleviate the difficulty. First, they can paraphrase or explain the concept as opposed to looking for the correct word (Gile 2009, p. 207). Thus, one might say "the time lag between the speaker and the interpreter's version of the speech" where one fails to remember the precise word "decalage". Second, they can substitute a general or descriptive term for the specific term that they cannot remember (Gile 2009, p. 206). For instance, if they cannot recall the exact word "Doppelbock" as a definition of a particular beer style, they can simply refer to it as a "dark beer" or a "strong beer". Finally, the interpreter can "transcode" the source language word or concept into the target language (Gile 2009, p. 208). As an example, where the interpreter cannot remember or does not know the French term for the "date of maturity" of a financial instrument, she can transcode this into French as "date de maturité" (Gile 2009, p. 208). In this example, as in the others, although the specific word is lost to the audience, the meaning of the word is conveyed and the interpreter can continue to interpret without falling behind or overtaxing her cognitive resources trying to solve a particularly acute problem of translation.

Sometimes interpreters simply do not understand what the speaker said, in that they know the sounds, but not the ultimate word. Here, the interpreter is taught two possibilities (aside from asking the speaker for clarification). On the one hand, the interpreter can simply echo the sounds that were made in the hope that the audience is familiar with the term, even if the interpreter is not (Gile 2009, p. 207). This strategy is particularly useful where the sounds likely refer to a name or a technical term, such as "opinio juris". A second strategy is to adopt the unknown word as a part of the target language and use it as if it were a legitimate target language word (Gile 2009, p. 207). An example would be an interpreter's use in German of "*downloaden*" (as opposed to the normal "*herunterladen*") as an equivalent to the English "to download".

In addition to these mainstream coping strategies, there also exist more aggressive or radical strategies. For instance, where interpreters miss an entire segment of speech, the interpreter may simply "*invent* a speech segment which is compatible with the rest of the speaker's statement" (Gile 2009, p. 211 [emphasis in original]). This is known as parallel reformulation (Gile 2009, p. 211). Of course, they also have the option of omitting that segment entirely, but this may risk the overall coherence of the speech

(Gile 2009, p. 210). Furthermore, instead of solving or evading a problem, interpreters are sometimes known to merely inform the listener of the problem, such as by saying "an author whose name the interpreter did not catch" (Gile 2009, p. 209). This allows the interpreter, as above, to avoid a possible roadblock and any resulting failure sequence. Another extreme coping strategy involves what is known as "form-based interpreting", or relying heavily on the source language structure and words to guide the target language output (Gile 2009, pp. 208–209). In other words, the interpreter effectively foregoes any consideration of the overall meaning of the speech and instead interprets word-for-word what has been said by the speaker, mirroring the grammatical structures and word sequencing of the source language in the target language. An example might be interpreting the German phrase "*gestern habe ich Golf gespielt*" into English as "yesterday have I golf played", which leaves something to be desired from a grammatical standpoint, but does convey the overall meaning. This strategy is generally used in moments of extreme interpreter fatigue or where the interpreter does not have the cognitive capacity to lag far enough behind the speaker to truly understand the overall meaning of the speech (Gile 2009, pp. 208–209). Although an extreme strategy, a recent study claims that this tactic is used more often than might be thought (Gile 2009, pp. 208–209).

There exist other coping strategies of a less extreme nature that are only useful in simultaneous interpreting. For instance, since simultaneous interpreters often work in pairs, they can ask their boothmate for help on a particularly complicated passage or word (Gile 2009, p. 202). Likewise, their boothmate can be proactive and consult resources such as dictionaries or pre-made glossaries when difficult words arise (Gile 2009, p. 202). The existence of a decalage also adds to the coping strategies that simultaneous interpreters may utilize in order to manage cognitive overload situations. As previously discussed, they may extend their decalage to allow for a better overall understanding of the speaker before they begin translating, or if their memory is overly taxed, they may shorten it to relieve their memory (Chabasse and Dingfelder Stone 2015, pp. 80–81; Gile 2009, p. 201). Since the decalage can be variable throughout the speech, interpreters may also practice "queuing", which refers to the habit of lagging further behind during sections of particularly dense speech only to catch up whenever easier speech arrives or the speaker pauses (González et al. 1991, p. 367).[5] There is some question, however, as to whether or not this strategy is actually useful with respect to cognitive overload (González et al. 1991, p. 367).

What is definitely helpful in relieving cognitive overload for simultaneous interpreters is a strategy known as segmentation. This involves breaking apart a complex source language sentence with embedded structures into several smaller, easier sentences that can be conveyed to the audience even before the original sentence is completed by the speaker or understood by the interpreter (Gile 2009, p. 205). For example, consider the following sentence:

> Given the difficulty of writing a long sentence, especially those sentences that are grammatically complex, which frequently occur in legal or technical writing, it is sometimes best to write shorter sentences.

Using segmentation, this sentence might be broken apart and translated to the audience in the following manner:

> Long sentences can be difficult to write. Particularly difficult is grammatically complex writing such as legal and technical writing. Thus, sometimes it is best to write short sentences.

Such segmentation allows the interpreter to provide immediate relief to her short-term memory (Gile 2009, p. 205). Instead of waiting for the entire sentence to finish before starting to interpret, resulting in a very significant decalage that would be prohibitively taxing on her memory effort, the interpreter can "unload" her short-term memory by conveying the individual segments of the sentence in neutral terms (Gile 2009, p. 205). However helpful this strategy may be at minimizing the interpreter's memory effort, it carries with it the risk of an increased production effort, since the larger sentence (of as yet unknown ultimate meaning)

[5] It should be noted, though, that some interpreters use the opposite approach: reducing their decalage during difficult segments, then lagging further behind during easier segments as a method of recuperation.

must be broken apart into smaller sections that are flexible enough to accept the speaker's ultimate meaning (Gile 2009, p. 205). This is not always an easy task, or an effective tradeoff, but in the right circumstances, segmentation can be a useful coping strategy for interpreters.

3.5.4 Conclusion

What should be noticeable from the above discussion is how uneasily some of these coping strategies fit with courtroom interpreting. Even the more mainstream tactics (such as paraphrasing or transcoding), while admittedly preserving the meaning of the speech segment, involve an ultimate loss of nuance and precision. It is exactly this precision and nuance that is of such importance to courtroom interpretation where the impact of the source language speech on the audience must be maintained and replicated as exactly as possible. Moreover, in some instances, the errors that the coping strategies seek to avoid are actually of less impact than the implementation of the strategy itself; for example, omitting a portion of speech that the interpreter did not fully understand is arguably more damaging to the legal process than having the interpreter interpret what she thinks she understood, even when the result is absolute nonsense or gibberish. At least in the latter case, the courtroom actors have the option of asking for clarification because they know that something was unclear. Naturally, following upon this logic, the more extreme coping strategies (such as parallel reformulation) are completely inappropriate in the courtroom.

By comparison, the techniques employed by interpreters to improve the efficiency of their interpreting efforts, and thus avoid any overload scenarios, are completely compatible with courtroom interpreting. They allow interpreters to handle complex situations and maintain an optimum work-product by avoiding the very cognitive overload that other interpreters must relieve using coping strategies. In fact, the very existence of coping strategies, and their general incompatibility with the courtroom interpreting, further emphasize the importance of employing interpreters who have the cognitive flexibility and training to avoid the overload scenarios that make such strategies necessary.

4 Conclusion

As can be seen from the foregoing discussion, court interpretation is far from an automatic process and court interpreters are not invisible machines effortlessly eliminating the language barrier for anyone who does not understand the language of the court. The entire situation is more complex than that. The act of interpreting involves the interpreter making a nearly infinite number of ethical and technical choices. Choices such as whether to explain to an individual what a particular term actually means or simply interpret what has been said. Choices such as which particular word in the target language best approximates what was said in the source language. Choices such as what coping strategy to use when the speaker isn't understandable. Choices such as to whether to take notes while interpreting consecutively or not. Each of these decisions, as well as many more, is made by a human, who is only as good as her experience, intelligence, and training have made her, and is eminently capable of error.

Yet, on top of those errors that arise from an interpreter's incorrect choices, practical evidence and theoretical discussions show that additional errors stem from the simple fact that interpreting is an inherently difficult process that stretches the cognitive capacities of the human brain. In short, there are only so many mental resources that an interpreter has at her disposal, and occasionally the task of interpreting demands more than can be supplied, resulting in the deterioration of the interpreter's performance. Seen in this light, interpreting errors are the inevitable byproduct of a tremendously complicated process. The more complex the interpreting task (thus demanding more cognitive resources) or the less skilled the interpreter (thus capable of supplying only limited cognitive resources), the more errors will occur. But the existence of such errors is, unfortunately, a given.

What remains to be seen is the impact of these errors on the overall process. Some errors are seemingly harmless, while others would appear to have a major effect on the trial. In order to better understand the extent to which interpreters can affect the trial process, and possibly endanger a defendant's right to a fair trial, it is necessary to first explore the right to a fair trial itself.

Bibliography

Andres, D. (2002). *Konsekutivdolmetschen und Notation*. Frankfurt am Main: Peter Lang.

Benmaman, V. (1992). Legal Interpreting: An Emerging Profession. *Modern Language Journal, 76*, 445–454.

Berk-Seligson, S. (1990). *The Bilingual Courtroom: Court Interpreters in the Judicial Process*. Chicago: University of Chicago Press.

Berk-Seligson, S. (2002). The Impact of Politeness in Witness Testimony: The Influence of the Court Interpreter. In F. Pöchhacker & M. Shlesinger (Eds.), *The Interpreting Studies Reader* (pp. 279–292). London: Routledge.

Cardenas, R. (2001). "You Don't Have to Hear, Just Interpret!": How Ethnocentrism in the California Courts Impedes Equal Access to the Courts for Spanish Speakers. *Court Review, 38*(Fall), 24–31.

Chabasse, C., & Dingfelder Stone, M. (2015). Capacity Management in Interpretation: Efforts, Directionality, and Language Pair Considerations. In D. Andres & M. Behrs (Eds.), *To Know How to Suggest…: Approaches to Teaching Conference Interpreting* (pp. 75–102). Berlin: Frank & Timmer.

Chang, W. B. C., & Araujo, M. U. (1975). Interpreters for the Defense: Due Process for the Non-English-Speaking Defendant. *California Law Review, 63*, 801–823.

Corsellis, A., & Fernández, L. F. (2001). Code of Ethics and Conduct and Guidelines to Good Practice. In E. Hertog (Ed.), *Aequitas: Access to Justice Across Language and Culture in the E.U.* (pp. 77–87). Antwerpen: Lessius Hogeschool.

Craney, G. (1989–90). Language v. the Law. *Barrister, 16*, 20–23, 27, 42.

Davis, L. W., & Hewitt, W. E. (1994). Lessons in Administering Justice: What Judges Need to Know About the Requirements, Role, and Professional Responsibilities of the Court Interpreter. *Harvard Latino Law Review, 1*, 121–176.

de Jongh, E. (1991). Foreign Language Interpreters in the Courtroom: The Case for Linguistic and Cultural Proficiency. *Modern Language Journal, 75*, 285–295.

de Jongh, E. (1992). *An Introduction to Court Interpreting: Theory & Practice*. Lanham: University Press of America.

de Jongh, E. (2008, July/August). Linguistic Presence v. Linguistic Absence. *Florida Bar Journal, 82*, 20–32.

Dingfelder Stone, M. (2015). The Theory and Practice of Teaching Note-Taking. In D. Andres & M. Behrs (Eds.), *To Know How to Suggest…: Approaches to Teaching Conference Interpreting* (pp. 145–166). Berlin: Frank & Timmer.

European Commission. (2009). *Final Report: Reflection Forum on Multilingualism and Interpreter Training*. Brussels: Commission of the European Communities.

Fowler, Y. (1995). The Courtroom Interpreter: Paragon and Intruder? In S. E. Carr, R. P. Roberts, A. Dufour, & D. Steyn (Eds.), *The Critical Link: Interpreters in the Community* (pp. 191–200). Amsterdam: John Benjamins.

Gile, D. (2002). Conference Interpreting as a Cognitive Management Problem. In F. Pöchhacker & M. Shlesinger (Eds.), *The Interpreting Studies Reader* (pp. 162–177). London: Routledge.

Gile, D. (2009). *Basic Concepts and Models for Interpreter and Translator Training* (Rev. ed.). Amsterdam: John Benjamins.

González, R., Vásquez, V. F., & Mikkelson, H. (1991). *Fundamentals of Court Interpretation: Theory, Policy, and Practice*. Durham: Carolina Academic Press.

Grabau, C. M. (1996). Court Interpreting: View from the Bench. *State Court Journal, 20*(1), 6–11.

Hale, S. (2001). The Complexities of the Bilingual Courtroom. *Law Society Journal, 2001*, 68–72.

Hale, S. (2002). How Faithfully Do Court Interpreters Render the Style of Non-English Speaking Witnesses' Testimonies? A Data-Based Study of Spanish-English Bilingual Proceedings. *Discourse Studies, 4*(1), 25–47.

Hale, S. (2004). *The Discourse of Court Interpreting: Discourse Practices of the Law, the Witness and the Interpreter*. Amsterdam: John Benjamins.

Hale, S. (2007). Challenges of Court Interpreting: Intricacies, Responsibilities and Ramifications. *Alternative Law Journal, 32*, 198–202.

Hayes, A., & Hale, S. (2010). Appeals on Incompetent Interpreting. *Journal of Judicial Administration, 20*(2), 119–130.

Heller, D. J. (1994–95). The Language Bias in the Criminal Justice System. *Criminal Law Quarterly, 37*, 344–383.

Ibrahim, Z. (2007). The Interpreter as Advocate: Malaysian Court Interpreting as a Case in Point. In C. Wadensjö, B. Englund Dimitrova, & A.-L. Nilsson (Eds.), *The Critical Link 4: Professionalisation of Interpreting in the Community* (pp. 205–213). Amsterdam: John Benjamins.

Ibrahim, Z., & Bell, R. T. (2003). Court Interpreting: Malaysian Perspectives. In L. Brunette, G. L. Bastin, I. Hemlin, & H. Clarke (Eds.), *The Critical Link 3: Interpreters in the Community* (pp. 211–222). Amsterdam: John Benjamins.

Jacobsen, B. (2003). Pragmatics in Court Interpreting: Additions. In L. Brunette, G. L. Bastin, I. Hemlin, & H. Clarke (Eds.), *The Critical Link 3: Interpreters in the Community* (pp. 223–238). Amsterdam: John Benjamins.

Kadric, M. (2000). Interpreting in the Austrian Courtroom. In R. P. Roberts, S. E. Carr, D. Abraham, & A. Dufour (Eds.), *The Critical Link 2: Interpreters in the Community* (pp. 153–164). Amsterdam: John Benjamins.

Laster, K., & Taylor, V. L. (1994). *Interpreters and the Legal System*. Sydney: The Federation Press.

LaVigne, M., & Vernon, M. (2003). An Interpreter Isn't Enough: Deafness, Language, and Due Process. *Wisconsin Law Review, 2003*, 843–936.

Mason, M. (2008). *Courtroom Interpreting*. Lanham: University Press of America.

Matu, P., Odhiambo, K., Adams, Y., & Ongarora, D. (2012). The Court Interpreters' Role Perception: The Case of English-Dholuo Interpreters in Subordinate Courts in Nyanza Province, Kenya. *Greener Journal of Social Sciences, 2*(4), 121–126.

Mikkelson, H. (1998). Towards a Redefinition of the Role of the Court Interpreter. *Interpreting, 3*(1), 21 [online]. Available at: https://works.bepress.com/holly_mikkelson/17/. Accessed 21 Nov 2017.

Mikkelson, H. (1999). Court Interpreting at a Crossroads. In *Annual Conference of the National Association of Judiciary Interpreters and Translators* [online]. Available at: http://works.bepress.com/holly_mikkelson/10/. Accessed 21 Nov 2017.

Mikkelson, H. (2000). *Introduction to Court Interpreting*. Manchester: St. Jerome Publishing.

Mikkelson, H. (2008). Evolving Views of the Court Interpreter's Role: Between Scylla & Charybdis. In C. Valero-Garcés & A. Martin (Eds.), *Crossing Borders in Community Interpreting: Definitions and Dilemmas* (pp. 81–98). Amsterdam: John Benjamins.

Mikkelson, H. (2010). "Verbatim Interpretation" Revisited. *Proteus, 19*(1), 1 [online]. Available at: https://works.bepress.com/holly_mikkelson/22/. Accessed 21 Nov 2017.

Morris, R. (1995). The Moral Dilemmas of Court Interpreting. *The Translator, 1*(1), 25–46.

Morris, R. (1999). The Gum Syndrome: Predicaments in Court Interpreting. *Forensic Linguistics, 6*(1), 6–29.

Morris, R. (2001). Eichmann vs. Demjanjuk or Plus c'est la même chose, plus ça change.... In *AIIC Court Interpreting Seminar – The Hague* [online].

Available at: https://40be6ebe-a-62cb3a1a-s-sites.googlegroups.com/site/ruthmorris13/AIICHagueEichmannvsDemjanjuk.pdf. Accessed 21 Nov 2017.

National Association of Judiciary Interpreters & Translators. (2005). *NAJIT Position Paper: Summary Interpreting in Legal Settings*. Washington, DC: NAJIT [online]. Available at: https://najit.org/wp-content/uploads/2016/09/SummaryInterpreting200609.pdf. Accessed 21 Nov 2017.

Pantoga, H. (1999). Injustice in Any Language: The Need for Improved Standards Governing Courtroom Interpretation in Wisconsin. *Marquette Law Review, 82*, 601–664.

Ramler, S. (2007). The Origin and Challenges of Simultaneous Interpretation: The Nuremberg Trial Experience. *Interpretation Studies, 7*, 7–18.

Riccardi, A. (2005). On the Evolution of Interpreting Strategies in Simultaneous Interpreting. *Meta, 50*(2), 753–767.

Safford, J. B. (1977). No Comprendo: The Non-English-Speaking Defendant and the Criminal Process. *Journal of Criminal Law & Criminology, 68*, 15–30.

Stern, L. (2011). Courtroom Interpreting. In K. Malmkjær & K. Windle (Eds.), *The Oxford Handbook of Translation Studies* (pp. 325–342). Oxford: Oxford University Press.

Taibi, M., & Martin, A. (2012). Court Translation and Interpreting in Times of the "War on Terror": The Case of Taysir Alony. *Translation & Interpreting, 4*(1), 77–98.

Tuck, B. M. (2010). Comment: Preserving Facts, Form, and Function When a Deaf Witness with Minimal Language Skills Testifies in Court. *University of Pennsylvania Law Review, 158*, 905–955.

4

The Right to a Fair Trial

1 Introduction

The right to a fair trial is based upon the Anglo-Saxon concept of "due process" and is a basic norm of international law (Nowak 2005, p. 305; Weissbrodt and Wolfrum 1997, p. v.). However, to discuss a singular "right" to a fair trial is somewhat misleading, as the "right" to a fair trial is actually a collection of other individual rights and principles meant to ensure the "proper administration of justice" (HRC General Comment No. 13, §1). Many of these individual rights, such as the right to be presumed innocent and the right to an appeal, have become so well-known and accepted throughout the world that they are familiar to both non-lawyers and lawyers alike. In fact, the wide-spread adoption of these rights into national legal systems has led many scholars to conclude that the right to a fair trial, and specifically its codification in Article 14 ICCPR, represents customary international law (Robinson 2009, pp. 6–7, 11; see also Doswald-Beck 2012). Some scholars have even advanced the proposition that the right to a fair trial qualifies as a peremptory norm (Boas et al. 2011, p. 12; Boas 2010, pp. 329–330; Robinson 2009, pp. 6–7, 11; Orakhelashvili 2006, p. 60; Turner 2005, p. 22).

J. H. Dingfelder Stone, *Court Interpreters and Fair Trials*,
https://doi.org/10.1007/978-3-319-75355-3_4

For the purposes of this work, however, it is not necessary to consider each of the individual fair trial rights in full. While the work of interpreters does impact a wide range of fair trial aspects, their influence stops short of being completely pervasive. Thus, this Chapter will limit itself to the explanation and analysis of those specific fair trial rights and principles that interpretation is most likely to affect: the right of equality before the court; the right to adversarial proceedings; the right to be informed of the charge; the right to adequate time and facilities to prepare a defense; the right to be tried without undue delay; the right to be present at one's own trial; the right to counsel; the right to examine witnesses; and the right to appeal. Having already been analyzed in Chap. 2, the right to an interpreter will not be addressed in this Chapter. In this context, a very brief overview will be given as to how these individual rights may influence the work of interpreters, as well as how the actions of interpreters generally can be seen to affect these rights. Naturally, a more detailed discussion of the impact of interpreters on these individual rights will occur in the following Chapters.

As was the case with Chap. 2 on the right to an interpreter, the specific focus when discussing the right to a fair trial under international law will be on Article 14 ICCPR. In determining the extent and scope of these rights, the views of the HRC will be given paramount importance, since it is the body tasked with the interpretation and implementation of the ICCPR. In this role, the HRC has developed a fairly substantial jurisprudence relating to fair trial matters (Weissbrodt 2001, p. 152; McGoldrick 1994, p. 437). Likewise, the HRC's Concluding Observations on individual State Reports are also of some value in this area.

However, some caveats with respect to the HRC, and the ICCPR generally, are in order. First, while McGoldrick (1994) may be correct in asserting that the overall "range and depth" of the HRC's caselaw as to fair trial rights is "impressive", it does not dispel the fact that certain aspects of the right to a fair trial have received more attention from the HRC than others (p. 437; see also Weissbrodt 2001, p. 152). Second, a significant portion of the HRC's Article 14 caselaw consists of default cases, where the State Party refused to participate, and therefore did not dispute the allegations of the individual author (McGoldrick 1994, p. 439). One must be careful in such cases not to place too much emphasis on the reported facts. Third, the HRC has endeavored to apply the provisions of the ICCPR to a rather formidable array of distinctive legal systems (McGoldrick 1994, p. 438). As such, while its decisions attempt to ensure a baseline level of fair trial guarantees, it must do so while accommodating the unique procedural systems of each State Party. The end result is that, on occasion, the language of the HRC cases may be less specific than one would like.

Given these weaknesses in the HRC's jurisprudence, it is useful to look to alternate sources of international law concerning the right to a fair trial. When analyzing the extent of the Article 14 (3) (f) ICCPR right to an interpreter in Chap. 2, ECtHR cases regarding the similarly worded Article 6 ECHR right were used to inform the eventual interpretation of the ICCPR right. This practice will be continued in this Chapter as well, since Article 6 ECHR is in many instances nearly identical to Article 14 ICCPR.

2 General Overview of the Right to a Fair Trial Under International Law

Before proceeding further, it is necessary to consider the right to a fair trial as a whole. Many of the general aspects of Article 14 ICCPR have already been analyzed with reference to the right to an interpreter (such as the concept of a "criminal charge"), and as such will not be further addressed in this Chapter. However, there exist still other general facets of the Article that require mentioning. Article 14 ICCPR, at least the parts relevant to this work, reads as follows:

1) All persons shall be equal before the courts and tribunals. In the determination of any criminal charge against him, or of his rights and obligations in a suit at law, everyone shall be entitled to a fair and public hearing by a competent, independent and impartial tribunal established by law…
3) In the determination of any criminal charge against him, everyone shall be entitled to the following minimum guarantees, in full equality:

(a) To be informed promptly and in detail in a language which he understands of the nature and cause of the charge against him;
(b) To have adequate time and facilities for the preparation of his defence and to communicate with counsel of his own choosing;
(c) To be tried without undue delay;
(d) To be tried in his presence, and to defend himself in person or through legal assistance of his own choosing; to be informed, if he does not have legal assistance, of this right; and to have legal assistance assigned to him, in any case where the interests of justice so require, and without payment by him in any such case if he does not have sufficient means to pay for it;
(e) To examine, or have examined, the witnesses against him and to obtain the attendance and examination of witnesses on his behalf under the same conditions as witnesses against him;
(f) To have the free assistance of an interpreter if he cannot understand or speak the language used in court;

5) Everyone convicted of a crime shall have the right to his conviction and sentence being reviewed by a higher tribunal according to law.

The initial aspect that should be noticed from Article 14 ICCPR is that subsection (1) guarantees several general principles to which the proceedings must adhere (such as "equality" and "fairness"), while the later subsections set out the more specific preconditions of a fair trial. Article 14 (3) ICCPR, in particular, is a reservoir of detailed procedural guarantees meant to ensure the overall fairness of the criminal proceedings. As explicitly stated, its entitlements are considered the "minimum" baseline protections. The procedural rights specifically asserted in the subsections of Article 14 are not, however, an exhaustive list of the protections necessary to ensure a fair trial (Nowak 2005, p. 321; McGoldrick 1994, p. 405). Nowak (2005) has correctly noted that "the right to a fair trial is … broader than the sum of these individual guarantees" (Nowak 2005, p. 321). In other words, a "fair trial" may require more from the State than simply adhering to those specific guarantees listed in Article 14 ICCPR. The underlying concept of "fairness", itself, may provide protections for an accused individual (McGoldrick 1994, pp. 416–417). This residual right to overall fairness in the proceedings must also be considered.

Another facet of some importance with respect to Article 14 ICCPR is that subsection (1) does not actually guarantee a "fair trial", but rather a "fair hearing". This wording necessarily implies that the protections of Article 14 go beyond the trial itself and protect the accused during earlier elements of the criminal proceedings as well. In conjunction with the "autonomous" approach to the definition of a criminal charge (as accepted in Chap. 2), it is possible to say that the temporal scope of the Article 14 ICCPR rights begin once "State activities substantially affect the situation of the person concerned" and end after the final appellate proceedings (Nowak 2005, pp. 318–319).

Finally, considering that the right to a fair trial is "a key element of human rights protection and serves as a procedural means to safeguard the rule of law" (HRC General Comment No. 32, §2), it is arguable that its provisions must not be interpreted restrictively. Rather, their importance to the overall object and purpose of the ICCPR arguably necessitates a broad interpretation. This is further evidenced by the accepted observation that the notion of fairness requires more of States than the particular protections listed within the article itself (Nowak 2005, p. 321). Approaching Article 14 ICCPR with such interpretational deference would be in line with the treatment that Article 6 ECHR receives from the ECtHR (Jacot-Guillarmod 2003, p. 403). Such a deferential definition of "fairness" must stop short, however, of requiring that trials be perfect (Robinson 2009, p. 5). As the HRC has stated, the Article 14 rights provide procedural equality; they are not meant to ensure the "absence of error on the part of the competent tribunal" (*B.d.B. et al. v. The Netherlands* [HRC 1989] §6.3). Thus, even when interpreted broadly, the Article 14 rights guarantee only a fair process, not necessarily a fair result (*B.d.B. et al. v. The Netherlands* [HRC 1989] §6.3).

3 Analysis of the Individual Rights

3.1 Equality Before the Court (Article 14 [1])

Article 14 (1) ICCPR states that everyone "shall be equal before the courts and tribunals." This general principle gives rise to two different, but related, rights of some importance in the context of courtroom interpreters: the right to equal access to the courts and the right to the equality of arms (HRC General Comment No. 32, §8). In essence, each of these specific rights requires that the accused be granted treatment that is equal to both the opposing party (the prosecution in criminal proceedings) and any other individuals similarly situated to the accused (HRC General Comment No. 32, §14; *Dudko v. Australia* [HRC 2007] §7.4).

3.1.1 Equal Access to the Courts

The concept that individuals must have equal access to the court system effectively guarantees that "no individual is deprived, in procedural terms, of his/her right to claim justice" (HRC General Comment No. 32, §9). In other words, everyone is entitled to avail themselves of the court system on equal terms and the State may not impose any distinctions between individuals that are not justifiable on "objective and reasonable grounds" (HRC General Comment No. 32, §9; Henrard 2000, p. 76; *Waldman v. Canada* [HRC 1999]).[1] Nor may the State systematically frustrate (either *de jure* or *de facto*) a person's ability to access the courts.

At first glance, this guarantee of equality of access might appear simply to function as a non-discrimination provision, meant mainly to protect individuals from obviously discriminatory anti-access practices based upon the "usual" classifications of race, sex, religion, etc. However, the HRC has made it fairly clear that States also may not draw a distinction (with reference to allowing access to the court system) based upon other,

[1] Holding that distinctions with respect to the similarly themed prohibition of discrimination "must be based on reasonable and objective criteria" (*Waldman v. Canada* [HRC 1999] §10.6).

less obvious, grounds, such as language or national origin (HRC General Comment No. 32, §9). With reference to several State Reports, members of the HRC have enquired as to the actions taken to ensure the removal of any linguistic barriers that might lead to unequal access to the courts (see for example HRC Concluding Observations: Namibia [2004] §21 [with respect to the existence of only one official language]; HRC Concluding Observations: Belgium [1998] §17 [emphasizing that suspects must be informed of their rights in a language they understand]; HRC Concluding Observations: Finland [1998] §19 [with respect to the Swedish-speaking minority]; HRC Concluding Observations: Portugal [1997] §17 [encouraging the accommodation of Chinese in the courts of Macau]; HRC Concluding Observations: Sudan [1997] §20 [concerning the inability to use local languages in court]).

3.1.2 Equality of Arms

The principle of equality before the courts also guarantees the "equality of arms". This is best understood as an entitlement that "the court cannot act in a way which gives the prosecution an advantage over the defence" (Weissbrodt 2001, p. 130). Put differently, the court must treat both parties to a proceeding equally, unless a distinction is made by law and "justified on objective and reasonable grounds" (HRC General Comment No. 32, §13; see also *Dudko v. Australia* [HRC 2007] §7.4). As seen in the context of equal access to the courts above, distinctions based upon language would not be considered reasonable.

The equality of arms is considered by some to be the most important of the rights protecting a fair trial (Nowak 2005, p. 321). In its practical application, it requires that both parties are entitled to submit evidence on equal terms, both have the same rights to inspect and analyze records, and both may present and question witnesses without procedural differences (Nowak 2005, pp. 321, 341). An example of its application can be seen in *Larrañaga v. The Philippines* (2006), where the HRC held that it was a violation of the equality of arms for the trial judge to cut short the accused's cross-examination of an important prosecution witness, where the judge had not previously placed any similar restrictions on the accusatory testimony of prosecution witnesses (§7.7). Similarly, though couched in the general term of "equality before the court", the HRC held in *Vojnovic v. Croatia* (2009) that it was a violation of Article 14 (1) ICCPR for the trial court, without giving any stated reasons, to refuse to hear the complainant's witnesses (as well as other favorable evidence) after allowing the opposing party to present its evidence (§§8.2–8.3).

In essence, the principle affords the accused a level of power within the courtroom equal to that of the State and its nearly unlimited resources. Of course, even with this guarantee, the circumstances surrounding both parties can never allow for true equality in the courtroom (Trechsel 2005, p. 96). For instance, the State will always have coercive measures of investigation at its disposal that the defense will not, and yet the defense will always be allowed to remain silent while the State bears the burden of proof (Trechsel 2005, p. 96). Therefore, the parties cannot truly maintain arms of identical caliber. At most, it can be said that they may arrive at positions of equal power through alternative means (Henrard 2000, pp. 76–78). Despite this, the court must treat them identically, and assure that they are as equal in overall power as is possible, given the specific circumstances. It should be noted, though, that the equality of arms does not affirmatively guarantee to either side any particular procedural rights; rather it guarantees only that when one side is granted a procedural right, the other must also be afforded the same treatment. As such, if the court decides to deprive both sides of an essential procedural right, the equality of arms will not have been violated since treatment was equal (Trechsel 2005, p. 97 [with respect to the ECHR]).

3.1.3 The Relationship Between Interpreters and Equality Before the Courts

With respect to individuals who do not speak the language of the court, the concepts of "equal access to the court" and "equality of arms" are fairly significant. Since language can neither be used as a reasonable basis for providing unequal access to the court system, nor as a reasonable justification for treating the defense differently from the prosecution, it is possible to say that linguistic minorities are substantially protected by this principle of equality. On the other hand, it is also possible to argue that the provision of a free interpreter (as guaranteed by Article 14 [3] [f] ICCPR) effectively ensures this equality, and in the context of linguistically incompetent defendants, nothing more is required.

Yet, the concept of "equality before the court" requires more. Specifically, if an individual who does not speak the language of the court is entitled to access the court on equal terms to an individual who does speak the judicial language, and likewise is entitled to equal procedural treatment, then the interpretation guaranteed must be of such a quality as to eliminate any distinction between the two parties. In other words, the guarantees of "equal access" and "equality of arms" support the conclusion that a non-summarized, comprehensive interpretation of the proceedings is required, otherwise a linguistically incompetent accused would not actually be placed in an equal position before the court as the individual who can understand and communicate freely with that court. This interpretation is bolstered by language from the HRC's General Comment No. 32. With reference to the equality of arms in civil proceedings, the HRC has noted that an indigent party might be entitled to a free interpreter, otherwise they "could not participate in the proceedings on equal terms" (HRC General Comment No. 32, §13). As such, "equality before the courts" can be seen to guarantee not just an interpreter, but a specific type of interpretation and level of interpreter accuracy.

Just as the right to equality before the court may be said to impact the actions and duties of an interpreter by entitling an accused to a comprehensive interpretation, it is equally clear that the inability of an interpreter to provide such a detailed interpretation will undermine the right itself. In this way, the skill level and actual performance of an interpreter throughout a proceeding can severely impact an accused's opportunity to access the courts on the same procedural footing as the opposing party, as well as negatively affect his ability to enjoy a true equality of arms with respect to the prosecutor.

3.2 Right to Adversarial Proceedings (Article 14 [1])

3.2.1 Defining the Right to Adversarial Proceedings

Article 14 (1) ICCPR also endows an accused with the right to an adversarial hearing before the court (Nowak 2005, p. 322). Though this right is not expressly stated in the article, the HRC has noted that the "concept of a fair hearing in the context of article 14 (1) of the Covenant should be interpreted as requiring a number of conditions, such as ... respect for the principle of adversary proceedings" (*Morael v. France* [1989] §9.3). Adversarial proceedings are considered essential to a fair trial for several reasons. First, hearing argumentation and explanation from both parties contributes to better decision-making by the court (Trechsel 2005, p. 89). Second, the adversarial concept allows both parties to participate in the proceedings, which not only lets the accused have some impact on and control over the process (as opposed to simply having the process happen to him), but also makes acceptance of the end result more likely for each side (since both contributed to, and ideally had some impact on, that outcome) (Trechsel 2005, p. 89).

Unfortunately, while the HRC has unambiguously recognized a right to adversarial proceedings, its jurisprudence in the area is regrettably limited. Only in *Wolf v. Panama* (1992) has the HRC actually addressed the content of the right in a meaningful manner, holding that the author's Article 14 (1) rights were violated where the State did not allow him to "properly instruct his legal representative" and also denied him the "opportunity to personally attend the proceedings" (§6.6). Though even in this instance, the HRC's decision is less helpful than it could be, since the Committee found that these actions led to a violation of both the equality of arms and the right to adversarial proceedings together. As such, the guarantee of "adversarial proceedings" contained in Article 14 (1) is nebulous at best. Nor is national caselaw of particular use in this respect, since many domestic systems guarantee the "adversarial" nature of their proceedings under different substantive rights.[2]

---

[2] For instance, with respect to American law, the adversarial nature is assured under other, more specific constitutional rights. See for example *Kentucky v. Stincer* (Supreme Court 1987) which reaffirms the right to confront and cross-examine adverse witnesses orally as well as reiterating that "a defendant is guaranteed the right to be present at any stage of the criminal proceeding that is critical to its outcome if his presence would contribute to the fairness of the procedure" (p. 745).

The caselaw concerning Article 6 ECHR, however, provides significant assistance in fleshing out the right. The ECtHR has stated that the "right to an adversarial trial means, in a criminal case, that both prosecution and defence must be given the opportunity to have knowledge of and comment on the observations filed and evidence adduced by the other party" (*Laukkanen and Manninen v. Finland* [2004] §34). In essence, the ECtHR caselaw characterizes the right to adversarial proceedings as a "right to be heard" or a right to challenge prosecutorial evidence before the court (Trechsel 2005, p. 89). A necessary result of this definition is that the State (and sometimes the court itself) has a duty to disclose certain evidentiary material, since the accused cannot challenge or comment to the court on evidence of which it is unaware (Trechsel 2005, p. 94). A further implication of such a right to be heard is the obligation that the court listens: ECtHR caselaw places a duty on the court to actually consider submissions from the accused (Trechsel 2005, p. 89).

3.2.2 The Relationship Between Interpreters and the Right to Adversarial Proceedings

In the context of interpretation, the right to adversarial proceedings as described by the ECtHR again provides some clues as to the manner of interpretation required. If the purpose of the right is the effective participation by the accused in the trial, then it is necessary that the accused be given an interpreter whose skill level can guarantee such participation. In this respect, the fact that the accused's attorney can effectively act on his behalf does not necessarily fulfill the purposes of the right. Where a poor interpretation in court is given (or a limited method, such as summary interpretation, is used), the accused will not have a full understanding of the proceedings, and thus will not necessarily feel as if he can affect the outcome. This undermines both his acceptance of the result, as well as his ability to actually be a factor in the ongoing proceedings. Furthermore, the specific knowledge of the accused (since he is the participant in the facts, not the attorney) can be of use in successfully challenging the evidence, but this as well requires that the accused actually understand the presented evidence in some detail through a full interpretation. Likewise, a satisfactory presentation of the defendant's side of the story, which contributes to the quality of the court's decision-making, is more likely to be achieved through a high-quality interpretation. In short, the element of effective participation embedded in the right to adversarial proceedings dictates both a high level of interpreter quality and a rigorous method of interpretation. Anything less would likely undermine the accused's right to be heard.

3.3 Right to an Oral Hearing (Article 14 Generally)

3.3.1 Defining the Right to an Oral Hearing

Under Article 14 ICCPR, an accused is entitled to an oral hearing before the court as part of the criminal proceedings. As with the right to adversarial proceedings, however, this right is not explicitly mentioned in the ICCPR. Rather, it has been considered implicit to different aspects of the right to a fair trial overall. Some scholars have argued that the right to a "public" hearing necessarily means that the hearing must be oral, so that the public aspect of the hearing actually has meaning (Nowak 2005, p. 324). One can also make the case that the oral presentation of evidence by witnesses (as opposed to the exclusive usage of written witness statements) allows the trier of fact to more accurately assess the credibility of the witness and the reliability of the evidence (Trechsel 2005, p. 305). In this respect, the right to an oral hearing could arise from the accused's right to examine witnesses. The HRC, for its part, has cited Article 14 (3) ICCPR as the source of the guarantee, stating that in order to "satisfy the requirements of the right to defence … all criminal proceedings must allow the accused the right to an oral hearing" (*Becerra Barney v. Colombia* [2006] §7.2). While the origins of the right are debatable, its existence is not: every accused is entitled to an oral proceeding.

The major question in this regard is the extent to which this guarantee applies. Here, unfortunately, the HRC's caselaw has been less definitive, consisting of only a handful of cases that have generally been concerned with fairly black-and-white fact patterns. A notable exception is *Rodríguez Orejuela v. Colombia* (2002), where the HRC emphasized that every accused must be afforded "an oral hearing, at which he or she may appear in person or be represented by counsel and may bring evidence and examine the witnesses" (§7.3). Another important case in this regard is *R.M. v. Finland* (1989), in which the HRC held that the right to an oral hearing does not extend to appellate proceedings (§6.4). The exclusion of appellate proceedings is of some interest, since it implies that the right to an oral hearing only extends to those proceedings involving questions of evidence or fact and not to those mainly concerned with determinations of law (see also Nowak 2005, p. 325 [highlighting a similar argument concerning the right to a public hearing]). This would align with the emphasis placed on the oral presentation of evidence in *Rodríguez Orejuela v. Colombia*, as well as ECtHR caselaw in the area (see for example *Fischer v. Austria* [ECtHR 1995] §44[3]; *Fredin v. Sweden (No.2)* [ECtHR 1994] §§20–22).[4]

3.3.2 The Relationship Between Interpreters and the Right to an Oral Hearing

Given that the right to an oral hearing includes the opportunity to present and question witnesses as to factual issues (and is linked to the accused's right to a defense), the mere existence of an oral hearing will not likely fulfill the guarantee. As such, any oral hearing will necessarily require the services of an interpreter for a linguistically incompetent defendant; he cannot be expected to effectively exercise his right to defense in a hearing which he cannot comprehend. Furthermore, since the interpreter is such an integral part of any oral hearing, her competence and skill level will have an outsized impact upon the accused's exercise of his right. Obviously, a poor interpretation that fails to help the accused understand the oral evidence at the proceeding will effectively negate the individual's right to that very hearing.

---

[3]Finding a violation where the accused's request for an oral hearing had been denied by the court, even where it reviewed "not only issues of law but also important factual questions".

[4]Holding that a violation occurred where the jurisdiction of a court of first instance extended to factual issues, but no opportunity for an oral hearing was granted.

3.4 Right to Be Informed of the Charge (Article 14 [3] [a])

3.4.1 Defining the Right to Be Informed of the Charge

Article 9 (2) ICCPR entitles an individual who is arrested to information as to the reason for his arrest and guarantees that he "shall be promptly informed of any charges against him." Article 14 (3) (a) ICCPR supplements this right by requiring that an accused be "informed promptly and in detail in a language which he understands of the nature and cause of the charge against him." In its General Comment No. 32, the HRC noted that this right applies not only to those individuals in State custody, but to all persons charged with a crime, regardless of their detention status (§31). The right does not, however, apply to individuals who are under investigation but have yet to be formally charged (HRC General Comment No. 32, §31). The purpose of the right is to allow an accused to defend himself, which can only be done if the individual, prior to the trial setting, has sufficient information concerning the subject matter of the prosecution to allow him to prepare a defense (Trechsel 2005, p. 193). Given this purpose, there are several key aspects to the right to be informed: namely, the timing as to when the accused is informed; the substance of the information given; and the form by which the accused is informed. Each of these will be dealt with separately.

Timing

With respect to the timing of the right, both Articles 9 (2) and 14 (3) (a) ICCPR entitle the accused to be informed of the charges "promptly." The HRC has interpreted this to mean that an accused must be supplied with information about the charge "as soon as the person concerned is formally charged" (HRC General Comment No. 32, §31). There are several reasons for such a requirement. First, the earlier an accused is given specific notice of the subject matter of the prosecution, the earlier he can begin preparing his defense. This should ensure that he has adequate time to make such preparations. Indeed, under HRC caselaw, the accused must be informed of the charge early enough before the trial setting so that he has the necessary time to actually prepare his defense (*Monguya Mbenge v. Zaire* [HRC 1983] §§14.1–14.2; see also Weissbrodt 2001, p. 113). Second, the ability to begin preparing a defense early in the proceedings has the added advantage that any evidence in the accused's favor will likely still be discoverable and is less likely to have gone stale. Finally, the early notification of the charge will allow the accused (and thus the court) to quickly address any procedural irregularities or errors in the accusation (Nowak 2005, p. 228 [with respect to Art. 9 (2) but equally applicable here]). In other words, if the authorities have made a mistake (either procedurally or substantively), it can be remedied earlier in the process.

Substance

Article 14 (3) (a) guarantees an accused the right to be informed of the "nature and cause" of the charges as well. Thus, the accused's notification must contain enough information concerning the allegation to allow him to understand that with which he is actually charged (Trechsel 2005, p. 200). In this regard, the underlying facts supporting the charge are an essential element of the notification, as is a detailed legal description of the alleged offense (Nowak 2005, p. 331). The information must be specific enough to allow the accused to take immediate steps to legally combat the charge (Weissbrodt 2001, p. 114). Furthermore, since the accused must comprehend all of this information in order for the right to provide any actual protection, the notification must be provided "in a language which he understands" (Art. 14 [3] [a] ICCPR). It goes without saying that the information contained in the notification must also be clear and correct (Trechsel 2005, p. 200). The key aspect in this regard, as with the timing requirement, is that the notification must place the accused in a position from which he can prepare his defense (Nowak 2005, p. 331). Any notification that does not give the accused information and facts adequate enough to allow such preparation is likely insufficient.

Form

Finally, there is arguably some minimal requirement as to the form of the notification. Specifically, the accused must be informed of the charge in writing at some point in the proceedings. Oral notification is sufficient, but only where a written version of the charge is later given as confirmation of the oral information (HRC General Comment No. 32, §31). Likewise, the HRC has noted that the responsibility for notification rests solely with the State and may not be discharged through other parties or means (*Monguya Mbenge v. Zaire* [HRC 1983] §14.2).[5] As such, there is an element of official governmental formality that is also necessary.

3.4.2 The Relationship Between Interpreters and the Right to Be Informed of the Charge

Where the accused does not understand the language of the court, the requirement that the notification be given in a language which he understands will invariably necessitate the involvement of an interpreter (for the reading of the charge) or translator (for the written charge). Since the driving purpose of the right is to allow the accused both sufficient time and adequate information in order to prepare a defense, his understanding of the information is crucial. It goes without saying that the interpreter's performance level in this context will also be key, since a poor interpretation or translation containing incorrect or incomplete information will effectively bar the accused from actually understanding the charge, and therefore set back his efforts to mount an early defense.

3.5 Right to Adequate Time and Facilities to Prepare a Defense (Article 14 [3] [b])

3.5.1 Defining the Right to Adequate Time and Facilities to Prepare a Defense

Article 14 (3) (b) ICCPR guarantees that an accused shall "have adequate time and facilities for the preparation of his defence and to communicate with counsel of his own choosing." Although the language of Article 14

[5] Holding that the accused's right to be notified of the charges against him was violated even where he had been given information from other sources as to the actual charges and underlying facts.

(3) (b) addresses both the rights to choose and communicate with counsel, these will be dealt with in the section on the right to counsel. For the purposes of this section, the two main aspects of the right (time and facilities) will be the focus. Each will be discussed below separately. Beforehand, however, some general, overlapping aspects of the right must be addressed.

First, the term "adequate" implies that the time and facilities granted need only be "good enough" to prepare a defense and not necessarily perfect (Trechsel 2005, p. 211). Second, the use of the term "adequate" also implies that, in order to show a violation of this right, the accused must demonstrate that he was denied some facility or amount of time and that this denial resulted in some harm to his defense (Trechsel 2005, p. 211; Weissbrodt 2001, p. 122). Logically, where the accused cannot show that the denial caused actual prejudice to his defense, then the facilities or time available were "good enough". Similarly, a failure to complain about the inadequacy of specific facilities or particular time limits at the trial court level represents an implied acceptance that the circumstances were adequate for the preparation of a defense. This aspect of the right can be seen as "very close to the obligation to exhaust domestic remedies" (Trechsel 2005, p. 215). Third, the "adequacy" of the resources and time guaranteed to an accused must of necessity change depending on the circumstances of the case: for example, complex cases require more time for preparation and cases with international actors require more resources to ensure the participation of witnesses. Thus, the meaning of "adequate" must be determined on a case-by-case basis (Weissbrodt 2001, pp. 121–122).

Adequate Time

The first main element of this right concerns the concept of adequate time. It is important to note that the key purpose of time is to allow the preparation of a defense and to communicate with counsel. Thus, the amount of time allotted to an accused will only be sufficient if it permits him to prepare his defense properly. In fact, in its General Comment No. 32, the HRC noted that courts have a positive "obligation to grant reasonable requests for adjournment" where "additional time for preparation of the defence is needed" (§32). Since the HRC evaluates the adequacy of time on a case-by-case basis, it is instructive to look at a few of its most recent precedents for guidance.

In *Ashurov v. Tajikistan* (2007), the author's request for extra time to study the case file with the help of an interpreter (since he did not speak the language of the court) was denied without explanation by the trial court; the HRC held this denial to be a violation (§6.6). Similarly, in *Quispe Roque v. Peru* (2005), the HRC found a violation where defense counsel was only given 30 minutes to review the case file (§7.3). In addition, in *Khostikoev v. Tajikistan* (2009), where defense counsel was not given the opportunity to review the case file before the actual trial, the HRC held that this (along with several other substantial irregularities) resulted in a violation of the "basic guarantees of a fair trial" (§§3.2, 7.2–7.3).

What is most telling from these cases is that, in each instance, a violation was found not simply where the author was rushed to trial, but rather where the author was denied time to perform a specific act that was necessary to the preparation of his defense. Thus, as explained by Trechsel (2005) in the context of the ECtHR caselaw in this area, "there is not one period of time needed for the defence," rather "there will be a succession of such instances" where adequate time is needed for the defense to take a specific act, such as answering a recently-filed prosecution motion or evaluating new evidence that has come to light (pp. 219–220). In each situation, the accused is likely entitled to extra time of sufficient length to allow his counsel to address the change in circumstances in the case. Furthermore, it is also apparent that the accused must request this extra time where he feels it is necessary, in order to allow the court the opportunity to grant his request (HRC General Comment No. 32, §32; Weissbrodt 2001, p. 123). Failure to do so may be taken as an admission that the original time given was adequate.

Adequate Facilities

The second primary element of the guarantee is that the accused is entitled to adequate "facilities". Here again, it must be noted that the preparation of the accused's defense is the unequivocal goal of the right, and thus the accused is guaranteed access to any facilities that are necessary for the preparation of that defense. However, this underlying goal not only acts as a guarantee of access, but also as a limitation, since under this right the defense is only entitled to those facilities that are helpful to their preparation and no more (Reid 2011, p. 124 [with reference to the same principle under the ECHR]). Naturally, this begs the question as to what types of facilities the defense is entitled.

In this context, the HRC has explicitly stated that the defense is guaranteed access to "all materials that the prosecution plans to offer in court against the accused or that are exculpatory" (HRC General Comment No. 32, §33). The HRC has further defined "exculpatory" materials to include not only those that help to prove the accused's innocence, but "also other evidence that could assist the defence" (HRC General Comment No. 32, §33). This is a fairly generous definition that, in combination with the explicit grant of access to evidence that will be presented in court by the prosecution, entitles the defense to access a very substantial portion of the State's evidentiary file. Despite this seemingly exhaustive entitlement, there are some limitations to the guarantee. First, the right is tied to the preparation of a defense; as such, it is important that the defense overall have access to the documents and evidence, not necessarily the accused personally. Thus, where the accused does not understand the language in which the evidence is presented, this will not be problematic so long as his counsel does understand (*Harward v. Norway* [HRC 1994] §9.5). Second, the State may deny the accused access to documents where necessitated by national laws protecting the public interest, privilege, or confidentiality (McGoldrick 1994, p. 421).

Another aspect of "facilities" concerns the accused's ability to contact his defense counsel, which is unambiguously protected by this guarantee. As previously mentioned, the right to communicate with counsel will be more fully analyzed in the context of the general right to counsel. However, it is important to note here that defense counsel itself is considered a "facility" under Article 14 (3) (b) ICCPR, and thus is something to which the accused is entitled to the extent necessary to prepare his defense (naturally, the overall right to counsel covers this as well). The same logic would seem to apply concerning access to a court interpreter: where an interpreter is necessary in order to prepare a defense (for example, questioning a potential witness before the trial), then the requirement of adequate facilities would arguably entitle the defense to have access to such an interpreter. Note that this entitlement would not simply mirror the right to an interpreter as analyzed in Chap. 2, since that right only applies to those individuals who do not speak the language of the court (*Guesdon v. France* [HRC 1990] §10.2; see also HRC General Comment No. 13, §13). Here, the entitlement would appear to apply to any accused, whether or not he speaks the language of the court, so long as interpretation services are needed to prepare the defense. However, as is true with respect to the translation of documents under *Harward v. Norway*, any guarantee of an interpreter likely hinges less on whether the accused is capable of understanding the language in which the evidence is presented, and more on whether his counsel can prepare a defense without such an interpreter.

3.5.2 The Relationship Between Interpreters and the Right to Have Adequate Time and Facilities

Naturally, if interpreters are considered a "facility", then their competence will necessarily have an effect on the adequacy of the facilities available to the defense. In much the same way that insufficient access to prosecution documents may undermine the preparation of a defense, the inability to break through a linguistic barrier to access potentially helpful evidence or witnesses may cause a similar result. In this respect, the competence of the interpreter, and thus her ability to effectively remove this language barrier, will be essential to the preparation of the defense and fulfillment of this right. Likewise, where the accused himself is behind the language barrier, and thus unable to effectively participate in the preparation of his own defense, the skill with which the interpreter can eliminate this obstacle and ensure the accused's helpful participation will be of similar importance. It is clear, however, that in either case, the experience and ability of the interpreter will play a key role in the provision of adequate facilities.

Furthermore, the existence of an interpreter for a foreign language accused, or in order to access evidence that is not linguistically accessible to counsel, will likely affect the amount of time necessary for the preparation of a defense (Schomburg 2009, p. 12 [noting this in the context of the international tribunals]). The usage of an interpreter, even if only for one witness or one piece of evidence, is a complicating factor that will necessitate not only extra time for the analysis of that evidence, but also impose increased logistical difficulties on everyone involved. In addition, if an interpreter is required in order to involve the accused in the entire preparatory process, then the logistical and scheduling difficulties will be further increased, as will the amount of time necessary for the evaluation of all the evidence. In short, the use of an interpreter carries with it the necessity of additional time; therefore, the evaluation of whether "adequate time" has been given to an accused will inevitably change where an interpreter is involved in the process.

3.6 Right to Be Tried Without Undue Delay (Article 14 [3] [c])

3.6.1 Defining the Right to Be Tried Without Undue Delay

While Article 14 (3) (b) ICCPR guarantees an accused an adequate period of time to prepare a defense for the eventual trial, Article 14 (3) (c) protects an accused from having the State take too much time before initiating that trial. Specifically, the accused is entitled to "be tried without undue delay". These two rights thus exist in a state of unique tension: on the one hand prohibiting the State from rushing an unprepared accused to trial, while simultaneously requiring the State to schedule the trial as soon as is reasonable (Trechsel 2005, p. 216).

There are several underlying reasons for ensuring that an accused is promptly tried. First, the right was "designed to avoid keeping persons too long in a state of uncertainty about their fate" (HRC General Comment No. 32, §35). Facing criminal charges is highly stressful and can significantly restrict the accused's ability to move forward with his life. Naturally, the sooner the charges are determined, the sooner these issues disappear (though, perhaps not always in the manner the accused would prefer). Second, guaranteeing an accused the right to a trial without undue delay is simply an extension of the right of access to the court system (Trechsel 2005, p. 136). If an accused must wait an unreasonable amount of time to have his charges determined in a court of law, then it is arguable whether his right to access was truly respected. Third, from a purely practical standpoint, evidence (and the ability to discover that evidence) tends to diminish with time: witnesses forget details and physical evidence can actually decay or be lost. While this may affect both the State and the accused equally, and thus does not automatically harm the accused's ability to prepare and present a defense (Trechsel 2005, p. 136), the decay of evidence does threaten the reliability of the ultimate decision, since that decision will be made on evidence that is either incomplete or unreliable due to age. In this respect, the general tension between "adequate time" and "without undue delay" serves to ensure a trial that is as complete as possible from a preparation standpoint, without having grown stale from excessive waiting.

The right to be tried without undue delay breaks down into several key aspects, each of which will be separately discussed below. At the outset, the question of applicability must be addressed. Following upon this will be a discussion as to what factors must be taken into consideration when determining whether a delay is "undue". Finally, the relationship between interpreters and the right to be tried without undue delay will be considered.

Applicability

As with most of the Article 14 (3) rights, the accused's right to be tried without undue delay arises once he has been criminally charged (Nowak 2005, p. 334). Its application, however, is not quite that straight forward, since Article 9 (3) ICCPR guarantees an individual who has been arrested or detained the right to a "trial within a reasonable time". The difference in the specific language used ("without undue delay" as opposed to "within a reasonable time") is not as important as it might appear at first, since the concept of "undue delay" has generally been reduced to a complicated question of reasonability (Trechsel 2005, pp. 134–135). Moreover, as has been previously discussed in Chap. 2, the concept of a criminal charge, while not entirely settled, can best be understood as the time when the accused is "informed that the authorities are taking specific steps to prosecute him or her" (Nowak 2005, p. 334). An official arrest or detention of the individual would necessarily qualify as a "specific step" towards prosecution, even where an actual charge is not forthcoming (*Bozize v. Central African Republic* [HRC 1994] §§5.2–5.3).[6] Thus, under Article 9 (3) and 14 (3) (c), the right to a trial without undue delay (or within a reasonable time) applies from the moment that an individual is either arrested or becomes aware that the State is taking steps to prosecute him. The determination of the official beginning of the right's application is especially important because the eventual decision as to whether undue delay existed necessarily revolves around the amount of time that has passed. Other factors also have an impact, but determining the moment at which the timer begins to count is crucial.

An important aspect of the right is its applicability throughout the various stages of the criminal process. Although Article 14 (3) (c) specifically refers to a right to be "tried", which might be assumed to grant a right to have a "trial" within a reasonable time, the right itself has been interpreted by the HRC to apply throughout the entirety of the criminal proceedings (HRC General Comment No. 32, §35). Thus, every stage of the criminal proceedings, from "first instance" up until the final appeal, must occur "without undue delay" (HRC General Comment No. 32, §35; see also Weissbrodt 2001, p. 125). As such, an unreasonable delay in a court's consideration of an accused's appeal of his conviction has previously been held to be a violation of Article 14 (3) (c) (*Pinkney v. Canada* [HRC 1985] §22). Likewise, where an appellate court failed for six years to issue a reasoned written judgment that would allow the accused to further appeal his conviction, the HRC found a violation (*Hamilton v. Jamaica* [HRC 1994] §9.1). In each instance, the violation was due not to the delay in the commencement of the accused being "tried", or even based on the overall length of time during which the criminal proceedings took place, but rather arose from the delay of

[6] Holding that Article 14 [3] [c] had been violated where the author was held in custody with neither a charge nor a trial for over four years.

one particular procedure out of the entire criminal process. In this respect, the right to be tried without undue delay bears an even stronger resemblance to the right to have adequate time to prepare a defense: just as the accused must be allocated sufficient time to perform every individual defense-related task throughout the process, the State may not take too much time during any one particular stage of the process. There is even some indication from the ECtHR that an unreasonably long trial itself might constitute a violation (Trechsel 2005, p. 146), though the HRC has yet to either confront or embrace this logic.

The Factors Concerning "Undue Delay"

The determination as to what constitutes "undue delay" is particularly dependent on the specific circumstances of the case, and is thus made on a case-by-case basis (HRC General Comment No. 32, §35). The HRC has developed a fairly extensive caselaw in this area, and has consistently engaged itself in the implementation of this standard at the national level through the critical evaluation of State Reports (McGoldrick 1994, p. 407). In this respect, it has identified several factors that must be taken into account, including the "complexity of the case, the conduct of the parties, the manner in which the case was dealt with by the administrative and judicial authorities, and any detrimental effects that the delay may have had on the legal position of the complainant" (*Lederbauer v. Austria* [HRC 2007] §8.1; see also HRC General Comment No. 32, §35). The HRC, as discussed above, does not look to the overall amount of time that has been spent on the case, but instead focuses on any delay present at a particular phase of the proceedings (Nowak 2005, p. 337). Where such a delay exists, the burden of justifying the delay falls on the State (Nowak 2005, p. 335). Throughout the entire process, it is the State's obligation to ensure that every stage of the criminal proceedings occurs without delay; the accused is under no obligation to press the court for a prompt proceeding (*Pratt and Morgan v. Jamaica* [HRC 1989] §13.4).

Unfortunately, even though the HRC has set out the specific factors to be considered in a determination of whether a delay is unreasonable, there has been little clarification as to the content of the factors themselves. Most of the HRC's jurisprudence in this area involves cases where the State made no attempt to justify its delay (McGoldrick 1994, p. 424). Thus, given that the burden of justification is placed upon the State, cases where no State explanation has been forthcoming result in very little argumentation concerning the specified factors. As such, the factors still lack clarification. For instance, the complex nature of a case may justify a longer delay in the proceedings, yet it is still unclear whether complexity arises from the complicated nature of the evidence itself (such as scientific evidence), the relative amount of the evidence and witnesses, the procedural difficulties inherent in a particular case (such as extensive motions hearings), or something else entirely. Likewise, while the HRC has left open the possibility that a procedural delay might be excused by "the manner in which the case was dealt with by the administrative and judicial authorities", there is very little caselaw clarifying the meaning of this factor either.

It is possible to look to the jurisprudence of the ECtHR for some guidance. Although the difference in wording between Article 14 (3) (c) ICCPR ("without undue delay") and Article 6 (1) ECHR ("within a reasonable time") is noticeable, as discussed with reference to Article 9 (3) ICCPR, the concept of "undue delay" has some equivalence to the idea of "reasonableness" embodied in Article 6 (1) ECHR. As such, the comparison is not entirely without merit and is quite helpful. The idea of complexity, for example, comes more clearly into focus. ECtHR jurisprudence has recognized that the complexity can arise from factual aspects such as the number of witnesses, the subject-matter of the case, and the volume of written evidence (Reid 2011, p. 206). Complexity that arises from procedural difficulties, however, does not excuse extra delays, since the State should be adept at utilizing the criminal procedures that it has created (Trechsel 2005, pp. 145, 147) and is under a positive obligation to organize its legal system to ensure no undue delay occurs (*Mansur v. Turkey* [ECtHR 1995] §68; *Zimmerman and Steiner v. Switzerland* [ECtHR 1983] §29).

Another significant factor clarified by ECtHR caselaw involves the impact of the conduct by both parties on any resulting delays. Here, the HRC has not been completely silent, holding in *Jessop v. New Zealand* (2011) that where the accused's attorney was out of the country and thereby caused a majority of the delay, no violation of the right was present (§8.4). Thus, an accused may not benefit from a delay (intentional or not) that he or his counsel have caused. The ECtHR, however, has dealt with this factor extensively. For instance, ECtHR case law has noted that since an accused has no obligation to assist the State in its prosecution, any unreasonable delays that result from a lack of cooperation on the part of the accused may still constitute a violation (Trechsel 2005, p. 143). Likewise, since the accused has an affirmative right to contest the case and seek procedural remedies, any delay resulting from these actions will not be imputed to the accused (Trechsel 2005, p. 143). Defensive actions, or lack of cooperation on the part of the accused, however, must remain within acceptable limits. Where the accused's actions are considered unreasonable (such as where he engages in a hunger strike, refuses to leave his cell, or actually flees the jurisdiction), any ensuing delay will be attributed to the accused (Trechsel 2005, pp. 143–144).

The conduct of the State must also be taken into account, and can have an impact on the determination of the reasonability of a delay. The baseline assumption is that it is the ultimate responsibility of the State to ensure that the criminal proceedings occur without delay (Weissbrodt 2001, p. 128). Where a delay occurs, the basic question is whether this delay should be excused or held against the State. A delay that arises from an event that is clearly beyond the control of the State is generally excused. For example, the ECtHR has held that delays attributable to public unrest or a lawyers' strike are justifiable (Trechsel 2005, p. 148). However, where the State has some modicum of control over the event that creates the delay, the State apparently will be held responsible for that delay. This is the case, as noted above with regard to the ECtHR, where the delay in the criminal proceedings arises from the complicated nature or relative newness of the criminal procedures of the jurisdiction (Trechsel 2005, p. 147). Since the State created these conditions, it is expected to diligently work within them.

The ECtHR has also held that any delays due to the general inefficiency of the overall criminal justice system are also attributable to the State (*Mansur v. Turkey* [ECtHR 1995] §68; *Zimmerman and Steiner v. Switzerland* [ECtHR 1983] §§29–32). This applies to the ICCPR as well, since, as McGoldrick (1994) has noted, "[m]atters of organization and administration will generally be the responsibility of the State" (p. 423; see also Nowak 2005, p. 335). Yet, even if the ICCPR envisions a baseline level of criminal justice expediency for which the State is ultimately responsible, not all States have equal means with which to achieve such efficiency. Some States have argued that their particular economic conditions and financial situation do not allow them to create a criminal justice system capable of meeting the HRC's temporal expectations under Article 14 (3) (c) ICCPR. The HRC, however, has refused to accept the economic situation of the country (Zambia) as a mitigating factor when determining the reasonability of a specific delay (*Lubuto v. Zambia* [1995] §7.3). Thus, regardless of whether the State has the fiscal or administrative means to create an efficient judicial system, it is nevertheless responsible for efficiently processing the claims of the accused under Article 14 (3) (c).

The HRC, though, has sent somewhat ambiguous signals in this area. For instance, in its first State Report, Australia asserted that the lack of interpreters and available courts in the "more remote and sparsely populated areas" of the country created delays that, while admittedly longer than ideal, were not considered unreasonable given the "special circumstances" presented by the particular area (quoted in McGoldrick 1994, p. 407). In its consideration of the report, the HRC expressed concern over the issue, but failed to take an overt stance as to whether these "circumstances" justified the admitted delays (HRC Concluding Observations: Australia [1983] §148). Leaving aside the HRC's uncertainty on the issue, it is difficult to accept Australia's apparent belief that the lack of available interpreters in the area is beyond its control to such an extent that its situation is markedly different from that of Zambia in the *Lubuto* case. It must be assumed that the lack of available resources to provide expedient trials in the remote areas of Australia is a function of that State's inability (or simple unwillingness) to provide the necessary funds to create enough courts and attract enough interpreters to staff them. If this is indeed the case, then the delays in Australia, at their essence, are no different from those in Zambia: they arise from insufficient financial allocation to the court system. Thus, the HRC's hesitancy with respect to Australia's assertions is confusing.

3.6.2 The Relationship Between Interpreters and the Right to Be Tried Without Undue Delay

As noted with respect to the concept of "adequate time", the inclusion of interpreters at the various stages of a criminal proceeding necessarily entails extra time. The interpretation itself requires more time (which is especially true where consecutive interpretation is involved), as does the preparation of the case for both sides. Furthermore, the added necessity of scheduling interpreters (some of whom can be very in demand due to either their obscure language combinations or exceptional competence) can increase the delays in an interpreted proceeding. These extra delays can further stress the efficiency of criminal justice systems that already struggle with expediency. In this manner, the involvement of interpreters can further complicate an accused's ability to be tried without undue delay. Moreover, the threat of creating such an unreasonable delay by waiting for the availability of an experienced interpreter may result in the usage of a less-qualified substitute. Thus, the interplay between interpreters and the right to be tried without undue delay can inadvertently impact the other fair trial rights as well.

Whether the use of an interpreter would be considered part of the "complexity" of a case such as to justify additional delays is not entirely settled. While the ECtHR's overall treatment of complexity, and the HRC's general disapproval of economic excuses in that regard, may make that outcome likely, the HRC's handling of the Australian State Report provides a note of caution. However, the fact remains that interpreters add to the length of proceedings and neither the HRC nor the ECtHR have explicitly stated that their inclusion in the process excuses an otherwise unreasonable delay. In addition, there is an excellent argument to be made that the State itself must bear some responsibility for the overall lack of quality interpreters available to the criminal justice system, since the State determines the level of compensation given to court interpreters. Given these circumstances, any evaluation of the reasonability of a delay in a case involving an interpreter must, to some extent, consider the impact of the interpreter on that delay.

3.7 Right to Be Present at Trial (Article 14 [3] [d])

3.7.1 Defining the Right to Be Present at Trial

Under Article 14 (3) (d) ICCPR, every accused has the right to be "tried in his presence". The right to be present at one's own trial is protected primarily as a part of a greater right to defend oneself in person before the court, though this defense can be (and usually is) delegated to legal counsel (Nowak 2005, p. 339). Although frequently underestimated by judicial actors, the importance of the accused to the actual presentation by his counsel of an effective defense at trial is substantial (Grabau 1996, p. 6). The accused is, among other things, in a unique position to verify the accuracy of witness statements and to provide meaningful lines of cross-examination (Reid 2011, p. 211). As such, even where represented by counsel, under most circumstances the accused is entitled to be present, and this entitlement arguably applies to the entirety of the trial (*Domukovsky and others v. Georgia* [HRC 1998] §18.9).[7]

It should be noted, though, that the accused's right to be "tried" in his presence does not have the same expansive reach throughout the criminal proceedings as his right to be "tried" without undue delay, which encompasses every stage of the process. In the context of Article 14 (3) (d), the word "tried" has been interpreted in a much more limited fashion. In *Gordon v. Jamaica* (1992), the HRC held that no violation occurred where the accused was not present during his appellate proceedings since he was competently represented by counsel (§6.2). The circumstances would appear to be different, however, where the accused is not represented by counsel, which was the case in *Dudko v. Australia* ([HRC 2007] §5.2). Though, oddly, the HRC found a "violation of the guarantee of equality before the courts" and not of the right to be present (*Dudko v. Australia* [HRC 2007] §§7.3–7.4). Of further interest is that the HRC in *Dudko* placed emphasis on the fact that the oral hearing at which the accused was not present also involved questions of fact, as opposed to

[7] Where the author was "forced to be absent during long periods of the trial", his right to be present under Article 14 [3] [d] was violated.

appellate questions of law (§7.3). This emphasis on questions of fact aligns with the ECtHR caselaw in the area (even though the language of the Article 6 ECHR right to be present is somewhat different), which stresses that the right to be present does not arise when only questions of law are to be determined (Reid 2011, p. 213; see for example *Sobolewski v. Poland (No. 2)* [ECtHR 2009] §41).

Along with limiting the scope of application of the right, the HRC has also stated that exceptions may exist where they are "in the interest of the proper administration of justice" (HRC General Comment No. 32, §36). Thus, in some circumstances, a trial might be allowed to continue even absent the presence of the accused. An obvious example of such a circumstance, though the HRC has yet to rule on this issue, would be where the accused purposefully disrupts the trial through his behavior (Trechsel 2005, p. 253 [noting ECtHR caselaw allows such an exception to the right]). In *Monguya Mbenge v. Zaire* (1983), the HRC speculated that where an accused was properly informed of the proceedings but voluntarily chose not to attend, continuation of the trial would be permissible (§14.1). In essence, the accused's decision not to be present at his own trial would be taken as a waiver of his right. As such, the right to be tried in one's presence is not absolute, though the permissible exceptions have yet to be fully fleshed out by the HRC.

3.7.2 The Relationship Between Interpreters and the Right to Be Present at Trial

At first glance, there would appear to be little impact upon the right to be present from the usage of interpreters. However, the concept of "presence" may not be as limited as it appears. For instance, if one accepts that the underlying purpose of the right is to allow the accused to help with the presentation of the defense and to assist in the verification of the evidences' accuracy, then one can see that the accused's right to be "present" at the trial must mean more than simply being physically present. In other words, the right to be present entails a necessary level of understanding and participation in the trial itself. An accused who requires an interpreter in order to understand the language of the court, and thus the trial proceedings, would not truly be "present" under Article 14 (3) (d) without the help of the interpreter (Schabas 2007, p. 289 [noting this within the context of the International Criminal Court]). It is with this in mind that some national courts have spoken of a necessity of "linguistic presence" as well as physical presence under the right (de Jongh 2008, p. 21; Heller 1994–1995, pp. 345–346).

Regardless of whether such an entitlement to "linguistic presence" exists, its parameters and requirements would likely align neatly with other aspects of the right to a fair trial. In other words, by granting an accused a competent interpreter as required under Article 14 (3) (f) and guaranteeing his effective participation in the proceedings on an equal basis with the State under Article 14 (1), the requirements of linguistic presence likely would already be satisfied as well. Still, it is important to note that the overall right to an experienced and competent interpreter is further buttressed by an accused's right to be present at trial, and furthermore that an incompetent interpreter may also contribute to a violation of this right along with numerous other fair trial rights.

3.8 Right to Counsel (Article 14 [3] [d])

3.8.1 Defining the Right to Counsel

The right to have legal counsel arises primarily from Article 14 (3) (d), which guarantees the accused not only the right "to defend himself in person or through legal assistance of his own choosing", but also the right to have appointed legal counsel if the "interests of justice so require." There are several reasons for protecting the right of an accused to have legal counsel during criminal proceedings. First, the law is complex and contains many technical elements that non-lawyers will not be able to navigate intelligently (Trechsel 2005, p. 245). Since the State will likely employ an attorney to manage its prosecution, provision of counsel for the defense can be seen as necessary for the equality of arms. Second, a defense counsel will not be as emotionally engaged in the case as the accused, and can provide a more neutral and knowledgeable viewpoint (Trechsel 2005, pp. 245–146). Third, criminal cases are naturally stressful for an accused, and the existence of an attorney will offer the accused an experienced individual to guide him through the emotional difficulties inherent in the process (Trechsel 2005, p. 246). Finally, the inclusion of counsel who will necessarily represent the accused's viewpoint allows the accused to feel a part of the process, rather than simply the object of that process. As discussed in the context of the right to adversarial proceedings, permitting the accused to participate actively in the proceedings can lead to better acceptance of any eventual judgment (Trechsel 2005, p. 89).

There are several different aspects of the right to counsel that are of importance with respect to the usage of interpreters. First, the applicability of the right will be discussed. Next, the choice of counsel and the accused's right to communicate with counsel will be examined. Lastly, the effectiveness and competence of counsel will be analyzed.

Applicability

When and to whom the right to counsel applies changes depending upon the level of crime with which the accused is charged. Capital crimes historically have demanded a higher level of scrutiny (Weissbrodt 2001, p. 116), and the HRC has stated that individuals charged with capital offenses are entitled to legal counsel at all stages of the criminal process (*Aliboev v. Tajikistan* [HRC 2005] §6.4). On the opposite end of the spectrum, individuals charged with trivial offenses are not entitled to legal counsel at all (McGoldrick 1994, pp. 428–429). In *O.F. v. Norway* (1984), for example, the HRC held that an accused who was subject to only a small fine was not entitled to legal assistance (§1.3).

In the middle of the spectrum, however, the moment at which an accused becomes entitled to an attorney is less straightforward. In *Levinov v. Belarus* (2011), the HRC held that no violation had occurred where the accused had been denied legal counsel after his arrest because he was afforded counsel during his actual trial (§8.3). By way of contrast, in *Iskandarov v. Tajikistan* (2011), where the accused had been denied "access to the legal counsel of his choice" for 13 days after his arrest, the HRC did find a violation even though the accused was later allowed counsel (§6.7). The main difference between these two cases, and the primary issue that appears to drive the HRC's analysis, was the level and type of interrogation or investigation that occurred while the accused was unrepresented. In the *Iskandarov* case, the accused was interrogated and required to participate in investigatory acts while unrepresented ([HRC 2011] §6.7), while in the *Levinov* case, no investigation took place while the accused was without counsel ([HRC 2011] §8.3). As such, it can be argued that in non-trivial, non-capital cases, an accused has the right to counsel once any form of interrogation or participatory investigative act commences. This is logical given that "the early stages of the arrest and investigation can be crucial and have lasting impact on the course of the trial" (Reid 2011, p. 188).

Choice of Counsel and the Right to Defend Oneself

Article 14 (3) (d) entitles an accused "to defend himself in person or through legal assistance of his own choosing". Thus, the accused has a right to act as his own defense counsel at trial, but if he decides not to do so, he has the right to choose his own representative. Although the language of Article 14 (3) (d) appears nearly absolute, the application of the right in practice is somewhat more limited. The HRC has stated that the interests of justice may require that counsel be assigned to an accused even where he desires to defend himself (HRC General Comment No. 32, §37). Specific examples given that would merit the appointment of counsel against the accused's wishes are where the accused has been "substantially and persistently" obstructive of the trial, faces a grave charge but is not able to act on his own behalf, or would further distress or intimidate a vulnerable witness by questioning them during the proceedings (HRC General Comment No. 32, §37).

Where counsel will represent the accused at trial, Article 14 (3) (d) entitles the accused to choose his own counsel. This right necessarily entails that the accused be given adequate time to engage private counsel if he wishes to do so (*Larrañaga v. The Philippines* [HRC 2006] §§7.5–7.6). The HRC has noted that where qualified counsel is chosen and privately compensated by the accused, the accused's choice of counsel must be respected (*Acosta v. Uruguay* [HRC 1984] §§2.6, 13.2). However, as with the right to defend oneself, this right to choose is not unlimited. For example, the State may require that the chosen representative have certain educational or professional qualifications, such as being a fully qualified attorney certified to practice law within the relevant jurisdiction (Trechsel 2005, p. 268 [ECtHR caselaw is in accord]). Likewise, the situation changes once the accused avails himself of the right to have legal assistance appointed at the expense of the State. Under these circumstances, the accused is not entitled to choose his own counsel, but must rather accept the counsel selected by the State, so long as this is not incompatible with the interests of justice (Weissbrodt 2001, p. 116). Counsel appointed by the State under a legal aid plan of this sort is, however, free of charge for the accused (Nowak 2005, p. 339). It must be noted, however, that under Article 14 (3) (d) the accused is only entitled to appointed counsel where "he does not have sufficient means to pay" for counsel of his own.

The Right to Communicate with Counsel

Under Article 14 (3) (b), as previously discussed with reference to the right to adequate time and facilities, the accused is guaranteed the right to communicate with his own counsel. The HRC has stated that access to counsel must be prompt and occur under "conditions that fully respect the confidentiality" of the communications (HRC General Comment No. 32, §34). With regard to the privacy of the communication, the HRC has suggested that a violation may occur where the accused is only allowed to contact his counsel in the presence of law-enforcement personnel (*Iskandarov v. Tajikistan* [HRC 2011] §6.7). The ECtHR has taken a similar stance, even though the ECHR contains no express right to communicate with counsel (*S. v. Switzerland* [ECtHR 1991] §48). Furthermore, since the accused is entitled to adequate time to prepare a defense, it is axiomatic that his communication with counsel must also be of a sufficient length of time to ensure that this preparation can take place. Similarly, it would also seem quite logical to assume that the necessity of investigating the charge and preparing a defense, as well as the aforementioned "promptness" requirement, would entitle the accused to communicate with his counsel as quickly as possible after he is charged. Although the HRC has not explicitly ruled on the issue, it has "suggest[ed] that an accused has a right to see an attorney at all times during the pre-trial period" (Weissbrodt 2001, p. 124; see also McGoldrick 1994, p. 406). At a minimum, cases such as *Iskandarov* indicate that the accused must be granted access to counsel whenever some form of interrogation or participatory investigative act will take place.

Effectiveness and Competence of Counsel

The right to counsel as envisioned in the ICCPR necessarily carries with it a requirement that the accused's counsel be competent and effective (HRC General Comment No. 32, §38). At a minimum, the individual representing the accused likely must be a qualified attorney (*Vasilskis v. Uruguay* [HRC 1983] §11). Furthermore, they must actually advocate on behalf of the accused, and not undermine his defense (Weissbrodt 2001, p. 120). In addition, since the accused is entitled to participate in the preparation of his defense, counsel is also required to consult with the accused on aspects of that defense (*Little v. Jamaica* [HRC 1991] §8.3). The HRC has also held on several occasions that counsel representing the accused is entitled to be free of State coercion or threats (*Iskandarov v. Tajikistan* [HRC 2011] §§2.8, 6.7; *Vargas Mas v. Peru* [HRC 2005] §6.4).

The right to competent and effective counsel, however, does not entitle the accused to representation that is perfect or free of errors. Attorneys are allowed to exercise their professional judgment, and their decisions will not automatically result in a violation simply because they ultimately end up being incorrect (Weissbrodt 2001, p. 120). Only in instances of "blatant misbehavior or incompetence", such as withdrawing an appeal in a death penalty case without consulting the accused or being absent when a witness testifies during a death penalty case, will the actions of a defense counsel create liability on the part of the State (HRC General Comment No. 32, §38). And even in these limited circumstances, the State will only be held responsible where the blatantly incompetent defense counsel was appointed by State authorities: the actions of a privately retained counsel "cannot be attributed to the State party" (*H.C. v.*

Jamaica [HRC 1992] §6.3). Thus, the accused himself is responsible for the actions of his private counsel, and may not complain of his own counsel's incompetence.

3.8.2 The Relationship Between Interpreters and the Right to Counsel

It is self-evident that where an accused who does not speak the language of the court chooses to represent himself at trial, as is his right, the competence and effectiveness of his interpreter will play a major role in the efficacy of his defense. Moreover, even where such an individual chooses to have counsel represent him, his ability to communicate with that counsel (if counsel does not speak the language of the accused) will depend entirely upon an interpreter as well. Given that effective communication with counsel is extremely important to the realization of the overall right to counsel (communication is necessary for consultation of defense strategy as well as the preparation of the defense with counsel), this makes the abilities and competence of the interpreter a necessary prerequisite to the fulfillment of that right as well.

In addition, examining the right to counsel in some detail assists in understanding the right to an interpreter itself. They are, in some elemental ways, highly analogous and caselaw that pertains to the right to counsel can often be highly persuasive with reference to similar issues involving interpreters. For instance, since defense counsel are considered "facilities" with respect to the accused's right to have adequate facilities for his defense, this right would likely encompass interpreters as well. Similarly, the HRC's ruling that the State is not responsible for the incompetence of privately retained counsel would also likely be applicable to privately retained interpreters. As such, interpreters can not only have an impact on the effective realization of the right to counsel, but the right to counsel can have a substantial impact on the rules surrounding the usage of interpreters.

3.9 Right to Examine Witnesses (Article 14 [3] [e])

3.9.1 Defining the Right to Examine Witnesses

Article 14 (3) (e) entitles an accused to "examine, or have examined, the witnesses against him", as well as "to obtain the attendance and examination of witnesses on his behalf under the same conditions as witnesses against him." In essence, the right guarantees to the accused the ability to both present his own witnesses, as well as to question those witnesses presented by the State. Furthermore, it also grants the accused a right to access other evidence associated with witnesses, so that he may question witnesses under the same conditions as the State. Each of these aspects of the overall right to examine witnesses will be discussed separately, along with the limitations or exceptions imposed upon Article 14 (3) (e). At the outset, however, it is necessary to consider both the definition of "witness", as well as the purposes of the right.

Who and what qualifies as a "witness" for the purposes of Article 14 (3) (e) is not entirely clear, since the HRC has yet to provide a clarification of the expression. Nor can the definition simply be left to national jurisdictions, as this would allow uncooperative domestic courts to severely limit the applicability of the right through a restrictive definition. As such, some form of autonomous definition is required, as is used in the ECtHR caselaw (Trechsel 2005, pp. 301–302). However, none has been forthcoming from the HRC. Rather, the concept of a "witness" has been shaped largely through the HRC's caselaw. As an obvious starting point, anyone who testifies (or wishes to testify) in court will likely be considered a witness. Yet, the concept appears much broader than that. In *Jessop v. New Zealand* (2011), the HRC entertained the possibility that reading a witness's unchallenged prior statement to the jury would have violated the accused's rights under Article 14 (3) (e) (HRC §8.6). Similarly, in *García Fuenzalida v. Ecuador* (1996), the HRC found a violation of Article 14 (3) (e) where the court refused to order an examination by an expert of biological evidence related to the case (§§3.5, 9.5). Both of these cases show that the concept of a "witness" would appear to extend beyond actual live testimony in court to encompass some forms of documentary evidence related to witnesses as well. Such an expansive definition would align with the ECtHR caselaw on the issue (Trechsel 2005, pp. 301–304).

The purposes behind the right to examine witnesses are also of some importance, and there are several. First, the right ensures that the accused is an active participant in the trial, and not a passive subject, making it more likely that he will accept the end result of the trial (Trechsel 2005, p. 293). As discussed earlier, such participation. Second, the ability to challenge evidence and present counter-evidence is necessary to uphold the right to adversarial proceedings (Trechsel 2005, p. 292). Finally, the continual questioning and probing of evidence by an accused (who is allegedly involved in the relevant incident and will therefore have first-hand knowledge of that incident) makes it more likely that the actual truth of the situation will be discovered (Trechsel 2005, p. 293). Likewise, the ability of the accused to present his own witnesses enables the presentation of a second, perhaps alternative, side to the story that might otherwise not be placed before the court. Each of these aspects promotes the ultimate establishment of justice in the case. It is also worth noting that where an accused cannot speak the language of the court, the fulfillment of each of these purposes likely requires the assistance of an interpreter.

The Right to Call Witnesses

The HRC has noted that the right to examine witnesses grants to an accused the "same legal powers of compelling the attendance of witnesses … as are available to the prosecution" (HRC General Comment No. 32, §39). In other words, the right is a manifestation of the equality of arms: the accused must be given the same techniques of legal coercion as the State in order that both parties are playing on a level field (HRC General Comment No. 32, §39; Nowak 2005, p. 341). From a practical standpoint, this means that the accused has the right to petition the court to require the attendance of witnesses "on his behalf". The language used ("on his behalf") does not appear to limit the allowable witnesses to only those who would testify in favor of the accused, but rather would also seem to encompass other witnesses that the accused wishes to call, such as those affiliated with the prosecution or neutral experts (Trechsel 2005, p. 323). This grant, however, is not unlimited: the accused is only entitled to call witnesses that "are relevant for the defence" (HRC General Comment No. 32, §39).

It is the duty of the State to see that requested witnesses are available to the accused, in the same manner that the State would ensure witness availability for the prosecution. For example, in *Grant v. Jamaica* (1994), the HRC found a violation of Article 14 (3) (e) where the State failed to provide transportation for a defense witness to attend and testify at the accused's trial (§8.5). The HRC stressed, though, that such a violation only exists where the inability to obtain the witness can be attributed to the State in some respect (*Grant v. Jamaica* [HRC 1994] §8.5). The accused here also has an obligation, since he likely must actually request the witness, and thereby bring the existence and desirability of the evidence or witness to the attention of the State (Weissbrodt 2001, pp. 136–137). Examples of instances where State actions have produced violations of Article 14 (3) (e) are fairly numerous: specifically, where the court "failed to ensure the presence and questioning of important witnesses" (*Iskandarov v. Tajikistan* [HRC 2011] §6.6); where the trial judge denied the accused's request to have certain witnesses testify (*Ashurov v. Tajikistan* [HRC 2007] §6.6); and where the court refused to order expert testimony concerning biological evidence crucial to the outcome of the case, in spite of the accused's request to that effect (*García Fuenzalida v. Ecuador* [HRC 1996] §9.5). The unifying theme in these cases is that the inability of the accused to present a witness was due directly to an action (or purposeful inaction) taken by the court, which imputed responsibility to the State.

The Right to Confront Witnesses

Along with the right to call witnesses, the accused also has the right to "examine" those witnesses called by the State. Thus, the accused must be given the opportunity to challenge any witness evidence put forward by the State (Trechsel 2005, p. 293). This is also implied by the guarantee of adversarial proceedings. The ability to challenge witness testimony is considered essential to a fair trial, since it is "well-known" that witness testimony and evidence "can be the source of many errors" (Trechsel 2005, p. 305) and confrontation of such witnesses can help refine and clarify their testimony. The centrality of this aspect of the right has been reinforced by HRC caselaw. In *Jessop v. New Zealand* (2011), the HRC noted that allowing a statement from a witness who had not been subject to cross-examination to be read to a jury would likely have resulted in a violation of Article 14 (3) (e) (HRC §8.6). Similarly, the HRC has used, in several cases involving Peru, the inability of an accused to question witnesses at trial as part of a group of infringements supporting a general violation of Article 14 (*Alegre v. Peru* [HRC 2005] §7.5; *Quispe Roque v. Peru* [HRC 2005] §7.3; *Vargas Mas v. Peru* [HRC 2005] §6.4). The ECtHR has also emphasized the importance of actual confrontation to the assessment of witness testimony (*Van Mechelen and Others v. The Netherlands* [ECtHR 1997] §59; *Kostovski v. The Netherlands* [ECtHR 1989] §42). What must be noted, however, is that the accused is only granted the "opportunity" to confront the witnesses: if he chooses not to do so, or does not press his claim, then he can be held to have waived his right to cross-examine that witness (Weissbrodt 2001, pp. 136–137).

The relative importance of the right to confront witnesses, however, does not mean that it is a continuing right throughout the entire proceedings. The HRC has noted only that the right to confront a witness must be afforded the accused "at some stage of the proceedings," which necessarily implies that the guarantee does not apply throughout every stage. As such, it is possible that so long as the accused was given the right to confront a witness at a preliminary proceeding, he might not be entitled to challenge the evidence of the witness if it is presented at trial. The logic and language employed by the HRC in the *Jessop* case would seem to support this conclusion, since the HRC did not unequivocally hold that a statement from the witness would not be admissible at trial, but rather that it would be, so long as the accused had previously been given a "proper opportunity to question and challenge" the witness (*Jessop v. New Zealand* [HRC 2011] §8.6). The allowance of such evidence, if previously contested at an earlier stage of the proceedings, would align with the jurisprudence of the ECtHR on the issue (Trechsel 2005, pp. 307–308). However, some account also must be taken of the principle of immediacy, which guarantees "the possibility of an accused to be confronted with the witness in the presence of the judge who ultimately decides the case" (*Pitkänen v. Finland* [ECtHR 2004] §58). This principle ensures that the court have the opportunity to personally assess the "demeanor and credibility of a witness" as exposed through confrontation (*Pitkänen v. Finland* [ECtHR 2004] §58). Thus, some balance must be found as to the exact method and timing of witness confrontation.

The Right to Access Related Evidence

In order to make effective an accused's right to question and confront witnesses, Article 14 (3) (e) contains an associated right for the accused to have access to evidence that is related to the witness's testimony. As previously discussed in the context of the right to adequate facilities, the accused is already guaranteed the right to examine any evidence that will be presented by the State in court, as well as any exculpatory material. If it is assumed that one of the main purposes of cross-examination is to uncover the truth through the vigilant questioning of a witness's testimony, it is logically necessary that the party engaged in that questioning should have access to, and knowledge of, any associated evidence that might inform their line of enquiry. While such evidence might well be considered "exculpatory" since it "could assist the defence" (HRC General Comment No. 32, §33), Article 14 (3) (e) would appear to provide a right of access independent of such considerations. This seems to be the course taken by the HRC in its caselaw. In *Peart and Peart v. Jamaica* (1995), a case concerning capital punishment, the State failed to make a witness's statement to the police available to the defense prior to their cross-examination of that particular witness (HRC §13). The HRC specifically held this to be an obstruction of the accused's ability to cross-examine the witness, and therefore a violation of Article 14 (3) (e) (*Peart and Peart v. Jamaica* [HRC 1995] §13). No consideration of the right to adequate facilities was involved. Nor, unfortunately, was there any detailed discussion as to what other types of documents must be provided to the accused prior to examination of a witness.

3.9.2 The Relationship Between Interpreters and the Right to Examine Witnesses

Just as access to evidence associated with a witness's testimony allows the defense to better inform its line of questioning, the active inclusion and participation of the accused in the process ensures that their assumed knowledge of the underlying incident will help inform the discovery of valuable facts. Indeed, each of the underlying motivations behind the right to examine witnesses (strengthening the adversarial nature of the proceedings and promoting the discovery of the truth) necessarily involves the participation of the accused throughout the proceedings. Obviously, where an accused does not understand the language of the court, this participation can only be obtained through the usage of a competent interpreter.

Yet, the mere existence of an interpreter is likely not enough to ensure the effective participation of a linguistically incompetent accused in the questioning process of a prosecution witness. Rather, the interpretation provided by that interpreter must likely rise to a very high standard indeed. It is arguable that anything less than a comprehensive interpretation will not be sufficient to satisfy the underlying purpose of having the accused engaged and actively monitoring the testimony of witnesses. The cross-examination of a witness, for instance, can be built upon the minor discrepancies between the facts as experienced by the witness, and those experienced by the accused. Without the ability to notice and instantly comment upon these minute differences to counsel, it is questionable whether the accused's participation will actually rise to a level sufficient enough to be of value. Thus, the accused's right to examine witnesses would seem to dictate the usage of a comprehensive interpretation technique as performed by an experienced and well-skilled interpreter.

The same is also likely true where the accused wishes to call a witness on his behalf who does not speak the language of the court. Here as well, not only will a court interpreter be necessary to allow the witness to present their evidence, but the standard of interpretation must be accurate enough that the fact-finder may view the evidence as if it were originally rendered in the language of the court. A lower standard, either through the employment of an unqualified court interpreter or the usage of a less detailed technique like summation of the evidence, will create a situation whereby the accused's right to call witnesses on his behalf will not be fulfilled at a level equal to that of the prosecution's witnesses, who will have presented their evidence in full detail with no aberrations. As such, with respect to the presentation of evidence through witnesses, at least, the accused's right to examine witnesses is to some degree tied to the capabilities of the court interpreter and the comprehensiveness of the interpretation.

3.10 Right to Appeal (Article 14 [5])

3.10.1 Defining the Right to Appeal

Article 14 (5) ICCPR guarantees "[e]veryone convicted of a crime ... the right to his conviction and sentence being reviewed by a higher tribunal according to law." This right to appeal one's conviction is intended to provide a means of oversight to ensure that the other, individual rights to a fair trial have been respected throughout the process (Marshall 2011, p. 17). To achieve this purpose, the HRC has noted that the right to appeal is not limited to the most serious crimes, but rather can include more minor infractions as well (HRC General Comment No. 32, §45; Weissbrodt 2001, p. 148). In *Salgar de Montejo v. Colombia* (1985), the HRC stated that the right to appeal applied even where the individual was only sentenced to one year of imprisonment (§§1.4, 10.4). Unfortunately, the HRC has stopped short of expressly stating that the right to appeal applies to all cases, thus leaving open the possibility that some truly minor infractions might be excluded (McGoldrick 1994, p. 431). However, what is clear from *Salgar de Montejo* and the HRC's General Comment No. 32 is that the determination of which crimes qualify for appellate review is not left to the discretion of the State. In this respect, the phrase "review[] by a higher tribunal according to law" is not meant to restrict the appellate review to that allowed under the State's domestic law, but rather concerns only the "modalities by which the review by a higher tribunal is to be carried out" (*Salgar de Montejo v.*

Colombia [HRC 1985] §10.4). In other words, the HRC determines whether appellate review for a conviction is mandatory, and the State is then left with the discretion how to implement the procedural mechanisms to carry out that review (McGoldrick 1994, p. 431).

Nature of the Tribunal

The latitude afforded the State concerning the manner in which the appellate review takes place extends to the composition of their appellate system as well (Marshall 2011, p. 18). For the most part, the State may design their appellate system as they wish, so long as adequate review by a higher tribunal is accessible to an accused (Marshall 2011, p. 19). In this regard, the concept of a "higher tribunal" necessitates review of a conviction or sentence by a court that is different than the original court that convicted or sentenced the accused (Trechsel 2005, p. 368; see also *Gelazauskas v. Lithuania* [HRC 1997] §7.6). Moreover, just as the State may not limit appellate review to a single level of the court system, nor may they artificially limit access to further levels of appellate review within an already established multi-level system (Nowak 2005, p. 351). In other words, where the domestic law generally provides for a third level of appeals, the accused must be granted access to that extra level as well (Weissbrodt 2001, pp. 148–149).

Extent of the Review

Likewise, the State must ensure that the appellate review that is provided to the accused is adequate. In this context, the HRC has stated that the right to appeal requires that the State substantively review both the conviction and the sentence, "both on the basis of sufficiency of the evidence and of the law" (HRC General Comment No. 32, §48). A review addressing only matters of law, as existed in *Domukovsky v. Georgia* (1998), has therefore been considered insufficient by the HRC (§18.11). The requirement that the sufficiency of evidence be considered, however, does not mean that the higher tribunal must effectively retry the case or rehear evidence. They must only provide "an evaluation of the evidence presented at the trial and of the conduct of the trial" (*Perera v. Australia* [HRC 1995] §6.4). Nor must the appellate tribunal always consider every possible aspect of the underlying proceeding; rather, Article 14 (5) will be fulfilled so long as the court considers every appellate point raised by the accused in his appeal (Marshall 2011, pp. 18–19; see for example *Pindado Martínez v. Spain* [HRC 2008] §6.5).

Effective Access to an Appeal

The State is also responsible for ensuring that the review eventually provided is effective (Marshall 2011, p. 21). Put differently, the State must establish a system whereby the individual can enjoy "effective exercise of the right to appeal" (*Lumley v. Jamaica* [HRC 1999] §7.5). From this requirement flow several specific obligations. First, the State must ensure that the individual has access to the appellate system. A system involving discretionary appeals will not necessarily violate this rule, as long as the consideration of the application for leave to appeal fully reviews the conviction and sentence (Marshall 2011, p. 19; Nowak 2005, p. 349). Second, the accused must have access to the documents necessary to prosecute the appeal (Marshall 2011, p. 21). Thus, the HRC has found violations of Article 14 (5) where the accused was unable to obtain a transcript of his trial (*Lumley v. Jamaica* [HRC 1999] §7.5; see also *Pinkney v. Canada* [HRC 1985] §35 [where a delayed transcript was also a violation]) or a duly-reasoned written judgment (*Henry v. Jamaica* [HRC 1991] §8.4; *Little v. Jamaica* [HRC 1991] §8.5).

3.10.2 The Relationship Between Interpreters and the Right to Appeal

On the surface, there would appear to be little overlap between the use of interpreters, which generally occurs in the eliciting of evidence, and a right to appeal which normally does not entail the reproduction or rehearing of evidence. However, the requirement that the State provide an effective, substantive review of the conviction necessarily implicates interpreter issues where one has been involved in the original trial. These issues generally arise in two appellate contexts: review of the adequacy of the interpreter's performance and the review of the original evidence.

With respect to the interpreter's performance, there is little opportunity to review the adequacy of the interpreter since no trial transcript of the source language is generally produced. Without a transcript or recording of the original evidence, no comparison can be made later by a neutral individual to judge the adequacy of the interpreter's work. As such, appellate oversight of the competence of an interpreter is normally limited to reviewing whether anyone complained about the interpretation during the trial, which is less an objective review of the performance by a higher tribunal than it is deference to the subjective opinion of the trial court. Keeping in mind that none of the other individuals involved in the trial are likely to be trained interpreters (or even bilingual), it is questionable if institutionalized deference to their contemporaneous reaction can truly be considered an effective review by a higher tribunal.

Moreover, where the appellate court is tasked with reviewing the sufficiency of evidence from a trial involving an interpreter, there is a genuine question as to whether the higher tribunal can effectively do so where that evidence came through an unsupervised interpreter. In the completion of this review, the appellate court will naturally rely on the written trial transcript, which will only include the interpreter's version of the evidence, and not the original source evidence itself. This is akin to judging the quality of a reproduced painting without having ever seen the original artwork: the new painting may appear excellent in its own right, but is it a faithful copy of the original? In effect, when reviewing the sufficiency of such evidence, the appellate court is relying almost entirely upon the product of an interpreter, the quality of which it has no actual capacity to check. Naturally, it is impractical to require the appellate court to review the evidence in its original form, since this will likely not be possible. However, the fact that an effective substantive review relies on second-hand evidence as related by an individual whose performance is beyond effective oversight is problematic. At a minimum, it shows how the performance of an interpreter can undermine not only the rights of an accused at the trial itself, but also the right to an appeal that is meant to ensure the effective implementation of those very rights.

3.11 Right to Overall Fairness in the Proceedings (Article 14 Generally)

3.11.1 Defining the Right to Overall Fairness in the Proceedings

As mentioned previously, the individual guarantees listed in Article 14 ICCPR set out specific procedural practices that are meant, through their implementation, to ensure the actual fairness of criminal proceedings. As such, they represent the minimum level of protection that must be afforded to accused individuals (Nowak 2005, p. 321; McGoldrick 1994, p. 405). It does not necessarily follow, however, that the simple fulfillment of each of these individual rights will inevitably guarantee the accused a fair hearing. Thus, a residual guarantee of overall fairness exists to ensure that, in the end result, the proceedings granted an accused considered as a whole were actually fair, regardless of whether the specific individual rights were fulfilled.

This overarching right to fairness can be seen clearly in the HRC's recent caselaw. In several cases involving Peru, the HRC, without explicitly considering the merits of claims as to specific violations of individual fair trial rights, found that the "there was a violation of article 14 of the right to a fair trial taken as a whole" (*Gómez Casafranca v. Peru* [HRC 2003] §7.3; see also *Alegre v. Peru* [HRC 2005] §7.5; *Quispe Roque v. Peru* [HRC 2005] §7.3; *Vargas Mas v. Peru* [HRC 2005] §6.4). Likewise, in *Gridin v. Russian Federation* (2000), the HRC emphasized the "fairness of the trial as a whole" in its determination of an Article 14 (1) violation (§8.4). Similar language can be found in numerous other recent HRC opinions (see for example *Akhadov v. Kyrgyzstan* [HRC 2011] §7.5; *Khostikoev v. Tajikistan* [HRC 2009] §7.3; *Tolipkhuzhaev v. Uzbekistan* [HRC 2009] §8.4). What is most impactful from these decisions is the insistence on evaluating the fairness of the proceeding "as a whole", as opposed to any specific aspect of the hearing. Thus, a violation of Article 14 can be found not only through the breach of one of the individual fair trial rights, but also where the overall fairness of the proceeding has been found wanting. This interpretation of Article 14 as containing a right to overall fairness mirrors the ECtHR's treatment of the analogous Article 6 ECHR (van Dijk and Viering 2006, p. 579; Trechsel 2005, pp. 86–88; Fawcett 1987, pp. 148–149). As such, the HRC's movement in this direction is neither without precedent nor wholly unexpected.

Its acknowledgment of a right to fairness is, however, somewhat problematic, specifically because it has been left rather vague. Although the HRC has issued several opinions in which the trial "as a whole" was found unfair due to an accumulation of "irregularities", it has failed to fully define the circumstances under which such "irregularities" fatally undermine the overall fairness of the proceeding. In the majority of the cases cited above, the HRC has simply declared a violation of Article 14 as a whole, with only a cursory listing of the author's allegations or the problematic "irregularities" provided (see for example *Quispe Roque v. Peru* [HRC 2005] §7.3).[8] The right to overall fairness, in these instances, can at times appear to function as a shortcut to a violation, saving the HRC from the messy task of actually considering the merits of the author's individual allegations. Regardless of the vagueness of the resulting right to fairness, what is certainly clear from these cases is that any determination as to whether an accused's hearing adhered to Article 14 standards must also evaluate the proceeding "as a whole". In other words, it is necessary to consider not only the impact of large, obvious issues on the fairness of a hearing under Article 14, but also the accumulated effect of numerous small, seemingly minor, problems as well.

3.11.2 The Relationship Between Interpreters and the Right to Overall Fairness

It is within the context of the right to overall fairness that the impact of the court interpreter is perhaps most deeply felt. As will be seen in the following Chapters, court interpretation is more likely to produce a lit-

[8] "With regard to the author's complaints in relation to article 14, the Committee takes note of his allegations that his trial was conducted by a court composed of faceless judges, that the interrogation of witnesses was not permitted and that his lawyer had only 30 minutes to examine the case file. In the circumstances, the Committee, recalling all of its previous jurisprudence in similar cases, concludes that article 14 of the Covenant as a whole was violated" (*Quispe Roque v. Peru* [HRC 2005] §7.3).

any of minor, seemingly unimportant, distortions than it is one severely impactful mistake. In isolation, these alterations may appear trivial and inconsequential, but over the course of an entire trial, their accumulated impact may be substantial. For example, an imperfect court interpreter may inhibit the communication between a foreign language defendant and his native counsel while simultaneously providing the defendant with a diluted and simplified translation of the court proceedings. Taken on their own, neither of these performance irregularities may rise to the level of a violation of an individual fair trial right (such as the right to counsel); yet considered together, the court interpreter's deficient translations may undermine the overall fairness of the proceedings "as a whole".

Likewise, the necessity of considering the fairness of the trial as a whole sets a rather daunting standard for the competency of court interpreters themselves. Since court interpreters are often involved in a variety of different aspects of the proceedings, any systematic weaknesses in their abilities will likely be multiplied throughout the trial. For instance, a court interpreter who habitually abbreviates her translations will do so throughout the proceeding, thereby systematically reducing the level of detail available to the foreign language participant or the court. Eliminating information by shortening a witness's reply may be unproblematic in any one particular incident, but will likely be severely impactful when replicated over the course of the proceedings. As such, any specific shortcoming in the court interpreter's abilities will be magnified when the hearings are analyzed "as a whole".

4 Conclusion

As has been shown in the foregoing analysis, the various elements of the right to a fair trial have aspects that either can be impacted by interpreter performance, or can themselves influence the performance of the interpreter. Although only the most pertinent facets of the right to a fair trial have been analyzed, even this small selection of relevant rights actually includes a substantial portion of the overall right to a fair trial. Guarantees such as the right to adequate time and facilities to prepare a defense, the right to adversarial proceedings and the right to examine witnesses are instrumental to the effectiveness of the fair trial protections. Furthermore, many of the rights detailed above place a heavy emphasis on the accused's understanding of, and effective participation in, the ongoing trial. Since the interpreter is a language incompetent defendant's only hope to comprehend or contribute to the proceedings, the fulfillment of these rights is entirely dependent upon the performance of the court interpreter. Thus, interpreter error can severely undermine not just the accused's right to an interpreter, but many of the other individual fair trial rights as well as the overall fairness of the proceedings themselves.

In addition, examining these rights in detail also has assisted in shedding some light on the legal requirements for interpreters. In order to effectively fulfill the overall right to a fair trial, it would appear that a comprehensive interpretation of the trial and the evidence is necessary. The principle of equality of arms dictates that the accused must be placed on an equal footing with the State, as well as other similarly situated defendants. Since both the State and linguistically competent defendants are able to understand and communicate freely with the court, the interpretation must, as far as is possible, place the accused in the same position. Furthermore, a comprehensive interpretation is likely also necessary to ensure a truly active participation on the part of the accused, as required by both the right to adversarial proceedings and the right to examine witnesses. Anything less arguably places the individual at too far a remove from the actual ongoings of the court to truly participate. The right to adequate facilities and the requirement that the accused be informed of the charge in enough detail to allow the preparation of his defense extend the necessity of a comprehensive interpretation into the pre-trial stages as well, since the effective participation of the accused in the preparation of his own defense will likely also demand a certain heightened level of understanding. Thus, it would appear that a comprehensive interpretation, which is the generally-accepted standard employed by court interpreters themselves if not by the ECtHR in *Kamasinski v. Austria* (1989), is also legally necessary to effectively fulfill the overall right to a fair trial.

Naturally, by embracing such a high standard, the legal expectations placed upon court interpreters likewise increases, as do the opportunities for interpreter error. The possible impact that an interpreter can actually have on these rights, as detailed above, was but a general overview, meant only to show the very tip of a much larger iceberg. Having set out in some detail the contours and requirements of each of these fair trial rights, and the associated expectations they place on interpreters, it is left now to consider in depth the actions of interpreters and how they can specifically impact these rights.

Bibliography

Boas, G. (2010). War Crimes Prosecution in Australia and Other Common Law Countries: Some Observations. *Criminal Law Forum, 21*(2), 313–330.

Boas, G., Bischoff, J. L., Reid, N. L., & Taylor, B. D., III. (2011). *International Criminal Procedure*. Cambridge: Cambridge University Press.

de Jongh, E. (2008). Linguistic Presence v. Linguistic Absence. *Florida Bar Journal, 82*, 20–32.

Doswald-Beck, L. (2012). Fair Trial, Right to, International Protection. In R. Wolfrum (Ed.), *The Max Planck Encyclopedia of Public International Law* (pp. 1104–1112). Oxford: Oxford University Press.

Fawcett, J. E. S. (1987). *The Application of the European Convention of Human Rights* (2nd ed.). Oxford: Clarendon Press.

Grabau, C. M. (1996). Court Interpreting: View from the Bench. *State Court Journal, 20*(1), 6–11.

Heller, D. J. (1994–95). The Language Bias in the Criminal Justice System. *Criminal Law Quarterly, 37*, 344–383.

Henrard, K. (2000). Language and the Administration of Justice: The International Framework. *International Journal on Minority and Group Rights, 7*, 75–108.

Jacot-Guillarmod, O. (2003). Rights Related to Good Administration of Justice (Article 6). In R. St, J. MacDonald, F. Matscher, & H. Petzold (Eds.), *The European System for the Protection of Human Rights* (pp. 381–404). Dordrecht: Nijhoff.

Marshall, P. D. (2011). A Comparative Analysis of the Right to Appeal. *Duke Journal of Comparative & International Law, 22*, 1–46.

McGoldrick, D. (1994). *The Human Rights Committee: Its Role in the Development of the International Covenant on Civil and Political Rights*. Oxford: Clarendon Press.

Nowak, M. (2005). *U.N. Covenant on Civil and Political Rights: CCPR Commentary* (2nd ed.). Kehl: Engel.

Orakhelashvili, A. (2006). *Peremptory Norms in International Law*. Oxford: Oxford University Press.

Reid, K. (2011). *A Practitioner's Guide to the European Convention on Human Rights* (4th ed.). London: Sweet & Maxwell.

Robinson, P. (2009). The Right to a Fair Trial in International Law, with Specific Reference to the Work of the ICTY. *Berkeley Journal of International Law Publicist, 3*, 1–11.

Schabas, W. A. (2007). *An Introduction to the International Criminal Court* (3rd ed.). Cambridge: Cambridge University Press.

Schomburg, W. (2009). The Role of International Criminal Tribunals in Promoting Respect for Fair Trial Rights. *Northwestern Journal of International Human Rights, 8*, 1–29.

Trechsel, S. (2005). *Human Rights in Criminal Proceedings*. Oxford: Oxford University Press.

Turner, J. I. (2005). Nationalizing International Criminal Law. *Stanford Journal of International Law, 41*, 1–51.

van Dijk, P., & Viering, M. (2006). Right to a Fair and Public Hearing (Article 6). In P. van Dijk, F. van Hoof, A. van Rijn, & L. Zwaak (Eds.), *Theory and Practice of the European Convention on Human Rights* (4th ed., pp. 511–650). Antwerpen: Intersentia.

Weissbrodt, D. (2001). *The Right to a Fair Trial Under the Universal Declaration of Human Rights and the International Covenant on Civil and Political Rights*. The Hague: Nijhoff.

Weissbrodt, D., & Wolfrum, R. (1997). Preface. In D. Weissbrodt & R. Wolfrum (Eds.), *The Right to a Fair Trial*. Berlin: Springer.

Other Documents

Convention for the Protection of Human Rights and Fundamental Freedoms. (1953). 213 UNTS 221, signed 4 November 1950, entered into force 3 September 1953.

Human Rights Committee. (1983, September 15). Concluding Observations of the Human Rights Committee: Australia. In: Human Rights Committee. *Report of the Human Rights Committee*, U.N. Doc. A/38/40.

Human Rights Committee. (1984, April 13) General Comment No. 13: Equality Before the Courts and the Right to a Fair and Public Hearing by an Independent Court Established by Law (Art. 14). U.N. Doc. A/39/40 at 143.

Human Rights Committee. (1997, May 5). Concluding Observations of the Human Rights Committee: Portugal. U.N. Doc. CCPR/C/79/Add.77.
Human Rights Committee. (1997, November 19). Concluding Observations of the Human Rights Committee: Sudan. U.N. Doc. CCPR/C/79/Add.85.
Human Rights Committee. (1998, April 8). Concluding Observations of the Human Rights Committee: Finland. U.N. Doc. CCPR/C/79/Add.91.
Human Rights Committee. (1998, November 19). Concluding Observations of the Human Rights Committee: Belgium. U.N. Doc. CCPR/C/79/Add.99.
Human Rights Committee. (2004, July 30). Concluding Observations of the Human Rights Committee: Namibia. U.N. Doc. CCPR/CO/81/NAM.
Human Rights Committee. (2007, August 23). General Comment No. 32: Right to Equality Before Courts and Tribunals and to Fair Trial (Art. 14). U.N. Doc. CCPR/C/GC/32.
International Covenant on Civil and Political Rights. (1976). 999 UNTS 171, adopted 16 December 1966, entered into force 23 March 1976.

List of Cases

Akbarkhudzh Tolipkhuzhaev v. Uzbekistan (HRC 2009). Communication No. 1280/2004 (22 July 2009) U.N. Doc. CCPR/C/96/D/1280/2004.
Antonino Vargas Mas v. Peru (HRC 2005). Communication No. 1058/2002 (26 October 2005) U.N. Doc. CCPR/C/85/D/1058/2002.
Antonio Viana Acosta v. Uruguay (HRC 1984). Communication No. 110/1981 (29 March 1984) U.N. Doc. A/39/40, p. 169.
Arieh Hollis Waldman v. Canada (HRC 1999). Communication No. 694/1996 (3 November 1999) U.N. Doc. CCPR/C/67/D/694/1996.
Aston Little v. Jamaica (HRC 1991). Communication No. 283/1988 (1 November 1991) U.N. Doc. CCPR/C/43/D/283/l988.
B.d.B. et al. v. The Netherlands (HRC 1989). Communication No. 273/1988 (30 March 1989) U.N. Doc. CCPR/C/35/D/273/1988.
Barry Stephen Harward v. Norway (HRC 1994). Communication No. 451/1991 (15 July 1994) U.N. Doc. CCPR/C/51/D/451/1991.
Bernard Lubuto v. Zambia (HRC 1995). Communication No. 390/1990 (31 October 1995) U.N. Doc. CCPR/C/55/D/390/1990/Rev.1.
Consuelo Salgar de Montejo v. Colombia (HRC 1985). Communication No. 64/1979 (24 March 1982) U.N. Doc. CCPR/C/OP/1 at 127.
Daniel Monguya Mbenge v. Zaire (HRC 1983). Communication No. 16/1977 (25 March 1983) U.N. Doc. CCPR/C/18/D/16/1977.

Denroy Gordon v. Jamaica (HRC 1992). Communication No. 237/1987 (5 November 1992) U.N. Doc. CCPR/C/46/D/237/1987.

Dieter Wolf v. Panama (HRC 1992). Communication No. 289/1988 (26 March 1992) U.N. Doc. CCPR/C/44/D/289/1988.

Dimitry L. Gridin v. Russian Federation (HRC 2000). Communication No. 770 (20 July 2000) U.N. Doc. CCPR/C/69/D/770/1997.

Dominique Guesdon v. France (HRC 1990). Communication No. 219/1986 (25 July 1990) U.N. Doc. CCPR/C/39/D/219/1986.

Dusan Vojnovic v. Croatia (HRC 2009). Communication No. 1510/2006 (30 March 2009) U.N. Doc. CCPR/C/95/D/1510/2006.

Earl Pratt and Ivan Morgan v. Jamaica (HRC 1989). Communication No. 210/1986 & 225/1987 (6 April 1989) U.N. Doc. Supp. No. 40 (A/44/40) at 222.

Elena Beatriz Vasilskis v. Uruguay (HRC 1983). Communication No. 80/1980 (31 March 1983) U.N. Doc. Supp. No. 40 (A/38/40) at 173.

Emelysifa Jessop v. New Zealand (HRC 2011). Communication No. 1758/2008 (29 March 2011) CCPR/C/101/D/1758/2008.

Fischer v. Austria (ECtHR 1995). Application No. 16922/90 (26 April 1995) Series A No. 312.

Francis Peter Perera v. Australia (HRC 1995). Communication No. 536/1993 (28 March 1995) U.N. Doc. CCPR/C/53/D/536/1993.

Francisco Juan Larrañaga v. The Philippines (HRC 2006). Communication No. 1421/2005 (24 July 2006) U.N. Doc. CCPR/C/87/D/1421/2005.

François Bozize v. Central African Republic (HRC 1994). Communication No. 428/1990 (7 April 1994) U.N. Doc. CCPR/C/50/D/428/1990.

Fredin v. Sweden (No.2) (ECtHR 1994). Application No. 18928/91 (23 February 1994) Series A No. 283-A.

Garfield Peart and Andrew Peart v. Jamaica (HRC 1995). Communications Nos. 464/1991 & 482/1991 (19 July 1995) U.N. Doc. CCPR/C/54/D/464/1991 & 482/1991.

H.C. v. Jamaica (HRC 1992). Communication No. 383/1989 (28 July 1992) U.N. Doc. CCPR/C/45/D/383/1989.

Jorge Luis Quispe Roque v. Peru (HRC 2005). Communication No. 1125/2002 (21 October 2005) U.N. Doc. CCPR/C/85/D/1125/2002.

José Luis García Fuenzalida v. Ecuador (HRC 1996). Communication No. 480/1991 (12 July 1996) U.N. Doc. CCPR/C/57/D/480/1991.

José Ramón Pindado Martínez v. Spain (HRC 2008). Communication No. 1490/2006 (30 October 2008) U.N. Doc. CCPR/C/94/D/1490/2006.

Kamasinski v. Austria (ECtHR 1989). Application No. 9783/82 (19 December 1989) Series A No. 168.
Kentucky v. Stincer (Supreme Court 1987). 482 U.S. 730 (United States).
Kestutis Gelazauskas v. Lithuania (HRC 1997). Communication No. 836/1998 (17 March 2003) U.N. Doc. CCPR/C/77/D/836/1998.
Kostovski v. The Netherlands (ECtHR 1989). Application No. 11454/85 (20 November 1989) Series A No. 166.
Larry James Pinkney v. Canada (HRC 1985). Communication No. 27/1978 (29 October 1981) U.N. Doc. CCPR/C/OP/1 at 95.
Laukkanen and Manninen v. Finland (ECtHR 2004). Application No. 50230/99 (3 February 2004).
Lenford Hamilton v. Jamaica (HRC 1994). Communication No. 333/1988 (23 March 1994) U.N. Doc. CCPR/C/50/D/333/1988.
Lloyd Grant v. Jamaica (HRC 1994). Communication No. 353/1988 (31 March 1994) U.N. Doc. CCPR/C/50/D/353/1988.
Lucy Dudko v. Australia (HRC 2007). Communication No. 1347/2005 (23 July 2007) U.N. Doc. CCPR/C/90/D/1347/2005.
Mansur v. Turkey (ECtHR 1995). Application No. 16026/90 (8 June 1995) Series A No. 319-B.
Manuel Francisco Becerra Barney v. Colombia (HRC 2006). Communication No. 1298/2004 (11 July 2006) U.N. Doc. CCPR/C/87/D/1298/2004.
Marlem Carranza Alegre v. Peru (HRC 2005). Communication No. 1126/2002 (28 October 2005) U.N. Doc. CCPR/C/85/D/1126/2002.
Miguel Ángel Rodríguez Orejuela v. Colombia (HRC 2002). Communication No. 848/1999 (23 July 2002) U.N. Doc. CCPR/C/75/D/848/1999.
Mukhammadruzi Iskandarov v. Tajikistan (HRC 2011). Communication No. 1499/2006 (30 March 2011) U.N. Doc. CCPR/C/101/D/1499/2006.
O.F. v. Norway (HRC 1984). Communication No. 158/1983 (26 October 1984) U.N. Doc. CCPR/C/23/D/158/1983.
Olimzhon Ashurov v. Tajikistan (HRC 2007). Communication No. 1348/2005 (20 March 2007) U.N. Doc. CCPR/C/89/D/1348/2005.
Otabek Akhadov v. Kyrgyzstan (HRC 2011). Communication No. 1503/2006 (25 March 2011) U.N. Doc. CCPR/C/101/D/1503/2006.
Pavel Levinov v. Belarus (HRC 2011). Communication No. 1812/2008 (26 July 2011) U.N. Doc. CCPR/C/102/D/1812/2008.
Peter Lumley v. Jamaica (HRC 1999). Communication No. 662/1995 (31 March 1999) U.N. Doc. CCPR/C/65/D/662/1995.

Pitkänen v. Finland (ECtHR 2004). Application No. 30508/96 (9 March 2004).

R.M. v. Finland (HRC 1989). Communication No. 301/1988 (23 March 1989) U.N. Doc. CCPR/C/35/D/301/1988.

Raphael Henry v. Jamaica (HRC 1991). Communication No. 230/l987 (1 November 1991) U.N. Doc. CCPR/C/43/D/230/l987.

Ricardo Ernesto Gómez Casafranca v. Peru (HRC 2003). Communication No. 981/2001 (22 July 2003) U.N. Doc. CCPR/C/78/D/981/2001.

S. v. Switzerland (ECtHR 1991). Application Nos. 12629/87 & 13965/88 (28 November 1991) Series A No. 220.

Sobolewski v. Poland (No. 2) (ECtHR 2009). Application No. 19847/07 (9 June 2009).

Valery Khostikoev v. Tajikistan (HRC 2009). Communication No. 1519/2006 (22 October 2009) U.N. Doc. CCPR/C/97/D/1519/2006.

Valichon Aliboev v. Tajikistan (HRC 2005). Communication No. 985/2001 (18 October 2005) U.N. Doc. CCPR/C/85/D/985/2001.

Van Mechelen and Others v. The Netherlands (ECtHR 1997). Applications Nos. 21363/93, 21364/93, 21427/93 & 22056/93 (23 April 1997) 25 EHRR 647.

Victor P. Domukovsky and others v. Georgia (HRC 1998). Communications Nos. 623/1995, 624/1995, 626/1995, 627/1995 (6 April 1998) U.N. Docs. CCPR/C/62/D/623/1995, CCPR/C/62/D/624/1995, CCPR/C/62/D/626/1995, CCPR/C/62/D/627/1995.

Wolfgang Lederbauer v. Austria (HRC 2007). Communication No. 1454/2006 (13 July 2007) U.N. Doc. CCPR/C/90/D/1454/2006.

Yves Morael v. France (HRC 1989). Communication No. 207/1986 (28 July 1989) U.N. Doc. CCPR/C/36/D/207/1986.

Zimmerman and Steiner v. Switzerland (ECtHR 1983). Application No. 8737/79 (13 July 1983) Series A No. 66.

5

Interpreter Error and Its Implications

1 Introduction

The act of interpreting requires a courtroom interpreter to make a nearly infinite number of ethical, technical, and linguistic decisions. It is, as one scholar has noted, an "extremely subtle and exacting art" (Heller 1994–1995, p. 379). The complexity and difficulty of the interpreter's task necessarily results in errors (McCaffrey 2000, p. 393), as well as an "inherent loss of meaning" between the source and target languages (Viljoen 1992, p. 69). Such distortions appear to be, in fact, a natural and inevitable part of the process. Once this is accepted, the question changes to whether or not interpreter accuracy is sufficient to ensure a fair trial.

Unfortunately, this appears to be a question that is rarely asked by judges or national legal systems themselves. The common practice is for a judge to assign an interpreter and then to assume (along with the participating attorneys) the competency of that interpreter (Davis and Hewitt 1994, p. 121; Heller 1994–1995, p. 367). By deferring to the trial court's discretion, and without a foreign language transcript from which to objectively review the interpreter's work, domestic appellate systems also effec-

J. H. Dingfelder Stone, *Court Interpreters and Fair Trials*,
https://doi.org/10.1007/978-3-319-75355-3_5

tively take interpreter competence for granted. In short, no one within the process considers the possible mistakes that are (or might have been) made, nor the frequency with which these mistakes regularly occur. This is highly problematic, since there are many different forms of interpreter error, and they occur within criminal proceedings at a significant rate.

This Chapter will outline the various types of mistakes and errors that interpreters can (and do) make during a criminal proceeding as well as analyze the possible implications of these individual errors on the right to a fair trial. In an attempt to make the multitude of different interpreter errors more comprehensible (and organized) for the legal community, this Chapter divides these errors into two separate sections: those mistakes related to the interpreters themselves and their conscious choices, and those mistakes predominately arising from the complexity and difficulty of languages and the interpreting process. It must be noted that this division is almost completely artificial, and many of the errors that will be discussed can and will bleed over into areas just as easily classified in some other manner. However, from an organizational standpoint, the different classifications prove more positive than negative.

2 Interpreter-Based Problems

2.1 Introduction

As previously mentioned, throughout the interpreting process the court interpreter faces a seemingly endless series of decisions, the determination of which both informs and influences the eventual target language output. These decisions can concern not only particularly thorny linguistic problems, but also ethical and procedural dilemmas. How a courtroom interpreter approaches these problems, and the eventual decisions she reaches, can have an impact not only on the quality of the interpretation itself, but also on the criminal proceeding as a whole. These conscious decisions are the main focus of this section.

2.2 Pragmatic Versus Verbatim Debate from the Legal Perspective

2.2.1 Introduction

Perhaps the most important decision that a courtroom interpreter must make concerns the level of accuracy and the interpreting standard to which she wishes to adhere. There are essentially two options from which the interpreter may choose: the word-for-word verbatim standard (focusing on the speaker's exact words) and the pragmatic standard (focusing on the meaning of the speaker's words) (see Chap. 3 for a more detailed discussion). It should be noted that both of these standards are effectively forms of a non-summarized, comprehensive interpretation. The relative advantages and disadvantages of each of these standards from the perspective of an "accurate" interpretation have already been discussed in Chap. 3. What remains to be analyzed in this context is the impact of the implementation of either standard on the right to a fair trial. In other words, the legal perspective must be taken into account.

2.2.2 Strengths and Weaknesses of Each Standard

The word-for-word verbatim standard meshes well with the role, as envisaged by the legal community and the court system, court interpreters are expected to play within the courtroom. They are seen as performing a mechanical process with a fixed, objective result, with little room for either judgment or decision-making (Stern 2011, p. 333; Mikkelson 2008, pp. 82–83; Morris 1995, p. 26). In this way, the process can be ignored, and the end product taken for granted (Morris 1995, p. 30). By relegating interpreters to a mechanical presence, they are not only denied the opportunity to exercise any judgment, but also effectively forbidden from taking an "active role in the communication process" (Morris 1995, p. 26). Given that judges rarely have any understanding of the interpreting process (Stern 2011, p. 341), and common law judges at least have historically demonstrated a very negative view towards the interpreting process and interpreters themselves (Morris 1995, pp. 25–26), the implementation of a standard that limits interpreter discretion is hardly surprising.

However, there is more to support the verbatim standard than the fear of interpreters and judicial misunderstandings of the interpreting process. The interpreter's output in the language of the court is the official record of the proceeding. As such, it is understandable that the legal actors expect and demand that the output be as close as possible to what was actually said by the foreign language participant. The meaning of what was said is, of course, helpful to the proceedings, but the meaning is nothing more than an individual's subjective understanding of the message that a string of words intends to convey (Morris 1995, p. 26). The actual, specific sequence of words employed by the foreign language speaker, however, is the backbone of that meaning, and that is the speech act that normally forms the record. This is true in monolingual trials as well: the actual words spoken by a person are part of the record, not a particular individual's subjective understanding of what they mean. For example, if the speaker states that he "shot himself in the foot", it is up to the listener to decipher whether this is a metaphorical statement (meaning the speaker made a mistake) or a literal statement (meaning he literally shot himself in the foot). "Interpreting" the intended meaning from a series of words is the job of the judicial fact-finder, not the courtroom interpreter. As such, the requirement that courtroom interpreters provide a word-for-word verbatim interpretation makes complete sense from a technical legal standpoint: to allow anything else would be to permit the interpreter to effectively usurp the role of the fact-finder.

On the other hand, blind adherence to a word-for-word verbatim standard invites error. Limiting the discretion of courtroom interpreters only works if such discretion is not necessary to the interpreting process. Yet, as previously noted, interpreting is not like mathematics: there is rarely a perfect linguistic match, rather only a series of different options each with its own merits and drawbacks (LaVigne and Vernon 2003, p. 868). The determination of which option is the closest match depends to a large extent on the meaning the speaker wished to convey by using that particular word in that specific context. For example, when legal counsel states that the case should be "continued", it is obvious from the identification of the speaker and the context of the remark that the case will be postponed until a later date. This translation, however, is in direct contravention with the normal understanding of the word "continue", which would imply to a listener that the case will proceed as normal. The interpreter in such circumstances cannot provide a word-for-word verbatim interpretation without consulting the meaning and truly "interpreting" what was said, because the word itself is misleading or untranslatable without reference to the speaker's intended meaning.

At least in the example above, the eventual interpretation of the word "continue" is still technically a word-for-word translation, even if it is informed by the context and the interpreter's judgment. However, the word-for-word standard is open to other, deeper criticisms. For instance, as noted in Chap. 3, to translate the German idiom "*ich verstehe nur Bahnhof*" literally produces "I only understand the train station". This would be a correct word-for-word translation, yet few would argue that it truly conveys what the German speaker actually said, which is more akin to the English idiom "it's as clear as mud to me". In such circumstances, the literal word-for-word translation as required by the verbatim standard would be hopelessly misleading to the ultimate fact-finder, and the resulting trial record would be illogical and unintelligible. In short, in certain situations, the word-for-word standard does more to obfuscate the record than to safeguard it.

That the word-for-word verbatim standard is capable of producing misunderstandings and impairing the development of an accurate record does not necessarily mean that the pragmatic standard wins by default. It too has significant disadvantages from the legal perspective. As previously noted, when the courtroom interpreter focuses on interpreting the meaning of statements to the detriment of the actual words spoken, she engages in a form of "interpretation" that is primarily reserved for the fact-finder. When an interpreter translates "he shot himself in the foot" as the equivalent of "he made a mistake", she has made a judgment as to the ultimate meaning of the speaker's words. The fact-finder in such a situation is denied not only the opportunity to make such a determination for themselves, but also denied the knowledge that such a determination was ever made for them by someone else. They are presented a factual *fait accompli*: someone is said to have "made a mistake" and this declaration is presented to the entire courtroom as a statement of fact, not one of judgment. In fact, no one aside from the interpreter is likely even aware that such a decision as to meaning was ever made, or even that the statement was open to interpretation in the first place. Moreover, this uncertainty is almost certainly not reflected in the record.

It might be argued that where the interpreter makes a mistake in the exercise of such judgment, that it will assuredly cause a disconnect in communication substantial enough that the judicial process will naturally clarify and correct it. The same, however, could be said for any misunderstandings arising from utilization of the word-for-word verbatim standard. The key point in this respect is that the pragmatic approach is utilized specifically to avoid such misunderstandings, and if it is subject to the same incidents of miscommunication as the verbatim standard, given that it also results in a record devoid of the actual words of the speaker, it is questionable whether it actually denotes an improvement over that earlier standard.

In addition, allowing courtroom interpreters to exercise such discretion, with little in the way of actual oversight, places a tremendous amount of faith in the abilities and judgment of interpreters. Given the high usage of untrained and inexperienced individuals as courtroom interpreters (Stern 2011, p. 339; see also Chap. 6 for a more in-depth discussion), this is perhaps a misplaced faith. Furthermore, even highly-qualified and experienced courtroom interpreters are likely not in a position to correctly decipher the intended meaning of a speaker's every statement. Lawyers, especially, use language as a tool, and the textual meaning of their statements or questions is sometimes not the most important aspect of their language (Mikkelson 2008, p. 82; Hale 2004, p. 31, 2007, p. 199). For instance, on the cross-examination of a witness, the examining attorney may pose a question in a particular manner for a variety of different reasons, such as to express disbelief with an earlier answer or even to confuse the witness (Hale 2004, p. 6). Court interpreters are often not well-placed to understand (or even notice) the true intent of such questions, leaving their eventual interpretation of meaning somewhat lacking.

2.2.3 Possible Alternatives

What is noticeable from this discussion is that neither the word-for-word verbatim standard nor the pragmatic standard is a perfect fit for judicial proceedings, especially where the interpreter's performance forms the permanent courtroom record. If the word-for-word verbatim standard is employed, then noticeable errors and misunderstandings will occur with the translation of metaphorical speech or cultural references. On the other hand, if the pragmatic standard is employed, an extra level of interpreter filtering and discretion will be placed between the foreign language participant's speech and the fact-finder. As such, both standards have obvious, and occasionally insurmountable, disadvantages from the legal perspective that can negatively affect the accused's right to a fair trial.

A possible solution to this problem would be to allow the interpreter discretion to employ different standards depending upon the situation. Where the interpreter's words form the permanent record, usage of the word-for-word verbatim standard as far as possible would help to preserve a detailed record, and save the "interpretation" of the evidence for the fact-finder. In other situations, where preservation of the record is not as high a priority or the interpreter's speech is only meant for the foreign language participant, preference for the pragmatic standard would allow for easier communication across the language barrier. However, even this muted solution creates numerous legal problems. First, it is not altogether clear that courtroom interpreters should be given even more discretion, given their general lack of qualifications. Second, encouraging or expecting interpreters to switch between two different standards during the interpreting process (or to utilize possible hybrid standards for which they are not trained) is to further complicate what is already a nearly impossible task. As previously argued, in its normal form, interpreting generally requires the maximum mental resources of even experienced interpreters; to add an extra variable to this process is to invite more errors, not less.

Third, communicative events are inter-related. The use of the pragmatic standard by an interpreter in an off-the-record capacity will still likely be an influence on any later on-the-record statements made in the proceeding. For example, if an attorney is questioning a foreign language witness, their question would be interpreted using the pragmatic standard in which the courtroom interpreter makes certain judgments as to the "meaning" of the question. The witness would then answer, and the interpreter would strictly interpret that answer for the record using the word-for-word verbatim standard in an effort to preserve the record as close to the witness's actual words as possible. However, the content of the witness's answer would have already been influenced by the interpreter's pragmatic "interpretation" of the attorney's question. In other words, the witness will answer the question that the interpreter believes the attorney asked, not necessarily what was actually asked. The word-for-word translation of that answer preserves it for the record, but a larger impact on the trial may have already occurred.

2.2.4 Conclusion

The end outcome of this discussion is that no perfect solution actually exists. Regardless of which standard the courtroom interpreter employs, the possibility for error and impact on the trial exists in arguably equal measure. The proceeding will be influenced in some manner by the mere usage of an interpreter, because either standard that the interpreter chooses to employ (pragmatic or word-for-word verbatim) creates legal issues: either the judgment of the fact-finder is occasionally usurped or the word-for-word translation sometimes renders incomprehensible gibberish. In short, it is not a question as to whether or not the interpreting standard chosen by courtroom interpreters will negatively influence a proceeding, but rather the extent to which such an influence will be felt. Naturally, this depends a great deal on the interpreter involved, and her ability to mitigate the weaknesses of her chosen standard. This presumes, of course, that the interpreter understands that these problems exist, which, given the high usage of unqualified and untrained interpreters in criminal proceedings, will not always be the case.

2.3 Stepping Outside the Neutral Role

2.3.1 Introduction

The role that the interpreter plays within the proceedings is also mostly a conscious decision on the part of the interpreter. While the legal system envisions an "impartial translation machine" (Mikkelson 1998, p. 8), and the generally accepted ethics applying to courtroom interpreters requires them to remain neutral both in fact and in appearance (Stern 2011, p. 335; Corsellis and Fernández 2001, p. 79; González et al. 1991, pp. 494–495), the reality of the situation is more complex. Courtroom interpreters frequently engage in activities during legal proceedings that, although often helpful to the efficient administration of the proceeding, go well beyond any understanding of "neutrality". Even more worrisome is that many foreign language professionals themselves believe that such actions are necessary in order to fulfill their legal role (Stern 2011, p. 333; Hale 2004, p. 8; Lindie 1993, p. 414). The purpose of this section is to explain and discuss these actions, as well as examine their impact on the right to a fair trial.

2.3.2 Adaptation

One of the major disadvantages of the pragmatic standard is that, on occasion, it requires the courtroom interpreter to convey the meaning of a phrase used, rather than the actual words, in an attempt to make the output language content more understandable for the listener. The concept of adaptation takes this practice a step farther; courtroom interpreters who use adaptation affirmatively "adapt" their interpretation to suit the language or educational level of their target audience (González et al. 1991, p. 18). In other words, courtroom interpreters will simplify or explain complicated language for a listener with a lower education level or elevate and correct grammatically incorrect language for a more educated audience (González et al. 1991, p. 18). Far from being the actions of a small minority of courtroom interpreters, such adaptations are "erroneously considered a necessary activity by a great number of interpreters"

(González et al. 1991, p. 18; see among others Matu et al. 2012, pp. 123, 125 [with respect to Kenya]; Stern 2011, p. 333 [generally]; Ibrahim 2007, p. 212 [with respect to Malaysia]; Kadric 2000, p. 157 [with respect to Austria]; Astiz 1986, p. 34 [speculating that a majority engage in this practice]). There are two main variations of adaptation for the purposes of this section: the simplification or explanation of difficult language; and the elevation or correction of simple or erroneous language.

Simplification and Explanation

There exists the common misconception amongst court interpreters that their primary role is to ensure communication within the courtroom (Hale 2001, p. 71). A necessary prerequisite for communication is the understanding by everyone involved of what was said. As such, instead of simply interpreting the words that have been spoken without consideration of the result, interpreters feel a responsibility that their target audience actually understands the content. This instinct can create significant problems in the context of a legal proceeding.

It goes without saying that legal language is more difficult than normal everyday language and is not always understandable for visiting or first-time courtroom participants. When faced with the task of interpreting dense legal language for a target audience from a different linguistic (and possibly legal) culture, the natural inclination of the courtroom interpreter is to simplify her language in an attempt to ensure that the foreign language participant actually understands what is occurring in the courtroom (Lindie 1993, p. 414; Astiz 1986, p. 34). This can be done by, for instance, substituting a "normal" word in place of a complicated legal word, or by rendering an intricate charging instrument into a simplified, narrative form (Moeketsi 1999b, p. 5).

In addition to simplifying difficult language, court interpreters also commonly explain key legal concepts to the foreign language participants (Hale 2004, p. 8; Moeketsi 1999b, p. 5; Lindie 1993, p. 414). The cross-cultural nature of interpreting situations presents many opportunities for such actions, since the legal culture of the foreign language participant may have no analogous linguistic term or concept that the interpreter can use for her translation, thus making an explanation all but necessary if the individual is meant to understand what is occurring (de Jongh 1991, p. 291; see also Moeketsi 1999b, pp. 5–6). Although the ethics of interpreting advocates simplification and explanation only as a measure of last resort, there is still an ongoing debate within the interpreting community as to their appropriateness (Mikkelson 2008, p. 8; Hale 2004, p. 8; González et al. 1991, p. 18).

There are also other reasons, aside from attempting to ensure communication, that courtroom interpreters may choose to simplify or explain complex legal terms and concepts. For example, given that many foreign language participants are in fact the defendants in criminal proceedings, there exists a strain of thought within the interpreting community that a duty exists to balance out the inherent disadvantages that such defendants encounter in a foreign language proceeding in order to achieve a form of social justice (Hale 2004, p. 8). Furthermore, as previously mentioned, there is a tendency for interpreters to sometimes identify with the foreign language participant (Berk-Seligson 1990, p. 109). Since the interpreter is the individual's only linguistic link to the proceeding, and thus the person's only means of understanding what is occurring, the interpreter can occasionally feel personally obligated to ensure that the individual truly comprehends. Moreover, the interpreter's adaptive actions do nothing more than meet the target audience's expectations, since most expect not only that the interpreter will help them understand the proceedings, but also that the interpreter will "provide assistance, advice and moral support" (Hale 2004, p. 11; see also Davis and Hewitt 1994, p. 140). Given these expectations, and the fact that most interpreters are aware that the foreign language participant is the most likely courtroom actor to challenge the accuracy of their translation, it is no surprise that at least one scholar has openly argued that courtroom interpreters sometimes use the adaptation role to ensure the satisfaction of the target audience in an attempt to forestall any such challenges (Astiz 1986, p. 35). Finally, it is not only the foreign language participant that expects a smooth communication process: many judges and attorneys actually assume the courtroom interpreter will take on a liaison role in order to facilitate communication across the language barrier (Ibrahim 2007, p. 212; Lindie 1993, pp. 413–414; González et al. 1991, p. 156). Fewer obvious breakdowns in communication help produce a more efficient proceeding, which all parties prefer; thus the interpreter has an incentive to streamline the process to appease everyone connected to the case.

Elevation and Style Correction

Just as court interpreters sometimes simplify their language in order to satisfy the needs of the target audience, they may also feel pressure to engage in the opposite action: consciously elevating their language to meet the requirements of a formal courtroom setting. The language employed in a courtroom is, by the very nature of the process, dense and complex. Interpreters speaking in such an environment may tailor their language in order to fit the surroundings, which can mean taking simple language from the foreign participant and making it sound more "at home" in the legal setting.

Such actions can be seen in several different forms. For example, where the foreign language speaker uses grammatically incorrect language, the natural tendency of the interpreter is to produce a grammatically correct version of the speaker's meaning (Jacobsen 2004, p. 248; Morris 1995, pp. 31–32). Similarly, expletives and other indecorous language are often removed from the version conveyed to the courtroom audience, since the interpreter may feel it is inappropriate to use such language in a formal setting (Mojuta and Arua 2016, p. 200; Namakula 2014, p. 135; Hovland 1992–1993, p. 476; Astiz 1986, p. 34). Interpreters also sometimes clean up and clarify any statements from the speaker that do not make obvious sense (González et al. 1991, pp. 479–480). It is important to note that these are generally actions that result from conscious decisions by the interpreter, not accidental or ingrained habits (such inadvertent edits will be dealt with later in this Chapter in the context of style alterations).

The reasons court interpreters make these changes are numerous. For one, just as the interpreter may develop an affinity for the foreign language participant and seek to help them understand the proceedings through explanation and simplification, this same feeling of kinship or sympathy may lead the interpreter to improve the speech to a level that reflects positively on the foreign language speaker. Furthermore, the interpreter's actions can be seen as a simple act of fulfilling expectations. The interpreter refrains from using obscenities in the courtroom because the target audience expects a certain level of decorum (González et al. 1991, p. 290). Likewise, since the judge and attorneys lay the burden of efficient communication at the feet of the interpreter, any incoherent translation or obvious misunderstanding is seen as evidence of the interpreter's incompetence rather than being taken as an accurate interpretation of an unintelligible statement or a genuine misunderstanding between the parties (Namakula 2014, p. 92; Jacobsen 2008, pp. 68–69; Heller 1994–1995, p. 373). In this manner, the expectations of the parties create a false incentive for the court interpreter to produce intelligent and logical translations rendered in appropriate language, since the perception of her competence (and her likelihood of future employment by the same officials) relies on creating a favorable impression (Hale 2007, p. 200). Finally, it is accepted practice in other areas of interpreting (especially conference interpreting) for the interpreter to produce an articulate version of what the interpreter believes the speaker meant to say, rather than accurately reproduce what was actually said (Morris 1995, p. 38; González et al. 1991, p. 27). Given that many interpreters are taught to improve speech (Hayes and Hale 2010, p. 121; Morris 1995, p. 38; González et al. 1991, p. 27), doing so helps an individual with whom they may feel some sympathy, and simultaneously fulfills the expectations of the courtroom participants, it is not surprising that such improvements and corrections take place.

Implications of Adaptation

As can be seen from the discussion above, adaptation helps to satisfy the previously formed expectations of nearly every party to a trial, ultimately leads to more coherent and efficient judicial proceedings, and ensures that the defendant or other foreign language participant actually understands the proceedings. If adaptation truly serves to advance these otherwise laudable objectives, then it might honestly be questioned why most judges and attorneys vehemently oppose, and court interpreting ethics forbid, the utilization of the adaptation role. The simple answer is that the simplification or improvement of speech by an interpreter during a trial fundamentally changes the nature of the entire proceeding, and in doing so, can significantly impact the fairness of that proceeding.

The adaptation role works to corrupt information throughout the process. When a court interpreter simplifies or explains a complex concept for a foreign language participant, she is necessarily changing the information that the individual receives. This can affect the individual's reaction to, or understanding of, that information. As such, when an interpreter simplifies a question to a witness, the witness will answer the simplified question, which is not necessarily what was asked by the attorney. For example, if the concept of a "charge" is too difficult for a particular foreign defendant to understand, the interpreter might seek to simplify the language, even though a direct equivalent exists in the defendant's native language and culture. But changing the question "Have you ever been charged with a crime?" to something less technical and more understandable (such as "Have you ever been brought before a court and accused of a crime?") risks losing the essence and importance of the question through simplification of a technical legal concept. A defendant who answers in the affirmative is not necessarily stating that he was ever officially "charged" with a crime, but only accused by a court.

Likewise, if an interpreter is both simplifying the translation for the foreign language participant and improving their statements to the court, then the information may be corrupted in both directions. In the example above, the defendant might answer evasively ("I can't exactly remember, but I don't think I was ever brought before a court for anything"), but the interpreter might improve the output to an extent that it reflects positively on the speaker ("I've never been brought before a court for anything"). Here, the attorney was asking about an official charge, and the eventual answer does not actually answer that question. Moreover, the certainty of the defendant's answer is strengthened, which may affect the fact-finder's impression of his honesty and integrity. Such little changes can result in a singular large discrepancy, or they can simply accumulate over time until the proceeding itself is appreciably different on either side of the language divide. An example would be the systematic elimination of rough language or obscenities from a foreign language participant's testimony, which might not in any one instance make an impact upon that witness's believability or credibility, but in the aggregate could result in a much more favorable reception of their testimony by the fact-finder (Hale 2007, p. 200; see also González et al. 1991, p. 477).

These alterations negatively impact a defendant's right to a fair trial. For example, if the interpretation involves a foreign language witness testifying against an accused, any act of speech improvement would implicate the defendant's right to truly examine and confront the witness (since the evidence produced by the witness would be filtered or altered by the interpreter). If the underlying reason behind the right to confront witnesses is to ensure the accuracy of the evidence produced by the witness through questioning (Trechsel 2005, p. 293), then surely any systematic act that undermines the accuracy of that evidence would be a violation. Furthermore, where the court interpreter's actions undercut the accuracy of evidence produced against an accused, this might infringe the overall fairness of the proceeding. Finally, if fulfillment of the right to an adversarial proceeding and the right to be present at one's trial require a full understanding of the ongoing proceedings so that the accused can effectively participate in the trial itself, then it is arguable that too much simplification can rob the accused of a detailed comprehension of the proceedings. However, it must be acknowledged that while the act of simplification may impair the accused's understanding of the trial's technical details, it may actually enhance his overall understanding of what has occurred. As such, a violation would appear to hinge mainly upon the particular circumstances in each case.

The practice of explanation also creates significant problems. Interpreters are not trained as lawyers, nor are they generally familiar with the underlying facts of the case (Stern 2011, p. 332; González et al. 1991, p. 156). Indeed, many court interpreters are unqualified and largely unfamiliar with legal matters (Stern 2011, pp. 333, 339; see also Chap. 6). As such, they are not well-placed to offer detailed explanations of legal terminology to foreign language participants. Their explanations may be incomplete, or even unequivocally wrong (Astiz 1986, p. 34). Naturally, the potential impact of such errors upon the defendant's right to a fair trial can be extensive. In the same way that simplification can lead a defendant to answer the wrong question, explanation can produce the same result. An example would be where the defendant is asked on cross-examination whether he "forged" someone's signature on a document. If the interpreter explains the concept of forgery to the defendant only as "signing someone else's name" (and thus overlooking the necessity that the signature be made with some intent to deceive), then a defendant might answer in the positive, effectively admitting his guilt to a technical legal term, even where his actions exhibited no intent to deceive. In such circumstances, it is obvious that the defendant's right to present a defense would be seriously jeopardized (Nowak 2005, pp. 337–341), and perhaps the principle of equality of arms, since the defendant would be handicapped by the interpreter in a manner not applicable to the prosecutor. However, even erroneous explanations of lesser importance could potentially undermine a variety of other fair trial provisions. For instance, a poor explanation of concepts to foreign language witnesses could negatively influence witness testimony, and thus impact the defendant's right to present or confront witnesses. Likewise, a faulty explanation of important elements of the charge might violate the accused's right to be informed of that charge.

In addition, even where the explanation is correct, it may be said to impact the proceedings. The provision of an explanation (or a simplification) assumes that the speaker intended that the foreign language participant actually understand what was said. Sometimes this is not the case; sometimes drama and confusion are the speaker's intended results, and an explanation that removes this confusion inadvertently neuters the speaker's intent and unnecessarily alters the proceedings (Hale 2004, p. 13). Furthermore, the act of correctly explaining a difficult legal concept to a foreign language defendant places that defendant in a privileged position of understanding that native language defendants do not enjoy (Mikkelson 2000, p. 2; Schweda-Nicholson 1989, p. 720; Astiz 1986, p. 34). This would have implications with respect to the principle of equality before the court. The same may also be said where interpreters simplify or improve language. Obviously, it is tricky to argue that a defendant's right to a fair trial has been violated where he was given a benefit or advantage through his interpreter. However, interpretation is only meant to place the defendant in the same position as a similarly situated defendant who speaks the language (Koo 2009, p. 216; Hale 2004, pp. 9–10); it is not meant to provide an advantage (Mikkelson 1998, p. 1). In practice, the provision of a systematic advantage to foreign language defendants might be seen, from the perspective of native language defendants, as a systematic disadvantage and unequal treatment.

Utilization of the adaptation role also compromises the neutrality of the interpreter. She no longer functions as an impartial liaison, but rather as an advocate or helper for the foreign language participant, thus becoming an active party to the proceeding (Hale 2004, p. 13). Such an imposition can upset the delicate balance that exists between the parties to an adversarial proceeding, introducing an extra (sometimes unnoticed) element into the equation (Hale 2004, p. 13). Since the defendant has the right to adversarial proceedings, which consists mainly of the right to be heard by the court and to challenge prosecutorial evidence (Trechsel 2005, p. 89), any variation that undermines the integrity of that process might negatively impact (even if indirectly) his right to those proceedings.

2.3.3 Other Breaches of Interpreter Role

Editing Content

In addition to "adapting" a speaker's statement, court interpreters also occasionally edit and "correct" their content (*Interpreters in the Courtroom* 2008 [Hale Statement]; Morris 1995, pp. 34–35). This can occur in a variety of different situations. For instance, when confronted with a word that they do not understand or cannot interpret, trained interpreters will revert to their learned coping strategies, nearly all of which involve editing the content of the original statement. However, less purposeful edits also occur. An example would be where the witness simply misstates a matter of fact, such as describing a rectangle as a triangle, and the interpreter corrects it in their rendition for the court (Morris 1995, p. 34). While perhaps helpful and made with the best of intentions, such a correction is nevertheless an alteration of the speaker's statement and violates the court interpreter's oath to interpret what was actually said (Morris 1995, pp. 34–35). Furthermore, since the interpreter is often the only bilingual individual in the courtroom, the fact that the witness originally misspoke will likely go unnoticed, even though such information may be of relevance to the credibility of the participant. Additionally, there is the possibility that the interpreter's correction may, in fact, be wrong. In the end, though, the truthfulness of the correction is irrelevant, since the interpreter is not meant to be a supplier of facts (correct or otherwise), but rather a neutral intermediary between the two linguistic parties.

Because interpreters step into the shoes of the speaker by using the first person ("I" as in the speaker, not the interpreter) when they interpret, they sometimes also feel the need to distance themselves from the speaker's words and thoughts (Morris 1995, p. 35). Thus, they may omit, for example, obscenities or racist statements (González et al. 1991, p. 290). For similar reasons, interpreters occasionally even use the third person ("he says…") to refer to the speaker instead (Hale 2004, p. 193). This too, in a slightly different manner, is an alteration of the speaker's content, because it inevitably involves the interpreter no longer repeating exactly what was said, but rather providing a description or paraphrase (Hale 2004, p. 192). Untrained interpreters are especially guilty of such practices (Hale 2004, p. 193).

Assisting the Court

Interpreters also occasionally feel obliged to break from their mandated role in order to assist the court (Stern 2011, p. 333). For instance, it is not unheard of for judges to require the interpreter to perform clerical tasks, such as photocopying (González et al. 1991, p. 502). This can make it appear to the foreign language participant that the interpreter effectively works for the court, and is therefore not necessarily neutral or on his side. Likewise, judges have been known to order the interpreter to explain something to the defendant, or to ask the interpreter to influence the defendant in certain decisions (Davis and Hewitt 1994, pp. 140–141). Such actions require the interpreter to engage in adaptive behavior that, as previously shown, can have a negative impact upon the fairness of the proceedings.

Furthermore, where miscommunication occurs in the courtroom due to cultural differences, interpreters sometimes feel it necessary to step in and explain the source of the misunderstanding (Mikkelson 1998, p. 1). Hispanics, for instance, may look at the floor when asked a question, which is meant as a sign of respect for the judge (de Jongh 1992, pp. 62–63). In an American courtroom, however, such an action could be understood by the fact-finder as an indication of guilt (Messier 1999, p. 1401; de Jongh 1992, pp. 62–63). Likewise, Aboriginals consider it impolite to make eye contact with the person speaking to them, a behavior which reflects poorly upon them in Australian courtrooms (Non-English Speaking Clients 2005–2006, p. 239). Court interpreters who are aware of both sides of these cultural situations may feel the need to explain the meaning of the speaker's actions. This is acceptable in inquisitorial legal systems, but not in common law systems (Nartowska 2015, p. 11), largely because it removes the interpreter from her traditional role of information transmitter and places her in the role of information supplier.

Implications of Other Violations

While adaptive behavior such as simplification and improvement deal with the alteration of how the speaker's message is conveyed, when a court interpreter edits the speaker's message itself, this is an action which strikes directly at the validity of the evidence. The interpreter's decision to change information that will be supplied to the fact-finder (even where the change is correct) effectively tampers with the evidence produced at the proceeding. The interpreter is substituting her understanding of the evidence in place of the speaker. Even where the change occurs into the foreign language, and thus is not part of the record, it is an alteration which will have an impact on the foreign language participant's response to that information. In either scenario, the interpreter is usurping the role of the fact-finder, by determining what the "correct" evidence shall be. The accused's right to present a defense and call witnesses on his behalf during an adversarial proceeding necessarily implies that the accused has a corollary right to have this information heard by the judge (Trechsel 2005, p. 89). Where the interpreter is correcting or editing the content of this testimony or evidence, this would not appear to be in keeping with the spirit of those rights.

It is self-evident that not correcting faulty information will inevitably lead to a misunderstanding or disrupt the proceeding. This, in turn, may reduce the efficiency of the trial and perhaps even negatively impact the credibility of whoever made the initial error. Such a result is normal in a monolingual proceeding. The interpreter's role is to interpret what has actually been said throughout the proceeding, in effect, to remove the language barrier between the two parties and produce just such a monolingual proceeding (Hale 2004, p. 12). This should, in turn, place the defendant in the exact same position as a similarly situated native language defendant. If anyone in the courtroom makes an erroneous statement, the error should be cleared up through the normal courtroom process, just as it would be in a proceeding that does not contain an interpreter (Hale 2004, p. 12). In this manner, the defendant receives equal (but not advantaged) access to the court.

The practice of stepping into different roles in the courtroom can also negatively affect an accused's right to a fair trial. An interpreter who explains a cultural difference to the court is assuming the role of a cultural expert witness (González et al. 1991, pp. 240–241). While this is generally allowed in inquisitorial legal systems (Nartowska 2015, p. 11), it is less acceptable in common law systems because interpreters are considered language experts with some cultural knowledge, not qualified cultural experts (González et al. 1991, pp. 502–503). From this viewpoint, the interpreter's statements in these areas are not necessarily reliable and can further undermine the accuracy of the evidence. In addition, as an interjection, her information would not automatically be subject to cross-examination or confrontation on the part of the accused, which would set up a possible violation of the right to examine witnesses as well. Furthermore, as her information will likely favor one party to the proceeding, the interpreter, by voluntarily offering that information, will undercut her own appearance of neutrality. This is also true of situations where the interpreter deviates from her prescribed role in order to assist the court itself in administrative or other matters. Weakening the interpreter's appearance of impartiality can reduce the level of trust that the foreign language participant has for the interpreter, making their active participation less likely. If the defendant is the foreign language individual, then anything that undermines his active participation in the proceedings has fair trial implications. Moreover, if the interpreter appears biased in any way, the fact-finder is more likely to believe that this bias will taint a witness's interpreted testimony, which will give that testimony less credibility (González et al. 1991, p. 495). Likewise, under Article 14 (1) ICCPR, the defendant is entitled to an impartial tribunal, and the appearance of interpreter bias would likely undercut confidence in the impartiality of the court's decision itself, not to mention the overall fairness of the proceedings.

2.3.4 Conclusion

Court interpreters are required to maintain neutrality both in appearance and in fact, an outcome that is generally accomplished by strictly adhering to their assigned role within the courtroom. However, their actions occasionally go beyond this role and thereby jeopardize the fairness of the proceedings. The practice of adapting their interpretation to fit the expectations or limitations of the target audience through simplification or elevation leads to an alteration of both the content and style of a speaker's message. These adaptations either directly or indirectly change the evidence adduced at trial. Similarly, court interpreters at times edit or "correct" information they assume to be either incorrect or inappropriate for the court. They also sometimes voluntarily provide information to the court in an attempt to clarify what they deem to be a misunderstood situation. Each of these activities, although they may increase the efficiency of the proceedings and may even be wanted or expected by the court participants themselves, substantially undermines the accuracy of the eventual interpretation: interpreters are no longer conveying exactly what the speaker said, they are instead providing their own version of the speech. By stepping outside their assigned role and attempting to help, court interpreters actually weaken the fair trial protections granted to the accused.

2.4 Issues of Control

2.4.1 Overview of the Issue

Occasionally, court interpreters must exert some control over the other participants in the courtroom (Stern 2011, p. 331; González et al. 1991, p. 395). In doing so, they step out of their idealized role as a mere conduit of information, and necessarily change the dynamics of the adversarial process. Such interferences in the process can occur in a variety of different situations.

As with court reporters, interpreters can only effectively handle the speech of one person at a time. Thus, when two individuals are speaking simultaneously, the interpreter must interrupt the proceeding (if the judge does not) in order to remind the participants of her limitations (Davis and Hewitt 1994, pp. 134–135). While such an interruption is normally the duty of the judge, the exercise of this power by the interpreter is fairly uncontroversial. The interpreter must protect her ability to interpret.

The main area, however, where interpreters exert control within the courtroom involves witness testimony. This can take the form of prompting the witness to answer a question more quickly (Viljoen 1992, pp. 68–69; Berk-Seligson 1990, p. 86), telling the witness to answer more briefly or to slow down (Hovland 1992–1993, p. 476), or asking the witness to repeat their testimony (González et al. 1991, p. 395; Berk-Seligson 1990, p. 89). Likewise, court interpreters commonly interrupt witnesses, as well as attorneys, when their answers or questions are too lengthy (Mason 2008, p. 41; Berk-Seligson 1990, p. 191). This is necessary, because court interpreters only rarely take notes while consecutively interpreting witness testimony (Mikkelson 2000, p. 72). As such, when the witness or attorney speaks for too long a period, the court interpreter must interrupt the speech; otherwise the limits of her short-term memory will not allow her to competently translate the entirety of what has been said. Even though such interruptions may appear necessary, their usage is controversial and not allowed under the current ethical standards for court interpreters (González et al. 1991, pp. 395–396). This ban can be blamed partly on the fact that unqualified interpreters have historically abused this practice to compensate for their lack of skill and training (González et al. 1991, p. 396).

2.4.2 Implications of Issues of Control

Where the court interpreter exerts control over a witness or attorney, her action necessarily changes the dynamics of the linguistic exchange and the proceeding in general (Berk-Seligson 1990, pp. 96, 196–197). By stepping outside of her prescribed role, the interpreter becomes an active part of the proceeding, as opposed to a passive facilitator. Her active role can have unintended consequences. For instance, the practice of asking a witness to repeat their answer inevitably alters that answer (González et al. 1991, p. 395). The witness will likely take more time with their second answer in order to make it more clearly understandable, specifically because the interpreter apparently did not understand it in the first instance. The witness may also change the answer because they fear that they have said something wrong or damaging the first time (González et al. 1991, p. 395). Finally, although the first answer is the original statement that should be included in the record, the interpreter will focus on the edited and altered second answer instead (González et al. 1991, p. 395). In this manner, such a simple action as requesting that the witness repeat their answer can corrupt the original testimony of the witness, which has obvious implications for the presentation of evidence and the right to examine witnesses.

Likewise, the common practice of prompting a witness to answer a question when they have otherwise shown hesitance to do so or have given an unintelligible answer also has fair trial implications. This is considered the most intrusive of the actions an interpreter can take with respect to a witness, and is therefore considered ethically inappropriate (Berk-Seligson 1990, pp. 88–89). In effect, unilaterally telling the witness to "please answer" is a form of managing the witness (Berk-Seligson 1990, p. 87). Such management can have an impact on the evaluation of the witness by the fact-finder in the proceeding. A study performed by Berk-Seligson (1990) involving mock juries has shown that, where an interpreter prompts the witness to answer correctly instead of attempting to interpret an otherwise unintelligible answer, the witness was held in higher regard by the jury (pp. 192–193). The same was also found to be true where the court interpreter felt it necessary to interrupt a witness who was speaking for too long a period. Specifically, a witness who is interrupted by the court interpreter is considered by mock jurors to be more "convincing, competent, and trustworthy" than the same witness who is allowed to continue speaking (Berk-Seligson 1990, p. 190).

With respect to interrupting attorneys, the court interpreter's actions produce the opposite effect. Berk-Seligson (1990) found that an interrupted attorney was rated by the mock jurors significantly lower with respect to his competence than a non-interrupted attorney (pp. 187–188). The interruptions by the interpreter are taken by the fact-finder as a veiled criticism of the attorney and both their sensitivity to the needs of, and their ability to work with, the interpreter (Berk-Seligson 1990, pp. 191, 195). Naturally, these changes in perception of the courtroom participants can have a consequence on the reception of the evidence by the fact-finder. An attorney that is not seen as credible will have a more difficult time convincing the fact-finder of the strength of his presented evidence. Such a result with respect to defense counsel, merely as a consequence of the interpreter's actions, would appear to undermine the accused's right to adequate counsel and the right to present a defense. In effect, the potential deficiencies of the interpreter (such as the inability of the interpreter's short-term memory to handle longer stretches of speech or the interpreter's need to have an attorney repeat technical legal terms that are unfamiliar to the interpreter) result in actions that harm the parties through their attorneys, and therefore weaken the accused's fair trial protections.

Similarly, an accused can be negatively impacted by the fact-finder's increased regard for an interrupted witness or a witness that is allowed to reformulate an answer because the interpreter failed to understand the original. In both instances, the credibility and believability of the witness may be enhanced in the eyes of the fact-finder. If the witness is testifying in favor of the accused, then this places the defendant in a more favorable position than a similarly-situated native defendant, thus raising issues of equality. On the other hand, if the witness is relating evidence against the defendant, then the potentially incriminating evidence has been corrupted or strengthened by the deficiencies of the interpreter. This has ramifications on the overall fairness of the proceedings, as well as on the ability of the accused to effectively confront the witness. It might be argued that any impact on the process is simply an inevitable risk associated with any witness or attorney, but this is not necessarily true since these same risks do not exist within the context of a monolingual proceeding. In short, these alterations in the perception of courtroom participants only apply when court interpreters are involved.

In addition to the impact such interpreter actions can have on the fact-finder, they can have an equal effect on the interpreters themselves. Interrupting a witness or attorney inevitably leads to an increased rate of interpreter error (Mason 2008, p. 45). In essence, when a courtroom participant speaks for a lengthy period, they place the court interpreter in a no-win situation. If the interpreter interrupts the speaker, the interruption itself will change the normal testimonial process: it affects the rhythm of the testimony by breaking it up into segments, and also gives the witness time to rethink the content and style of what they wish to say in the next segment (González et al. 1991, p. 396). On the other hand, if the interpreter does not interrupt the speaker, then her short-term memory will quickly become overloaded by excess information, leading to an increase in errors as her cognitive capacity struggles to adapt (Mason 2008, p. 46; see generally Gile 2009). The end result is that a so-called "sweet spot" exists where the interruption has a minimal effect on the process (Mason 2008, pp. 42–45; González et al. 1991, p. 397). However, even the task of trying to apprise when this moment arrives draws valuable cognitive capacity away from the interpreting process itself, making the achievement of a minimally-impactful interruption somewhat akin to hitting a moving target (Mason 2008, p. 45). As such, even though interruptions are common, interpreters rarely achieve this goal, normally waiting too long into the process (Mason 2008, p. 45).

The consequences of interpreter interruptions on the interpreters themselves are not merely hypothetical enemies based upon Gile's theory of cognitive overload. Rather, they are a real and measurable phenomenon, primarily resulting in an increased level of omissions on the part of the interpreter. Mason has studied this area extensively and found that "for every 100 interruptions, interpreters will make 86 omissions" (Mason 2008, p. 46). These omissions, some large and some small, are simply the price that interpreters must pay in order to effectively handle the increased length of speech, and yet their presence (if such a thing can be said of an omission) necessarily affects the evidence that is produced in the courtroom. In summary, interpreter interruptions (again due at least partially to deficiencies in the courtroom interpreters themselves) inevitably result in the loss of testimonial evidence from witnesses or the abbreviation of courtroom statements being interpreted for the foreign language participant. From the perspective of the right to a fair trial, neither of these outcomes is acceptable. The loss of evidence threatens the ability of the defendant to present a defense or confront witnesses, and the truncation of information to a foreign language defendant undermines his ability to effectively participate in the proceedings through a compromised understanding of the courtroom activities. An obvious and possible solution to this problem would be for the participants to proactively use shorter statements. However, any attempt by the judge to enforce this rule would still likely result in interruptions from the bench that would carry the same risk of alteration of fact-finder perception as interpreter interruptions, if not more risk (since the judge is a more authoritative figure than the interpreter). Likewise, while this tactic might decrease interpreter error, it would necessarily change the dynamics of any trial involving interpreters, which again raises issues of equality before the court.

2.5 Coping Strategies

Aside from interruptions, which are a deliberate strategy taken to alleviate the burden placed on the interpreter's short-term memory, there are other conscious actions utilized by court interpreters specifically to limit, or relieve, potential cognitive overload. Just as with interruptions, these purposefully employed strategies can have a substantial effect on the accuracy of the interpreter's work, and likewise weaken the accused's fair trial protections. These "coping strategies" break down into two categories: those employed exclusively in simultaneous interpretation and those utilized in both simultaneous and consecutive. Many of these strategies, as well as their inherent disadvantages, have previously been discussed in more detail in the context of Chap. 3's examination of court interpreting theory. As such, it suffices in this section to focus mainly on the impact these strategies can have on the right to a fair trial.

2.5.1 Strategies for Simultaneous Interpretation

As previously discussed, simultaneous interpretation involves a variety of concurrent tasks (listening, processing, and speaking) all of which must be completed within a limited timeframe. While the interpreter successfully produces the translation of one speech segment, the next segment is already arriving. Thus, the interpreter must be able to keep up with the pace of the speaker, for if she cannot, she will fall behind and be unable to continue interpreting.

There are two coping strategies used mainly to enhance simultaneous interpretation. The first is known as "form-based interpreting" (or "literal interpretation"), wherein the interpreter stops attempting to perform a complete translation of the speaker's meaning or grammar, instead opting to merely interpret the words spoken (Gile 2009, pp. 208–209; González et al. 1991, p. 311). Eliminating any effort at analysis of the speech allows the interpreter to speed up her own output to match the pace of the speaker. The end result is a word-for-word translation that generally follows the grammatical structure of the speaker's language; as can be imagined, this has the potential to result in "marked losses" of meaning from the original statement (Gile 2009, pp. 208–209). A second strategy employed by simultaneous interpreters is known as segmentation. This involves the interpreter effectively dismantling any complex sentences used by the speaker into several smaller and easier sentences (Gile 2009, p. 205). Segmentation allows the interpreter to begin conveying the meaning of the complex sentence before the speaker has even finished, thus relieving her short-term memory and preventing cognitive overload. The downside to segmentation is that the complexity and depth of the original sentence is literally lost in translation, taking a complicated sentence and turning it into several independent, uncomplicated thoughts.

2.5.2 Strategies for Both Forms of Interpretation

While simultaneous interpretation is performed under a constant time pressure, consecutive places an unremitting demand on the interpreter's memory. In the context of a court proceeding, the consecutive interpreter must simply remember everything until it is her turn to produce her translation. The coping strategies employed in this context revolve mainly around managing the efficiency of the translation and limiting the strain placed upon her short-term memory. As such, the majority of these strategies are equally useful to both consecutive and simultaneous interpreters.

One coping strategy that has already been discussed in depth is the tactic of interrupting a long-winded speaker. Likewise, obvious tactics such as asking someone to repeat an answer or to speak more slowly have also been examined above. Among those that have yet to be analyzed, note-taking is perhaps the most normal. However, as previously mentioned, court interpreters rarely take notes; thus it has little practical impact on trial proceedings (Mikkelson 2000, p. 72). One coping strategy employed frequently by both simultaneous and consecutive interpreters is anticipation, which involves the interpreter making an educated guess as to what the speaker will say next, based upon what has come before (González et al. 1991, pp. 364–365). This can take the form of anticipating the usage of a particular word, grammatical structure, or specific content (González et al. 1991, pp. 364–365). Doing so allows the interpreter to move forward with her analysis without having to actually wait for the specific term to be used, thus freeing up additional mental resources. Another strategy employed for this purpose entails the reordering of speech segments or elements (translating the most recent information first), since this is thought to relieve pressure on the interpreter's short-term memory (Gile 2009, pp. 205–206).

The act of omitting information or words is also a coping strategy employed by both simultaneous and consecutive interpreters, though its use is not without controversy (Gile 2009, p. 210). In situations where interpreters are overloaded with information and can only remember a limited amount, they are taught to discard the least important pieces of information in order to preserve those of more consequence (Gile 2009, p. 210). Interpreters are also trained that it is appropriate to omit information "if something grossly inappropriate was said and the interpreter feels strongly that if reproduced, it will cause major harm to the speaker's interests" (Gile 2009, p. 210). It is generally agreed upon, however, that such a strategy is improper in a courtroom setting (Stern 2011, p. 334; González et al. 1991, p. 313). In contrast to information overload, interpreters must also deal with situations where they have either missed or not understood a word or important piece of information. Here, as well, omission is sometimes seen (Gile 2009, p. 210). Another option is for the interpreter to reconstruct the lost information from the surrounding context; in effect reporting, based upon her knowledge of the subject matter and the speaker, what she believes the speaker said as opposed to what was actually said (Gile 2009, p. 201). Or, the interpreter can simply "invent a speech segment which is compatible with the rest of the speaker's statement;" a process that is known as parallel reformulation and is reserved only for the most extreme situations (Gile 2009, p. 211). Where the interpreter heard, but did not understand the word used, a slightly less adventurous option is to "echo" the sound heard (Gile 2009, p. 207). For example, in a legal setting, if the interpreter heard "*res judicata*" but did not understand the term, she could simply use the term in her translation in the hopes that the other party would know it.

Numerous coping strategies exist to handle the occasional inability of an interpreter to remember or find the exact term for a source language concept. When this occurs, interpreters have several options. As discussed earlier in a different context, the interpreter may explain (or even paraphrase) the term instead (Gile 2009, p. 207). She may also substitute a general term in place of the specific term (for instance, using "tree" instead of "oak tree") (Gile 2009, p. 206). Another possibility is for the interpreter to adopt the source word as part of the target language; this is known as naturalization (Gile 2009, p. 207). Thus, the English word "driver" referring to a particular type of software, might be translated into French as "*driver*" (pronounced as a French word: "dreevair") (Gile 2009, p. 207). A related strategy, known as transcoding, involves literally translating the phrase into the target language word-for-word (Gile 2009, p. 208). Thus, an interpreter might translate the "maturity date" of a financial instrument into French as "*date de maturité*", which, while not technically correct, would still be close enough to convey the concept (Gile 2009, p. 208).

2.5.3 Implications of Coping Strategies

The implications of each of these coping strategies differ based upon their usage in the courtroom. The employment of coping strategies in connection with simultaneous interpretation is less problematic, since this form of interpretation is mostly used to convey information about the proceedings into the foreign language, which is not part of the official evidence in the case (Davis and Hewitt 1994, p. 131; de Jongh 1992, p. 45). As such the practices of segmentation and literal translation likely have only a moderate impact on the accused's right to a fair trial, unless the loss of details inherent to the practice of both strategies becomes so pronounced as to limit the accused's ability to actively participate in the proceedings.

The more troublesome aspects of the coping strategies arise in connection with consecutive interpretation, since this is typically used during the interpretation of witness testimony (Davis and Hewitt 1994, pp. 130–131; González et al. 1991, p. 163). Each of these strategies acts distorts the accuracy of any evidence that is produced. In some instances, the distortion may be negligible (such as replacing "oak tree" with "tree"), in others it may be disastrous (such as any usage of parallel reformulation). Naturally, this depends largely upon the context and the information that is corrupted by the interpreter's strategy. Whether the interpreter uses "tree" or "oak tree" for the record may be completely irrelevant to the proceeding, or it may be the key to the prosecution's entire case. At the end of the day, interpreters are rarely in a position to know the value of specific pieces of information to a case, since they do not often have an overview of the entire situation (Stern 2011, p. 332; González et al. 1991, p. 156). As such, the use of these strategies, so far as they are not absolutely necessary, is problematic, because they invariably corrupt the testimonial evidence. This can easily work to undermine the accused's right to examine witnesses and to present a defense, since there can be no assurance that the translation put forward by the interpreter is actually the exact evidence produced by the witness. Even more inappropriate is the usage during a criminal proceeding of aggressive coping strategies such as parallel reformulation, reconstruction from context, or omission, since these result either in the actual fabrication or in the wholesale loss of evidence. Yet, these are tactics that are taught to, and therefore presumably employed by, interpreters (Gile 2009, pp. 201, 210–211).

However, it is important to remember that these strategies exist for the express purpose of salvaging an otherwise impossible situation. Where an interpreter did not understand or even hear a part of the speech, she has nothing to interpret. In other words, she starts from a position of absolute failure, and any tactic or strategy that brings the interpretation closer to what was actually stated must be considered an improvement over the complete loss of that information. Thus, it must be accepted that, under certain circumstances, coping strategies are an appropriate reaction to a difficult interpreting situation. On the other hand, it must also be acknowledged that these strategies only exist to overcome such situations. Moreover, it must further be recognized that the less qualified and less experienced an interpreter is, the more likely she is to encounter an interpreting difficulty that requires the employment of a coping strategy. In other words, these strategies exist, in part, in order to compensate for the specific deficiencies in an interpreter's knowledge and preparation. For example, if an interpreter did not adequately prepare for the testimony of an expert medical witness, then she will need to use a variety of coping tactics (explanation, transcoding, etc…) to overcome her lack of appropriate vocabulary. And, if properly employed, noone other than the interpreter will ever know the incident occurred, or that the depth and detail of the original evidence has ever been compromised. Thus, the interpreter is consciously altering testimonial evidence specifically in order to overcome or hide her inability to competently handle the interpreting assignment. From a legal standpoint, where the preservation and accuracy of evidence is a paramount interest, such actions must be of grave concern.

2.6 Conclusion

Throughout the criminal proceeding, a court interpreter makes numerous conscious decisions that can substantially impact the fairness of the end proceeding. Whether the interpreter chooses to use the verbatim word-for-word standard (as expected in many jurisdictions) or the pragmatic standard (as preferred by interpreters themselves), the proceeding itself will be negatively impacted in some manner. Likewise, court interpreters who fail to understand the importance of their role within the process will also undermine the fairness of the proceeding. Those who explain, simplify, improve or edit testimonial statements effectively corrupt the evidence; and those who overzealously interrupt speakers in the courtroom run the risk of doing so as well. Finally, the frequent use of coping strategies to overcome difficult interpreting situations, while occasionally necessary, sacrifices the accuracy of the proceeding in favor of more efficient communication. Each of these conscious decisions is taken by court interpreters with the sole purpose of improving the courtroom proceeding. And yet, the good intentions of the interpreter cannot overcome the practical negative consequences that stem from these practices: the accuracy of evidence is necessarily degraded; witness testimony is influenced and compromised; and the accused's ability to follow the proceedings is undermined through both the loss of detail and the inaccuracy of the eventual interpretation. These results, taken together, represent a real threat to the fairness of an accused's trial.

3 Language-Based Problems

3.1 Introduction

As problematic as interpreter-based issues may be, they stem from the conscious decisions that interpreters make throughout the process. Thus, they are arguably correctable through training and experience. Perhaps the more significant problems are those that are unintentional or simply inherent in the process itself. These difficulties have much to do with the nature of language and the intrinsic difficulty of interpreting between languages and cultures. Such problems will be the focus of this section, and for the ease of discussion will be broken down into two separate subdivisions: those related to content and those related to style.

3.2 Content Problems

3.2.1 Introduction

In a criminal proceeding, the content of the evidence is determinative above all else, since it is upon the substance of the evidence that a court's verdict will be based. As such, the accuracy of the interpretation is paramount. Yet, within the context of interpreting, "accuracy" is a difficult concept to define, hence the debate surrounding the verbatim and pragmatic standards (Hale 2002, p. 25). Beyond that, however, it is fair to ask whether true accuracy is even possible, since "no two languages in the world interpret word for word" (LaVigne and Vernon 2003, p. 869) and some concepts and meanings have no proper analog outside of their home cultural framework (de Jongh 1992, p. 59). It is the purpose of this subdivision to examine the impact such difficulties can have on the fairness of the proceedings.

3.2.2 The Nature and Difficulty of Courtroom Language

As previously mentioned, languages do not match up perfectly (LaVigne and Vernon 2003, p. 869). Thus, the act of interpreting "entails an inherent loss of meaning" (Viljoen 1992, p. 69; see also Steytler 1993, p. 207). Interpreters are aware of this reality, and are trained to minimize such losses. However, the language used in criminal court proceedings is distinct from the language used in normal, everyday situations in a variety of important ways. These distinctions create a specific subset of problems that are native to criminal proceedings and make the accurate retention of content problematic for court interpreters, especially those untrained in courtroom procedures.

Legal Language

Legal language is "a profession-specific, relatively antiquated, and anomalous category" of language (González et al. 1991, p. 253). It is characterized by several different distinctive features. For instance, the grammatical structure of legal language tends to be significantly more complicated than the normal version of the language, with a higher number of complex and causative verbs (de Jongh 1992, p. 115; González et al. 1991, p. 271). In addition, its vocabulary is both more intricate and esoteric (Stern 2011, pp. 329–330; de Jongh 1992, p. 115). An important portion of this vocabulary may consist of foreign words (such as the prevalent usage of Latin and French phrases in English legalese), as well as terms of art (Stern 2011, p. 329; de Jongh 1992, p. 115). These terms of art, when employed by legal practitioners, can appear as seemingly simple words or phrases, yet they actually represent much larger, complex arguments or thoughts (González et al. 1991, p. 257). For example, in American courtrooms, an attorney might object to witness testimony simply by stating the single word "nonresponsive", which would in fact represent the argument that the witness's statement did not respond to the specific question asked. Legal vocabulary also contains latent ambiguities that, when used by attorneys and judges, are frequently intentional (de Jongh 1992, p. 116). Finally, legal language invariably includes numerous phrases and words that are culturally bound, meaning that they have little significance outside of the legal environment of their native language (Stern 2011, p. 337; González et al. 1991, p. 242). In other words, phrases such as "due process of law" have a specific, detailed connotation that does not carry over directly into other languages.

Given the increased complexity of legal language, interpreters who set foot in a courtroom without the benefit of specific training in the areas of law or legal language, operate under a supreme disadvantage. They are liable to either not understand an unfamiliar vocabulary term specific to legal speech (such as "estoppel" or "garnishment") or incorrectly interpret a normal term with a particular legal meaning that they mistakenly believe they do understand (such as "obscene" or "alien"). Moreover, despite the difficulties presented by legal language, and the importance of its accurate translation, little work has been done to standardize foreign language equivalents in court, even with respect to the most common of language combinations (Stern 2011, p. 337; de Jongh 1992, p. 117). As a result, different interpreters translate the same legal terms differently, and these variations can lead to confusion.[1] Furthermore, it must be remembered that this distinctive legal language and culture must not only be understood by the court interpreter, but she must endeavor to translate its meaning, as far as possible, into the legal language of the target language as well, which will naturally have its own cultural and legal idiosyncrasies. Thus, in order to translate legal language correctly, and retain all of its inherent complexities, the court interpreter must be comfortable with the legal terminology and culture of both languages. This, naturally, is no small task.

Jargon, Argot and Slang

Legalese is not the only subset of language used in a criminal proceeding. Police and investigative officers also have their own "jargon", or specialized form of vocabulary (González et al. 1991, p. 249). Some may be full terms of art, such as "fingerprinting", "booking", or "to flip", while others may simply be frequently-used acronyms or abbreviations, such as "DOA" (dead on arrival), "PC" (probable cause), or "NCIC" (National Crime Information Center) (González et al. 1991, pp. 250, 284). And, as with legal terms, every language and law enforcement culture will likely have its own internal vocabulary. In many instances, given that most evidence detrimental to the accused will originate from law enforcement officials, these abbreviations and terms will represent the most significant elements of information that the fact-finder hears (González et al. 1991, p. 284). As such, their accurate translation is essential not only to the

[1] For example, the German term *Gefährdungshaftung* is often translated into English as either "strict liability" (Romain 1983, p. 301), "absolute liability", (Noack 2007, p. 595), or both (Dietl and Lorenz 2005, p. 336; Lister and Veth 2002, p. 82; von Beseler and Jacobs-Wüsterfeld 1991, p. 635). Strict and absolute liability are not, however, interchangeable concepts (Vandall 2011, p. 156).

State's case against the accused, but also to the accused's ability to both understand and challenge the evidence against him.

In addition, criminal proceedings are not limited to legal language and law enforcement jargon either. Normal everyday witnesses use slang and other informal language (Heller 1994–1995, p. 370). Probation reports will contain socio-psychological language particular to that forum (de Jongh 1992, p. 114). Forensic reports will employ detailed scientific language (de Jongh 1992, p. 68). Expert witnesses of various specialties will each use the language specific to their particular field (González et al. 1991, p. 251). Likewise, as criminal proceedings necessarily involve activities of an illicit nature, the jargon of the criminal underworld, known as "argot", is also common. A specific trait of argot is that it frequently employs otherwise normal words to represent illegal activity (de Jongh 1992, p. 80); thus, words such as "mule" (a person who transports drugs) and "burner" (a disposable cell phone) must be understood in their criminal context, otherwise they cease to truly represent the speaker's intention (González et al. 1991, p. 284). Interpreters working in a criminal court proceeding are liable to come into contact with, and be required to both understand and accurately translate in and out of both languages, each of these different specialized vocabularies.

Geographical Variations and Dialects

Dialects and geographical variations within a language can also complicate the interpreting process. The Spanish spoken in Mexico is distinct from that which is spoken in Spain, and both are dissimilar to Chilean Spanish (Kaufman 2007, p. 24). These differences can be seen not only in pronunciation and grammar, but also in the usage of specific words. For instance, a Colombian will refer to a small commercial warehouse as a "*bodega*", whereas to a Cuban this would signify a very small local store (de Jongh 1992, p. 81). Similarly, a common word such as "*taco*" denotes a popular food item in the United States and Mexico, a short and stocky individual to a Chilean, and literally means "swearword" to someone from Spain (de Jongh 1992, p. 82). Nor is Spanish the only language afflicted by such variations; they exist in the dialects of many languages.

A "fag" in the United Kingdom refers to a cigarette, but is a highly derogatory term for a homosexual in the United States. These variations carry through into the specialized jargons of each language as well: a duffel bag (a specific drug-related term referring to the means of transporting illicit drugs) is a "*gusano*" in Cuba, but a "*tula*" in Colombia (de Jongh 1992, p. 82). Thus, an interpreter must not only be capable of interpreting out of and into all of the various jargons within each of the two languages used in the proceeding, but also all of the possible dialects and their separate jargons as well.

Implications of the Nature and Difficulty of Language

The dialects, jargons and other variations within a language create a multitude of problems for court interpreters. Not only must they be familiar with each of these possible permutations, but they must also be capable of effectively translating each. That court interpreters possess these capabilities is often taken for granted by the court. Unfortunately, such skill is not always present. Of those court interpreters who sit for the interpreter's exam to gain certification to practice in the United States' federal court system, the most frequently reported problem is a lack of general and specialized vocabulary (González et al. 1991, p. 284). Given that only 8% of applicants actually pass this particular certification exam (and that not every nation or jurisdiction actually has such exams), it should not be assumed that all interpreters possess such knowledge.

Yet, the lack of specialized vocabulary can be very detrimental. The small differences in connotation between argot and standard language, for instance, may represent extremely important evidence in a trial. For example, if a Spanish-speaking witness notes that the accused had a "*bolita*", this could mean either that he possessed a little ball, or a packet of cocaine (de Jongh 1991, p. 291). The interpreter's familiarity with criminal argot in the particular dialect of the speaker can be instrumental in identifying the exact information the speaker wishes to convey. Conversely, if an interpreter is unfamiliar with these specialized terms, it can demonstrably undermine the accuracy of the evidence produced, as well as severely hinder the fact-finder's ability to gather and evaluate that evidence. Furthermore, in an attempt to compensate for these deficiencies in knowledge, the interpreter may resort to a coping strategy, thus introducing even more variables into the accuracy of the interpretation.

Nor does the interpreter have the option of eliminating or homogenizing any particular idiosyncrasies of the speaker's message. The nuances of the speaker's statement must be conveyed into the target language in its entirety (González et al. 1991, p. 284). Likewise, the use of dialect, jargon or slang by an individual must also be preserved for the fact-finder, since its mere usage carries pertinent information about the speaker himself: their country of origin, their education level, and their background, among others. Stated differently, the words used by the speaker convey not only the dictionary meaning, but associated information as well, all of which must be retained by the interpreter (González et al. 1991, p. 247). This is a daunting task, and not one that unskilled interpreters can efficiently manage with any regularity. As one court interpreting textbook has noted:

> It becomes very obvious when interpreters cannot deal with particular realms of language. They begin to paraphrase, define, invent, omit, guess, and very often lead the testimony into a web of confusion. … [M]ore often than not, communication collapses totally, leaving many critical portions of testimony uninterpreted. (González et al. 1991, p. 284)

Such breakdowns of testimony naturally have a substantial effect on the accurate production of evidence. In a sense, though, these collapses are the best case scenario, since they are immediately noticeable and can be fixed. Smaller, subtler errors that do not result in an obvious miscommunication, however, can be just as dangerous, if not more so, specifically because they go unnoticed and therefore permanently corrupt the record.

Alone, these minor discrepancies in the evidence may appear inconsequential; however, in the aggregate, they can be significant. Missing the illicit connotation of an otherwise normal phrase, failing to understand the ambiguities of a legal term used during witness questioning, or misunderstanding the geographic origin of a particular term: each of these seemingly minor errors can multiply into a much larger disconnect between the account of a trial translated for a foreign language defendant and the version conveyed to the fact-finder. Such discrepancies undermine the ability of a defendant to truly understand the details of the trial and effectively participate in the proceedings. Likewise, where the interpreter is unfamiliar with the specialized vocabulary in usage, particularly in the case of a foreign language witness employing criminal argot, it is questionable whether her interpretation of the presented evidence will be accurate enough to safeguard the accused's right to examine and confront that witness. Similarly, the foreign accused may have difficulty effectively testifying on his own behalf where his specific dialect or jargon is not well understood by the interpreter, thereby undercutting his right to present a defense. The linguistic difficulties inherent in a criminal proceeding provide a wealth of opportunities for interpreters to accidentally damage the fairness of a proceeding, many times in ways that will neither be noticed nor understood by the legal actors themselves.

3.2.3 Lack of Equivalents

Introduction

Difficulties arising from the specialized forms of language used in criminal proceedings are only one source of content errors attributable to court interpreters. Even where the court interpreter is familiar with the specialized vocabulary of a language, accuracy problems can still be alarmingly widespread. Faithfulness to the original spoken message is "an illusive concept" that can be difficult to achieve (Hale 2007, p. 198). The lack of direct equivalence between languages is partly to blame.

Linguistic Equivalence

Linguists argue that the terms and ideas presented in one language are unique to that language, and cannot be translated completely into a different language (de Jongh 1992, p. 59). According to this theory, any translation is inherently imperfect, because the words of the target language will necessarily lack the exact meaning of the original source language. This general problem in interpreting between languages has long been recognized, and it consequently also creates difficulties for court interpreters (Stern 2004, p. 63, 2011, p. 337; Hale 2001, pp. 71–72). The lack of equivalence between languages manifests itself in a variety of different ways.

For instance, one particular language may use only one or two words to describe an object or idea to which another language devotes an entire vocabulary. The most well-known (though perhaps apocryphal) example is the multitude of Eskimo words available to discuss what in English is primarily known as "snow" (González et al. 1991, p. 308). Likewise, Spanish is rich in words to describe the exact relationships that exist within an extended family, whereas English lacks terms of equivalent particularity (González et al. 1991, p. 308).[2] The differences that exist between languages in these areas create a problem for interpreters, since the precise word used in one language will lose its precision when translated into the more general target language equivalent. Similarly, translating "snow" into Eskimo may be impossible, since the original English word does not contain enough implicit information for the interpreter to pick an accurate, precise equivalent.

Furthermore, some languages lack any possibility of an equivalent. French, for example, has no direct equivalent for the concept of a "motion to dismiss" (Stern 2001, p. 9; see also Stern 2011, p. 337). The German word "*Schadenfreude*", more often than not, is directly incorporated into many English sentences because the only feasible English translation is an explanation (taking enjoyment in the misfortune of others) that is too cumbersome to accommodate. Examples of such holes in different languages are too legion to mention, but their existence is problematic for interpreters.

Even where an equivalent word exists, it is unlikely that the corresponding word is truly equal in meaning to the original (Stern 2011, p. 337; González et al. 1991, p. 307). An example is the word "arm". In English, this can refer to, amongst other definitions, (1) an appendage of

[2] For example, the Spanish term *concuñado* specifically means the "spouse of one's own spouse's sibling", which is a relationship not entirely captured by the English equivalent "brother-in-law".

the human body or (2) a weapon (for example, "the right to bear arms"). The German equivalent "*Arm*" can also denote the same human appendage (1), but it does not encompass the possible meaning of "weapon" (2). As such, the semantic area of the German word only partially overlaps with the equivalent English term. To further complicate matters, however, the German word has an associated meaning of its own that is not represented by the English word, since in its adjectival form, "*arm*" means to be "poor". The existence of substantial overlap between equivalent words does not guarantee an accurate translation either. Equivalent words may represent the same basic meanings and concepts, but the connotations associated with each may be strikingly different. For instance, the Bosnian-Croatian-Serbian word "*poznal*" can be translated into English as "[I] knew [someone]", however this equivalent English phrase fails to render the necessary connotation that the person known was specifically not a friend (Stern 2001, pp. 10–11). Nor do "cozy" or "comfortable" truly capture the full positive connotation of the German "*gemütlich*". Thus, even when a source language word appears to have a readily available equivalent in the target language, it is possible that certain aspects of meaning or connotations associated with the word will literally be lost in the interpretation.

Legal Equivalence

If the lack of linguistic equivalents between languages is difficult under normal circumstances, it is even more problematic in legal proceedings. As previously discussed, the language used in criminal proceedings can be highly technical and extremely complex in its specialization. The very preciseness of legal language (and the other specialized jargons previously discussed) is what makes it especially difficult to accurately translate, since the equivalent words and phrases in the target legal language will likely be just as precise, but in a way that does not directly correspond with the original.

Partially this is due to the fact that the legal terms used in a courtroom correspond directly to the legal system in which they are employed. Yet, just as languages do not match up directly, neither do legal systems (Stern 2004,

p. 63, 2011, p. 329). Thus, even where a seemingly direct equivalent exists, the match will be inherently flawed in its particulars. For example, the concept of dismissing a case may exist in both the original and target legal systems, but because the legal systems are distinct, the exact meaning of dismissing a case will vary based upon the systems themselves. In one, dismissing the case may be a final, irrevocable act; in the other, it may simply be a temporary end. Unfortunately, foreign participants in a courtroom often make false assumptions as to the meaning of what has occurred by incorrectly drawing an analogy to their home legal system (Griffin and Cole 2007, p. 5). Interpreters who carelessly draw direct equivalence between legal terms in both languages only reinforce this error.

Perhaps even more troublesome than the existence of partial equivalence is the complete lack of legal equivalents that exist between some languages. For example, the non-existence of direct legal equivalents between French and English is well-known, and has been cited as one of the most difficult aspects of interpreting at the International Criminal Tribunal for the Former Yugoslavia (Stern 2004, p. 65). Unfortunately, this is also true of a great many language and legal system combinations. Spanish, for instance, lacks the ability to linguistically distinguish between the common law concepts of 1st and 2nd degree murder (Mikkelson 1995, p. 208). Conversely, the English term "involuntary manslaughter" encompasses two separate Spanish language concepts: "*homocidio culposo*" and "*homocidio preterintencional*" (Mikkelson 1995, pp. 211–212). The absence of equivalent terms for legal language can be a significant handicap for court interpreters, as it often requires them to explain the concept to the foreign language participant (which, as previously mentioned, is an activity fraught with risk).

False Friends

Further compounding the lack of equivalents is the existence of those words that appear to be, but are not actually, equivalent terms. These are known as either "false cognates" or "false friends", and their usage is one of the most common mistakes that court interpreters make (de Jongh 1992, p. 77). Examples, unfortunately, are not difficult to find. For instance, when asked why she did not report a particular crime, a Spanish-speaking witness replied "*Yo lo ignoraba*" (which translates as "I was unaware of it") (de Jongh 1991, p. 291). The interpreter, using the false cognate, interpreted this for the court as "I ignored it", which obviously alters the content of the speaker's testimony (de Jongh 1991, p. 291). In another representative incident, a witness was asked whether he had a "discussion" with his uncle; the interpreter translated the question into Spanish using the false cognate "*discutir*", which means "to argue" (de Jongh 1992, p. 78). Thus, when the witness eventually answered in the negative, he was stating that they had not argued, while the court understood his testimony to be that they had not had a discussion (de Jongh 1992, p. 78). Here again, the distinction is of some importance.

Such false friends reside in abundance in many language combinations,[3] and are the bane of every language student's existence. If only beginning language students fell victim to the lure of false cognates, then their impact on courtroom interpreting would be minimal indeed. However, court interpreters are not immune, and the mistaken usage of false cognates is a very common problem for court interpreters (de Jongh 1992, p. 77). Language deficient interpreters, particularly those who lack sufficient knowledge of specialized vocabulary or jargon, are especially prone to the usage of false friends, specifically because they lack the dedicated knowledge to identify that the obvious solution is actually false (González et al. 1991, p. 285). In this manner, even highly-qualified and experienced interpreters can fall blindly into errors because they lack the particular subset of knowledge that the witness's testimony demands.

Non-literal Language

Another area where true equivalence is hard to find involves non-literal language, such as idioms and metaphors. An idiom is an "expression whose meaning (as a whole) cannot be inferred from the meanings of

[3] For instance, in German, to highlight only a few from a much longer list: *aktuell* does not mean "actually", but rather "currently"; *fast* means "almost", not "fast"; and *Mörder* refers to a "murderer" rather than the "murder" itself. Likewise, in French: *attendre* does not mean "to attend", but rather "to wait"; *travail* has nothing to do with "travel", but everything to do with "work"; and a *librairie* is not a "library" but a "bookstore" instead.

its elements (or parts)" (de Jongh 1992, p. 62). The English phrase "You can't judge a book by its cover" is an example of an idiom, since its true meaning (that one cannot accurately judge something based solely on how it appears from the outside) is not necessarily apparent from the actual words used in the phrase (González et al. 1991, p. 244). A metaphor is similar to an idiom in the sense that its intended meaning also does not match the individual meanings of the words used in the phrase (González et al. 1991, p. 246). However, unlike an idiom, the actual words that comprise a metaphor make no literal sense on their own: an example would be the phrase "lame duck congressman" (González et al. 1991, p. 246).

The use of such non-literal speech is routine in the courtroom. Attorneys and judges regularly use idiomatic expressions, especially in those legal systems where juries are involved (González et al. 1991, p. 241). Likewise, witness testimony is "replete with these casual everyday expressions that facilitate communication" (González et al. 1991, p. 286). The abundance of idiomatic speech in the courtroom causes several major problems for interpreters. First, since the meaning of idiomatic language is not literal, interpreters are required to use their judgment as to the actual meaning of the expression (González et al. 1991, p. 244). As discussed in the context of the pragmatic standard, interpreting the meaning of a phrase and not the actual words used not only infringes upon the role of the fact-finder, but also arguably distorts the record. Second, understanding idiomatic speech is generally difficult for interpreters, because such non-literal speech normally is not taught at the formal educational level (González et al. 1991, p. 286). Finally, properly translating non-literal expressions into the target language is an extremely challenging task, since it requires that the interpreter keep the meaning of the idiom while simultaneously conveying to the target audience that an idiom of a particular nature was used (González et al. 1991, p. 310). The latter fact is especially important because the use of an idiom by the speaker indirectly communicates information to the audience about the speaker himself (such as his background, sense of humor or perspective) (González et al. 1991, pp. 286–287). Thus, in order to find the perfect legal equivalent for an idiom, the court interpreter would ideally use an idiom in the target language that corresponds with the original in both meaning and sophistication (de Jongh 1992, p. 62; González et al. 1991, p. 310). For interpreters, this is an incredibly delicate task, given that it requires a mastery and understanding of both source and target language idioms. This assumes, of course, that an equivalent non-literal expression actually exists in the target language, which will not always be the case.

Implications of the Lack of Equivalents

The equivalency issue is particularly problematic for court interpreters because it serves to distort the content of criminal proceedings in a variety of ways, thus undermining the interpreter's efforts to accurately remove the language barrier. For instance, where no direct equivalent exists for an idiom or word, the interpreter is left in a position where no accurate word-for-word translation is even possible. The only options available for the interpreter are to either explain the concept or omit it entirely. Neither of these options is particularly appropriate, given that they each distort the record and the evidence in their own unique ways. Likewise, the mistaken use of a false friend can similarly misrepresent the speaker's statement.

Yet, even the success of finding a seemingly appropriate equivalent is oftentimes simply an exercise in papering over the cracks. For instance, both "*komandir*" and "*komandant*" (Bosnian-Serbian-Croatian) can be comfortably translated into English as "commander", but that English expression will not accurately reflect the fact that a "*komandant*" outranks a "*komandir*" (Stern 2001, p. 7). Similarly, the English term for "back" encompasses two distinct anatomical phrases in Spanish: "*espalda*" (upper back) and "*cintura*" (lower back) (González et al. 1991, p. 308). By using the accepted equivalent, an element of precision inherent in the original may be lost, or conversely, a level of detail may be added where none was previously present. One possible solution is for interpreters to use multiple words in the target language to cover every area of meaning that arises in the source word (González et al. 1991, p. 308). The difficulty in this regard is that adding extra clarifying words may actually make the speaker appear hesitant or confused (González et al. 1991, p. 308). For example, a Spanish-speaking witness who states that she observed a "*camioneta*", would appear less certain of her eyesight if she was translated as having seen "a pick-up truck or station wagon" (González et al. 1991, p. 308).

In addition to maintaining the full breadth of meanings associated with a word or phrase, the interpreter must also find an equivalent that retains the nuances of those meanings as well. Such nuances can be critical to the accurate translation of courtroom testimony (González et al. 1991, p. 477). For example, in an experiment where subjects were shown a film of an automobile accident and then asked questions about the accident, the particular words employed in the questions were shown to substantially impact the resulting answers. Thus, those individuals who were asked to estimate the speed the cars were travelling when they "smashed into each other" produced a "significantly higher" estimate than those who were asked how fast the cars were going when they "hit each other" (Berk-Seligson 1990, p. 25). Asking a question using a word with violent connotations ("smash") as opposed to one with much weaker connotations ("hit") influenced the test subjects' description of the event (Berk-Seligson 1990, p. 25). Minor nuances of meaning such as these can therefore have an outsized impact on the trial itself. The accurate preservation of the speaker's intent, in all of its subtlety and detail, is thus paramount to the effective production of evidence.

Translating a word or phrase can also strip it of any deliberate ambiguity, or add extra layers of ambiguity where none were intended. Legal practitioners frequently and purposefully use ambiguous language in the courtroom (de Jongh 1992, p. 116). A perfect example would be the question "Did you have anything to drink in the car?". The word "drink" is ambiguous here; in the context of a criminal proceeding, it could refer to any liquid beverage or specifically to alcoholic drinks. Furthermore, the question itself has multiple interpretations: it can be asking whether the person possessed something to drink in the car or whether they actually drank something while in the car (González et al. 1991, p. 486). For a court interpreter to successfully interpret this sentence, she must either retain each of these possible meanings in the final product (which will likely be impossible), use her judgment and discretion to pick which question she believes the speaker is actually asking (which will automatically undercut the speaker's intended ambiguity and likely the overall question as well), or ask the questioner to clarify (which will certainly eliminate any deliberate ambiguity and perhaps reflect negatively upon the attorney). Under these circumstances, even though a literal word-for-word equivalent seems to exist, in reality this translation is fraught with danger.

The translation of idioms also comes with risk. A literal word-for-word equivalent may exist, but since the idiom's meaning is not tied to the literal words, such a translation would not truly be equivalent. Choosing to use a corresponding idiom from the target language is generally considered to be the appropriate solution, however, by focusing on the interpretation of the idiom's meaning, the interpreter falls prey to the same difficulties that exist with the pragmatic standard: usurpation of the fact-finder's role as "interpreter" of testimony and the intentional distortion of the permanent record. Perhaps even more troublesome, the interpreter will be exercising her discretion and judgment in an area that requires a native (or near-native) understanding of both the source and target languages (González et al. 1991, p. 309). The successful translation of an idiom is a high-wire act that only the most qualified and experienced interpreters are likely to consistently perform correctly, and yet (as will be seen later), the average court interpreter falls far below that standard of excellence. Again, this all assumes that a perfect equivalent even exists.

Conclusion

The truth of the matter is that, arguably, no such thing as a "perfect" equivalent can exist between languages (de Jongh 1992, p. 59). In the translation of every word in every sentence, some indeterminate loss of meaning will inevitably occur (Viljoen 1992, p. 69). A nuance, connotation, or intended ambiguity will fail to make the transition from one language to another. In this manner, interpretation acts akin to a filter that eliminates any external, associated speech elements outside of the main, intended meaning preserved by the interpreter. This is the curse of linguistic equivalence, and it is especially destructive in a context where the interpreter's job is to preserve every single element contained in the speaker's original statement. In a criminal proceeding where these very nuances and ambiguities can not only be integral parts of the evidence themselves, but also directly influence the testimony of witnesses and the production of that evidence, the loss of these speech elements is particularly troublesome. That such losses are systematic, widespread, and unavoidable is doubly problematic.

The nature of a legal proceeding also contributes to these problems. Specialized vocabularies and the extra difficulty of finding cross-cultural equivalents for native legal terms make the possibility of locating a satisfactory equivalent even more remote. The routine usage of non-literal language by courtroom participants further complicates the interpreter's task. The end result is that the eventual translated version of statements and evidence is, at best, an altered version of the original event. This reality calls into question whether a foreign language defendant can actively participate in proceedings from which he is linguistically divided, as the version of events conveyed to him through the interpreter will necessarily be different from what has actually occurred. Likewise, evidence that has originated in a foreign language and been translated for the court by an interpreter will necessarily be distorted and have suffered a loss of meaning. Whether the evidence incriminates or exculpates an accused, the fairness of using that evidence depends exclusively on the level of distortion present. In these small and imperceptible ways, the production of evidence through an interpreter will inevitably influence an accused's trial, potentially weakening his right to examine witnesses, his ability to present a defense, or his overall right to fairness.

However, whether the alterations to the evidence are irrelevant to, or determinative of, the outcome of the trial is almost beside the point: the mere existence of such alterations marks out an interpreted trial as fundamentally different from a normal proceeding. Moreover, an interpreted proceeding is subject to a greater level of risk that a significant error will occur. In these ways a proceeding involving an interpreter is not equal to one that does not, and an accused who is subjected to an interpreted trial is not treated equally before the court because his experience is substantially different in a manner that places him at greater risk of an unjust result. Nor is it sufficient to argue that the inevitability of distorted evidence in interpreted trials must be acceptable because no other alternative exists. This is akin to arguing that, so long as one tries very hard, the end result is irrelevant. International law standards establish an acceptable level of fairness for criminal proceedings that may not vary based upon the language used during the proceeding (HRC General Comment No. 32, §9). To allow such variation would be to discriminate against the foreign language participant. When that participant is also the accused, such discrimination would be the direct opposite of equal treatment before the court.

3.2.4 Other Content Issues

The demands of specialized vocabularies and the issue of equivalency provide the most fertile areas from which content errors and distortions may arise. However, these are not the only causes of content problems. Other interpreting issues also exist that can lead to the alteration of evidence.

Simple Interpreting Error

Obviously, sometimes interpreters simply make mistakes. Given the virtual impossibility of the task, and the accepted fact that it requires nearly all of an interpreter's mental resources, errors will be made. In some instances, such mistakes can be traced back to a specific origin, such as an interpreter's lack of specialized vocabulary or the necessity of employing a coping strategy to overcome a specific deficiency. Yet, sometimes, mistakes occur for which no obvious reason exists. These, too, can be detrimental to an accused's fair trial protections.

For example, the difference between being "famous" and "notorious" can be highly relevant for a trial (González et al. 1991, p. 284). Translating "Do you waive further notice of this date?" into Spanish as "Do you wave [good-by] to receiving other information about this case?" is an error that can have significant impact upon an accused (de Jongh 1992, p. 29). Furthermore, translating "arms" in a drug context as a bodily appendage instead of as "weapons" would also be problematic (González et al. 1991, p. 282). Such mistakes might arise from a lack of vocabulary, or they may simply result from the interpreter consciously but incorrectly choosing between several different known meanings of a word. Unfortunately, mistranslation distortions such as these are "quite prevalent" among untrained or developing interpreters, though they also afflict experienced interpreters as well (González et al. 1991, p. 287).

Grammatical issues can also be troublesome for interpreters and highly impactful on the proceedings. For instance, where an interpreter translates a witness as admitting that he "would have killed" someone as opposed to "could have killed" someone, the difference is highly significant, but is in truth only a simple error of verb tense (González et al. 1991, p. 7). Likewise, switching past tense ("They wanted to kill me") and present tense ("They want to kill me") can completely distort the actual meaning of a statement (González et al. 1991, p. 283). The confusion of active form ("He threw a bottle at me") with passive form ("A bottle was thrown at me") is also a widespread practice of court interpreters, though the ramifications of this will be considered more thoroughly with respect to style issues below (Berk-Seligson 1990, p. 116). Even seemingly insignificant changes can have substantial consequences on the production of evidence. After being shown a film of an automobile accident, experimental subjects were asked about the existence of a broken headlight (that did not actually exist) (Berk-Seligson 1990, p. 25). Those who were asked whether they had seen "the broken headlight" were much more likely to answer in the affirmative than those who were asked whether they had seen "a broken headlight" (Berk-Seligson 1990, p. 25). In their own way, such minor changes in grammar can dramatically alter the content of not only the speaker's message, but also indirectly change the substance of witness and audience reactions to those statements as well.

Omissions of Content

The existence of interpreter omissions has previously been discussed in several different contexts, such as its use as a coping strategy. However, the omission of words and phrases exists as an independent phenomenon as well, normally with respect to the elimination of specific types of information in the courtroom. As either a coping strategy or a standalone problem, omissions exist in the work of both developing and experienced court interpreters (Gile 2009, p. 157; González et al. 1991, p. 288). And it is not only isolated words or phrases that are omitted by court interpreters, but sometimes "clauses, ideas, sentences, or large portions of discourse" (González et al. 1991, p. 288).

As previously noted, when an interpreter's cognitive resources are overloaded, any new information that arises is a likely target for omission (either conscious or accidental). Likewise, specialized vocabulary that is unknown or concepts that are not understood may also be omitted as a strategic choice (González et al. 1991, p. 288). Particularly technical legal language is especially prone to omission, because the interpreter either fails to understand its importance or does not understand the term (González et al. 1991, p. 288). Profanity, too, is sometimes eliminated by the court interpreter (Hovland 1992–1993, p. 476). Each of these has been discussed previously, however there are other types of information that are also likely to be omitted.

The same instinct that motivates court interpreters to improve upon a speaker's statement (Morris 1995, pp. 31–32), also likely induces them to omit information. For example, particularly repetitious phrases are subject to omission by court interpreters who deem them to be superfluous extra information. When an attorney asks a witness for a clarification ("So, you say you were walking along Main Street. Which direction were you going?"), the witness will oftentimes begin their clarification by repeating information that has already been clearly established ("Yes, I was walking along Main Street going east."). Interpreters will sometimes shorten these answers by eliminating the repetitive information ("I was going east.") (Berk-Seligson 1990, pp. 128–129). In addition, courtroom testimony and speech does not always proceed in a clean and tidy manner (González et al. 1991, p. 478). Rather, it can, and frequently does, contain false starts, fragmentary sentences, hesitations, grammatical mistakes and backtracks among other things (Berk-Seligson 1990, p. 130). Errors in grammar are often corrected or omitted by interpreters, because to translate them accurately would require the interpreter to use grammatically incorrect statements in the target language as well, which would not only be difficult to achieve, but might also impair the court's perception of the interpreter's competence with the language (Jacobsen 2004, p. 248; Morris 1995, pp. 31–32; see also Heller 1994–1995, p. 373). Furthermore, the impulse to clarify information in order to foster communication can lead interpreters to alter the organization of the answer and eliminate meandering language (Berk-Seligson 1990, p. 130). Thus, disorganized testimony such as "I don't remember, difficult to think about that, perhaps, but I don't think so" might become a simple "I don't think so", which replicates the witness's final thought, but fails to contain the entirety of the answer. In addition to the omitted content, the hesitancy in such an answer has also been eliminated and may have an effect on the fact-finder's perception of the witness, but this is a style consideration that will be dealt with in some detail later in this section.

Additions of Content

Court interpreters not only omit content, they also sometimes add extra elements. This is often seen with information that is understood to exist, but has not been explicitly stated (Berk-Seligson 1990, pp. 132–133). For example, when a witness is asked whether a person has a beard, they might simply answer "Yes", but this might be interpreted to the court as "Yes, he does" or even "Yes, he does have a beard" (Berk-Seligson 1990, p. 133). In these instances, the court interpreter is simply making explicit what was implicit, and although it may subtly change the emphasis of the answer, it does not necessarily add any content that did not otherwise exist. This, however, is not always the case. When an interpreter inserts "understood" information into an answer, it is the interpreter's understanding of the situation that is being added, not necessarily the witness's. Thus, the answer "No" might be rendered as "Never" or "I never did", which substantially changes the content of the answer (Berk-Seligson 1990, p. 134). Perhaps this is exactly what the witness meant, but it is not what was said.

Another area where interpreters add information is in their insertion of synonyms in order to cover every possible meaning of a word. As such, the German word "*Blatt*" (with reference to paper) might be interpreted as a "sheet or page". The use of two words instead of one is a strategy meant to compensate for the interpreter's inability to find an exact equivalent (which may not exist anyway) (González et al. 1991, p. 308). However, since most words have multiple nuances and meanings, the addition of an extra synonym (such as "page") in order to cover a significant portion of "*Blatt*'s" semantic area, also potentially adds the extra information associated with the second synonym. Thus, the translation's use of "page" creates the possibility that the "*Blatt*" referenced by the witness could be part of a book (as a page may be), whereas the German word does not actually allow for this option (a page in a book is a "*Seite*", never a "*Blatt*"). In this manner, the addition of an extra word meant to clarify can mislead instead.

Structural Issues

The respective structures of the two languages involved in a courtroom proceeding can also create issues that may lead to content alterations. It is generally well-known that languages "follow a great deal of variation with respect to how the elements of a sentence are ordered" (Mason 2008, p. 26). The structure of one language, while perhaps not problematic on its own, can become so when paired with another language that has a drastically different structure (Chabasse and Dingfelder Stone 2015, pp. 85–88).

The dissimilar structures native to German and English, for instance, do not pair well, especially when simultaneous interpretation is involved. Complex German sentences tend to feature the operative verb at the very end of the sentence; thus forcing a simultaneous interpreter to wait with her translation until she is certain as to the overall meaning of the statement (which will be defined by the verb) (Mikkelson 2000, pp. 74–75). Likewise, the existence of separable prefixes in German verbs such as "*aufmachen*" (which means "to open") and "*zumachen*" (which means "to close") may require the same delaying tactics: the interpreter must suspend her translation of the main verb ("*machen*") until the prefix ("*auf-*" or "*zu-*") arrives at the end of the sentence to further clarify it. Such complicated grammatical structures, when coupled with a language such as English that typically requires a verb much sooner in the sentence structure, can lead to drastic changes in the target language output in order to accommodate the dissimilarities (Mikkelson 2000, p. 75). One tactic, as previously discussed, is segmentation, where the longer sentence is broken into more manageable, standalone pieces

(Gile 2009, p. 205). Another is the dramatic reorganization of the source language information, to allow the interpreter to convey the information that is complete while awaiting the clarification of any incomplete information (Gile 2009, pp. 205–206; Mason 2008, p. 29). Neither of these strategies necessarily distorts a statement's content, but the mere alteration of the statement's structure has the potential to do so in every instance, especially with respect to the connation and nuance inherent in the original language.

Implications of These Other Issues

Content problems can arise from a variety of different sources in courtroom interpreting. The fact that interpreters are confronted with a never-ending array of subtle decisions that must be made concerning the correct word or the right phrasing inevitably means that they will occasionally choose the wrong option. In some instances, this leads to a distortion in meaning, in others to a grammatical mistake that affects the content of the statement. Regardless, both mistakes have the potential to seriously impact a criminal proceeding. Errors concerning the past and present tense of verbs can be especially impactful, since the timeline of when a witness saw or did something is invariably important to the case.

Similarly, intentional omissions may have a negative influence on the evidence produced at trial. Filtering out repetitive statements may help create a more efficient proceeding, but it also results in an inaccurate presentation of the witness's actual testimony. Likewise, there may be legitimate reasons that the witness or speaker repeated information, perhaps for emphasis or out of emotional involvement (Berk-Seligson 1990, pp. 127–128). Removing these repetitions undermines the speaker's intent or neuters their testimony of an indirect sign of sincerity. In either case, the accuracy of the speaker's statement has been compromised by the interpreter's actions. Furthermore, eliminating false starts and grammatical errors paints an unrealistic portrait of the foreign language speaker for the fact-finder. The production of a smoother, more coherent text does not accurately reflect what was actually said, nor does it retain the entirety of the original content. Among the speech elements eliminated by the interpreter may be something of real, important value to the speaker, questioner or fact-finder. It is neither the interpreter's role to make determinations as to what constitutes superfluous information, nor is she in a knowledgeable enough position with respect to the overall case to do so.

Additions are no less problematic. The insertion of "understood" information makes explicit something that the witness left implicit or unsaid. It is not beyond reason that the witness intentionally left out the information that the interpreter considers to be implicit. For example, if a witnesses is asked whether they saw a particular man walking down Main Street, and answers "Yes, I saw him walking", it is entirely possible that the witness has chosen to limit his answer to only a partial affirmation of the question. Thus, the witness is purposefully saying that they saw the man walking, not that they saw the man walking down Main Street. For an interpreter to answer "Yes, I saw him walking down Main Street" as an "understood" addition would therefore place the witness in a position of affirming something that they may have intentionally left ambiguous. The same result is true where the court interpreter omits repetitive information and translates only a "Yes", since this too affirms the question in its entirety. Perhaps the major difficulty with both intentional additions and omissions is that the court interpreter is substituting her understanding of the evidence in place of what was actually said. Such an action is problematic because this is the responsibility of the fact-finder, not the interpreter. In addition, the interpreter may very well be wrong.

Finally, the complicated interaction of language structures can produce situations wherein the interpreter feels it is necessary to alter the organization of a speaker's statements. This can take the form of reorganizing information or of restructuring the grammar. In either case, the rearrangement of substantive information can subtly alter the content and impact of a witness's testimony. For example, if a witness is describing the actions he took as soon as he realized his house was on fire, and states "I woke up my daughter, grabbed my laptop computer and our photo albums, and then left the house", but the interpreter translates this as "I grabbed my laptop computer, my photo albums, and also woke up my daughter before leaving the house", the change is only one of minor reorganization, yet it makes the witness appear to value his laptop more than his daughter. The speaker may have organized their statement in a particular way for a specific reason and the interpreter is not in a position to second-guess or correct the arrangement of the information within that statement. As Hale has stated, "[t]hose who speak through an interpreter have a right to express their message in whatever way they like and for it to remain unaltered in the process" (Hale 2004, p. 8).

Yet, each of these other issues fails to allow the speaker to convey the full extent of their information in the manner of their choice. By eliminating what she considers to be superfluous or repetitive information, reorganizing speech elements, or even adding what she believes is implicit, the interpreter is overriding the speaker's intent while simultaneously usurping the fact-finder's role as the ultimate arbiter of meaning. Furthermore, she is distorting and corrupting the production of evidence in the courtroom. These actions can significantly impact the accused's right to present a defense, since the evidence produced through an interpreter may not actually be the evidence the accused wishes to present. Moreover, this can undermine the right to examine and confront foreign language witnesses because any questioning must occur through an interpreter who is consciously altering the flow and substance of information, often without the knowledge of the participants. Finally, with respect to interpretation for a foreign language defendant as to the content of the proceeding, the actions of the interpreter in this context draw a false portrait of what has actually been said or occurred, making it more difficult for an accused to actively participate in the proceedings.

3.2.5 Conclusion as to Content Problems

The accurate interpretation of the substantive content of the evidence in a criminal proceeding is central to the fairness of an accused's trial. Where interpreters alter or modify the substance of the evidence, the ultimate outcome is a distorted proceeding using inaccurate information. Whether these alterations occur because of the inherent difficulty of the language used in the courtroom or because the interpreter lacks the specialized knowledge to find a suitable equivalent is ultimately less important than the fact that they do indeed occur on a regular basis. That these distortions are largely the result of subtle and seemingly insignificant changes that happen outside the cognizance of the courtroom participants is especially troublesome, since it leaves little ability for anyone directly involved in the process to correct the problems as they arise. Without this self-correction, it is questionable whether the accuracy of the evidence produced in interpreted proceedings is truly sufficient to provide a fair trial.

3.3 Style Problems

3.3.1 Introduction

The question of content accuracy is only one ingredient in a much larger problem. The evidence in adversarial proceedings is mainly produced orally, through the testimony of witnesses who are questioned by the attorneys or judge during the proceeding (Hale 2007, p. 199). The credibility and persuasive power of a witness's testimony is due as much to their demeanor and mannerisms as it is to the content of their statements (Viljoen 1992, p. 71).[4] As such, how a witness says something is often as important as what they actually say (Stern 2011, pp. 337–338; González et al. 1991, p. 16). In other words, the content of an interpreter's translation may be perfectly complete, but if that translation is delivered to the fact-finder in a manner that is inconsistent with the witness's actual mannerisms and demeanor, then its overall accuracy will be substantially compromised. Unfortunately, interpreters constantly alter the speech style of witnesses in their eventual translations (Hale 2002, pp. 43–44; Berk-Seligson 1990, p. 142; see also Stern 2011, p. 338). These alterations take a variety of different forms, each of which will be addressed in this section, along with their potential impact on the fairness of the proceedings.

[4] Lord Shaw's famous quote explains this best: "witnesses without any conscious bias towards a conclusion have in their demeanour, in their manner, in their hesitation, in the nuance of their expressions, in even the turns of the eyelid, left an impression upon the man who saw and heard them which can never be reproduced in the written page" (*Clarke v. Edinburgh and District Tramways Company Limited* [1919] p. 36).

3.3.2 General Issues of Style

The Overall Concept of Speech Style

The manner in which a speaker delivers their content, or "how they say" what they say, is known as their "speech style" (Hale 2007, p. 200). It can include a variety of aspects, such as the existence of hesitations, the use of the passive voice, the complexity of the vocabulary, and even the level of politeness. Each of these elements combines to create a "style" that is personal to the speaker. Since fact-finders in adversarial proceedings base their conclusions upon the presentation of oral evidence, it is no surprise that a witness's speech style can have an impact upon the credibility and persuasiveness of their testimony (Stern 2011, p. 337; Hale 2007, p. 200). However, the particular details as to how different speech styles impact fact-finder perception are somewhat more surprising.

A study performed at Duke University has shed some light on this phenomenon as it occurs in the English language. The research group found that the speech style of uneducated, non-professional individuals had certain common features: excessive use of hedges ("sort of", "kind of", etc.), fillers ("basically", "you know", etc.), hesitations ("uhm", "well", etc.), and intensifiers ("very", "definitely", etc.); overuse of polite forms ("sir", "ma'am", etc.) and exaggerated adjectives ("divine", "glorious", etc.); and the use of a rising question intonation when making a statement (Hale 2001, p. 70; González et al. 1991, p. 276). This speech style was labeled "powerless", by way of contrast with the "powerful" speech style of educated, professional individuals, which was found to not have these characteristics (Hale 2001, p. 70; González et al. 1991, p. 276). Armed with this information, the research group orally presented witness testimony of identical content to mock jurors using the two distinctive speech styles (Hale 2001, p. 70). Without exception, the witnesses who used the "powerful" style of speech were considered by the jurors to be "more truthful, more intelligent, more convincing, more competent, and more trustworthy than those who used the powerless style" (Hale 2001, p. 70).

This finding has particular relevance to the work of court interpreters and the right to a fair trial because, generally speaking, court interpreters present testimony in their own speech style, and not that of the witness (Hale 2007, p. 200). In doing so, they invariably change the impact of that testimony. For instance, a witness statement full of hesitations and uncertainty in Spanish such as "*Yo solamente le vi la hojita, que, o sea como, como brillosa, no más, y eso*" (which translates as "I only saw the little blade, that, I mean, like like it was shiny, that's all… and that") will be translated for a court as "I just saw the shiny blade of the knife" (Hale 2001, p. 70, 2007, p. 200). Such a transformation of style, while not necessarily affecting the content, inevitably leads to the fact-finder having a more favorable perception of the witness's credibility and competence than they would if the original speech style was maintained (Hale 2007, p. 200). Yet, interpreters rarely preserve the original speech style.

There are several reasons for this. For instance, many untrained or developing court interpreters are unaware of the importance of doing so (Hale 2001, pp. 70–71). In addition, the sheer variety of distinctive speech styles that are regularly used in a courtroom proceeding (for example, an attorney's legal formalism or an uneducated witness's slang) can be difficult for even a highly-experienced court interpreter to successfully mimic (Hale 2001, p. 71). Thus, many choose not to try. Furthermore, as with the debate over the pragmatic standard, some interpreters feel that it is their role to foster communication, and any speech elements that impede this goal are removed (Hale 2001, p. 71). Economic pressures and the expectations of the court participants also play a role in the abandonment of witness speech styles. Lawyers frequently assess the competence of the interpreter based upon the coherence of the interpreter's translations (Hale 2007, p. 200). As such, where an interpreter faced with the Spanish witness above remains faithful to the hesitant and partially incoherent style of the testimony, that interpreter risks being considered incompetent (Hale 2007, p. 200). In this manner, a poorly-trained and unqualified court interpreter who cleans up untidy testimony will be considered more competent by the judge and attorneys than a highly-qualified and experienced court interpreter who translates such statements faithfully. This creates an economic incentive for interpreters to abandon any elements of style that reflect poorly on their performance, regardless of the ultimate impact on the witness's credibility.

Implications of General Style Issues

Scientific studies have shown that, content being equal, an individual's speech style directly affects the listener's assessment of "the speaker's social status, personality, intelligence, trustworthiness and competence" (Hale 2002, p. 26). As such, the preservation of a witness's speech style is an important component of the court interpreter's task, since this style will help determine the fact-finder's perception of the witness and their testimony. Unfortunately, several scholars have shown that court interpreters fail to preserve the witness's style of speech, unintentionally replacing it with their own speech style instead (Hale 2002, pp. 43–44, 2007, p. 200; González et al. 1991, p. 291; Berk-Seligson 1990, p. 142).

This substitution can have grave consequences for the fairness of a proceeding. Consider a witness who testifies that "I only saw the little blade, that, I mean, like like it was shiny, that's all… and that" as opposed to the witness who testifies, "I merely observed the shiny, rather diminutive edge, of the blade". The first, exhibiting many of the characteristics of "powerless" speech, will appear much less credible and intelligent than the second, which is erudite, confident and "powerful". Yet, in the courtroom, both will largely take on the speech style of the court interpreter and become "I just saw the shiny blade of the knife." This is significant, because it has been shown that fact-finder perceptions of witnesses are based upon the demeanor and style of the court interpreter rather than the witnesses themselves (Berk-Seligson 2002, pp. 288–289). As such, regardless of the actual intrinsic persuasiveness of their testimonial style and personality, both will be assessed equally, based upon the credibility and believability of the interpreter (Hale 2002, p. 27). Such an outcome, in an adversarial proceeding where evidence is primarily presented orally through witness testimony, is highly problematic. That the trustworthiness and persuasiveness of a witness should be determined so substantially by the natural demeanor of the court interpreter significantly undermines the accuracy of the evidence produced in such a proceeding.

There is more, however, to the issue of speech style than the simple transposition of the interpreter's style for that of the witness's. Since speech style is personal to every individual, every interpreter has a different collection of speech elements that comprise her individual style. Interpreters, as a group, are neither "powerful" nor "powerless". Nor do witnesses, as a whole, exhibit any one particular style of speech. Thus, the substitution of speech styles does not lead to any one particular outcome; it may either hurt a witness's credibility or help it, depending upon the individual characteristics of the witness and the interpreter. As such, in order to fully understand the impact that speech style alteration can have on the fairness of a criminal proceeding, it is necessary to consider the various different ways in which a witness's speech style is altered.

3.3.3 Register

The Concept of Register

Speech register refers to the formality of language used by individuals in different settings (González et al. 1991, p. 248; Berk-Seligson 1990, p. 169). This includes not only the vocabulary and complexity of grammar used, but also the level of intimacy employed by the speaker. In the courtroom, the formality of language can vary drastically from speaker to speaker, in some instances even fluctuating moment to moment within the same speaker's statements (González et al. 1991, pp. 248–249). For example, consider the following three statements:

> His performance was on the uppermost regions of the normal curve.
> He is very intelligent.
> He's a brain. (González et al. 1991, p. 249)

The basic content of these three statements is virtually identical: the individual has higher than average intelligence. However, the different levels of formality, as indicated by the vocabulary and sentence complexity employed, are very distinct. Court interpreters, in order to maintain the accuracy of their interpretation, must be able to cover the entirety of possible registers (González et al. 1991, p. 248). The necessity of shifting through the various levels of formality all within a short period of time makes conservation of register one of the most difficult aspects of a court interpreter's job, even for those who are highly qualified and experienced (González et al. 1991, p. 286).

The Implications of Register

The preservation of a speaker's register is not an empty requirement; its loss in the interpretation process has real-life implications. Higher levels of formality equate with powerful speech, and produce a more favorable rating from jurors (Berk-Seligson 1990, pp. 172, 175–176). In contrast, lower levels of formality reflect poorly upon witnesses. As such, the conservation of the witness's register is important to a representative conveyance of their speech style, and the ability of the fact-finder to make an accurate appraisal of their believability and persuasiveness. Unfortunately, as with many elements of speech style, "systematic changes in register are often made in the interpreting process" (Berk-Seligson 1990, p. 172). Thus, it is questionable whether witnesses presented at interpreted trials are accurately portrayed by court interpreters.

In addition to the direct distortion of a witness's testimony through loss of register, there is also the likelihood that court interpreters may indirectly determine the register with which the witness answers in the first place. It has been shown that the formality of a question can set the register of the answer (Hale and Gibbons 1999, p. 212). In other words, a question phrased in an informal manner will likely elicit an answer at a similar level of formality. As such, if an attorney asks a formal question, and the court interpreter lowers the register through interpretation to a more casual level, the witness will then answer casually. In response to a formal question, the witness's informality may be even more damaging. Likewise, if the question's register was an attempt on the part of the attorney to elevate the discussion's formality in order to improve the fact-finder's reception of the witness, then the interpreter's alteration would be entirely counterproductive. Of course, if the interpreter is not preserving speaker register anyway, then the formality of the witness's answer is somewhat beside the point.

Nevertheless, fact-finders assess the credibility and persuasiveness of witnesses based, in part, on the formality and appropriateness of their speech register. That court interpreters often systematically alter speech register weakens the ability of the fact-finder to accurately evaluate the probative value of evidence. This, in turn, has the potential to seriously undermine the overall fairness of the proceedings.

3.3.4 Active and Passive Voices

The Concept of Active and Passive

The active and passive verb forms represent a difference in emphasis using the same basic information but different sentence structures (Mason 2008, p. 27). For example, in an active form sentence such as "Bob threw the bottle", there is a clear "Actor-Verb-Object" structure (González et al. 1991, p. 238). In the passive construction, "The bottle was thrown by Bob", the structure is altered: "Object-Verb-Actor" (González et al. 1991, p. 238). The alteration in organization changes the focus of the sentence: in an active construction, the focus is on the actor (Bob), whereas in a passive construction, it is on the action itself (the bottle being thrown) (Berk-Seligson 1990, p. 111). This change in focus can result in a modification of responsibility as well, since the action is placed in the foreground, and the actor in the background (Mason 2008, p. 28; Berk-Seligson 1990, p. 97). This is even more true if the actor is not retained in the passive construction at all, as is normal. Such a result can clearly be seen in the difference between "Bob threw the bottle" and "The bottle was thrown" (Berk-Seligson 1990, p. 115). In the first, Bob is clearly indicated as the responsible actor; yet in the second, Bob is no longer even mentioned, as the action (rather than the actor) is the primary focus of the sentence.

The change in emphasis on different aspects of information that is inherent in the active and passive forms makes their retention in any eventual translation of paramount importance. However, court interpreters fail to differentiate between the two forms, routinely changing active to passive and vice-versa (Berk-Seligson 1990, p. 116). Berk-Seligson

(1990) has characterized this practice as "widespread" (p. 116). Indeed, in her influential study on the subject, she found that over 20% of the court interpretations analyzed involved such an alteration in voice; the majority (70%) of changes entailed a switch from passive to active, while a minority (30%) concerned active to passive (Berk-Seligson 1990, p. 116). Such alterations are generally believed to be unintentional on the part of court interpreters (Berk-Seligson 1990, p. 118).

The Implications of the Active and Passive Voices

As mentioned above, the usage of the active or passive voice can alter the apportionment of responsibility for an action. For the fact-finder, the difference between "Bob threw the bottle" and "The bottle was thrown" is of obvious importance, as one assigns blame for the action, and other does not. This is a clear alteration of the evidence. Furthermore, even where the interpreted sentence correctly identifies the actor, such as "The bottle was thrown by Bob", the movement of the action to the foreground changes the emphasis of the statement away from the actor. Such a modification of style can also impact the fact-finder's perception of the evidence.

Likewise, the movement from passive to active (which was the majority of alterations identified in Berk-Seligson's study) occasionally requires the insertion of an actor where none existed in the original statement. Thus, the interpreter who changes "The bottle was thrown" to an active statement "Bob threw the bottle", must necessarily identify Bob as the actor to throw the bottle. If the witness did not explicitly state this in their testimony, then the change to active form may result in the interpreter inserting her understanding of the culpable party into the evidence. Regardless of whether her perception of the evidence is correct, making explicit what the witness left implicit is a significant alteration.

Furthermore, the usage of the passive or active by a witness may impact how the fact-finder views their evidence. In English, for instance, the passive voice has been found to negatively impact a juror's estimation of the witness's intelligence and trustworthiness (Berk-Seligson 1990, pp. 184–185). Yet, it is important in this context to understand that, as with the "powerful" and "powerless" demarcations, this impact is likely language specific: usage of the passive in another language may be viewed as a positive, rather than a negative, marker. This is true because the relative usage rates of passive and active forms varies from language to language, and thus they have different connotations within that linguistic culture (González et al. 1991, pp. 238–239). For example, passive constructions are used extensively in English, while in Spanish, the active is preferred (González et al. 1991, p. 238). This makes the interpretation of active and passive forms rather problematic, because the interpreter, while charged with retaining the style and structure of the original statement, may not blindly retain every active or passive construction, because doing so might give the listener a false impression of the speaker's register or style. Carrying over into English every active construction used by a Spanish speaker, for instance, will produce an interpretation that does not sound native, reemphasizing the foreign nature of the speaker (González et al. 1991, p. 238). The interpretation of the active and passive voices, therefore, involves fairly complex decision-making. That court interpreters largely appear to ignore these complicated dynamics, while still engaging in the widespread alteration between active and passive voices, is unfortunate. Likewise, it is a practice which has the potential to severely undermine the reliability of evidence and the assessment of responsibility through that evidence.

3.3.5 Question Forms

The Concept of Question Forms

It is well-established that attorneys (and judges) in an adversarial proceeding exercise significant control over witnesses and the flow of information during testimony (González et al. 1991, p. 273). One specific illustration of this can be seen in how attorneys use different forms of questions in order to elicit varying styles of answers (Hale 2004, p. 35). For example, the query "You took the money, didn't you?" is more an accusation than an attempt to obtain a true answer (Hale and Gibbons 1999, pp. 214–215). Phrased differently, such as "You took the money, have I understood that correctly?", the question is much less coercive. As such, the form of a question does more than simply enquire, it can also accuse the listener of something, command them to do something, or demand something from them (Moeketsi 1999a, p. 55; González et al. 1991, p. 274). Language, in such an instance, is used by attorneys as a weapon (Hale 2004, p. 13; Fowler 1995, p. 194; González et al. 1991, p. 18).

These varying roles of the question form can cause problems for court interpreters, particularly with relation to languages where direct equivalents for question types do not align well. One prominent example is the difficulty in English and Spanish with "tag questions", which are a statement followed by a negative or positive tag: "He doesn't like reading, does he?" or "You took the money, didn't you?" (Hale 2004, p. 45). The nature of these questions can change not only with the modification of the tag at the end, but also with the alteration of the intonation used by the questioner (Hale 2004, p. 45). Scholars have identified seven different varieties of tag questions in English, only one of which has a direct equivalent in Spanish (Hale 2004, pp. 45–46). This lack of equivalence can be offset using various different methods of interpretation; however each of these alters the impact of the original in some way (Hale 2004, pp. 49–54). Likewise, the complexity of overcoming an inherent lack of equivalents, along with the abundant use of such questions in adversarial proceedings, makes their translation especially difficult for courtroom interpreters (Hale 2004, p. 44). The solution to this problem as practiced most often by interpreters is to simply omit the tag all together; one prominent study found that the "tag" aspect of a tag question was eliminated in over 52% of the interpretations analyzed (Hale 2004, p. 44).

Other aspects of question form can also cause difficulties for court interpreters. For instance, where an attorney asks a witness to confirm a piece of information with a negative question, such as "So, she wasn't at the bar that night?", the relative grammatical differences between languages can be especially problematic (Berk-Seligson 1990, p. 73). In Spanish, the information can be confirmed with either a "*No*" (as in "No, she wasn't there") or a "*Sí*" (as in "Yes, you are correct: she wasn't there") (Berk-Seligson 1990, p. 73). This is not the case in English, where only a "No" actually affirms the premise of the question (Berk-Seligson 1990, p. 73). Thus, if the court interpreter translates the Spanish witness's "*Sí*" as a "Yes", the actual meaning of the answer will be reversed from what the speaker intended. This confusion arises directly from the form of the question, and the inherent differences between two distinct languages. Unfortunately, the difficulty of finding a suitable equivalent for a grammatical structure that does not exist in the target language is not confined to Spanish. Other languages also lack the ability to replicate tag questions in all of their connotations (de Jongh 2008, p. 27; Hale 2004, p. 46, 2007, p. 200).

The Implications of Question Form

The form given to a question by an attorney generally serves a specific purpose, or is meant to elicit a particular type of response (Hale 2004, p. 35). In spite of the general care taken by attorneys to choose the right language and the correct question form for their purposes, the combination of a lack of equivalent grammatical structures in the target language and the unawareness of interpreters as to the importance of these details means that the form of a question is often altered by court interpreters (Hale 2001, p. 68, 2004, p. 36). One extreme example of this phenomenon is the omission in Spanish of most tags from English tag questions, and the necessary rephrasing of the question that results. Such actions are not without impact. Translating "That's because you still wanted to fight him, is that correct?" as "Did you still want to fight him?" preserves the basic content of the question, but reduces its coerciveness and aggressiveness considerably (Hale and Gibbons 1999, p. 214). This change in the tenor of the question will necessarily influence the tone of the answer as well,[5] thus directly influencing the course of the proceeding while indirectly altering the actual evidence produced. Neither outcome is acceptable in a criminal proceeding where the "[c]onstruction of questions with the desired level of coercion during examination is a highly developed skill" among attorneys (Hale and Gibbons 1999, p. 218).

Furthermore, in the same manner that the subtleties of a word used in a question ("smash" as opposed to "hit") can actually influence the resulting testimony, the form given to a question can do the same. Asking an

[5]This has been found to be especially true of witnesses and individuals from lower social classes who are less comfortable interacting with attorneys and judges (González et al. 1991, p. 274).

individual how "tall" a particular person is, as opposed to how "short", results in a larger estimation of their size (Loftus 1996, p. 94). Similarly, asking study subjects who recently viewed a video that contained no dog, whether they saw "the" dog as opposed to "a" dog makes it more likely that they will claim to have seen a dog that did not actually exist (Loftus 1996, p. 95). In each instance, the question content is basically identical, only the form of the wording has changed. Yet, the result, the aspect that will be most important in a criminal proceeding, has been altered by the question and the assumptions made in its form.

Research has also found that the "form in which a question is put to a witness exerts a strong influence on the quality of the answer" (Loftus 1996, pp. 90–91). For example, open-ended questions that allow the witness to choose their own details result in a narrative style answer containing a less comprehensive set of details, but a lower rate of errors as to those details (Loftus 1996, pp. 90–91). Conversely, questions that call for specific details generally produce a more comprehensive answer, but do so at the expense of a higher rate of errors and a fragmented style (Loftus 1996, pp. 90–91). In other words, the structure of the question affects the accuracy of the answer. It also influences the style of answer given by the witness, and thus also indirectly affects the perception that the fact-finder will have as to the credibility and persuasiveness of that answer: narrative answers are more favorably received by juries than those given in a fragmentary style (González et al. 1991, p. 276).

As can be seen from the discussion above, the form of a question is highly important to the adversarial process. The coerciveness of the question, its ability to draw out an accurate remembrance of events, and its influence on the perceived persuasiveness of the answer make its successful interpretation key. The relative inattention paid to question form by court interpreters has the potential to significantly impact the outcome of a criminal trial. Changes in question form can not only distort the testimony of a witness and introduce errors, but likewise alter the fact-finder's perception of a witness and their evidence. These are not inconsequential alterations, but rather strike at the heart of the right to a fair trial. An accused's right to confront witnesses is made somewhat irrelevant where the ability to ask coercive questions is severely limited. Likewise, the ability to present evidence through witnesses in the manner that best supports one's case is undermined by the unreliable translation of question form, since it can negatively affect the accuracy of the answers that result. Finally, an accused's equality before the court is also threatened where he experiences a proceeding that is fundamentally different in a negative manner from other similarly-situated defendants.

3.3.6 Politeness

The Concept of Politeness

Just as the level of a witness's formality can either aid or detract from their credibility before the fact-finder, so too can their level of politeness (Berk-Seligson 2002, p. 287). In other words, as mothers everywhere advise their children: being polite has its advantages. In the context of criminal proceedings, being polite and speaking in complete sentences has been shown to increase an accused's chances of being acquitted (Berk-Seligson 1990, p. 149). Politeness in the courtroom primarily involves the level of respect and deference participants afford each other, and the language they use when addressing someone. Certain politeness markers or courteous phrases are typical indicators of polite speech: in English, for instance, "sir"; "ma'am"; "please"; and "thank you" (Berk-Seligson 2002, p. 279). Likewise, in languages with formal and informal forms of address (such as "*du*" and "*Sie*" in German, or "*tu*" and "*vous*" in French), use of the formal may be seen as an indicator of respect and politeness.

The addition or omission of politeness markers by court interpreters is not uncommon. Mason has found that when speech or question lengths exceed 10 words, politeness markers toward the beginning of the speech segment are invariably omitted, while other politeness markers may be added in a different area (Mason 2008, p. 24). Likewise, due to the natural limitations on their short term memory, court interpreters make a habit of condensing longer segments of speech into shorter pieces. Thus, a question such as "Mr. Gomez, could you please give your name?" may be interpreted as "State your name" (Hale and Gibbons 1999, p. 211). The loss of the politeness marker, as well as the witness's title and surname, render the target language translation much less polite than the original (Hale and Gibbons 1999, p. 211). Due to the prevalence of longer, denser questions, the cross-examination of witnesses is especially prone to such omissions and additions (Mason 2008, p. 24).

Furthermore, Berk-Seligson (1990) has found that court interpreters (especially Spanish language interpreters from Latin America) frequently use politer forms of address with foreign language witnesses than those used by the English language attorneys (p. 150). In part, this alteration is due to the heightened level of politeness exhibited in Latin American Spanish, but also partly to the natural inclination to attempt to place the foreign witness at ease (Berk-Seligson 1990, p. 150). Court interpreters also add extra politeness markers when interpreting for a judge; thus, a "Yes" answer will become "Yes, sir" or "Yes, ma'am" (Berk-Seligson 1990, p. 154). It is assumed that, as with the phenomena of conscious language improvements, interpreters feel obliged to address the judge respectfully, even where the foreign language participant has not, due to the general level of formality in the courtroom (González et al. 1991, p. 479). Additionally, since the approval of the judge may make a significant difference in their future job prospects in that jurisdiction, it is logical that the court interpreter would not wish to use impolite forms of address (Berk-Seligson 2002, p. 281).

The Implications of Politeness

Court interpreter alterations in levels of witness and speaker politeness change the perception that the fact-finder has of the witness. Where a witness exhibits politeness in the original language, but the court interpreter fails to maintain these politeness markers or forms of respect, then the witness will appear to the fact-finder as if they were impolite. Similarly, if the witness is rude, but the translation inserts politeness markers, then the fact-finder will assess the witness as polite. This is because the fact-finder bases their perception of the witness on the speech style of the interpreter, not the witness (Berk-Seligson 2002, pp. 288–289). As such, the intrinsic politeness of the court interpreter matters more than that of the witness.

Moreover, the court interpreter can also influence the levels of politeness shown by the witness in their answers. Generally speaking, the register and politeness of the question informs and influences the politeness of the eventual answer (Hale and Gibbons 1999, p. 212). However, the witness answers the court interpreter's version of the question, which is oftentimes more polite than the attorney's version. The witness then matches the increased politeness shown by the court interpreter, who then conveys this politeness back to the court (Berk-Seligson 1990, p. 150). The same politeness cycle can work in reverse as well. For instance, in the example given above where a polite question was reduced to "State your name", the witness might simply respond with his name, which might seem impolite to the fact-finder given the politeness of the attorney's initial question. Such interpreter-induced alterations may be especially damaging or helpful to the perception of the witness, since it creates a situation where the politeness or impoliteness shown by the witness does not match that of the questioner.

Perhaps even more important, changes in witness politeness generate a disconnect between the actual politeness displayed by the witness, and that shown to the fact-finder and recorded on the record. This is highly significant because the politeness of the witness plays an important role in the formation of the fact-finder's impression of that witness (Berk-Seligson 2002, p. 279). A study by Berk-Seligson (2002) has shown that juries find polite witnesses to be "significantly more convincing, competent, intelligent, and trustworthy" than those who do not exhibit politeness markers (p. 286). Thus, the addition or omission of politeness markers in a witness's testimony, or the indirect alteration of witness politeness through the addition or omission of politeness markers in an attorney's question, can have a substantial impact on the probative value given to that witness's testimonial evidence. As such, changes in politeness, which may appear a very minor modification on the part of a court interpreter, can dramatically affect an accused's right to examine or present witnesses, since these changes may fundamentally alter the perceived strength of any evidence produced through an interpreter. This, again, establishes the possibility of unequal court proceedings based solely on the participation of an interpreter.

3.3.7 Discourse Markers

The Concept of Discourse Markers

Discourse markers are "words or phrases which are seemingly meaningless in content, but carry strong assumptions and can affect the tone, tenor, force and coherence of utterances" (Hale 2001, p. 69). Examples in English would be "you see", "now", "actually", and "well" (Hale 2002, p. 34). Their chief usage is during the examination of a witness, where they allow the attorney to link their questions to prior answers and indirectly convey to witnesses that their answers were not sufficient or relevant with respect to the questions asked (Hale 2004, p. 76). For instance, in the question "Well, is it correct that you have no prior convictions?", the usage of the discourse marker "well" acts similarly to saying "yes, but …" (Hale 2001, pp. 69–70). In other words, its inclusion in the question signifies a level of disapproval with the prior answer, while also attempting to link the new question and its subject matter to the answer that came before. Discourse markers thereby serve as linguistic tools, allowing attorneys to assert control over the narrative of a line of questioning or increase the combativeness or aggression of a statement or question (Hale 2004, p. 62). They are frequently employed in adversarial proceedings (Hale 2001, p. 69).

Unfortunately, they are also systematically ignored or omitted by court interpreters (Hale 2004, p. 62; see also Hale 2001, p. 69; Berk-Seligson 1990, p. 180). The question related above, for example, would likely be interpreted simply as "Is it correct to say that you had no previous convictions?". Thus, the discourse marker "well" would be omitted, depriving the question of much of its illocutionary force, since it would no longer actually express the questioner's dissatisfaction with the previous answer. Likewise, consider the following exchange:

Witness: We talked about the price a little.
Attorney: You see, I put it to you that you had an argument, isn't that correct?

In this context, the "you see" is used to express overt disapproval or disbelief of the prior statement (Hale 2001, pp. 69–70). In connection with the phrase "I put it to you", the combination introduces an alternative scenario that challenges that presented by the witness. If the interpreter translates the attorney's follow-up question as "You had an argument, isn't that correct?", much of these nuances will be lost on the witness: a strong accusation that the witness was withholding the true nature of the incident would be transformed into a simple question related to the prior statement. Naturally, these are not equivalent questions. That interpreters ignore discourse markers because they appear irrelevant is further evidenced by the fact that they not only omit those used by the speaker, but they also insert their own into translated statements (Hale 2002, p. 34). As such, a witness's answer such as "*Es una casa chica*" ("It's a small house") becomes "Well, it's a small house" (Berk-Seligson 1988, p. 32, 1990, p. 141). The addition of the discourse marker in this instance converts an otherwise clear and definite description into one tinged with uncertainty (Berk-Seligson 1988, p. 32, 1990, p. 141).

The omission or addition of discourse markers is not an infrequent occurrence; one study found that only eight (13.5%) of the 59 discourse markers used in the original statements were actually translated into the target language (Hale 2002, p. 34). The other 51 markers, along with their associated meanings, were simply omitted. This was the case even where an adequate and appropriate target language equivalent existed (Hale 2004, pp. 80, 84–85). By way of contrast, the court interpreters inserted 18 new discourse markers of their own creation into the translations (Hale 2002, p. 34). Thus, the court interpreters introduced twice as many new markers to the target language statements than they actually carried over from the original speech segments.

The Implications of Discourse Markers

The seemingly random insertion and elimination of discourse markers carries with it the potential to significantly alter the meaning of testimonial evidence. Although most discourse markers will likely arise in the questions of attorneys, and thus their elimination will not directly alter evidence, the subtle change in the meaning of the question as related to the foreign language witness will in many instances influence the resulting answer, which is evidence (Hale 2004, p. 86). Likewise, the questioner's ability to control and guide the examination of a witness will be negatively affected, since the interpreter will be eliminating the linguistic tools used to tie together disparate questions and answers into a complete narrative (Hale 2001, p. 70). For instance, reconsider the exchange related above, where the "You see, I put it to you…" was omitted, leaving the attorney's question as "You had an argument, isn't that correct?". Here, the resulting answer would not be a spirited defense by the witness of their earlier characterization of the discussion as a "talk", because the witness would have no way of knowing that the attorney was actually challenging that characterization. Rather, the resulting follow-up question about having an argument would likely confuse the witness, as it assumes a description of the incident that the witness has never actually provided, and lacks the discourse markers that indicate this alternate portrayal was put forward by the attorney.

The elimination of these seemingly minor details can substantially undermine the coherence and tone of the proceedings, and corrupt the evidence provided by witnesses (Hale 2002, p. 39). As previously detailed, the accused has a right to examine and confront witnesses on equal terms with both the prosecution as well as other similarly situated defendants. Where the court interpreter is inadvertently distorting the practice and coherence of questioning witnesses, it is difficult to say that this right has been substantially protected. Furthermore, the likelihood that witness evidence is being altered or influenced through the elimination or addition of discourse markers is a significant concern, given the importance of these speech elements in establishing the tenor or tone of questioning and their systematic alteration by court interpreters.

3.3.8 Hesitations, Hedges, and Fillers

The Concept of Hedges and Fillers

A hedge is a word or phrase that is used to increase the vagueness or reduce the strength of a statement (Hale 2002, p. 29). For example, in the declaration "Heidelberg, I think, is a beautiful city", the phrase "I think" is meant to reduce the absolute nature of the statement. Other examples of English language hedges are "sort of", "more or less", "probably", and "maybe" (Hale 2002, p. 30). Fillers, in contrast, are words or phrases "used to fill a pause in the utterance" (Hale 2002, p. 30). Hesitations are random speech particles which do the same. In other words, they each "fill" the empty space in a statement. Prominent examples of fillers are "basically", "in fact", "really", "you know" and "I mean" (Hale 2002, p. 30). Representative hesitations are "uh", "uhm", and "well" (Berk-Seligson 1990, p. 140). These can evidence a lack of eloquence on the part of the speaker, or they may even be used similarly to a hedge under the right circumstances (Hale 2002, p. 30).

As with many other style elements, interpreters tend to leave the speaker's hedges, hesitations and fillers out of their resulting translations (González et al. 1991, p. 291; Berk-Seligson 1990, p. 140). Occasionally, this is the result of the systematic elimination of information that is seen as repetitive or meaningless, but it can also simply occur because court interpreters shorten answers to limit the strain on their short-term memory or just do not pay attention to their existence and preservation (Berk-Seligson 1990, p. 143). Thus, as related previously, "*Yo solamente le vi la hojita, que, o sea como, como brillosa, no más, y eso*" (which translates as "I only saw the little blade, that, I mean, like like it was shiny, that's all… and that") will be conveyed to the court as "I just saw the shiny blade of the knife" (Hale 2001, p. 70, 2007, p. 200). The elimination of the hedges and fillers in this translation changes an uncertain and scattered answer into a concise and powerful statement (Hale 2002, p. 30). The omission of hesitations effectively does the same (Berk-Seligson 1990, p. 140). Unfortunately, such omissions and eliminations are not an uncommon occurrence. In her study of court interpretations, Hale (2002) found that the interpreters omitted every single hesitation contained in the original statements (p. 40). In addition, the study noted that the "interpreted answers showed 37.2% fewer hedges and fillers than the original answers" (Hale 2002, p. 30).

The reduction in overall numbers of these speech elements in interpreted answers, however, does not tell the entire story, because court interpreters routinely insert their own hedges, hesitations and fillers into the answers as well (Hale 2002, p. 30). Thus, a witness answer such as, "*Un promedio de veintiuno*" ("An average of twenty-one") will become "Uh, probably an average of twenty-one" (Berk-Seligson 1990, p. 141). Likewise, a witness answer such as "No, that wasn't discussed" will be interpreted as "I don't think so, that wasn't discussed" (Hale 2004, p. 112). In each instance, the insertion of hedges, hesitations or fillers adds an element of uncertainty or indecision to an otherwise definite and clear answer. Insertions are especially prevalent with respect to hesitations, where studies have shown that no correlation exists between the hesitations present in the target language translation and those originally present in the speaker's statement (Berk-Seligson 1990, p. 140). In effect, the extra hesitations are the interpreter's own, the unintentional byproduct of an unconscious coping strategy meant to provide the interpreter with extra time to handle situations arising because of "their own performance deficiencies" (Berk-Seligson 1990, pp. 140–141; Hale 2002, pp. 40, 43).

The Implications of Hesitations, Hedges and Fillers

The preservation of hedges, hesitations and fillers in witness testimony is instrumental to the accurate assessment of that witness's credibility. A hedge, by definition, increases the vagueness, while decreasing the absoluteness, of a statement. As such, it creates the impression that the speaker is somehow uncertain as to the ultimate accuracy of his or her own statement (Berk-Seligson 1990, p. 181). Hesitations do the same (Mason 2008, p. 22; González et al. 1991, p. 481). Naturally, the certainty exhibited by witnesses is important to the persuasiveness of their testimony, as well as to their overall credibility (Hale 2002, p. 30). In addition, hedges, hesitations and fillers can even be interpreted by the fact-finder as evidence that the witness is attempting to conceal the full truth behind hedged statements (Berk-Seligson 1990, p. 181). In line with these assumptions, the Duke study previously referenced determined hedges, hesitations and fillers to be representative of "powerless" speech, the usage of which results in lower assessments of a witness's truthfulness, competence, trustworthiness and intelligence (Hale 2001, p. 70; see also González et al. 1991, p. 276). This finding is supported by studies specifically related to court interpretation, which have found that omitting the hedges and fillers from a translation makes the witness appear significantly more convincing, competent, intelligent, and trustworthy (Hale 2002, pp. 30, 43; Berk-Seligson 1990, p. 181). It should therefore not be surprising to note that the insertion of additional hedges, hesitations and fillers, where none existed previously, undermines the overall credibility of a witness as well (Hale 2002, p. 33).

If it is a given that hedges, hesitations and fillers substantially affect the credibility and persuasiveness of testimony, and that court interpreters engage in the widespread omission or insertion of these speech elements in interpreted testimony, then it must also be true that the power and probative value of the resulting testimony may not bear any actual resemblance to the believability of that testimony due to the interpreter's alterations. In other words, the fact-finder in an interpreted trial may be basing their evaluation of the evidence on speech mannerisms and words that originate with the interpreter rather than the witness. By potentially rendering an unbelievable witness believable (or vice-versa), the court interpreter may not be distorting the content of the evidence, but rather indirectly influencing and inadvertently manipulating the strength of that evidence. Such an outcome would be a substantial misrepresentation of testimony, and would again weaken the accused's ability to examine and confront witnesses, as well as the overall fairness of his trial.

Likewise, where the court interpreter's running translation of the proceedings for a foreign language accused randomly omits or adds hedges, hesitations and fillers to her account of the testimony, the accused may not be in a position to successfully contribute to the proceedings, since his assessment of the strength of the evidence produced at trial will likely vary substantially from the fact-finder's assessment, which will be based on the original testimony. That is to say, the court may have heard an unconvincing and hesitant witness, but the account given to the accused by the interpreter may present the evidence as more definite and certain. Under these circumstances, the accused's ability to actively participate will be limited, because the proceedings that he is following through the interpreter will be significantly different from the real proceedings. Such a disconnect calls into question whether the accused's right to adversarial proceedings, among others, will have been upheld.

3.3.9 Non-verbal Elements of Communication

The Concept of Non-verbal Communication

Language communication is not limited to the words used, but rather includes non-verbal elements as well (González et al. 1991, p. 480). Body language, such as facial expressions and gestures, must also be taken into account when determining the actual meaning of a speaker's words (de Jongh 1992, p. 58; González et al. 1991, p. 480). Likewise, paralinguistic elements like gasps, sighs, or the speed and volume of speech also further refine the speaker's message, as do emotional qualities in the speaker's voice, such as anger, doubt or surprise (González et al. 1991, p. 480). An example of how non-verbal communication can affect the ultimate meaning of a speaker's words can be seen in the phrase, "You look really nice today." When spoken in a sincere and level tone with normal body language, the sentence would appear to pay the intended listener an honest compliment. However, when the tone of voice turns angry and is accompanied by a shake of the head and a large sigh, the speaker's words might be taken to convey the exact opposite: that the listener has never looked worse and that the speaker is not pleased by this development. By way of contrast, the same sentence, delivered with a knowing smile and a laughing voice might be taken as mere sarcasm and a good-natured joke at the listener's expense. Three different sets of non-verbal elements applied to the same sentence result in three completely different messages. The court interpreter must be sensitive to these different non-verbal elements. Successfully conveying the speaker's message occasionally involves going beyond the speaker's words, not only in deciphering the speaker's statements, but also in translating them into the target language (de Jongh 1992, p. 58; González et al. 1991, p. 480).

The difficulty, of course, is determining the extent to which court interpreters should emulate or consciously communicate the speaker's non-verbal communication. This debate is far from settled in the interpreting community (González et al. 1991, p. 481). Some interpreters believe that all elements of the speaker's message must be retained and conveyed to the audience. Thus, where the speaker yells, so should the court interpreter; where the court interpreter hears fear in the speaker's voice, then she must attempt to sound afraid for the court as well (González et al. 1991, p. 481). On the opposite side of the debate are those interpreters who believe that only the words of the speaker are of consequence, and that interpreters must refrain from including any non-verbal elements (González et al. 1991, p. 481). To a limited extent, the debate in this area mimics the arguments surrounding the pragmatic and word-for-word verbatim standards. A court interpreter who conveys all of the non-verbal elements of a speaker's communication is inserting her understanding of what each of these elements means into the translation (González et al. 1991, p. 483). As with the pragmatic standard, this can be seen as usurping the fact-finder's role of interpreting the meaning of the testimony. On the other hand, to exclude non-verbal elements that significantly alter the content of the message, such as presenting sarcasm as sincere, is to render an incomplete and misleading translation. In this respect, both sides of the debate have merit; thus the general standard for court interpreters is to use their judgment and conserve as much of the original message as possible while exercising extreme caution (González et al. 1991, pp. 481, 483).

The Implications of Non-verbal Communication

The implications of non-verbal communication on the right to a fair trial depend, in large part, on which side of the debate the specific court interpreter embraces. As no significant studies have been undertaken on the impact of the various methods of interpretation in this area, there is as yet no resolution or common practice. Every court interpreter handles non-verbal communication differently.

That no set practice exists does not, however, mean that the non-verbal elements have no actual impact on the proceedings. Each side of the debate brings its own advantages and disadvantages to the table. For instance, when a court interpreter conserves every element of the speaker's message (and thus shouts, yells, and does what is necessary to convey the non-verbal elements), she provides for the court a hyper-detailed view of the speaker's statement. Yet, in so doing, she makes a variety of personal assumptions as to what each of those non-verbal elements actually means, and then communicates these assumptions to the fact-finder fully formed. If the court interpreter believes that the speaker's tone of voice and body language indicate that he is lying, then the translation will carry elements that make clear it is a lie. This effectively negates the fact-finder's role in determining the credibility of witnesses and the persuasiveness of evidence (González et al. 1991, p. 483).

On the other hand, eliminating all non-verbal elements also brings with it significant disadvantages. As previously noted, presenting sarcastic words as earnest is misleading to the fact-finder. Likewise, as discussed earlier, failing to preserve hesitations and non-verbal politeness markers can similarly misrepresent a witness's testimony. Gestures, too, provide an area where some overt conservation of the non-verbal meaning may be necessary, because not all gestures are interpreted the same in every culture (de Jongh 1991, p. 290). For example, some Spanish speakers (especially those with a Latin American background) may look at the floor when asked a question out of respect for the court; yet in an American courtroom, this non-verbal act might well be understood by the fact-finder as an indication of guilt (de Jongh 1992, pp. 62–63). Allowing the fact-finder to erroneously interpret such a gesture would be to consciously permit the distortion of evidence; however, explaining this gesture carries with it serious risks as well. One possible solution that is often put forward is to allow the attorneys or the judge to explain the significance of any relevant non-verbal elements (González et al. 1991, p. 483). This option, too, has significant drawbacks, since it assumes that the courtroom officials are competent to recognize, understand, and explain the meaning of non-verbal elements intrinsic to a culture they may only rarely have encountered.

From the standpoint of court interpreters, the general standard (if one can even be said to exist) treads the middle ground: the interpreter's version should exercise extreme caution when dealing with non-verbal elements, but should generally retain anything necessary to convey the underlying meaning of the speaker's statement (González et al. 1991, pp. 481, 483). Thus, the tone of a speaker's voice should be emulated, but only in a "conservative, unexaggerated manner" (González et al. 1991, p. 481). Even this rather moderate and cautious standard has its problems, mainly that it places an extra burden on court interpreters to exercise their personal judgment, yet provides them with very little guidance in how to do so appropriately. This extra task, placed on top of an already highly-taxing interpreting process that stretches the mental resources of even the most competent court interpreters, would appear to invite the type of overloading of cognitive resources that leads to interpreter error. In addition, as will be seen in Chap. 6, many individuals used as court interpreters are untrained and unqualified, and are thus not necessarily well-placed to exercise such significant discretion (Stern 2011, p. 339).

The end result is that, regardless of which approach is taken, there exists the strong potential that an accused's right to a fair trial will be impacted. Allowing an interpreter to substitute her judgment in place of the fact-finder when it comes to matters of evidence substantially undermines the overall fairness of the proceedings while also damaging their adversarial nature. Furthermore, it limits the accused's ability to examine and confront witnesses, since the practice of questioning witnesses will invariably be distorted by the interpreter's short-circuiting of that process. Ignoring non-verbal elements also weakens these same rights, because it significantly distorts the presentation of evidence and occasionally strips witness testimony of its actual meaning. The proposed middle ground, which allows interpreter discretion, would appear to be the best solution. Yet, it too has the potential for substantial impact on the presentation of evidence, since it relies heavily on court interpreters acting conservatively and making the right decision, but provides no real standard to guide these decisions. Nor, in any particular case, would the courtroom participants be aware whether the non-verbal elements of communication that they see (such as a sigh, or a hesitation) originated with the witness or with the interpreter. Thus, irrespective of which side of the debate eventually prevails, the existence of non-verbal communication will continue to undermine and complicate the efforts made to preserve the right to a fair trial where a foreign language participant is involved.

3.3.10 Conclusion as to Style Problems

The content of an individual's speech or a witness's testimony is of obvious importance to a criminal proceeding. In an adversarial proceeding, such statements may form a valuable part of the evidence. However, the probative value awarded to that evidence is based not only on its content, but also on the fact-finder's estimation and assessment of the individual speaking. The truthfulness, trustworthiness, intelligence, and general competence of the speaker all play a part in the persuasiveness of the speaker's evidence. In this respect, the witness's demeanor and the style in which they speak are of central importance to the fact-finder's eventual perception of the speaker. Court interpreters, unfortunately, pay little attention to the speech style of a witness, primarily because the individual elements of style (hedges, fillers, politeness, discourse markers, register, and others) are not considered to be of significance (Stern 2011, p. 338; Berk-Seligson 1990, p. 143). However, research has shown that the inclusion or exclusion of these style elements can significantly alter the persuasiveness of a witness's testimony. As such, the court interpreter has the ability to substantially influence how a witness or speaker is perceived by the fact-finder (Berk-Seligson 1990, p. 145). That court interpreters disregard these extremely significant aspects of courtroom speech when interpreting is highly problematic for fair trial protections. The unwarranted insertion or omission of these elements corrupts testimonial evidence, distorts witness credibility, and calls into question whether an accused under such circumstances truly has full access to a fair trial.

3.4 Conclusion

As previously mentioned, the style in which something is asserted is nearly as important as the content of the assertion itself (Stern 2011, pp. 337–338; González et al. 1991, p. 16). Unfortunately, the inherent difficulties related to language, combined with the involvement of court interpreters, creates the potential for alterations in both of these aspects. The content of a speaker's statement may be inadvertently changed due to the court interpreter's lack of specialized vocabulary or inability to find a suitable target language equivalent. Likewise, the seemingly insignificant elements of a speaker's style may be omitted or altered by the court interpreter, thus producing a translation that fails to adequately convey the true levels of competence, intelligence or trustworthiness of the witness. The fundamental complexities of language create a series of problems for court interpreters, both with relation to content and style, that can frequently lead to inaccurate or misleading translations.

These unintentional modifications of the courtroom proceedings and the evidence produced therein, however, are but one portion of a larger picture. Whether choosing a standard of accuracy, deliberately stepping outside of their assigned role, or utilizing various coping strategies, court interpreters also transform trial proceedings by conscious design. In isolation, these actions (both intentional and unintentional) may appear insignificant with respect to the general accuracy of the translation or the overall fairness of the trial. Yet, considering the relative frequency of their occurrence, it is doubtful that such errors are isolated in nature. Rather, they appear pervasive and their impact likely accumulates throughout the trial. In this manner, the interpreter errors discussed in this Chapter exert a substantial influence on the integrity of interpreted criminal proceedings.

Bibliography

Astiz, C. A. (1986). But They Don't Speak the Language: Achieving Quality Control of Translation in Criminal Courts. *The Judge's Journal, 25*, 32–35, 56.

Berk-Seligson, S. (1988). The Importance of Linguistics in Court Interpreting. *La Raza Law Journal, 2*, 14–48.

Berk-Seligson, S. (1990). *The Bilingual Courtroom: Court Interpreters in the Judicial Process*. Chicago: University of Chicago Press.

Berk-Seligson, S. (2002). The Impact of Politeness in Witness Testimony: The Influence of the Court Interpreter. In F. Pöchhacker & M. Shlesinger (Eds.), *The Interpreting Studies Reader* (pp. 279–292). London: Routledge.

Chabasse, C., & Dingfelder Stone, M. (2015). Capacity Management in Interpretation: Efforts, Directionality, and Language Pair Considerations. In D. Andres & M. Behrs (Eds.), *To Know How to Suggest…: Approaches to Teaching Conference Interpreting* (pp. 75–102). Berlin: Frank & Timmer.

Corsellis, A., & Fernández, L. F. (2001). Code of Ethics and Conduct and Guidelines to Good Practice. In E. Hertog (Ed.), *Aequitas: Access to Justice Across Language and Culture in the E.U.* (pp. 77–87). Antwerpen: Lessius Hogeschool.

Davis, L. W., & Hewitt, W. E. (1994). Lessons in Administering Justice: What Judges Need to Know About the Requirements, Role, and Professional Responsibilities of the Court Interpreter. *Harvard Latino Law Review, 1*, 121–176.

de Jongh, E. (1991). Foreign Language Interpreters in the Courtroom: The Case for Linguistic and Cultural Proficiency. *Modern Language Journal, 75*, 285–295.

de Jongh, E. (1992). *An Introduction to Court Interpreting: Theory & Practice*. Lanham: University Press of America.

de Jongh, E. (2008, July/August). Linguistic Presence v. Linguistic Absence. *Florida Bar Journal, 82*, 20–32.

Dietl, C.-E., & Lorenz, E. (2005). *Wörterbuch für Recht, Wirtschaft und Politik – Teil II Deutsch-Englisch*. München: Beck.

Fowler, Y. (1995). The Courtroom Interpreter: Paragon and Intruder? In S. E. Carr, R. P. Roberts, A. Dufour, & D. Steyn (Eds.), *The Critical Link: Interpreters in the Community* (pp. 191–200). Amsterdam: John Benjamins.

Gile, D. (2009). *Basic Concepts and Models for Interpreter and Translator Training* (Rev. ed.). Amsterdam: John Benjamins.

González, R., Vásquez, V. F., & Mikkelson, H. (1991). *Fundamentals of Court Interpretation: Theory, Policy, and Practice*. Durham: Carolina Academic Press.

Griffin, P. W., & Cole, S. J. (2007). *White Paper on Court Interpretation: Fundamental to Access to Justice*. Conference of State Court Administrators [online]. Available at: http://cosca.ncsc.org/~/media/Microsites/Files/COSCA/Policy%20Papers/CourtInterpretation-FundamentalToAccessToJustice.ashx. Accessed 21 Nov 2017.

Hale, S. (2001). The Complexities of the Bilingual Courtroom. *Law Society Journal, 39*, 68–72.

Hale, S. (2002). How Faithfully Do Court Interpreters Render the Style of Non-English Speaking Witnesses' Testimonies? A Data-Based Study of Spanish-English Bilingual Proceedings. *Discourse Studies, 4*(1), 25–47.

Hale, S. (2004). *The Discourse of Court Interpreting: Discourse Practices of the Law, the Witness and the Interpreter*. Amsterdam: John Benjamins.

Hale, S. (2007). Challenges of Court Interpreting: Intricacies, Responsibilities and Ramifications. *Alternative Law Journal, 32*, 198–202.

Hale, S., & Gibbons, J. (1999). Varying Realities: Patterned Changes in the Interpreter's Representation of Courtroom and External Realities. *Applied Linguistics, 20*(2), 203–220.

Hayes, A., & Hale, S. (2010). Appeals on Incompetent Interpreting. *Journal of Judicial Administration, 20*(2), 119–130.

Heller, D. J. (1994–95). The Language Bias in the Criminal Justice System. *Criminal Law Quarterly, 37*, 344–383.

Hovland, D. L. (1992–93). Errors in Interpretation: Why Plain Error Is Not Plain. *Law and Inequality, 11*, 473–503.

Ibrahim, Z. (2007). The Interpreter as Advocate: Malaysian Court Interpreting as a Case in Point. In C. Wadensjö, B. Englund Dimitrova, & A.-L. Nilsson (Eds.), *The Critical Link 4: Professionalisation of Interpreting in the Community* (pp. 205–213). Amsterdam: John Benjamins.

Interpreters in the Courtroom. (2008). [Radio Program] ABC Radio National: Damien Carrick.

Jacobsen, B. (2004). Pragmatic Meaning in Court Interpreting: An Empirical Study of Additions in Consecutively Interpreted Question-Answer Dialogues. *Hermes – Journal of Language and Communication in Business, 32*, 237–249.

Jacobsen, B. (2008). Court Interpreting and Face: An Analysis of a Court Interpreter's Strategies for Conveying Threats to Own Face. In D. Russell & S. Hale (Eds.), *Interpreting in Legal Settings* (pp. 51–71). Washington, DC: Gallaudet University Press.

Kadric, M. (2000). Interpreting in the Austrian Courtroom. In R. P. Roberts, S. E. Carr, D. Abraham, & A. Dufour (Eds.), *The Critical Link 2: Interpreters in the Community* (pp. 153–164). Amsterdam: John Benjamins.

Kaufman, D. (2007). What Did You Say? The Perils of Clients Who Don't Speak English. *GPSolo, 24*, 22–25, 53.

Koo, A. (2009). Truth Through Court Interpreters. *International Journal of Evidence & Proof, 13*, 212–224.

LaVigne, M., & Vernon, M. (2003). An Interpreter Isn't Enough: Deafness, Language, and Due Process. *Wisconsin Law Review, 2003*, 843–936.

Lindie, B. (1993). Inadequate Interpreting Services in Courts and the Rules of Admissibility of Testimony on Extrajudicial Interpretations. *University of Miami Law Review, 48*, 399–433.

Lister, R., & Veth, K. (2002). *Taschenwörterbuch Recht: Deutsch-Englisch*. München: Hueber Verlag.

Loftus, E. (1996). *Eyewitness Testimony* (2nd ed.). Cambridge: Harvard University Press.

Mason, M. (2008). *Courtroom Interpreting*. Lanham: University Press of America.

Matu, P., Odhiambo, K., Adams, Y., & Ongarora, D. (2012). The Court Interpreters' Role Perception: The Case of English-Dholuo Interpreters in Subordinate Courts in Nyanza Province, Kenya. *Greener Journal of Social Sciences, 2*(4), 121–126.

McCaffrey, A. (2000). Don't Get Lost in Translation: Teaching Law Students to Work with Language Interpreters. *Clinical Law Review, 6*, 347–398.

Messier, F. (1999). Alien Defendants in Criminal Proceedings: Justice Shrugs. *American Criminal Law Review, 36*, 1395–1419.

Mikkelson, H. (1995). On the Horns of a Dilemma: Accuracy vs. Brevity in the Use of Legal Terms by Court Interpreters. In M. Morris (Ed.), *Translation and the Law* (pp. 201–218). Amsterdam: John Benjamins.

Mikkelson, H. (1998). Towards a Redefinition of the Role of the Court Interpreter. *Interpreting, 3*(1), 21 [online]. Available at: https://works.bepress.com/holly_mikkelson/17/. Accessed 21 Nov 2017.

Mikkelson, H. (2000). *Introduction to Court Interpreting*. Manchester: St. Jerome Publishing.

Mikkelson, H. (2008). Evolving Views of the Court Interpreter's Role: Between Scylla & Charybdis. In C. Valero-Garcés & A. Martin (Eds.), *Crossing Borders in Community Interpreting: Definitions and Dilemmas* (pp. 81–98). Amsterdam: John Benjamins.

Moeketsi, R. H. (1999a). *Discourse in a Multilingual and Multicultural Courtroom: A Court Interpreter's Guide*. Pretoria: van Schaik.

Moeketsi, R. H. (1999b). Redefining the Role of the South African Court Interpreter. *Proteus, 8*(3–4), 12–15.

Mojuta, K., & Arua, A. (2016). The Lexical Problems of Court Interpreters in a Botswana High Court. *Botswana Note and Records, 48*, 193–204.

Morris, R. (1995). The Moral Dilemmas of Court Interpreting. *The Translator, 1*(1), 25–46.

Namakula, C. (2014). *Language and the Right to a Fair Hearing in International Criminal Trials*. Heidelberg: Springer.

Nartowska, K. (2015). The Role of the Court Interpreter: A Powerless or Powerful Participant in Criminal Proceedings? *The Interpreters' Newsletter, 20*, 9–32.

Noack, A. (2007). *Business Essentials: Fachwörterbuch Deutsch-Englisch/Englisch-Deutsch*. München: Oldenbourg.

Non-English Speaking Clients. (2005–06). *Thomas M. Cooley Journal of Practical and Clinical Law: Special Edition, 8*, 235–269.

Nowak, M. (2005). *U.N. Covenant on Civil and Political Rights: CCPR Commentary* (2nd ed.). Kehl: Engel.
Romain, A. (1983). *Wörterbuch der Rechts- und Wirtschaftssprache: Teil II – Deutsch-Englisch*. München: Beck.
Schweda-Nicholson, N. (1989). *Ad Hoc* Court Interpreters in the United States: Equality, Inequality, Quality. *Meta, 34*(4), 711–723.
Stern, L. (2001). At the Junction of Cultures: Interpreting at the International Criminal Tribunal for the Former Yugoslavia in the Light of Other International Interpreting Practices. *The Judicial Review, 5*(3), 255–274.
Stern, L. (2004). Interpreting Legal Language at the International Criminal Tribunal for the Former Yugoslavia: Overcoming the Lack of Lexical Equivalents. *Journal of Specialised Translation, 2*, 63–75.
Stern, L. (2011). Courtroom Interpreting. In K. Malmkjær & K. Windle (Eds.), *The Oxford Handbook of Translation Studies* (pp. 325–342). Oxford: Oxford University Press.
Steytler, N. C. (1993). Implementing Language Rights in Court: The Role of the Court Interpreter. *South African Journal on Human Rights, 9*, 205–222.
Trechsel, S. (2005). *Human Rights in Criminal Proceedings*. Oxford: Oxford University Press.
Vandall, F. J. (2011). *A History of Civil Litigation: Political and Economic Perspectives*. Oxford: Oxford University Press.
Viljoen, F. (1992). Look Who's Talking, in the Courtroom, Too! *South African Law Journal, 109*, 64–76.
von Beseler, D., & Jacobs-Wüsterfeld, B. (1991). *Law Dictionary: Technical Dictionary of the Anglo-American Legal Terminology Including Commercial and Political Terms – German-English*. Berlin: Walter du Gruyter.

List of Cases

Clarke v. Edinburgh and District Tramways Company Limited. (1919). Court of Sessions Cases (Scotland), House of Lords 35.

6

Systemic Issues

1 Introduction

The previous Chapter set out a wide-ranging list of specific issues and problems that can develop with respect to court interpreters. Some of these have their origins in the conscious decisions taken by court interpreters, while others arise often inadvertently from the inherent difficulties associated with language and the interpreting process. However, regardless of their specific origin, each of these issues ultimately evolves from a variety of systemic practices and problems that affect the work of court interpreters. In this Chapter, these obstacles will be examined.

2 Fatigue

2.1 Overview

The average simultaneous interpreter will process between 120 and 180 words per minute, and consecutive interpretation is considered by many interpreters to be even more difficult (de Jongh 1991, p. 290; González

J. H. Dingfelder Stone, *Court Interpreters and Fair Trials*,
https://doi.org/10.1007/978-3-319-75355-3_6

et al. 1991, p. 379). The concentration required to accurately perform both is extreme, and working interpreters operate at the edge of their cognitive abilities with little or no margin for error (Gile 2009, p. 182; González et al. 1991, p. 360). The end result is that court interpreters become fatigued very quickly, which can negatively impact their ability to concentrate and accurately interpret. Studies have shown that the quality of performance steadily decreases, and the rate of errors in the interpretation progressively increases, as the interpreter approaches 30 minutes of work (Mason 2008, p. 8; Vidal 1997, p. 1). After 30 minutes "on task", a considerable increase in the number of errors occurs, representing a "significant decline in output" (Mason 2008, p. 9). Working past 60 minutes raises the error rate even higher (Mason 2008, p. 8). Considering Gile's theory on cognitive resources, these results make complete sense: as interpreters fatigue, they suffer a decline in processing capacity, which reduces their ability to juggle the many mental processes necessary to accurately interpret. For this reason, many professional interpreting associations and interpreting scholars recommend that interpreters work no longer than 30–45 minute stretches without a break (Hale 2001, pp. 71–72; Mikkelson 2000, p. 61; Edwards 1995, p. 74; de Jongh 1992, p. 52; González et al. 1991, p. 510). Indeed, 30 minutes is considered the standard amount for United Nations interpreters (Karton 2008, p. 30; Grabau and Gibbons 1996, p. 296).

Conference interpreters can realize this ideal because they generally work in pairs, and thus may alternate as required by fatigue (Mason 2008, p. 8; González et al. 1991, p. 510). This is not a luxury normally afforded to courtroom interpreters (Stern 2011, p. 332; Mason 2008, p. 8; González et al. 1991, p. 176). In fact, even though courtroom interpreting is considered to be "more demanding and stressful" (Vidal 1997, pp. 2–3; see also Laster and Taylor 1994, p. 21) than conference interpreting, courtroom interpreters are commonly required to work several hours without the benefit of a break (Stern 2011, p. 332; Mason 2008, p. 8). Nor is a lunch break even assured to court interpreters, as attorneys will occasionally enlist the interpreter for lunchtime interviews or translations (González et al. 1991, p. 177). In one extreme situation, an Arabic interpreter in an American drug case interpreted for 12 uninterrupted hours (Craney 1989–1990, p. 42).

2.2 Implications of Fatigue

While it may seem normal, or even heroic, for other professionals to work long hours without a break or work through lunch, such a practice can be disastrous for the court interpreter. Any external factors, such as fatigue, that reduce the mental resources available to a court interpreter will invariably increase the number of errors that she produces. Just as a tired soccer player is less likely to be accurate in their passing, a fatigued court interpreter is less likely to make an accurate translation. In this manner, fatigue can contribute substantially to, or simply create, the difficulties discussed in the previous Chapter. For example, where the court interpreter is unable to find a suitable linguistic equivalent in the target language, it may be because one does not exist, or it may be that the court interpreter is too fatigued to remember the one perfect equivalent that does. Likewise, fatigue may limit an interpreter's short-term memory, and thus necessitate the interruption of a long-winded speaker.

The longer a court interpreter interprets without a break, the more fatigue she will feel, and the more errors she will make. This is true for both experienced and inexperienced interpreters alike, though trained interpreters with courtroom experience will likely handle the fatigue better (Mikkelson 2000, p. 74). Yet, the standard practice in courtrooms is to stretch the work periods of court interpreters well beyond the recommended time limit, thereby inviting the very errors that undermine the fairness of the trial. Moreover, this practice, and the attendant stress and exhaustion that accompanies it, may deter otherwise qualified interpreters from accepting courtroom work. This too can have significant consequences on the quality of interpretation.

3 Lack of Preparation Time and Documents

3.1 Overview

The language and concepts used in a courtroom are especially complex and problematic for court interpreters (see Chap. 5). Many of the linguistic complexities, such as the peculiarities of legal language, exist in every court case, and are therefore known quantities for which an interpreter can and should prepare. However, that is not always the case. The specialized vocabulary of a specific expert witness or subject matter, or the particular dialect of a certain witness, can vary from case to case. Just as an attorney prepares beforehand for every proceeding, so should a court interpreter (Malmberg 2006, p. 21; Grabau 1996, pp. 9–10; Davis and Hewitt 1994, p. 133; González et al. 1991, p. 177). Having a detailed grasp on the facts and novel language involved in a case allows the interpreter to focus less on these difficulties while interpreting, and more on other areas of her performance (Gile 2009, p. 175). This is also true with respect to any documents that need to be sight translated: being able to preview the document can lead to a better result (González et al. 1991, p. 179).

The provision of relevant materials, such as witness statements, to the interpreter in advance of a court proceeding is standard practice at the international level (Elias-Bursać 2015, p. 74; Stern 2011, p. 332). Indeed, some scholars have argued that the ability to prepare in advance is one of the keys to the successful interpretation of an international proceeding (Stern 2001, pp. 20–21). Unfortunately, attorneys and judges at the domestic level rarely provide court interpreters with preparation materials, or even a summary of the subject matter, in advance (Stern 2011, p. 332; *Interpreters in the Courtroom* 2008 [Foley Statement]; Miguélez 1999, p. 2; Moeketsi 1999a, pp. 143–144; González et al. 1991, pp. 176–177; Craney 1989–1990, p. 27). Thus, a court interpreter may be called upon to handle an expert witness on the science of DNA, but not be given enough warning to learn the specialized vocabulary the witness will employ. Likewise, documents that will need sight translation (such as the formal charge) are rarely made available to interpreters ahead of time (Moeketsi 1999b, p. 5).

3.2 Implications of the Lack of Preparation Time and Documents

Stated simply, the inability to prepare beforehand for the particular complexities of a criminal proceeding leads to a reduced ability to interpret accurately (Hale 2007, p. 201). An interpreter who has been able to arm herself in advance with a thorough knowledge of the subject matter and the specifics of the case is more likely to quickly recognize and understand the meaning of what would otherwise be difficult vocabulary and concepts (de Jongh 1992, p. 48). Reducing the mental resources that are necessary to handle these details frees up cognitive capacity to focus on other areas, which results in improved overall performance (Gile 2009, p. 175; Edwards 1995, p. 89). An unprepared interpreter simply may not know the words or concepts used during the trial, leading to an avoidable mistake such as translating "a leading question" as the "the main question" (Craney 1989–1990, p. 27), or confusing a "mule" in a drug case with a normal pack animal. Prior preparation with respect to the sight translation of a document can also greatly reduce the cognitive capacity required for a suitable translation (Gile 2009, p. 181).

Yet, courts only rarely provide the materials that would allow for improved interpreter performance. In fact, in some instances, courts actively work to ensure that the court interpreter has no prior knowledge of the case or its subject matter. In Australia, for instance, "it is considered desirable, if not compulsory, to use a court interpreter who has not been 'contaminated' by any prior information about the case" (Stern 2001, p. 20). The concern in this area is that an interpreter with foreknowledge of the case may become biased in some manner (Stern 2001, p. 20, 2011, p. 332; *Interpreters in the Courtroom* 2008 [Foley Statement]). Moreover, there is always the risk that an interpreter who has become aware of the facts of the case as presented in witness statements and police reports will have difficulty impartially interpreting the actual testimony of these witnesses in court (González et al. 1991, pp. 506–507). In other words, an interpreter with advanced knowledge of the case is more likely to interpret what she believes the witness meant to say (as evidenced by their prior statement) than what the witness actually did say. As such, while court interpreters assume the positive value of being prepared, not every jurisdiction is in accord.

However, the risk of bias, weighed against the near certainty of errors that will arise where preparation is limited, would appear to be the smaller of the two threats to interpreting accuracy. A lack of preparation can exacerbate many of the issues referred to in Chap. 5. For instance, the inability to find a suitable equivalent for a legal term or to understand the particular terminology native to a specific dialect is both symptoms of inadequate preparation. Likewise, preparation can alleviate the systematic demands on an interpreter's mental resources, thus producing fewer random mistakes and reducing the necessity of employing inappropriate coping strategies. That court officials fail (or refuse) to assist court interpreters in their pre-trial preparations constitutes a weakness in the current system, one that contributes to inaccurate interpretations.

4 Poor Working Conditions

4.1 Overview

The lack of preparation materials is not the only way in which court officials handicap interpreters. There also often exists a lack of understanding on the part of courts as to how to properly accommodate court interpreters so that they can most effectively and accurately interpret (Stern 2011, pp. 332, 341; Helmerichs 2005, pp. 187–188). The conditions under which court interpreters work can have a significant impact on their ability to perform. For instance, an interpreter cannot interpret what she cannot hear: the more the interpreter must strain to hear the speaker, the more difficult it will be to maintain her accuracy (Morris 2008, p. 21; Vidal 1997, p. 3; González et al. 1991, p. 175). Volume level is important, but the concept goes far beyond that. The ability of the court interpreter to accurately interpret will be negatively impacted where someone does not speak clearly or where two individuals talk at the same time (Hale 2004, p. 201; Vidal 1997, p. 3; Grabau 1996, p. 10; Davis and Hewitt 1994, p. 135; González et al. 1991, p. 509). Likewise, the speed at which an individual speaks is also very important: courtroom speech has been measured at up to 220 words per minute, which is a rate of speed impossible for court interpreters to handle (Morris 2008, p. 21; González et al. 1991, p. 176). In addition, background noise from the audience or other court participants can both reduce the interpreter's ability to hear what has been said and also interrupt her concentration (Benmaman 1995, p. 183; González et al. 1991, p. 386). The placement of the court interpreter within the courtroom can either alleviate, or exacerbate many of these problems (Malmberg 2006, p. 21; González et al. 1991, p. 511).

Furthermore, the types of speech and vocabulary employed by the participants can be immensely impactful. As previously discussed, the legal language used in a courtroom can be very problematic for court interpreters; yet attorneys and judges rarely make an effort to simplify or curb their technical language to accommodate the necessity of interpretation (González et al. 1991, p. 257). Similarly, even though complex questions, double negatives and culture-bound references inevitably cause interpreters problems, little attempt is made by courtroom participants to minimize the usage of these constructions (Edwards 1995, pp. 93–94; González et al. 1991, p. 180). Even something as straightforward as using names instead of pronouns can make a difference for court interpreters (Edwards 1995, p. 93).

The facilities made available to the court interpreter are also of some importance. Court interpreters require water, since they invariably speak more than anyone else in the courtroom (*Interpreters in the Courtroom* 2008 [Hale Statement]; Hale 2007, p. 202; Davis and Hewitt 1994, p. 136). Likewise, seemingly minor amenities, such as a place to sit or a quiet room where the interpreter can work or rest during times when she need not interpret, can go a long way towards preventing fatigue (*Interpreters in the Courtroom* 2008 [Hale Statement]; González et al. 1991, p. 178). Unfortunately, these facilities are not always available for court interpreters. The courtroom is set up for the normal court participants, not necessarily for interpreters (Stern 2011, p. 332; Mason 2008, p. 53). Water and a work space many not be immediately offered (Laster and Taylor 1994, p. 21). More importantly, the positioning of the interpreter within the courtroom may not be of her choosing, making it difficult for the interpreter to hear everyone and for everyone to hear the interpreter.

Courtroom participants also occasionally lack an understanding for the ethics and role of the court interpreter (Stern 2011, p. 333; Mikkelson 2000, pp. 55–56; Edwards 1995, p. 68). For example, an attorney may ask the interpreter during a break whether she personally believes the foreign language witness was telling the truth, an assessment the interpreter is obligated not to convey (Stern 2011, p. 335; Corsellis and Fernández 2001, p. 79; Rasmussen and Martinsen 2001, p. 96; Davis and Hewitt 1994, p. 140). Or the judge may order the interpreter to explain certain legal documents to a foreign language defendant, which is beyond the scope of the interpreter's expertise (Davis and Hewitt 1994, pp. 140–141). In each instance, the courtroom participant is unknowingly asking or requiring the court interpreter to violate her ethical standards, which can both compromise the interpreter's appearance of impartiality and require her to perform a task for which she has no actual training.

It must be understood, however, that court interpreters also have some responsibility to improve the conditions under which they work, since they know what they need to perform adequately, and the court personnel likely do not (González et al. 1991, p. 509). This, of course, assumes that the court interpreter has enough experience to understand the necessities of her craft, and has enough confidence in her professional abilities to request the needed changes. Given the relative inexperience and lack of training of many court interpreters, this is not always the case. Nor are such suggestions always welcomed by the court; they may be seen as unnecessary or even inappropriate (Cardenas 2001, p. 24). In one somewhat famous case, the judge informed a court interpreter who had complained about her inability to hear that "You don't have to hear, just interpret!" (Cardenas 2001, p. 24). As such, court interpreters regularly find themselves doing "the best they can under appalling working conditions" (Hale 2007, p. 202; see also Stern 2001, pp. 331–333).

4.2 Implications of Poor Working Conditions

The implications of inadequate working conditions can be fairly serious. Since the task of interpreting already strains the mental resources of those involved, peak environmental conditions are a necessity to maximizing their performance (González et al. 1991, p. 386). Where an interpreter has difficulty clearly hearing the words spoken, she will inevitably make more mistakes, as she must deduce from the surrounding words what was actually said. This can lead to omissions or conjecture. In addition, an inability to clearly hear the speaker forces the interpreter to concentrate more on the listening aspect of the interpreting process, thereby drawing extra cognitive capacity away from the other tasks that must be fulfilled. As such, the interpreter's capacity to focus on finding a suitable equivalent, or remembering the full extent of the discourse markers used by the speaker may be negatively impacted, thus spawning more distortions or inaccuracies. Likewise, the less accommodating attorneys and judges are with respect to their linguistic choices, the more likely it is errors will occur in the interpretation.

External stimuli, such as background noise or unexpected movements, or a lack of comfort due to poor seating or a dry throat, can interrupt the concentration of the interpreter and obstruct her short-term memory (González et al. 1991, p. 386). A reduced memory may require the interpreter to interrupt the speaker, thereby causing distortions in the court proceeding. Likewise, it may lead to further omissions or a systematic shortening of the speaker's statements. Other coping strategies employed to overcome the reduced memory capacity also can have an impact on error production. Requiring an interpreter to concentrate more on one particular aspect of the interpreting process, or to perform an activity outside of her specific expertise or ethical role, draws valuable cognitive capacity from the other elements of that process, thereby reducing the efficiency and accuracy of those related elements. This, it would seem, is a rather steep price to pay for relatively fixable problems.

5 The Overall Level of Court Interpreters

5.1 Introduction

Not all court interpreters are equally skilled and experienced (Stern 2011, pp. 326–327; LaVigne and Vernon 2003, p. 869). Thus, there exist degrees of competence among the individuals who interpret in courtroom proceedings. Given the multitude of interpreting issues that can surface in a court, the skill set for a competent court interpreter must be wide-ranging indeed. As a basic starting point, the individual must have superior command of both languages that will be used (Stern 2011, p. 334; Laster and Taylor 1994, p. 26; González et al. 1991, p. 19). This includes not only perfect understanding of the grammar and everyday vocabulary, but also a deep knowledge of specialized vocabularies covering a variety of different subject matters that may arise in court (Laster and Taylor 1994, p. 26; González et al. 1991, p. 19). Her familiarity with the languages must also allow the interpreter to comfortably shift between different registers and speech styles as the necessity arises, as well as understand what these particular styles of speech represent in the target and source languages (Stern 2011, p. 330; Laster and Taylor 1994, p. 26; González et al. 1991, p. 19). The individual also must have an in-depth understanding of both cultures (that of the court's location and the foreign language participant), so as to fully comprehend the likely impact her interpreted words will have on the fact-finder or the participant (Laster and Taylor 1994, p. 26; de Jongh 1991, p. 286; González et al. 1991, p. 19). Likewise, she must be fully acquainted with the legal cultures and procedures of both jurisdictions, otherwise her interpretation of legal terms of art will potentially be misleading (Stern 2011, pp. 326, 334; de Jongh 1991, p. 286).

In addition to these basic linguistic and cultural requirements, the individual must be trained and skilled in the art of interpreting. Being bilingual and bicultural no more makes an individual an interpreter than speaking a single language qualifies one as a professional speaker or having two hands makes one a concert pianist: the individual must be taught how to use the raw tools they possess and they must refine the acquired skills through repetition and practice (Stern 2011, p. 339; Navarro 2006, p. 2; Cardenas 2001, p. 26). This includes training in simultaneous and consecutive interpretation, sight translation, as well as any and all of the associated interpreting skills necessary to perform these tasks efficiently (such as notetaking). Furthermore, the individual must be instructed on the proper role of the courtroom interpreter and the ethical canons under which she should operate (Stern 2011, p. 334; González et al. 1991, p. 19). Finally, a certain minimum level of intelligence and adaptability is required, as well as excellent short-term memory skills (Griffin and Cole 2007, p. 6; Laster and Taylor 1994, p. 26). As should be highly evident from the above list of necessary characteristics, individuals capable of competently interpreting in courtrooms are exceptionally rare.

5.2 The Reality of the Interpreting Market

That so very few people possess the required skill set of a court interpreter creates a shortage of supply. This is especially true concerning rare languages, and in rural areas (Lore 2010, p. 2; Mikkelson 1998, p. 6; Craney 1989–1990, p. 22). The lack of capable individuals is further exacerbated by the fact that, as with many professions, court interpreters operate within the context of a free market (eds. Hertog and van Gucht 2008, p. 195; González et al. 1991, p. 23). This means that courts must compete on the open market for the services of these highly-qualified individuals, nearly all of whom have a variety of other career options at their disposal. Their skill sets allow them to operate as conference interpreters, legal secretaries, or even translators in many instances. Since being a court interpreter often entails performing in poor working conditions under high stress while generally earning a comparatively low level of pay, there is little to recommend the profession (Laster and Taylor 1994, p. 22; González et al. 1991, p. 23). Additionally, many court interpretation jobs are short-term, so court interpreters tend to be freelance, which offers minimal job security and fairly unsteady employment (Svongoro 2016, p. 110; eds. Hertog and van Gucht 2008, p. 195; Heller 1994–1995, p. 380; Laster and Taylor 1994, p. 20). There is also the possibility that successful court interpreters, once they become comfortable with the legal process, transition into law school to become attorneys (which increases their earning power and professional status) (Moeketsi 1999b, p. 4). The end result is that it is difficult if not impossible to retain competent court interpreters (Griffin and Cole 2007, p. 6; Laster and Taylor 1994, p. 22), because the very skills that make them competent also make them highly desirable as private-sector interpreters on the open market (see for example Ibrahim and Bell 2003, p. 216; *Court Interpreter's Job Is No Easy Task* 2002; De Mas 2001, p. 5; Laster and Taylor 1994, p. 22).

Further compounding the lack of supply is an ever-increasing demand: as movement between countries has increased, so too has the demand for interpreters generally, and court interpreters in particular (Helmerichs 2005, p. 188; de Jongh 1992, pp. xvi–xvii; Berk-Seligson 1990, p. 1). In a normal competitive free market setting, high demand and low supply would lead to an increase in salaries. This, however, has not been the case in the court interpreting market, as pay levels remain stubbornly low. The primary reason is that courts fail to distinguish between qualified and unqualified interpreters, and settle for individuals who are "close enough" (Shepard 2007, p. 646). Given that most judges lack the linguistic training to identify incompetent interpretation (Mikkelson 2000, p. 16; Shulman 1993, p. 187), many operate under the false assumption that bilingualism qualifies someone to be a court interpreter, and have historically appointed individuals accordingly (Svongoro 2016, p. 109; Griffin and Cole 2007, p. 6; Grabau 1996, p. 6; Moeketsi 1999b, p. 7; Laster and Taylor 1994, pp. 15, 91; Benmaman 1992, p. 448; González et al. 1991, p. 51; Berk-Seligson 1990, p. 26). Yet bilingual individuals lack not only court interpreter training and ethical instruction (Mikkelson 1998, p. 5; Hewitt and Lee 1996, p. 23), but in many instances they represent heritage speakers, meaning that they acquired one language from a parent or their environment and therefore generally possess neither a sophisticated vocabulary level nor perfect grammar (Malmberg 2006, pp. 20–21; Mikkelson 1998, p. 5). In addition, bilingualism does not automatically make the individual bicultural (de Jongh 1992, p. 59). Lowering the qualification threshold for court interpreters in such a significant manner exponentially increases the supply of acceptable individuals, thus allowing low pay levels to continue.

However, this state of affairs has several important consequences. First, as mentioned, the limited earning potential for court interpreters cannot attract qualified interpreters away from higher earning fields, thus virtually eliminating from the supply those individuals most desirable to the court system. Second, making bilingualism the main qualification necessarily results in the employment of individuals who are not trained as court interpreters. This has turned out to be the case in a variety of different jurisdictions (Stern 2011, p. 339), such as the United States (Romero 2008–2009, p. 21; Grabau and Gibbons 1996, pp. 234–235; González et al. 1991, p. 20), Australia (Hale 2004, pp. 28–29), China (Tursun 2010, p. 562), Israel (Morris 1998, p. 8), Botswana (Mojuta and Arua 2016, p. 196), Kenya (Odhiambo et al. 2013, p. 913), Nigeria (Michael 2016, p. 231), Zimbabwe (Svongoro 2016, p. 109), Malaysia (Ibrahim 2007, p. 212), Greece (Apostolou

2012, p. 216), Ireland (Waterhouse 2009), Spain (Taibi and Martin 2012, p. 79), many other nations of the European Union (Hertog and Vanden Bosch 2001, pp. 6, 10), and even some international courts (de Bertodano 2004, p. 88 [with respect to the East Timor Tribunal]). Third, since judges are largely incapable of distinguishing between good and bad interpreters and remunerate both equally, there is virtually no incentive for working court interpreters to invest their own resources in professional development training (Choolun 2009, p. 30; Hale 2001, p. 72, 2007, p. 201). Anecdotal evidence suggests, in fact, that few court interpreters appreciate the importance of continuing skills development (Ostarhild 2001, p. 69; Astiz 1986, p. 56).

The final reality of the interpreting market is that the demand for court interpreters far outstrips the available supply of those capable of performing the task. Unable to cope with this shortage of supply, and largely unable to identify incompetent interpreters, courts appoint a significant number of untrained and unqualified bilingual individuals to act as court interpreters on a one-time-only basis (so called *ad hoc* interpreters) (Lindie 1993, p. 410; Schweda-Nicholson 1989, p. 711). For example, there are numerous cases where the individual appointed was a relative or friend of the accused or a witness (Craney 1989–1990, p. 22; Schweda-Nicholson 1989, p. 712), a building janitor (Shepard 2007, p. 646; Serrano 1990, p. 1), a clerk in the courthouse (Shepard 2007, p. 646), a local high school language teacher (Taylor 2002, p. 1), university professor (Moeketsi 1999a, p. 124), or even a child (*Interpreters in the Courtroom* 2008 [Hale Statement]; Shepard 2007, p. 646; Craney 1989–1990, p. 22). Employment of such untrained individuals results in a "wide variation in the competency of interpreters" (Heller 1994–1995, p. 376). Unfortunately, very few countries have a system in place to verify or guarantee the competency of those individuals who actually work as court interpreters (Stern 2011, pp. 327, 339; eds. Hertog and van Gucht 2008, p. 197). In many instances, the decision is left to the discretion of the trial judge, who is unlikely to have sufficient linguistic training to adequately oversee the interpreter's abilities (Tuck 2010, p. 940; Mikkelson 2000, p. 16). Even in those jurisdictions where quality control systems exist, they are often rendered meaningless by circumstances or non-enforcement (Hertog and Vanden Bosch 2001, p. 11; Hovland 1992–1993, p. 495).

For example, the United States federal court system requires certification for court interpreters, but only actively administers the qualification exams in Spanish (though it has also offered Navajo and Haitian Creole in the past), and allows the appointment of an uncertified individual where no certified interpreter is available (de Jongh 2008, p. 25; Kahaner 2008–2009, p. 228).

Aside from the evidence of actual, specific examples of interpreter error prevalent in criminal proceedings as detailed in Chap. 5, and the basic assumption that untrained and unqualified individuals likely lack the necessary competence to act as court interpreters, the circumstances surrounding certification examinations in the U.S. provides further evidence of the likely shortcomings of court interpreters. The U.S. federal certification examination is a two-year procedure consisting of both a written and oral examination, both of which must be passed (United States Courts 2017; de Jongh 1992, pp. 122–123). As such, it is a demanding process with high expectations that is not to be taken lightly. Given the time commitment involved and the difficulty of the examinations, it is logical to assume that those who choose to register for the exams consist primarily of working court interpreters wishing to solidify their ability to practice in the federal courts. The overall certification rate for the federal exams as of 2008, however, was approximately 8% (de Jongh 2008, p. 25). It must be understood that the certification exam is not considered to be so difficult as to unreasonably exclude otherwise competent interpreters; rather, the low pass rate is thought to be representative of the difficulty of the interpreting process and the lack of interpreters with sufficient training (Griffin and Cole 2007, p. 8; Hewitt and Lee 1996, p. 26). As such, the necessary conclusion to be drawn from the certification exams is that 92% of those working court interpreters who were ambitious enough to attempt federal certification were actually not considered to be automatically competent to work in the federal court system. If this is true, then the competence of those interpreters who do not even attempt to achieve certification must also be considered highly questionable at best, not to mention the abilities of the *ad hoc* interpreters who likely have no training or experience whatsoever. Yet, it must be assumed that the 92% who failed did not simply choose a new profession, but rather continue to work as court interpreters (either at the state level or in federal courts where no certified interpreter is reasonably available) (Hammond 1993).

Therefore, it is reasonable to conclude that the vast majority of working court interpreters, even in a nation with a noteworthy certification procedure, falls below what is considered the basic minimum level of aptitude. This results from a combination of inter-related factors. First, the demand for qualified individuals is growing, both within the private sector and the court system. Second, there exist a limited number of qualified individuals to satiate this demand, thus causing a noticeable shortage. Third, tight governmental budgets do not allow for effective competition on the marketplace for qualified individuals (Schweda-Nicholson 1989, p. 711), and yet judicial demand for their services is obligatory and continues to grow. Fourth, the court personnel involved in employment decisions lack the necessary linguistic training to identify accurate and nuanced interpretation. As such, it is nearly inevitable that, given the choice between a trained interpreter they cannot afford and an untrained individual they can, both of whom produce work product that appears to be of equal quality, courts on a limited budget will hire the untrained but affordable individuals who appear on the surface to be capable, but whose competency is far from assured.

5.3 Implications of the Overall Level of Court Interpreters

The implications of consistently employing untrained and unqualified individuals as court interpreters in criminal proceedings cannot be overstated. A lack of training in the art of interpreting can be seen as a systemic contributor to the specific issues examined in Chap. 5. An untrained interpreter may be deficient in either (or both) the source or target languages, thus leading to simple and avoidable content errors. Furthermore, she will generally lack the specialized legal vocabulary and training in courtroom procedures that is required to accurately interpret the legal terms of art often used in criminal proceedings. However, even where her language skills are sufficient, an untrained interpreter will still likely struggle with the procedural aspects of the job (such as listening and speaking at the same time). Having to focus too much on these fundamental aspects of the process (which should be second nature to trained interpreters) will necessarily affect her substantive performance on linguistic elements as her available cognitive resources will be diverted away from the linguistic elements of the interpretation. As such, even where the individual in fact knows the suitable target language equivalent for a source language word, the concentration expended on basic interpreting tasks may rob her of the ability to actually remember it at the time it is needed. For this reason, it is well-known that untrained interpreters make more mistakes than those who have been adequately trained (Stern 2011, p. 336; González et al. 1991, p. 281). Similarly, a lack of training can lead to ethical violations as well. It becomes understandable how the adaptation role can be thought acceptable, since the ethical questions involved are likely unknown to a significant number of working court interpreters. Likewise, the widespread alteration or omission of speech style elements may owe its origins to the simple fact that many court interpreters were never trained as to their importance to the assessment of witness credibility. The usage of untrained and inexperienced court interpreters is a fundamental problem, since the lack of training can be said, at a minimum, to exacerbate, if not entirely explain, every inconsistency or problem set out in the previous Chapter.

Beyond the effect untrained interpreters can have on the rate of interpretation errors seen in court proceedings, the actual shortage of trained interpreters can directly impact an accused's right to a fair trial itself. For instance, the lack of qualified interpreters in a jurisdiction can lead to the constant rescheduling and inevitable delay of a criminal proceeding. Even though this might not be considered an overt violation of the right to a trial without undue delay under the HRC's rather hesitant interpretation of that principle, the continual rescheduling of proceedings can still have an adverse effect on the ability to obtain witnesses or evidence. Moreover, where a jurisdiction has limited interpreting options (such as in a rare language combination), this may lead to the usage of an interpreter with connections to either the case or the individuals involved. The appointment of such an interpreter would naturally raise concerns as to bias and the accuracy of the interpretation, but may be unavoidable given the constraints of the pool of available interpreters.

In addition, a shortage of qualified interpreters can limit the ability of the court to choose an individual appropriate to the particular circumstances. For example, the sex of the interpreter may make a difference: it can be disconcerting to fact-finders if a female witness testifies about being raped through a male interpreter (Kaufman 2007, p. 24). Similarly, it may soften the impact of a particularly aggressive male witness if his interpreter is a petite female. The accent with which an interpreter speaks is also important, given the trustworthiness and credibility of the witness will partially be drawn from the impression that the interpreter makes on the fact-finder. In Canada, it has been shown that a witness speaking through an interpreter using European French is viewed more positively by French Canadian fact-finders than where the interpreter's accent is Canadian French (Berk-Seligson 1990, p. 146). Likewise, in the United Kingdom, interpreters with more prestigious accents provide a favorability boost to witnesses as compared to those interpreters with less prestigious accents (Berk-Seligson 1990, p. 146). For similar reasons, Mexican-accented English has been shown to negatively impact a witness's favorability in the United States (Berk-Seligson 1990, p. 146). Furthermore, since distinctive dialects contain different meanings for the same words and their own particular slang terms, being able to select an interpreter native to that dialect can be an important consideration. Not being able to appoint an interpreter appropriate to the circumstances can directly affect the accuracy of the evidence produced and the fact-finder's assessment of its probative value, and therefore negatively impact the fair trial rights of the accused.

5.4 Conclusion

In the end, the specific realities of the court interpreting market work against the fairness of interpreted criminal proceedings by systematically increasing the likelihood that an unskilled and inexperienced court interpreter will be appointed. Such individuals cost less and their incompetence goes unnoticed by monolingual court participants unfamiliar with court interpreting. This leads to the inevitable result that most individuals working as court interpreters lack the necessary training and ability to properly minimize (or even understand) the numerous errors and issues identified in Chap. 5. Indeed, being untrained and inexperienced, their appointment virtually guarantees the presence of interpreting errors affecting every facet of the trial or hearing. As such, the poor overall level of appointed court interpreters is a considerable impediment to ensuring the fairness of interpreted criminal proceedings.

6 Lack of Impartiality

6.1 Overview

Another systemic problem arises where the court interpreter has a real or perceived conflict of interest or bias. As previously discussed in Chap. 3, under the generally accepted ethical standards applicable to court interpreters, the interpreter must retain the appearance of neutrality as well as remain neutral in fact (Stern 2011, 335; Corsellis and Fernández 2001, p. 79; González et al. 1991, p. 494). This turns out to be a rather difficult task.

6.2 Actual and Perceived Bias

As discussed above, untrained court interpreters often adopt the adaptation role, which is explained by Hale as the belief that

> [T]he role of the interpreter is to help disadvantaged non-English speakers to succeed in their case. This arises out of a sense of social justice and justifies deviating from the source language utterance to give explanations to the non-English speaker to ensure clear understanding or to embellish the answers to help gain a more favourable result. (Citations omitted; Hale 2004, p. 8)

Thus, proponents of adaptation advance the principle that court interpreters should act as advocates for the foreign language participant, assisting them in a manner that is beyond what would normally be permitted by the court. Such actions place the interpreter in a decidedly non-neutral position, and represent an extreme form of overt bias within the courtroom. A more subtle form arises from the close relationship that court interpreters naturally form with the foreign language participant (Mikkelson 2008, p. 83). In such circumstances, it is possible that the natural sympathy that develops toward the participant may subconsciously influence the court interpreter's work. The end result may work in the accused's favor (where the accused is the foreign language speaker) or to his detriment (where the foreign language participant is a prosecutorial witness).

In addition, it is not uncommon for court interpreters who frequently work in criminal proceedings to actually develop negative feelings towards defendants in general. In one Canadian study, regular court interpreters admitted their past experiences with criminal defendants and recent immigrants had led them to assume that most were guilty (Heller 1994–1995, p. 358). Although the studied interpreters insisted that they never let these feelings affect their impartiality, it is legitimate to question whether such hidden biases might inadvertently cloud their judgment during the interpreting process (Heller 1994–1995, p. 359).

The appointment of *ad hoc* court interpreters also presents ripe opportunities for bias and conflict of interest. Courts "commonly appoint or allow relatives and friends of a defendant to act as *ad hoc* interpreters" (Schweda-Nicholson 1989, p. 712; see also Moeketsi 1999b, p. 3). Likewise, it is not uncommon for courts to utilize police officers or other law enforcement officials as court interpreters; court clerks and even the accused's defense attorney have also been used (Schweda-Nicholson 1989, pp. 713–714). Judges have also been known to select as *ad hoc* interpreters obviously biased individuals such as the defendant's girlfriend (Davis et al. 2004, p. 22), a witness for the prosecution, or even a co-defendant in the very same case (Schweda-Nicholson 1989, p. 716). In two rather notorious cases, the accused husband in a spousal-abuse case was asked to interpret for his wife, the victim (Taylor 2002, p. 2; McCaffrey 2000, p. 375). Although many of these appointments may be outliers, they reinforce the sentiment that courts often fail to understand the importance of a trained and impartial court interpreter (Stern 2011, p. 327).

However, in some instances, the court may have little or no choice but to select a potentially conflicted individual. In close-knit linguistic communities especially, there may exist so few interpreting options as to necessitate the employment of a relative or friend of an interested party (Hammond 1993, pp. 480–481). This has occasionally been the case in aboriginal communities in both Canada and Australia, though the practice is either frowned upon or explicitly forbidden (Choolun 2009, p. 28; *Interpreters in the Courtroom* 2008 [McCormack Statement]; Heller 1994–1995, p. 359). Nevertheless, the necessity of securing a court interpreter within a reasonable timeframe, along with the lack of readily available options, can lead to the appointment of unsuitable individuals as interpreters.

Even where the court interpreter proves to be unbiased, such inappropriate appointments inevitably undermine the appearance of neutrality. Actions of the court interpreter within the courtroom can also create an appearance of bias, such as engaging in conversations with the foreign language participant outside of the normal proceedings (Stern 2011, p. 335; González et al. 1991, p. 495), answering inappropriate questions from the attorneys (Corsellis and Fernández 2001, p. 79; Rasmussen and Martinsen 2001, p. 96; Davis and Hewitt 1994, p. 140), or stepping outside of her role to assist the court in some manner (González et al. 1991, p. 502). The fear of appearing biased has also prompted some interpreting scholars to argue that court interpreters should never interpret for both the accused and any prosecution witnesses in the same proceeding, because doing so "would seriously undermine the relationship of trust that must exist between interpreter and client" (González et al. 1991, p. 496). However, this argument appears to misunderstand the interpreter's role within the courtroom: she is an officer of the court, and while she may interpret for the accused, the accused is not her client (Grabau 1996, p. 7; González et al. 1991, p. 494). The main risk in such a situation is that the interpreter handling the witness will not be able to interpret any sidebar communications for the defendant at the same time, nor help the defendant communicate with his attorney during the testimony (Chang and Araujo 1975, pp. 821–822). In addition, there is the possibility that confidential information obtained by interpreting attorney-defendant communications or helping prepare the defense will inadvertently affect the court interpreter's judgment with respect to her later interpretation of prosecutorial witnesses (Chang and Araujo 1975, pp. 821–822).

6.3 Implications of Actual and Perceived Bias

Little need be said about the impact of bias on a proceeding. Whether such bias results from the appointment of an obviously conflicted interpreter or an untrained interpreter acting as an advocate is largely irrelevant: an interpreter who wishes to influence the trial in a particular direction certainly can. Furthermore, the interpreter's alterations and distortions can work either in favor of the accused or to his detriment.

Irrespective, such actions would obviously undermine the concept of equality before the court, as well as the overall fairness of the proceeding. To allow the victim's testimony to be interpreted by a friend of the defendant (or the defendant himself) brings an uncertainty to the accuracy of the evidence that is simply unjustifiable at any level. Moreover, since the interpreter is likely the only person in the courtroom capable of understanding both languages, any alterations probably would go unnoticed (Hale 2004, p. 163).

More subtle, though just as important, are instances where the bias is subconscious, rather than overt. Consider the situation where the court interpreter feels a natural sympathy for the defendant and his side of the story. When interpreting the victim's testimony, she may very well do so in a manner that undermines its believability, since she herself does not actually believe it. If done for the fact-finder and the record, the interpreter's speech mannerisms will convey to the fact-finder her internally held belief that the testimony is untrustworthy. As seen in the section on speech style, this can have a significant impact on how much probative value the fact-finder assigns to that evidence. However, even if the interpretation of the witness is meant only to keep the defendant informed as to the proceedings of the court, it can be seriously detrimental to the accused's ability to actively participate in the trial. The defendant will register the lack of believability of the victim's testimony (as conveyed by the interpreter), and will assume that the fact-finder will interpret its trustworthiness in a similar manner. This presents a situation where there exists a disconnect between the trial as it is actually occurring, and the version of the trial communicated to the accused.

Inadvertent bias can also cause alterations in content. For example, an interpreter who is subconsciously biased against an accused might translate the German testimonial statement "*der Angeklagte hat ihn geschlagen*" as "the defendant beat him up" instead of "the defendant hit him", both of which would be technically correct since the German verb "*schlagen*" is ambiguous enough to encompass both meanings. However, the use of the stronger target language equivalent ("to beat") over the weaker equivalent ("to hit") would significantly change the fact-finder's impression of the seriousness of the defendant's action. In this manner, the court interpreter's personal feelings may accidentally result in several of the content issues previously discussed, thereby impacting the evidence produced at trial.

The erosion of the appearance of impartiality also can create interpretation issues. Where the interpreter appears biased, the accuracy of her interpretation may be second-guessed by the fact-finder (González et al. 1991, p. 495). Perhaps even more impactful, since the credibility and trustworthiness of the witness relies in significant part on the demeanor of the interpreter (Berk-Seligson 2002, pp. 288–289), the degradation of the court interpreter's appearance of impartiality may bleed over to the witness's credibility. In other words, if the fact-finder distrusts the interpreter, they may by default transpose those feelings on any witness or defendant, since the interpreter is the public voice of those individuals. Furthermore, as noted above, where the interpreter's neutrality is called into question, this will automatically reflect poorly on the impartiality of the court as well as the overall proceedings.

7 Conclusion

Many, if not all, of the specific issues identified in Chap. 5 can be traced back to one of the systemic issues discussed here. Fatigue and poor working conditions, for instance, both undermine the court interpreter's ability to concentrate and therefore increase the potential for incorrect decisions and imprecise interpretations. Furthermore, the lack of preparation materials and time makes it more likely that a court interpreter will be unprepared for the specific vocabulary necessary for a proceeding, and thus less likely to make an accurate translation of testimony. The prevalence of untrained and inexperienced court interpreters has a truly systemic effect on the accuracy of interpretations, since such interpreters are probably unaware of the ethical obligations or standards of accuracy required of court interpreters. Likewise, being untrained, such interpreters generally lack the specialized knowledge and depth of vocabulary to find genuinely suitable equivalents, thus increasing the likelihood of distortions and inaccuracies. Compromised impartiality can also result in many of the specific issues previously discussed. Subconscious bias will affect the interpreter's decisions and may slant a translation in an improper direction, while the appearance of such bias will undermine the fact-finder's trust of that interpreter's renditions of testimony or evidence. In each instance, these systemic issues either create the specific issues discussed in Chap. 5, or at a minimum increase the likelihood of their existence. As such, the recognition and identification of these pervasive issues is key to limiting the prevalence of interpreter error during criminal proceedings.

Bibliography

Apostolou, F. (2012). Interpreting Services for Immigrants: A New Reality in Greece. *The Interpreters' Newsletter, 17*, 213–222.

Astiz, C. A. (1986). But They Don't Speak the Language: Achieving Quality Control of Translation in Criminal Courts. *The Judge's Journal, 25*, 32.

Benmaman, V. (1992). Legal Interpreting: An Emerging Profession. *Modern Language Journal, 76*, 445–454.

Benmaman, V. (1995). Legal Interpreting by Any Other Name Is Still Legal Interpreting. In S. E. Carr, R. P. Roberts, A. Dufour, & D. Steyn (Eds.), *The Critical Link: Interpreters in the Community* (pp. 179–190). Amsterdam: John Benjamins.

Berk-Seligson, S. (1990). *The Bilingual Courtroom: Court Interpreters in the Judicial Process*. Chicago: University of Chicago Press.

Berk-Seligson, S. (2002). The Impact of Politeness in Witness Testimony: The Influence of the Court Interpreter. In F. Pöchhacker & M. Shlesinger (Eds.), *The Interpreting Studies Reader* (pp. 279–292). London: Routledge.

Cardenas, R. (2001, Fall). "You Don't Have to Hear, Just Interpret!": How Ethnocentrism in the California Courts Impedes Equal Access to the Courts for Spanish Speakers. *Court Review, 38*, 24–31.

Chang, W. B. C., & Araujo, M. U. (1975). Interpreters for the Defense: Due Process for the Non-English-Speaking Defendant. *California Law Review, 63*, 801–823.

Choolun, N. (2009). Lost in Translation? An Examination of Court Interpreting in Australia. *Queensland Law Student Review, 2*(1), 20–31.

Corsellis, A., & Fernández, L. F. (2001). Code of Ethics and Conduct and Guidelines to Good Practice. In E. Hertog (Ed.), *Aequitas: Access to Justice Across Language and Culture in the E.U* (pp. 77–87). Antwerpen: Lessius Hogeschool.

Court Interpreter's Job Is No Easy Task. (2002, August 26). Japan Policy & Politics.

Craney, G. (1989–90). Language v. the Law. *Barrister, 16*, 20–23, 27, 42.

Davis, L. W., & Hewitt, W. E. (1994). Lessons in Administering Justice: What Judges Need to Know About the Requirements, Role, and Professional Responsibilities of the Court Interpreter. *Harvard Latino Law Review, 1*, 121–176.

Davis, L. W., McKell, M. N., Oldroyd, J. R., & Steed, B. C. (2004). The Changing Face of Justice: A Survey of Recent Cases Involving Courtroom Interpretation. *Harvard Latino Law Review, 7*, 1–25.

de Bertodano, S. (2004). East Timor: Trials and Tribulations. In C. P. Romano, A. Nollkaemper, & J. K. Kleffner (Eds.), *Internationalized Criminal Courts and Tribunals: Sierra Leone, East Timor, Kosovo and Cambodia* (pp. 79–98). Oxford: Oxford University Press.

de Jongh, E. (1991). Foreign Language Interpreters in the Courtroom: The Case for Linguistic and Cultural Proficiency. *Modern Language Journal, 75*, 285–295.

de Jongh, E. (1992). *An Introduction to Court Interpreting: Theory & Practice.* Lanham: University Press of America.

de Jongh, E. (2008, July/August). Linguistic Presence v. Linguistic Absence. *Florida Bar Journal, 82*, 20–32.

de Mas, S. (2001). Translation, Interpreting & Legal Rights within the European Union: The Law & Reality. In *Critical Link 3 – Interpreting in the Community: The Complexity of the Profession – Montreal* [online]. Available at: https://static1.squarespace.com/static/52d566cbe4b0002632d34367/t/5347f5f0e4b0bccee306dac1/1397224944878/CL3_deMas.pdf. Accessed 21 Nov 2017.

Edwards, A. B. (1995). *The Practice of Court Interpreting.* Amsterdam: John Benjamins.

Elias-Bursać, E. (2015). *Translating Evidence and Interpreting Testimony at a War Crimes Tribunal.* London: Palgrave Macmillan.

Gile, D. (2009). *Basic Concepts and Models for Interpreter and Translator Training* (Rev. ed.). Amsterdam: John Benjamins.

González, R., Vásquez, V. F., & Mikkelson, H. (1991). *Fundamentals of Court Interpretation: Theory, Policy, and Practice.* Durham: Carolina Academic Press.

Grabau, C. M. (1996). Court Interpreting: View from the Bench. *State Court Journal, 20*(1), 6–11.

Grabau, C. M., & Gibbons, L. J. (1996). Protecting the Rights of Linguistic Minorities: Challenges to Court Interpretation. *New England Law Review, 30*, 227–336.

Griffin, P. W., & Cole, S. J. (2007). *White Paper on Court Interpretation: Fundamental to Access to Justice.* Conference of State Court Administrators [online]. Available at: http://cosca.ncsc.org/~/media/Microsites/Files/

COSCA/Policy%20Papers/CourtInterpretation-FundamentalToAccessToJustice.ashx. Accessed 21 Nov 2017.

Hale, S. (2001). The Complexities of the Bilingual Courtroom. *Law Society Journal, 39*, 68–72.

Hale, S. (2004). *The Discourse of Court Interpreting: Discourse Practices of the Law, the Witness and the Interpreter*. Amsterdam: John Benjamins.

Hale, S. (2007). Challenges of Court Interpreting: Intricacies, Responsibilities and Ramifications. *Alternative Law Journal, 32*, 198–202.

Hammond, R. (1993, October 24). Lost in Translation; For Immigrants in Court, Bad Interpreters Rig the Jury. *Washington Post*, p. C3.

Heller, D. J. (1994–95). The Language Bias in the Criminal Justice System. *Criminal Law Quarterly, 37*, 344–383.

Helmerichs, C. (2005). Court Interpreting: The U.S. v. E.U. – A Brief Comparison of Our Realities. In H. Keijzer-Lambooy & W. J. Gasille (Eds.), *Aequilibrium: Instruments for Lifting Language Barriers in Intercultural Legal Proceedings* (pp. 185–189). Utrecht: ITV Hogeschool voor Tolken en Vertalen.

Hertog, E., & van Gucht, J. (Eds.). (2008). *Status Quaestionis: Questionnaire on the Provision of Legal Interpreting and Translation in the E.U.* Antwerpen: Intersentia.

Hertog, E., & Vanden Bosch, Y. (2001). Access to Justice Across Language and Culture in the E.U. In E. Hertog (Ed.), *Aequitas: Access to Justice Across Language and Culture in the E.U* (pp. 5–21). Antwerpen: Lessius Hogeschool.

Hewitt, W. E., & Lee, R. J. (1996). Behind the Language Barrier, or "You Say You Were Eating an Orange?". *State Court Journal, 20*(1), 23–31.

Hovland, D. L. (1992–93). Errors in Interpretation: Why Plain Error Is Not Plain. *Law and Inequality, 11*, 473–503.

Ibrahim, Z. (2007). The Interpreter as Advocate: Malaysian Court Interpreting as a Case in Point. In C. Wadensjö, B. Englund Dimitrova, & A.-L. Nilsson (Eds.), *The Critical Link 4: Professionalisation of Interpreting in the Community* (pp. 205–213). Amsterdam: John Benjamins.

Ibrahim, Z., & Bell, R. T. (2003). Court Interpreting: Malaysian Perspectives. In L. Brunette, G. L. Bastin, I. Hemlin, & H. Clarke (Eds.), *The Critical Link 3: Interpreters in the Community* (pp. 211–222). Amsterdam: John Benjamins.

Interpreters in the Courtroom. (2008). [Radio Program] ABC Radio National: Damien Carrick.

Kahaner, S. M. (2008–2009). The Administration of Justice in a Multilingual Society – Open to Interpretation or Lost in Translation? *Judicature, 92*, 224.

Karton, J. (2008). Lost in Translation: International Criminal Tribunals and the Legal Implications of Interpreted Testimony. *Vanderbilt Journal of Transnational Law, 41*, 1–54.
Kaufman, D. (2007). What Did You Say? The Perils of Clients Who Don't Speak English. *GPSolo, 24*, 22–25. 53.
Laster, K., & Taylor, V. L. (1994). *Interpreters and the Legal System*. Sydney: The Federation Press.
LaVigne, M., & Vernon, M. (2003). An Interpreter Isn't Enough: Deafness, Language, and Due Process. *Wisconsin Law Review, 2003*, 843–936.
Lindie, B. (1993). Inadequate Interpreting Services in Courts and the Rules of Admissibility of Testimony on Extrajudicial Interpretations. *University of Miami Law Review, 48*, 399–433.
Lore, M. (2010, March 1). Certified Interpreters in Short Supply Throughout Minnesota Court System. *The Minnesota Lawyer.*
Malmberg, N. (2006, May). How to Get the Most from Working with a Court Interpreter. *The Nebraska Lawyer*, pp. 20–24.
Mason, M. (2008). *Courtroom Interpreting*. Lanham: University Press of America.
McCaffrey, A. (2000). Don't Get Lost in Translation: Teaching Law Students to Work with Language Interpreters. *Clinical Law Review, 6*, 347–398.
Michael, C. O. (2016). Communication of an Interpreter and Fair Trial Under Nigerian Criminal Justice System. *International Journal of Legal Discourse, 1*(1), 213–233.
Miguélez, C. (1999). Current Issues in Court Interpreting: Spain, a Case Study. *Proteus, 8*(2), 1–4.
Mikkelson, H. (1998). The Court Interpreter as Guarantor of Defendant Rights. In *First European Congress on Court Interpreting and Legal Translation – Graz* [online]. Available at: http://works.bepress.com/holly_mikkelson/8/. Accessed 21 Nov 2017.
Mikkelson, H. (2000). *Introduction to Court Interpreting*. Manchester: St. Jerome Publishing.
Mikkelson, H. (2008). Evolving Views of the Court Interpreter's Role: Between Scylla & Charybdis. In C. Valero-Garcés & A. Martin (Eds.), *Crossing Borders in Community Interpreting: Definitions and Dilemmas* (pp. 81–98). Amsterdam: John Benjamins.
Moeketsi, R. H. (1999a). *Discourse in a Multilingual and Multicultural Courtroom: A Court Interpreter's Guide*. Pretoria: van Schaik.
Moeketsi, R. H. (1999b). Redefining the Role of the South African Court Interpreter. *Proteus, 8*(3–4), 12–15.

Mojuta, K., & Arua, A. (2016). The Lexical Problems of Court Interpreters in a Botswana High Court. *Botswana Note and Records, 48*, 193–204.

Morris, R. (1998). Justice in Jerusalem – Interpreting in Israeli Legal Proceedings. *Meta, 43*(1), 110–118.

Morris, R. (2008). Taking Liberties? Duplicity or the Dynamics of Court Interpreting. In D. Russell & S. Hale (Eds.), *Interpreting in Legal Settings* (pp. 1–25). Washington, DC: Gallaudet University Press.

Navarro, L. (2006, June 5). Commentary: The Need for Interpreters in South Carolina Courts. *South Carolina Lawyers Weekly*.

Odhiambo, K., Kavulani, C. K., & Matu, P. M. (2013). Court Interpreters View of Language Use in Subordinate Courts in Nyanza Province, Kenya. *Theory and Practice in Language Studies, 3*(6), 910–918.

Ostarhild, E. (2001). Continuing Professional Development. In E. Hertog (Ed.), *Aequitas: Access to Justice Across Language and Culture in the E.U* (pp. 66–72). Antwerpen: Lessius Hogeschool.

Rasmussen, K. W., & Martinsen, B. (2001). Interdisciplinary Conventions with the Legal Services. In E. Hertog (Ed.), *Aequitas: Access to Justice Across Language and Culture in the E.U* (pp. 93–101). Antwerpen: Lessius Hogeschool.

Romero, B. G. (2008–09). Here Are Your Right Hands: Exploring Interpreter Qualifications. *University of Dayton Law Review, 34*, 15–33.

Schweda-Nicholson, N. (1989). *Ad Hoc* Court Interpreters in the United States: Equality, Inequality, Quality. *Meta, 34*(4), 711–723.

Serrano, B. A. (1990, November 30). Courts Shy on Interpreters to Help Immigrants, Jurors. *The Seattle Times*, p. C1.

Shepard, R. T. (2007). Access to Justice for People Who Do Not Speak English. *Indiana Law Review, 40*, 643–657.

Shulman, M. B. (1993). No Hablo Ingles: Court Interpretation as a Major Obstacle to Fairness for Non-English Speaking Defendants. *Vanderbilt Law Review, 46*, 175–196.

Stern, L. (2001). At the Junction of Cultures: Interpreting at the International Criminal Tribunal for the Former Yugoslavia in the Light of Other International Interpreting Practices. *The Judicial Review, 5*(3), 255–274.

Stern, L. (2011). Courtroom Interpreting. In K. Malmkjær & K. Windle (Eds.), *The Oxford Handbook of Translation Studies* (pp. 325–342). Oxford: Oxford University Press.

Svongoro, P. (2016). Court Interpreter Training at the Crossroads: Challenges and Future Prospects for Zimbabwe. *Mediterranean Journal of Social Sciences, 7*(2), 106.

Taibi, M., & Martin, A. (2012). Court Translaton and Interpreting in Times of the "War on Terror": The Case of Taysir Alony. *Translation & Interpreting, 4*(1), 77–98.

Taylor, L. (2002, April 22). Attorneys, Some Judges Say Poor Interpretations Botch Convictions. *Lexington Herald Leader*, p. A1.

Tuck, B. M. (2010). Comment: Preserving Facts, Form, and Function When a Deaf Witness with Minimal Language Skills Testifies in Court. *University of Pennsylvania Law Review, 158*, 905–955.

Tursun, G. (2010). The Protection of Minorities in Court Proceedings: A Perspective on Bilingual Justice in China. *Chinese Journal of International Law, 9*, 537–563.

United States Courts. (2017). *Federal Court Interpreter Certification Examination* [online]. Available at: http://www.uscourts.gov/services-forms/federal-court-interpreters/federal-court-interpreter-certification-examination. Accessed 21 Nov 2017.

Vidal, M. (1997). New Study on Fatigue Confirms Need for Working in Teams. *Proteus, 6*(1), 1.

Waterhouse, K. (2009). Accessing Justice Through an Interpreter in Ireland's District (Criminal) Courts. In *EULITA Conference – Antwerp* [online]. Available at: http://www.eulita.eu/sites/default/files/Accessing%20Justice%20through%20an%20Interpreter%20in%20Ireland.pdf. Accessed 21 Nov 2017.

7

Analysis

1 Introduction

Having detailed in the previous two Chapters an extensive list of errors and problems (both individual and systemic) associated with court interpreting, as well as how these specific issues may impact particular fair trial rights, it is left now to bring this information together to determine how the totality of these court interpreting issues may affect an accused's ability to receive a fair trial. As such, this Chapter will reanalyze the individual fair trial rights, and the likelihood of their infringement, in the light of the interpreting issues and systemic failures previously discussed in this work. In order to accommodate this discussion and minimize unnecessary repetition, it is helpful to frame this Chapter around the concept of evidence, since it is through the interaction between court interpreters and the evidence at trial that an individual's right to a fair trial appears to be most significantly impacted. As such, this Chapter will group the fair trial rights into several different categories: those related to the production of evidence; those related to the understanding of evidence; and those miscellaneous aspects unrelated to evidence. Naturally, some rights will appear in more than one grouping, as they maintain a multifaceted relationship to trial evidence.

J. H. Dingfelder Stone, *Court Interpreters and Fair Trials*,
https://doi.org/10.1007/978-3-319-75355-3_7

2 Rights Related to the Production of Evidence

2.1 Introduction

Several of the individual rights to a fair trial appear to be most concerned with the accurate production of evidence at trial. For example, the right to an oral hearing (Article 14 ICCPR) guarantees to an accused that the evidence against him will be presented orally, most likely through witnesses in a formal setting. The right to examine witnesses (Article 14 [3] [e]) secures for the accused the ability to challenge and question these witnesses as to their information, as well as the right to present witnesses and evidence of his own. Furthermore, the right to adversarial proceedings (Article 14 [1]) grants the accused the ability to challenge any evidence presented by the government. Finally, the right to adequate time and facilities to prepare a defense (Article 14 [3] [b]) assures the accused sufficient time and resources to organize and plan his defense, both with respect to strategy and evidence. In their own way, each of these individual rights works to create a procedural system focused on the production of accurate and truthful evidence, mainly by enabling the accused's ability (either procedurally or from a resource standpoint) to challenge and dispute any evidence against him. Through this oral adversarial process of questioning and challenging witnesses or presenting witnesses of one's own, some semblance of the truth is expected to emerge, thereby allowing the fact-finder to make an accurate and reliable assessment of the accused's guilt (Trechsel 2005, p. 293). It is self-evident that the trustworthiness and correctness of the fact-finder's ultimate determination will depend heavily on the accuracy of the evidence produced at trial. It is in this context that the interjection of a court interpreter into the process may wreak havoc.

2.2 The Common Occurrence of Interpreter Error

As the previous Chapters have highlighted, court interpreters can distort and influence the trial evidence in a variety of ways. While maintaining the obvious potential to cause serious evidentiary discrepancies under the right circumstances, an occurrence that most attorneys and judges perhaps falsely believe they will notice, mostly these distortions appear trivial in impact and isolated in nature. However, in order to fully understand the cumulative effect these errors actually can have on a criminal proceeding, it is helpful to focus on the frequency with which each distortion or alteration may occur.

At the outset, every court interpreter must decide whether to adhere to a pragmatic (meaning-based) or verbatim (word-for-word) standard for interpretation during the proceeding. Thus, either the court interpreter occasionally usurps the fact-finder's judgment as to the meaning of evidence (pragmatic standard) or she faithfully renders idiomatic speech into occasionally incomprehensible word-for-word translations (verbatim standard). The decision between these two competing theories, and their respective outcomes, is unavoidable and will systematically undermine the accuracy of the evidence, one way or another, throughout the entire proceeding.

Likewise, the prevalence of the adaptation role in court interpretation will also undoubtedly impact the proceedings. Court interpreters who practice adaptation affirmatively change their interpretation to suit the language or educational level of the target audience; thus either simplifying or explaining difficult language so a listener may understand, or elevating and correcting erroneous language for a more educated audience (González et al. 1991, p. 18). In either case, the court interpreter's work will not be representative of what was actually stated. Depending upon the specific jurisdiction studied, such instances of "adaptation" may "invariably" occur (Jacobsen 2004, p. 248), be practiced by a majority of the court interpreters employed (Moeketsi 1999, p. 5; Astiz 1986, p. 34) or even be "regularly" expected by the court itself (Ibrahim 2007, p. 212; González et al. 1991, p. 156). Given the pervasiveness of this practice, it is unlikely that the production of evidence through a foreign-language witness will not be systematically distorted through simplifications, explanations or corrections as the interpreter attempts to adapt her interpretation for the sake of the foreign-language witness.

These, unfortunately, are not the only alterations of evidence likely to be encountered in an interpreted trial. The omission of words, phrases, and even entire sentences or parts of paragraphs is a "frequent error" (González et al. 1991, p. 288). Likewise, where untrained or unqualified interpreters are involved, the omission of specialized or legal vocabulary is the most commonly used coping strategy, and general mistranslations that "distort the overall or partial meaning of the original message are quite prevalent" (González et al. 1991, pp. 287–288). The mistaken usage of false friends is a "common" pitfall for interpreters (de Jongh 1992, p. 77), and the modification of verb tense between active and passive forms is a "widespread" practice (Berk-Seligson 1990, p. 116). Court interpreters also "often" add information to their translation where they are uncertain of the original term used (González et al. 1991, p. 289). Similarly, they "often" incorrectly interpret idiomatic speech (González et al. 1991, p. 286). Each of these common errors can and does result in the inaccuracy and misrepresentation of witness testimony, since every testimonial statement given by a foreign-language witness (as well as the question presented to that witness) must run the gauntlet of these widespread practices. As such, the content of a witness's testimony, as relayed through a court interpreter, is likely to have inaccuracies and distortions, due simply to the prevalence of these interpreting issues.

The accurate portrayal of the content of a witness's testimony, though, is but one aspect in a successful interpretation; the interpreter must accurately recreate the witness's speech style as well. As exhaustively detailed in Chap. 5, this is an aspect of court interpretation where most interpreters fail miserably. They "constantly" alter witness speech style (Hale 2002, p. 43), "generally" ignoring the witness's speech mannerisms and substituting their own style instead (Hale 2007, p. 200). Likewise, "systematic changes" in the level of formality employed by a speaker "are often made" as well (Berk-Seligson 1990, p. 172). Numerous scientific studies have determined that the style of a witness's testimony directly affects the fact-finder's assessment of the credibility and persuasiveness of that testimony (Hale 2002, p. 26). It has also been shown that fact-finders base their perceptions as to witness credibility on the demeanor and style of the court interpreter rather than that of the witness (Berk-Seligson 2002, pp. 288–289). As such, the systematic alteration of a witness's speech style invariably misrepresents the actual trustworthiness and probative value of trial evidence.

The substantial impact of these general habits can be seen more clearly by focusing on several prominent speech style characteristics that are systematically ignored by court interpreters. For instance, the original hesitations, hedges and fillers are "very rarely" maintained in the interpreted version of a speaker's speech, thereby eliminating any ambiguities and uncertainty naturally inherent in a witness's testimony. Instead, court interpreters "often" insert their own unrelated hesitations, hedges and fillers into the translated testimony (Hale 2002, p. 43; Berk-Seligson 1990, p. 140); thus adding new and misrepresentative information into the testimonial record and further obscuring the fact-finder's ability to accurately assess the reliability of the witness's information. Politeness markers are also "often" or "frequently" altered (Berk-Seligson 1990, pp. 150–154), and are omitted in "almost every instance" where the speech segment at issue is longer than 10 words (which would encompass the vast majority of the questions and answers involved in the production of testimonial evidence) (Mason 2008, p. 24). The result is that the fact-finder perceives a foreign-language witness or accused as either less or more polite than they actually were, via the alterations of the court interpreter. This altered perception is important, since polite witnesses are viewed as "significantly more convincing, competent, intelligent, and trustworthy" (Berk-Seligson 2002, p. 286). The same "significantly" enhanced credibility has also been found where interpreters omit hedges and fillers from a witness's testimony (Hale 2002, pp. 30, 43; Berk-Seligson 1990, p. 181).

Court interpreters can also influence the production of evidence in less direct ways. For example, discourse markers, an element of speech style frequently employed by attorneys to direct or influence witnesses during testimony, are likewise both eliminated "almost systematically" by court interpreters and reinserted anew at an alarming rate according to the court interpreter's own personal style choices (Hale 2004, p. 62; see also Hale 2002, p. 34). Similarly, court interpreters have been found to change the form of an attorney's questions at a substantial rate, specifically with relation to so-called "tag questions" (Hale 2004, p. 44). These modifications not only change the attorney's ability to control the presentation of evidence, but may also distort the actual meaning and intention of the attorney's line of questioning.

It must be stressed again in this context that the errors and distortions highlighted above are neither rare nor occasional, but rather are seen "often" or "invariably" or even "systematically". Nor does the employment of a highly-qualified court interpreter alleviate many of these concerns, since the frequency levels noted in many of these studies arose through the study of actual qualified interpreters. Thus, it must be expected that the usage of unqualified and untrained court interpreters, which appears to be the norm in even the most heavily regulated jurisdictions (see Chap. 6), will lead to even higher rates of error than those mentioned above. In other words, these practices are not the exception to the rule, but instead represent the basic reality of court interpreting.

2.3 The Legal Implications of Interpreter Error on the Production of Evidence

Errors are inherent in the process, and they are common. That there are so many different possible errors that each occur at an elevated rate of frequency leads one to necessarily conclude that the distortion of witness testimony is an unavoidable side-effect of interpreting that testimony. The end result is that the production of evidence through an oral, adversarial examination of interpreted witnesses will virtually always contain distortions of both content and style, to an extent that the fact-finder's evaluation of that evidence will be based chiefly on perceptions and understandings that are largely distinct from the reality of the witness's native language testimony.

Such inefficiencies in the production of evidence carry legal implications. For example, in *Gridin v. Russian Federation* (2000), the HRC found a violation of Article 14 (1) where the atmosphere in the courtroom was so hostile that the author was unable to effectively cross-examine the State's witnesses or present his defense (§8.2). Although little explanation is given for the decision, it can be assumed that the potential distortions in the evidence arising from the difficult environmental factors resulted in an unfair hearing. In other words, the author's ability to effectively cross-examine witnesses in order to clarify their testimony or assess their credibility was fatally undermined by the inability to successfully communicate with that witness given the circumstances of the courtroom. This placed the author in a situation not dissimilar to those defendants attempting to examine a witness through a court interpreter. Where an ineffectual interpreter hinders the examination process through an elevated rate of distortions and errors, her effect on the reliability of the evidence produced will be just as impactful, though much less noticeable, than the circumstances that produced a violation in *Gridin*.

Indirect guidance as to the legal impact of court interpreter errors can also be found in a line of ECtHR cases involving the use of anonymous witnesses. In *Kostovski v. The Netherlands* (1989), the ECtHR found a violation of the right to examine witnesses and the overall right to a fair trial where the State presented evidentiary statements from two anonymous witnesses at trial and the applicant had only been allowed to submit written questions for one of the witnesses to answer through an examining magistrate (§42). Furthermore, the trial court judges themselves were kept ignorant about the identities of the witnesses; a situation the ECtHR found distressing, since it limited the court's ability to judge witness reliability (*Kostovski v. The Netherlands* [ECtHR 1989] §43). Similarly, the ECtHR found a violation in *Van Mechelen v. Netherlands* (1997) where the applicant was only allowed to examine two anonymous witnesses through a sound link from a separate room (§59). In each instance, the ECtHR found a fair trial violation based on the idea that anonymity of a witness would deprive the defense "of the very particulars enabling it to demonstrate that [the witness] is prejudiced, hostile or unreliable" (*Kostovski v. The Netherlands* [ECtHR 1989] §42). The loss of such particular information, the sort that normally forms the backbone of an effective examination, exists in equal if not greater measure in interpreted testimony: style changes conceal the witness's actual demeanor and content distortions will eliminate the specific details of their testimony. While an interpreted witness may not be unseen or anonymous, the interpreter-created alterations to perceived reliability and understood content make the witness just as difficult to examine as the anonymous witnesses in *Kostovski* and *Van Mechelen*. If a fair trial violation exists with respect to one, it is likely it exists in respect to both.

The HRC, for its part, also follows a similar strain of logic with respect to the details necessary to ensure effective examination. In *Peart and Peart v. Jamaica* (1995), the State failed to make available to the defense a prior statement by the only eye-witness which contained highly exculpatory information that would have undermined that witness's testimony (HRC §11.5). The HRC held that the failure to provide this statement to the author "seriously obstructed the defence in its cross-examination of the witness" and therefore violated his right to a fair trial (*Peart and Peart v. Jamaica* [HRC 1995] §11.5). As with the ECtHR cases, the absence of specific information pertinent to the examination of a damaging witness was sufficient to render the resulting trial unfair. Naturally, given the extreme exculpatory nature of the evidence considered in *Peart and Peart*, it is difficult to draw a direct analogy between it and the evidentiary distortions and omissions introduced by a court interpreter. However, *Peart and Peart* does reinforce the ECtHR principle that contextual details are essential to the effective examination of witnesses. The inability of court interpreters to consistently and faithfully retain such information places defendants in a disadvantaged position similar to those faced by the effected individuals in *Peart and Peart*, *Kostovski*, and *Van Mechelen*.

The omission or alteration of evidence doesn't only affect a defendant's right to examine witnesses, though. The ability to present a defense and the overall fairness of a trial may also be placed in jeopardy by such errors. Court interpreters engage in persistent and nearly systematic alterations of evidence and the perceived reliability of that evidence. These distortions occur mainly in little incidents, spread out over the entirety of a witness's testimony and rendered largely unnoticeable by the complete lack of oversight. Gathered together, however, these alterations and omissions create a significant hole in the evidence not unlike the complete absence of a witness relevant to the defense, which would be a fair trial violation (*Iskandarov v. Tajikistan* [HRC 2011] §6.6; *Ashurov v. Tajikistan* [HRC 2007] §6.6; *García Fuenzalida v. Ecuador* [HRC 1996] §9.5). Similarly, systematic distortions may create a disconnect between the reality of a witness's evidence in their native language (the evidence that the defendant intends the fact-finder to hear) and the actual evidence as heard by the fact-finder (via the interpreter). Although the court may indeed go through the procedural formalities of calling and hearing the defendant's requested witness, in actual fact, they will have only heard the interpreter's distorted version of that person. Where the interpreter's performance is inconsistent and unfaithful enough, it is as if the court had never actually heard the defendant's witness at all. Again, this would likely call into question the fairness of the proceedings (*Iskandarov v. Tajikistan* [HRC 2011] §6.6; *Ashurov v. Tajikistan* [HRC 2007] §6.6; *García Fuenzalida v. Ecuador* [HRC 1996] §9.5).

There are also precedents that can shed light on the possible legal implications of interpreter error as to speech style. The principle of immediacy, as outlined by the ECtHR, dictates that the accused should "be confronted with the witness in the presence of the judge who ultimately decides the case" (*Pitkänen v. Finland* [ECtHR 2004] §58). Doing so allows that judge to make direct observations "about the demeanour and credibility of the witness" which "may have important consequences for an accused" (*Pitkänen v. Finland* [ECtHR 2004] §58). As noted above, scientific studies show that fact-finders evaluate the credibility of witness testimony based upon the demeanor and speech style of the interpreter, rather than the witness (Berk-Seligson 2002, pp. 288–289). Given that interpreters "generally" substitute their speech style for that of the witness (Hale 2007, p. 200), the end result is that judges and other fact-finders in interpreted trials are effectively cut off from direct observation of the interpreted witness. This is similar to the situation in *Kostovski v. The Netherlands* (1989) where the ECtHR found a fair trial violation based in part on the fact that the trial courts were never allowed to directly observe the demeanor of the anonymous witnesses and therefore could not form an independent impression of their credibility (§43). Although interpreted witnesses can be physically seen, the fact-finder is actually shielded from making an accurate assessment of witness credibility by the interpreter's speech style alterations. Perhaps even more impactful is that, unlike in *Kostovski* where the trial court was cognizant that it lacked the information to judge witness credibility, the fact-finders in an interpreted trial are entirely unaware that the witness presented to them through the interpreter is not an accurate representation. Thus, they confidently form an opinion as to the reliability of the witness's evidence without the knowledge that they are doing so from systematically distorted or altered information. This lack of awareness means that the trial court will fail to realize the risk of an inaccurate credibility evaluation, and therefore will take no procedural steps to counteract that risk (as it would, for instance, in the case of an anonymous witness) (see for example *Van Mechelen and Others v. The Netherlands* [ECtHR 1997] § 62; *Kostovski v. The Netherlands* [ECtHR 1989] §43).

2.4 Conclusion

The legal implications of court interpreter practices on the production and assessment of evidence are subtle and largely unexplored, yet still of great significance. Given that each of the rights discussed in this section are meant to ensure the fact-finder's ability to accurately assess the evidence and arrive at the truth of the matter, the existence of so many "frequent" and "common" errors by interpreters places an accused's right to a fair trial in substantial risk. Indeed, fair trial violations have been found by both the HRC and the ECtHR in a variety of different analogous situations. Yet, it is impossible to argue that the interpreting process itself necessarily creates an automatic violation of an accused's fair trial rights whenever a witness testifies through a court interpreter. The importance of the specific witness to a trial, as well as the actual extent of the distortions to that evidence, will obviously dictate the resulting fairness of the proceedings. However, what can be said is that the act of interpreting witness testimony necessarily distorts the substance and probative value of the witness's testimonial evidence, arguably to a very significant extent. This simple fact casts a considerable shadow over the fair trial rights discussed in this section. The right to call and examine witnesses in an oral hearing, the right to prepare and present a defense, and the right to challenge governmental witnesses in an adversarial proceeding are all appreciably undermined where the witnesses in question are unable to be accurately understood or assessed by the fact-finder.

3 Rights Related to the Understanding of Evidence

3.1 Introduction

While several individual fair trial rights focus on ensuring the accurate production of evidence, others seek to guarantee the ability of the accused to both understand and participate in the criminal proceeding. For instance, the right to be present at trial (Article 14 [3] [d]) guarantees the accused the opportunity to defend himself and to participate in the proceedings, which naturally requires a certain level of understanding of the courtroom activities and evidence as well. The right to be informed of the charge (Article 14 [3] [a]) also entails an element of linguistic understanding. Although they may not explicitly guarantee that the accused understands and can participate in the proceedings, the logical fulfillment of other fair trial rights would appear to necessitate just such an outcome. As an example, consider the previously discussed rights to an adversarial proceeding (Article 14 [1]), to examine witnesses (Article 14 [3] [e]), and to an oral hearing (Article 14). Each involves some element of participation on the part of the accused: to assist in challenging evidence or witnesses in an oral hearing, the accused must necessarily understand the orally presented evidence and the proceedings themselves. The effective fulfillment of these rights requires that the proceedings and the evidence be accurately interpreted not only for the fact-finder (as detailed above), but also for the accused himself, so that he may understand enough to actively participate in his own defense.

3.2 The Common Occurrence of Interpreter Error

As may be imagined, many of the same errors and mistakes detailed above with respect to the production of evidence apply in equal measure to the understanding of the evidence by the accused. Every interpreter must choose between the pragmatic and verbatim standards, the simplification and explanation of courtroom language to an accused is a basic and regular occurrence in some jurisdictions (Moeketsi 1999, p. 5; González et al. 1991, p. 156; Astiz 1986, p. 34), content omission is a "frequent" error, mistranslations are "quite prevalent", idiomatic speech is "often" misrepresented (González et al. 1991, pp. 286–288), and speech style elements are either "automatically ignore[d]" (Hale 2001, p. 71), "very rarely" maintained (Hale 2002, p. 43), or "almost systematically" omitted (depending on the element itself) (Hale 2004, p. 62). In summation, just as with the interpretation of witness testimony, the translation of the proceedings for an accused results in systematic and comprehensive distortions.

However, the impact these errors may have on the right to a fair trial is substantially different because the context in which the errors occur will be largely distinct from what was previously discussed. For example, where the testimony of a foreign-language witness is interpreted for the fact-finder, the interpreter's translation essentially is the evidence upon which the fact-finder will base their determination. By way of contrast, where the accused is the foreign language participant for whom the court interpreter is required, the interpretation of witness testimony will not be part of the official record and will only be for the accused himself; the fact-finder will base their determination upon the witness's actual uninterpreted testimony. Interpreter error in the latter situation does not directly affect the accuracy or reliability of the fact-finder's decision, rather it merely serves to undermine the accused's ability to understand the evidence and participate in his own defense.

3.3 The Legal Implications of Interpreter Error on the Understanding of Evidence

That the interpreter errors detailed in this section do not directly distort the production of evidence does not, however, mean that they are of less importance to an accused's right to a fair trial. It is a question of difference, rather than degree. The adaptation role, for instance, revolves around the active alteration of content in order to help the foreign-language accused better understand the proceedings. However, its efficiency in accomplishing this task is largely dependent upon the abilities and training of the court interpreter performing the alterations. Given that most court interpreters are untrained and unqualified, it is just as likely that the explanations and simplifications are uninformed or incorrect, and therefore actively counter-productive to the accused's practical understanding of the situation. Furthermore, the same content omissions and mistranslation errors that plague witness testimony are just as commonplace in interpretations for defendants, leading to a situation where the accused's perception of the evidence as presented will be substantially different from the fact-finder's perception of that same testimony.

The same is also true with respect to the constant loss of speech style. The fact-finder's evaluation of credibility and trustworthiness will be based upon the witness's actual speech style, whereas the accused will perceive the witness's credibility through the distorting filter of the court interpreter's speech style. Considering the frequency with which court interpreters substitute their own speech style in place of a witness's, it is logical to assume that the foreign-language accused, from the perspective of witness credibility and the probative value of testimonial evidence, will in fact experience a completely different trial from that of the fact-finder and the court at large. In effect, the ubiquity and frequency of interpreter distortions creates two separate courtroom realities: the actual trial as experienced by the fact-finder and those who speak the courtroom language, and the trial as experienced by the accused through the courtroom interpretation.

This is not a tenable outcome. In *Van Mechelen*, the ECtHR noted that even where an investigating judge is given the chance to assess the credibility and demeanor of anonymous witnesses, such "measures cannot be considered a proper substitute for the possibility of the defence to question the witnesses in their presence and make their own judgment as to their demeanour and reliability" (*Van Mechelen and Others v. The Netherlands* [ECtHR 1997] §62). It is the accused's right to participate in the evaluation and confrontation of a witness through his attorney. The effective exercise of this right requires that he have the opportunity to experience the exact same trial as the fact-finder and form his own judgments as to the evidence. Where a foreign language defendant is reliant on an interpreter throughout his trial, he will be denied complete access to the entirety of the evidence, not just two witnesses as was the case in *Van Mechelen*. While it is possible to argue that the presence of a defense attorney who understands the trial language may substitute in this instance and ameliorate this legal deficit, accepting this argument begs the question as to why the defendant is then even afforded an interpreter in the first place, since he need not personally understand his trial.

Furthermore, the accused cannot be expected to effectively contribute to his own defense where his perception of the proceedings is markedly different from what has actually taken place. For instance, consider the cross-examination of a governmental witness who is relating facts about the case damaging to the accused. As the person accused of the crime, the defendant is often in the best position to know whether these damaging facts are actually true, or in what way they may best be combatted or refuted by his attorney (Trechsel 2005, p. 309). However, if the accused lacks an understanding of the precise details of the witness's testimony or has a false impression as to what that testimony actually entailed, his ability to effectively instruct defense counsel as to the proper facts or a useful cross-examination strategy will be substantially negated. In this instance, the accused's predicament is similar to those discussed in the anonymous witnesses cases above. However, in cases such as *Van Mechelen* and *Kostovski*, the accused was legally denied his right to examine a specific witness because the anonymity of that witness had deprived him of the "very particulars" necessary for the examination. Where an accused experiences his trial through an interpreter, he is denied those "particulars" with respect to all of the evidence produced at his trial rather than simply a single witness. His ability to assist his attorney in the examination of witnesses is therefore systematically abridged, which undermines the fairness of a proceeding much more substantially than mere isolated incidents.

That the accused experiences a different trial from that of the fact-finder also creates a legal problem with respect to the accused's right to be present at the trial. Although the accused may be physically present during the proceedings, he may not actually be receiving the same information and contextual clues as the other courtroom participants. As such, his understanding of the proceedings may be only partial at best, which may not be sufficient. In *Domukovsky v. Georgia* (1998), the HRC held that the authors had been denied the right to be present at their trial where they had been "forced to be absent during long periods of the trial" (§18.9).[1] Although the HRC did not clarify its reasoning for the result, it can be assumed that the right to be present at one's trial requires that one be present throughout, so as to have the opportunity to listen to all of the evidence, and not only random segments. If the essential aspect of the right is the opportunity to comprehend the evidence in its entirety, defendants who must follow their proceedings through an interpreter are largely denied this right due to widespread interpreter distortions.

3.4 Conclusion

Here again, however, the context and seriousness of the errors are of great importance. Even given the prevalence of interpreter error discussed above, it would be overstating the case to say that the general level of interpretation is so incompetent as to automatically render any fair trial impossible. Some interpreters will be excellent and some will be terrible. Some distortions will be minor and some will be catastrophic. In short, the particular circumstances of each proceeding, and the specific abilities of each interpreter, will dictate whether or not the accused is able to understand and effectively participate in his own proceeding. Yet, given the frequency and seriousness of the errors discussed in the previous Chapters and the existence of cases in both HRC and ECtHR jurisprudence wherein analogous situations have led to fair trial violations, it is clear that the ability of a foreign-language accused to understand and participate in the proceedings is more at risk than previously imagined.

4 Rights Unrelated to Evidence

4.1 Introduction

Although court interpreters appear to mainly impact the right to a fair trial through their complicated relationship with the production or understanding of evidence, they may also negatively influence other, non-evidence related, fair trial rights. Specifically, the right to equality before the court (Article 14 [1]), the right to be tried without undue delay (Article 14 [3] [c]), the right to counsel (Article 14 [3] [d]), the right to an interpreter (Article [3] [f]), and the right to appeal (Article 14 [5]) may be placed in jeopardy by improper court interpretation. This section will focus on each of these rights separately and in turn, as they each present unique issues.

4.2 Equality Before the Court

Article 14 (1) guarantees every accused equality before the court. In practice, this means that the accused must have equal access to the court, and must be granted treatment before the court equal to that given to both the opposing party as well as any other similarly situated individuals (HRC General Comment No. 32, §14; *Dudko v. Australia* [HRC 2007]

§7.4). Where the State wishes to treat individuals or parties differently, it must provide "objective and reasonable grounds" to justify the distinction (HRC General Comment No. 32, §9; *Dudko v. Australia* [HRC 2007] §7.4). Variable treatment based upon language or national origin has not been considered justifiable by the HRC (HRC General Comment No. 32, §9). As such, a foreign-language accused is entitled to the same treatment and standards from the court and the criminal justice system as an accused who speaks the language of the court. Likewise, an accused whose proceeding includes foreign-language testimony would appear to also be guaranteed the same treatment granted to any other accused in the legal system. That each of these accused individuals must be regarded by the court on equal terms with the prosecution also goes without saying. Similarly, it must be assumed that an accused in a non-interpreted trial is entitled to any preferential or advantageous treatment afforded an accused in an interpreted proceeding. The end result is that every accused, regardless of language considerations, is entitled to the same procedural protections and to have his proceeding measured against the same overall fairness standards.

The practical implications of interpreter participation, however, make the procedural guarantee of equality difficult to maintain. As demonstrated in the preceding sections and Chapters, interpreted trials are prone to a variety of "frequent" and "common" errors. Where a witness's testimony is interpreted for the court, these errors effectively distort and alter the evidence used against (or in favor) of the accused. Where the entire proceeding itself must be interpreted for a foreign-language accused, the presence of court interpreter alterations undermines the accused's ability to understand and participate in the proceedings. The presence of an interpreter is not, however, always negative for the accused. Court interpreters who utilize the adaptation role may simplify and explain complex legal concepts for a foreign-language accused, thereby providing an advantage that does not exist for a "normal" defendant. In this instance, it is possible for the accused in a non-interpreted trial to argue that he is receiving unequal and detrimental treatment vis-a-vis a similarly-situated foreign-language defendant. Yet, even if it is assumed that none of these situations necessarily results in automatic fair trial violations, it is difficult to argue, given the evidence discussed in the preceding Chapters, that the employment of a court interpreter does not effectively change the dynamics and accuracy of a proceeding. Even the best court interpreters make errors, and the unqualified and untrained individuals normally employed by courts make many more.

It is therefore necessary to assume that a proceeding involving a court interpreter contains an inherent level of distortion or inaccuracy that does not exist in non-interpreted proceedings. As such, an accused whose proceeding is interpreted will have a fundamentally different qualitative experience than a similarly-situated defendant exposed to a monolingual trial. This disparity in accuracy and trustworthiness between interpreted and non-interpreted proceedings is problematic from an equality standpoint, since every accused is theoretically entitled to equal treatment. Yet a trial that necessarily must contain errors and distortions cannot be considered of equal quality to one that is devoid of these problems. Likewise, a court interpreted proceeding that produces an advantage for the accused will not be equal to one that does not, at least as far as the disadvantaged "normal" defendant is concerned.

The question, naturally, is what level of court interpreter-induced inaccuracy is necessary to render a violation of an accused's right to equality before the court. On one hand, this is a question that is all but impossible to answer, given the relative paucity of HRC jurisprudence in the area. On the other hand, it is not entirely clear that it need be answered at all. One may presume that any interpreted trial that contains sufficient enough inaccuracies as to trigger a violation of the right to equality before the court will likely also produce violations of the previously discussed individual fair trial rights as well. In other words, if the court interpreter commits enough errors to produce an unequal trial, then the magnitude of her errors likely also undermines the evidence (or the accused's ability to understand the proceedings) to an extent that the trial must be considered unfair on other grounds as well. Thus, the question of equal treatment may have little practical value in this context.

It might also be argued that, even though the accused is afforded an imperfect trial vis-à-vis a similarly-situated monolingual defendant, the provision of a court interpreter (unqualified or otherwise) is preferable to the alternative scenario where no interpretation is given at all. Put differently, having a poor interpreter is better than having no interpreter at all, at least as far as "equality" is concerned. This argument, however, overlooks the fact that Article 14 sets baseline fair trial standards to which an interpreted trial must also adhere: if the State wishes to place an individual's right to liberty at risk, it may only do so while maintaining certain minimum standards. "Equality before the court" cannot be interpreted to allow "better than nothing" anymore than the right to competent counsel can be said to guarantee "better than no counsel at all". However, given the unsettled nature of the right to equality before the court, and the wide variance in frequency and magnitude of interpreter errors in criminal proceedings, it is not possible to definitively state that every court interpreted proceeding is of such an unequal nature as to necessarily produce a violation of that right. On the other hand, the fact that every court interpreted proceeding will automatically, to at least some extent, involve inequalities before the court is highly problematic when equal treatment is guaranteed by right.

4.3 Right to Be Tried Without Undue Delay

Article 14 (3) (c) grants an accused the right "to be tried without undue delay." HRC jurisprudence has interpreted this right to apply to not only the amount of time it takes for the State to actually begin the accused's trial, but also to every stage of the criminal proceedings (HRC General Comment No. 32, §35; Weissbrodt 2001, p. 125). Thus, the elapsed time between each of the stages in a criminal proceeding must also be reasonable. When determining the reasonability of any delay, the HRC will consider the particular circumstances of the case, focusing on its complexity, the conduct of both parties, the manner in which the authorities handled a case, and any detrimental effects on the accused's legal position caused by the delay (*Lederbauer v. Austria* [HRC 2007] §8.1; see also HRC General Comment No. 32, §35). At the end of the day, however, it is the ultimate responsibility of the State to ensure that the proceedings are not unreasonably delayed (Weissbrodt 2001, p. 128).

Determining whether the involvement of court interpreters may lead to a violation of the right to be tried without undue delay is a deceptively difficult task. On one hand, where an accused suffers an unreasonable delay in his proceeding due to the inability of the court to procure a competent court interpreter, this would, on the surface at least, appear to be the responsibility of the State. However, in its Concluding Observations on Australia's first State Report, wherein Australia claimed that the shortage of available court interpreters in certain remote areas of the country was a special circumstance that justified longer than normal delays (McGoldrick 1994, p. 407), the HRC did not definitively contradict Australia's claim of an exception (HRC Concluding Observations: Australia [1983] §148). Their hesitancy in this respect leaves open the possibility that the State may not ultimately be responsible for otherwise unreasonable delays caused by the unavailability of court interpreters.

This outcome, however, appears largely illogical and counterproductive. If States may be held liable for unreasonable delays arising from the general inefficiency of their courts (Nowak 2005, p. 335) and therefore possess a positive duty "to organise their legal systems" such that a trial can be had without undue delay (*Mansur v. Turkey* [ECtHR 1995] §68; see also *Zimmerman and Steiner v. Switzerland* [ECtHR 1983] §29), then it is difficult to see why States would not be held responsible for the inability to employ a suitable court interpreter, which is an inefficiency created by inadequate structural incentives. Consider, for instance, the case of *Lubuto v. Zambia* (1995), where the HRC sympathized with the difficult economic situation in Zambia, but held that this did not excuse the unreasonable delay caused by the overall underfunding of its criminal justice system (§7.3). Jamaica as well has been criticized by the HRC for the inadequacy of its legal aid program, due at least partly to the insufficiency of compensation given to legal aid attorneys (Weissbrodt 2001, pp. 119–120). The unifying factor in both of these instances is the State's unwillingness (or inability) to adequately fund its criminal justice system and its ultimate responsibility for that decision. In the case of court interpreters, the failure to employ a suitable interpreter within a reasonable amount of time comes down, in part, to a reluctance by the State to pay the market rate for a qualified individual. This is a conscious choice, by the State, to sacrifice the accused's rights as a cost-saving measure. Such a tradeoff is generally not allowed under Article 14. Yet, to date, there has been no explicit indication from the HRC (or the ECtHR) that a lengthy delay attributable to the lack of a court interpreter will be held against the State.

4.4 Right to Counsel

An accused is guaranteed the right to counsel under Article 14 (3) (d). A significant aspect of this guarantee is not only the accused's right to have such counsel, but also to effectively communicate with his counsel (which is specifically protected in Article 14 [3] [b] as well). The degradation of such communication has been cited as a possible Article 6 ECHR violation by the ECtHR. In *Sakhnovskiy v. Russia* (2010), the ECtHR noted that a violation would exist where an accused and his counsel were unable to adequately communicate over a video-link because of technical difficulties (§98). While the inclusion of a court interpreter may not appear as obviously distorting to the communication process as malfunctioning communication technology, given that judges often treat interpreters as communication "machines", the applicability of the precedent is not absurd. Much as the sheer number and importance of errors made by court interpreters can undermine the accused's ability to understand his criminal proceedings, these errors can likewise distort any communication between the accused and his counsel. To cite but two examples from the multitude discussed above, the "frequent" omission or "prevalent" mistranslation of the sort of specialized legal vocabulary employed by counsel, as well as the common practice of explanation and simplification of such terms by adaptive court interpreters, will invariably weaken the accused's true capacity to effectively communicate with his counsel with respect to the details of his defense. In this respect, a poor interpreter is actually very similar to faulty technical equipment of the sort envisioned by the ECtHR, and would arguably create a similar violation.

Communication may also be undermined by the mere insertion of an interpreter between an accused and his counsel. It is well-established that an accused has the right to consult with his attorney outside the hearing of a third party (*Iskandarov v. Tajikistan* [HRC 2011] §6.7; *S. v. Switzerland* [ECtHR 1991] §48; see also van Dijk and Viering 2006, p. 639; Weissbrodt 2001, p. 122). While the confidentiality of lawyer-client communication is generally considered to be the paramount reason for retaining absolute privacy, such privacy also works to facilitate effective communication. In *Sakhnovskiy v. Russia* (2010), the ECtHR accepted that "the applicant might legitimately have felt ill at ease" discussing his case with counsel over video-link technology, given the questionable nature of its ability to provide sufficient privacy (§104). As such, the possibility that the conversation will be overheard by someone else inhibits effective communication and undermines the right to consult with one's attorney. Although it is true that court interpreters are bound to maintain the confidentiality of private communications (Stern 2011, p. 335; González et al. 1991, pp. 498–499), the practical effectiveness of this obligation relies on the usage of interpreters who are aware of these ethical canons, which is far from assured in practice. It is even more doubtful that the accused will be aware of the interpreter's ethical responsibilities. Therefore, even assuming interpreter confidentiality, the mere presence of the interpreter as a third-party may still cause an accused to be less candid with his attorney, thereby further weakening the accused's right to communicate with his counsel. This will especially be the case where the apparent and actual neutrality of the interpreter has been compromised in some manner.

An accused is also guaranteed counsel that is effective and competent (HRC General Comment No. 32, §38). Yet, those "frequent" and "common" interpreter errors discussed above will regularly interfere with the preparation of an accused's defense along with his participation at trial. The inability to communicate with the accused will render defense counsel less effective than the attorney of a similarly-situated defendant without communication difficulties. Furthermore, interpreter actions can negatively affect counsel's actual effectiveness during the proceedings. For instance, court interpreters "quite often" interrupt attorneys (Mason 2008, p. 41), a practice that renders the attorney significantly less competent in the eyes of the fact-finder (Berk-Seligson, 1990, pp. 187–188). This can affect the attorney's ability to persuade the fact-finder as to the innocence of his client. Interpreters also interrupt and exercise control over witnesses, as well as altering the content and style of their testimony. These habits undermine a defense attorney's ability to control the production of testimonial evidence, thereby negatively impacting the ultimate effectiveness of an accused's counsel.

Naturally, it is virtually impossible to determine outright that the common errors of court interpreters automatically violate an accused's right to counsel. The individual circumstances of each case must necessarily be considered. However, as with the other rights discussed above, the frequency of these errors and their potential impact upon the right to counsel is a worrying complication.

4.5 Right to an Interpreter

As examined in Chap. 2, every accused is entitled to the "free assistance of an interpreter if he cannot understand or speak the language used in court" (Art. 14 [3] [f] ICCPR). As can be seen from the text of Article 14 (3) (f), only an accused who is unable to understand or communicate in the language of the court is entitled to the appointment of a court interpreter; thus the right to an interpreter does not apply to witnesses or other parties who may find such assistance of value.[2] The appointment of a court interpreter by right, however, also necessarily guarantees that the court interpretation will meet certain minimum levels of quality (Nowak 2005, p. 344). In short, the right to a court interpreter also means a right to competent interpretation.

The focus is placed upon the end interpretation and its adequacy, as opposed to the general competence of the individual providing the interpretation. This has been the approach taken by the ECtHR in *Kamasinski v. Austria* (1989), and it makes logical sense, because it is the actual performance of the interpreter that allows the accused to understand and communicate in the language of the court, not her particular qualifications. This emphasis on the end result helps fulfill the overall purpose of the right, which is not to provide a well-qualified assistant, but rather to provide excellent assistance that alleviates any linguistic difficulties that "may constitute a major obstacle to the right of defence" (HRC General Comment No. 32, §13). Thus, it is the result that is of importance, not the process. The right to an interpreter would appear to be fulfilled where that result involves the removal of the linguistic barriers that prevent the accused from "understand[ing] or speak[ing] the language used in court" (Art. 14 [3] [f] ICCPR). As such, the standard for "competency" in this context would seem to align quite closely to the standard discussed above with reference to the understanding of evidence: the foreign-language accused must be able to understand and participate in the proceedings.

The requirement that a foreign-language accused be able to both understand and participate in his proceeding is, as previously noted, problematic at best. There is little utility in reexamining at length each of the errors and problems associated with court interpreters that work to undermine this outcome. It is enough to note here, again, that the prevalence and general magnitude of these distortions and errors is sufficient to call into question whether a foreign-language accused who is provided a court interpreter is actually experiencing and taking part in the same proceeding as the other courtroom participants. This being the case, the general deficiencies of court interpreter performance may be said to substantially undermine the actual right to an interpreter as well. This is even more the case where, as happens regularly in numerous jurisdictions, those individuals employed as interpreters lack both training and qualifications in the field (Stern 2011, p. 339; see Chap. 6). Such interpreters have acknowledged deficiencies that significantly reduce the likelihood of an adequate end result.

Of course, the appointment of an untrained interpreter does not necessarily equate to a violation of the right any more than the employment of a highly-qualified interpreter automatically safeguards it. The ultimate fulfillment of the right hinges on the competence of the actual interpretation provided. Thus, every individual performance must be evaluated to determine whether the inevitable errors inherent in the process reach a threshold whereby they subvert the accused's understanding of, and participation in, the proceeding. However, given the relative inability of the appellate system to provide effective oversight as to the linguistic competence of an interpreter's work, the pervasiveness of interpreter distortions (from both trained and untrained interpreters) leaves the right to an interpreter in significant danger.

4.6 Right to Appeal

Article 14 (5) ICCPR grants "everyone convicted of a crime" the right to have their conviction and sentence "reviewed by a higher tribunal according to law." For the purposes of this section, the most important aspects of this guarantee are that the appeal be both adequate and effective. The "adequacy" of an appeal requires the higher tribunal to consider not only those questions of law raised by the appellant, but also to consider, when asked, whether the evidence was sufficient to uphold the conviction (HRC General Comment No. 32, §48; *Domukovsky and others v. Georgia* [HRC 1998] §18.11). In other words, the court must consider those points of appeal (both procedural and factual) raised by the appellant, so long as they are pertinent to the case (Marshall 2011, p. 20; see also

Kharkhal v. Belarus [HRC 2007] §6.5). This would seemingly include any appellate complaints focused on any of the individual fair trial rights encompassed in the domestic law, such as the right to counsel or the right to examine witnesses. In fact, the original intention of the right to appeal was to ensure, through appellate oversight, that the other, individual fair trial rights were respected throughout the process (Marshall 2011, p. 17).

Where the right to appeal becomes somewhat awkward with respect to court interpreters involves the guarantee that the right be "effective", which means that the appellant must have non-discretionary access not only to an appellate court generally, but also to all of the documents necessary to prosecute his appeal (Marshall 2011, pp. 19–21; Nowak 2005, p. 349). Here, the State has an "obligation to preserve sufficient evidential material" to allow for appellate review (*Robinson v. Jamaica* [HRC 2000] §10.7). The HRC has held in *Lumley v. Jamaica* (1999) that the trial transcript is one of the documents necessary to prosecute an appeal (§7.5), since without a transcript there is no evidentiary material on which to base an appeal. In the context of an interpreted trial, such a requirement is problematic because there generally exists no documents or records on which to base an appeal of evidence that has been interpreted. A witness who testifies through an interpreter leaves no evidence of their original testimony in the record, since the trial record documents only the court interpreter's version in the language of the court (Stern 2011, p. 336; Kahaner 2008–2009, p. 226; de Mas 2001, p. 4; Messier 1999, p. 1408; Morris 1998, p. 4). Yet, presumably, an accused would be entitled to allege on appeal that he was denied an effective right to call or cross-examine a foreign language witness due to faulty or incompetent interpretation. However, with no trial record of the witness's original testimony in the foreign language, there would be no means by which to ascertain the court interpreter's performance. As such, the accused would effectively be denied any practical ability to prosecute this point on appeal.

Furthermore, there is generally no record at all of any of the foreign language statements made in court. Thus, although the accused is logically entitled to a competent court interpreter, there is little evidence in the record with which the accused might directly challenge this competency after the fact. Without the ability to consult a foreign language record and pinpoint each and every mistake of importance for the court, as well as extrapolate the potential consequences of these mistakes on the eventual outcome of the trial, the accused is left with no evidence on which to rest his claims. In effect, his predicament is little different than a normal appellant from a monolingual trial seeking to raise an appeal where no trial transcript at all has been preserved. This exact scenario was found to be a violation of the right to appeal in *Lumley v. Jamaica* ([HRC 1999] §7.5). It is not absurd to think that, where a trial involves a court interpreter, the lack of a bilingual record might constitute a violation as well. Given that such bilingual records are a rarity at best, the existence of an interpreted trial presents substantial problems for an accused's eventual right to appeal.

4.7 Conclusion

As can be seen, the impact of court interpreter error is not restricted to those fair trial rights primarily related to the production or understanding of evidence. Its influence extends much deeper. Interpreters can negatively impact an accused's right to equality before the court, infringe upon the right to counsel, and render the right to appeal virtually ineffective. Where a court interpreter is unskilled and untrained, there lack of competence may violate the very right that led to their appointment in the first place: the right to an interpreter itself. The inability to appoint an interpreter in a timely manner may also inadvertently cause an unreasonable delay in the trial proceedings. These rights, though perhaps less obviously impacted than those relating to evidence, are no less important and appear equally threatened by improper court interpretation.

5 Conclusion and Reflections on Overall Fairness

5.1 The Individual Fair Trial Rights

The analysis above has examined several different, but related, problems with respect to the right to a fair trial and the employment of court interpreters. These errors can best be described as alterations of content or style, and their impact can be felt on both the production and understanding of the evidence during a proceeding, as well as in other areas of importance. The accumulated effect of these distortions on an accused's fair trial rights is highly problematic.

From a content-perspective, court interpreters systematically distort the substance of a speaker's remarks. At the outset, the choice of the verbatim (word-for-word) or pragmatic (meaning-based) interpreting standard influences the interpreter's eventual accuracy, while the common usage of the adaptation role (simplification and explanation) leads to distortions and inequality among defendants (see Chap. 5). Furthermore, the mistaken use by court interpreters of "false friends" is "common" (de Jongh 1992, p. 77), the incorrect modification of a speaker's verb tense is "widespread" (Berk-Seligson, 1990, p. 116), and idiomatic speech is "often" mistranslated (González et al. 1991, p. 286). In addition, court interpreters "frequently" omit content while "often" adding their own substance, and the mistranslation of both general and specialized vocabulary is "prevalent" (González et al. 1991, pp. 287–289). Taken together, these "frequent" and "common" practices must invariably lead to significant distortions in the content of a speaker's speech.

Court interpreters also "constantly" alter the style of a speaker's comments (Hale 2002, p. 43), "generally" replacing an individual's speech mannerisms with their own speech style instead (Hale 2007, p. 200). In this context, interpreters "systematically" change levels of formality (Berk-Seligson 1990, p. 172), "very rarely" maintain a speaker's hesitations, hedges and filler while "often" inserting their own (Hale 2002, p. 43; Berk-Seligson 1990, p. 140), "frequently" alter politeness markers (Berk-Seligson 1990, pp. 150–154), "almost systematically" eliminate discourse markers (Hale 2004, p. 62), and change the form of an attorney's questions at a substantial rate (Hale 2004, p. 44). While these alterations may seem fairly harmless at first, distortions in speech style directly influence a fact-finder's or individual's perception of the value of the information conveyed. In other words, although these distortions do not change the substance of the speech, they make it substantially more or less likely that the listener will believe that substance.

Each of these errors affects the individual fair trial rights in its own unique, perhaps minimal, way. However, considered together, they can be of great significance. For example, with respect to the production of testimonial evidence, the alterations of content endemic to an interpreter's performance can lead to a divergence between what the witness's testimony actually alleged, and what the fact-finder actually understood. Moreover, the widespread modification of the witness's style will invariably alter the fact-finder's perception of that testimony as well (Hale 2002, p. 26). These distortions undermine an accused's right to adversarial proceedings, to an oral hearing, to examine witnesses, and to have adequate time and facilities to prepare a defense. They likewise weaken a foreign-language accused's right to be present at his own trial, as well as his right to counsel and to have a competent interpreter, since the same interpreter practices that distort the production of evidence will also consistently undermine that accused's ability to communicate with his counsel and to understand and participate in his interpreted proceedings.

The standard practices and common errors of court interpreters also call into question the equality of interpreted proceedings, since these will consistently invite a heightened risk of a fair trial violation that does not otherwise exist in non-interpreted proceedings. In addition, common practices such as simplification and explanation will invariably produce advantages (or disadvantages) for a foreign-language accused that other, similarly situated defendants will not enjoy. Furthermore, the relative scarcity of trained and qualified court interpreters may also lead to unequal treatment before the court, since it places the court in the position of either employing an unqualified individual (along with the increased risks associated therewith) or tolerating an otherwise unacceptable delay in the proceedings. Such a delay can also negatively affect witness recollection and the accurate production of testimonial evidence. And even though the HRC has not definitively decided the issue, the weight of its prior logic in the area indicates that the State may be held responsible for otherwise unreasonable delays associated with court interpreter unavailability.

Finally, the involvement of court interpreters in a proceeding has a significant impact on the ability of an accused to appeal certain aspects of his trial. The lack of a bilingual record renders the effective oversight of a court interpreter's work at the appellate level virtually impossible, since there is no mechanism by which to gauge the correctness of the interpretations after the fact. This emasculates the right to appeal with respect to interpretation issues. Furthermore, the lack of effective appellate oversight also eliminates any preventative effect the right to an appeal might have on court interpreters (Trechsel 2005, p. 362): since no one can actually check their work, there is little incentive to invest in the accuracy of their interpretations or their further training and education. Thus, with respect to court interpreters, the practical diminishment of the right to appeal has systemic knock-on effects throughout the entirety of the right to a fair trial.

5.2 The Right to Overall Fairness

While it cannot be said definitively that any of the individual fair trial rights is necessarily violated by the common practices and errors of court interpreters, since these are determinations that must be made on a case-by-case basis, it is important to recollect that the right to a fair trial consists of more than these individual rights. In fact, the individual rights are meant, at their most basic level, mainly to ensure the overall fairness of the trial itself through the protection of specific procedural aspects common to a fair proceeding. As such, it is necessary to gauge the overall fairness of the end proceeding itself. The HRC commonly engages in such an evaluation by looking at the trial "as a whole" (see for example *Akhadov v. Kyrgyzstan* [HRC 2011] §7.5; *Khostikoev v. Tajikistan* [HRC 2009] §7.3; *Tolipkhuzhaev v. Uzbekistan* [HRC 2009] §8.4).

It is in this context that the actions of court interpreters are most alarming. Each of the errors discussed in this work, on their own in any specific, isolated incident, may appear meaningless and unimportant. However, when repeated consistently throughout a proceeding, they take on greater significance. Yet, court interpreters do not limit themselves to the "frequent" repetition of one particular form of interpreter error; rather they commonly make a variety of different alterations and distortions (depending upon their abilities and training) throughout a proceeding. Taken together, these distortions of both style and substance add up to produce a collection of mistranslations and misrepresentations that is specific to a particular proceeding and interpreter. These alterations, depending upon their magnitude and prevalence, may or may not violate one of the individual fair trial rights. To a certain extent, however, this is beside the point. The systemic nature of many of these errors is such that they may simultaneously undermine a wide variety of other individual fair trial rights without ever fully breaching any one of them. This cumulative degenerative effect upon each of the fair trial rights individually may actually render the overall proceeding unfair. In other words, taken "as a whole", the (incomplete) undermining of each of the individual rights may ultimately infringe the overall fairness of the trial.

In a sense, a single interpreter error is similar to a small fingerprint smudge on a glass window pane. On its own, this fingerprint will not impede an individual's ability to see through the window, and will thus appear insignificant in isolation. However, if the window acquires enough such "insignificant" smudges, its functionality becomes questionable, since any attempt to look through the window will produce a highly distorted representation at best. The same is true of an interpreted trial, where enough minor errors throughout the proceeding will produce a highly distorted end result, even where the errors themselves appear meaningless in isolation. Making matters worse, since the court interpreter is often the only bilingual individual involved in the proceeding and no bilingual record is kept, the other participants (as well as the appellate court) are not even aware that the window is actually smudged. Rather, the highly distorted view is accepted by everyone as the proper representation of reality. Given the importance of accuracy in a criminal proceeding, it is difficult to accept this distorted outcome as objectively "fair".

5.3 Conclusion

It is obvious that court interpreters affect an accused's right to a fair trial. The errors and distortions inherent in the normal process of interpreting, especially considering their frequency and seriousness, either substantially undermine or outright infringe the individual rights necessary to ensure a fair trial. Likewise, in their accumulated state, these widespread distortions significantly jeopardize the overall fairness of a proceeding as well. While the wide variance in court interpreter ability and performance level make it impossible to say that the mere employment of an interpreter necessarily violates an accused's right to a fair trial, the risk of violations is substantial enough that the issue must, and should, be taken more seriously.

Notes

1. It is important to note in this context that *Domukovsky* was a death penalty case, which may play some role in the HRC's decision.
2. This is not to say, of course, that an accused who speaks the language of the court would not be entitled to an interpreter for witnesses on his behalf that do not. It is likely that the accused's right to adequate facilities to prepare defense, as well as the equality of arms, would guarantee such assistance.

Bibliography

Astiz, C. A. (1986). But They Don't Speak the Language: Achieving Quality Control of Translation in Criminal Courts. *The Judge's Journal, 25*, 32–35, 56.

Berk-Seligson, S. (1990). *The Bilingual Courtroom: Court Interpreters in the Judicial Process*. Chicago: University of Chicago Press.

Berk-Seligson, S. (2002). The Impact of Politeness in Witness Testimony: The Influence of the Court Interpreter. In F. Pöchhacker & M. Shlesinger (Eds.), *The Interpreting Studies Reader* (pp. 279–292). London: Routledge.

de Jongh, E. (1992). *An Introduction to Court Interpreting: Theory & Practice*. Lanham: University Press of America.

de Mas, S. (2001). Translation, Interpreting & Legal Rights within the European Union: The Law & Reality. In *Critical Link 3 – Interpreting in the Community: The Complexity of the Profession – Montreal* [online]. Available at: https://static1.squarespace.com/static/52d566cbe4b0002632d34367/t/5347f5f0e4b0bccee306dac1/1397224944878/CL3_deMas.pdf. Accessed 21 Nov 2017.

González, R., Vásquez, V. F., & Mikkelson, H. (1991). *Fundamentals of Court Interpretation: Theory, Policy, and Practice*. Durham: Carolina Academic Press.

Hale, S. (2001). The Complexities of the Bilingual Courtroom. *Law Society Journal, 39*, 68–72.

Hale, S. (2002). How Faithfully Do Court Interpreters Render the Style of Non-English Speaking Witnesses' Testimonies? A Data-Based Study of Spanish-English Bilingual Proceedings. *Discourse Studies, 4*(1), 25–47.

Hale, S. (2004). *The Discourse of Court Interpreting: Discourse Practices of the Law, the Witness and the Interpreter*. Amsterdam: John Benjamins.

Hale, S. (2007). Challenges of Court Interpreting: Intricacies, Responsibilities and Ramifications. *Alternative Law Journal, 32*, 198–202.

Ibrahim, Z. (2007). The Interpreter as Advocate: Malaysian Court Interpreting as a Case in Point. In C. Wadensjö, B. Englund Dimitrova, & A.-L. Nilsson (Eds.), *The Critical Link 4: Professionalisation of Interpreting in the Community* (pp. 205–213). Amsterdam: John Benjamins.

Jacobsen, B. (2004). Pragmatic Meaning in Court Interpreting: An Empirical Study of Additions in Consecutively Interpreted Question-Answer Dialogues. *Hermes – Journal of Language and Communication in Business, 32*, 237–249.

Kahaner, S. M. (2008–09). The Administration of Justice in a Multilingual Society – Open to Interpretation or Lost in Translation? *Judicature, 92*, 224–231.

Marshall, P. D. (2011). A Comparative Analysis of the Right to Appeal. *Duke Journal of Comparative & International Law, 22*, 1–46.

Mason, M. (2008). *Courtroom Interpreting*. Lanham: University Press of America.

McGoldrick, D. (1994). *The Human Rights Committee: Its Role in the Development of the International Covenant on Civil and Political Rights*. Oxford: Clarendon Press.

Messier, F. (1999). Alien Defendants in Criminal Proceedings: Justice Shrugs. *American Criminal Law Review, 36*, 1395–1419.

Moeketsi, R. H. (1999). Redefining the Role of the South African Court Interpreter. *Proteus, 8*(3–4), 12–15.

Morris, R. (1998). Justice in Jerusalem – Interpreting in Israeli Legal Proceedings. *Meta, 43*(1), 110–118.

Nowak, M. (2005). *U.N. Covenant on Civil and Political Rights: CCPR Commentary* (2nd ed.). Kehl: Engel.

Stern, L. (2011). Courtroom Interpreting. In K. Malmkjær & K. Windle (Eds.), *The Oxford Handbook of Translation Studies* (pp. 325–342). Oxford: Oxford University Press.

Trechsel, S. (2005). *Human Rights in Criminal Proceedings*. Oxford: Oxford University Press.

van Dijk, P., & Viering, M. (2006). Right to a Fair and Public Hearing (Article 6). In P. van Dijk, F. van Hoof, A. van Rijn, & L. Zwaak (Eds.), *Theory and Practice of the European Convention on Human Rights* (4th ed., pp. 511–650). Antwerpen: Intersentia.

Weissbrodt, D. (2001). *The Right to a Fair Trial Under the Universal Declaration of Human Rights and the International Covenant on Civil and Political Rights*. The Hague: Nijhoff.

Other Documents

Convention for the Protection of Human Rights and Fundamental Freedoms. (1953). 213 UNTS 221, signed 4 November 1950, entered into force 3 September 1953.

Human Rights Committee. (1983, September 15). Concluding Observations of the Human Rights Committee: Australia. In: Human Rights Committee. *Report of the Human Rights Committee,* U.N. Doc. A/38/40.

International Covenant on Civil and Political Rights. (1976). 999 UNTS 171, adopted 16 December 1966, entered into force 23 March 1976.

List of Cases

Akbarkhudzh Tolipkhuzhaev v. Uzbekistan (HRC 2009). Communication No. 1280/2004 (22 July 2009) U.N. Doc. CCPR/C/96/D/1280/2004.

Bernard Lubuto v. Zambia (HRC 1995). Communication No. 390/1990 (31 October 1995) U.N. Doc. CCPR/C/55/D/390/1990/Rev.1.

Dimitry Kharkhal v. Belarus (HRC 2007). Communication No. 1161/2003 (31 October 2007) CCPR/C/91/D/1161/2003.

Dimitry L. Gridin v. Russian Federation (HRC 2000). Communication No. 770 (20 July 2000) U.N. Doc. CCPR/C/69/D/770/1997.

Garfield Peart and Andrew Peart v. Jamaica (HRC 1995). Communications Nos. 464/1991 & 482/1991 (19 July 1995) U.N. Doc. CCPR/C/54/D/464/1991 & 482/1991.

José Luis García Fuenzalida v. Ecuador (HRC 1996). Communication No. 480/1991 (12 July 1996) U.N. Doc. CCPR/C/57/D/480/1991.

Kamasinski v. Austria (ECtHR 1989). Application No. 9783/82 (19 December 1989) Series A No. 168.

Kostovski v. The Netherlands (ECtHR 1989). Application No. 11454/85 (20 November 1989) Series A No. 166.

Lucy Dudko v. Australia (HRC 2007). Communication No. 1347/2005 (23 July 2007) U.N. Doc. CCPR/C/90/D/1347/2005.

Mansur v. Turkey (ECtHR 1995). Application No. 16026/90 (8 June 1995) Series A No. 319-B.

Michael Robinson v. Jamaica (HRC 2000). Communication No. 731/1996 (29 March 2000) U.N. Doc. CCPR/C/68/D/731/1996.

Mukhammadruzi Iskandarov v. Tajikistan (HRC 2011). Communication No. 1499/2006 (30 March 2011) U.N. Doc. CCPR/C/101/D/1499/2006.

Olimzhon Ashurov v. Tajikistan (HRC 2007). Communication No. 1348/2005 (20 March 2007) U.N. Doc. CCPR/C/89/D/1348/2005.

Otabek Akhadov v. Kyrgyzstan (HRC 2011). Communication No. 1503/2006 (25 March 2011) U.N. Doc. CCPR/C/101/D/1503/2006.

Peter Lumley v. Jamaica (HRC 1999). Communication No. 662/1995 (31 March 1999) U.N. Doc. CCPR/C/65/D/662/1995.

Pitkänen v. Finland (ECtHR 2004). Application No. 30508/96 (9 March 2004).

S. v. Switzerland (ECtHR 1991). Application Nos. 12629/87 & 13965/88 (28 November 1991) Series A No. 220.

Sakhnovskiy v. Russia (ECtHR 2010). Application No. 21272/03 (2 November 2010).

Valery Khostikoev v. Tajikistan (HRC 2009). Communication No. 1519/2006 (22 October 2009) U.N. Doc. CCPR/C/97/D/1519/2006.

Van Mechelen and Others v. The Netherlands (ECtHR 1997). Applications Nos. 21363/93, 21364/93, 21427/93 & 22056/93 (23 April 1997) 25 EHRR 647.

Victor P. Domukovsky and others v. Georgia (HRC 1998). Communications Nos. 623/1995, 624/1995, 626/1995, 627/1995 (6 April 1998) U.N. Docs. CCPR/C/62/D/623/1995, CCPR/C/62/D/624/1995, CCPR/C/62/D/626/1995, CCPR/C/62/D/627/1995.

Wolfgang Lederbauer v. Austria (HRC 2007). Communication No. 1454/2006 (13 July 2007) U.N. Doc. CCPR/C/90/D/1454/2006.

Zimmerman and Steiner v. Switzerland (ECtHR 1983). Application No. 8737/79 (13 July 1983) Series A No. 66.

8

Conclusions and Proposals

1 Introduction

The goal of this study was to assess the impact of court interpreters on the right of an accused to be afforded a fair trial. An analysis of the various distortions and mistakes introduced by court interpreters, as well as the systemic issues that arise with the usage of court interpreters generally, leads to the inevitable conclusion that the right to a fair trial is at substantial risk during interpreted trials. The widespread distortion of witness testimony, as well as the routine modification of their speech style, significantly alters both the fact-finder's understanding of the evidence, as well as their assessment of the reliability of that evidence. In addition, the same distortions and modifications undermine a foreign-language accused's ability to effectively understand and participate in his criminal proceeding by cutting him off from the actual evidence that is heard by the court. These same interpreter complications likewise weaken an accused's ability to communicate with his counsel and self-evidently jeopardize his actual right to an interpreter. Furthermore, the prevalence of court interpreter errors and alterations creates a trial that is invariably unequal to that given to a similarly situated defendant, and in many instances fails to

J. H. Dingfelder Stone, *Court Interpreters and Fair Trials*,
https://doi.org/10.1007/978-3-319-75355-3_8

allow an affected accused the opportunity to interact with the court on the same terms as the prosecutor. That all of these difficulties exist largely free from any meaningful, contemporaneous oversight and are also not retained in a bilingual record that would allow for any oversight after the fact, clearly endangers an accused's right to effective appellate review. The sheer frequency and magnitude of the difficulties arising from the employment of a court interpreter, and their systematic undermining of the individual fair trial rights, calls into serious question whether the overall fairness of proceedings involving an interpreter can meet international standards.

That court interpretation will automatically lead to a violation of an accused's right to a fair trial, though, is not an inevitable result. Aside from the fact that some interpreters are simply more competent than others, there is also the fact that the impact of a court interpreter on a criminal proceeding can be minimized through effective management of both the individual situation and the overall process. It is true that some aspects of interpreting, such as the lack of perfect linguistic equivalents, will necessarily lead to distortions in the record. These imprecisions are natural and unavoidable. Yet, their frequency and significance can likewise be mitigated in a variety of different ways. Thus, there is nothing inherent in the process itself that necessarily proves fatal to the fairness of any and all interpreted proceedings.

Rather, in many instances, it is the insertion of a court interpreter into a criminal justice system that is ill-prepared to accommodate her, and the process by which this interpreter is appointed, that exacerbates or even produces many of the difficulties identified and discussed in this study. As such, the specific errors and mistakes detailed in Chap. 5 arise not only from the complexities of the interpreting process itself, but also from a variety of other systemic issues. The pervasiveness and significance of these problems is often attributable to factors that exist beyond the control of the interpreter. However, they are within the control of the criminal justice system, and can be modified. Addressing these underlying issues may drastically reduce the negative impact court interpreters have on fair trial rights. The proposals presented in this Chapter are made with this goal in mind.

2 Better Informed Courtroom Actors

2.1 Overview

As has been noted, judges and attorneys lack a clear understanding of the court interpreter's role within the judicial process (Stern 2011, p. 341), and invariably underestimate the importance of the court interpreter to the accuracy of the proceedings (Davis and Hewitt 1994, pp. 121, 131; González et al. 1991, p. 5). In some instances, this lack of knowledge can have a highly negative impact upon the interpreter's ethical obligations or work product, such as where the judge does not realize the significance of the interpreter's placement within the courtroom, or where the courtroom actors expect the interpreter to act as their liaison with the foreign language participant (Mason 2008, p. 53; Lindie 1993, p. 414). Furthermore, the continuing assumption by judges and attorneys that interpreting is similar to mathematics, and that one correct translation actually exists in any given situation (LaVigne and Vernon 2003, p. 868), blinds them to the actual indeterminacy and vagueness of the process as well as to the importance of ascertaining a qualified interpreter to perform it. The obvious solution to these problems is the improved education and training of courtroom personnel as to the interpreting process and the work of court interpreters (Stern 2011, p. 341; Choolun 2009, p. 30; Fowler 1995, p. 200; Davis and Hewitt 1994, p. 145). Likewise, some educational development in the area of foreign languages and cultures generally can help increase awareness among courtroom actors concerning the myriad difficulties they can produce within the courtroom (Moeketsi 1999, p. 181; Mikkelson 1998b, p. 12). Better informed court personnel can increase the efficiency and accuracy of interpreted proceedings in a variety of ways.

2.2 Better Working Conditions

Where the courtroom actors more completely understand the interpreter's role within the process and her professional needs, working conditions for court interpreters should improve. Thus, interpreter placement within the courtroom should cease to be a problem because judges will be aware of its importance with respect to the interpreter's ability to hear the speaker. In addition, more essential infrastructure (such as water, seating, etc…) will likely be made available, since the courtroom actors will better understand the interpreter's work necessities. Moreover, informed attorneys will be less likely to object to the provision of advance materials, since they will comprehend the advantage of having a fully-prepared interpreter (Stern 2011, p. 341; Moeketsi 1999, p. 180; Davis and Hewitt 1994, p. 133). It would also be hoped that improved judicial awareness of interpreter needs would result in increased cooperation and assistance on the part of the judiciary, which is not always currently the case (Mikkelson 1998b, p. 12; Edwards 1995, p. 89).

2.3 Reduction in Problematic Actions

Attorneys with an enhanced understanding of the interpreting process and its inherent difficulties will be more likely to monitor the speed, clarity, and length of their speech, thus reducing the potential for errors and the likelihood of interpreter interruptions (Stern 2011, p. 341; Berk-Seligson 1990, pp. 188, 191; González et al. 1991, p. 179). Furthermore, given that the inherent difficulties of language and the complexity of finding suitable equivalents produce substantial issues for court interpreters, informed attorneys will be better able to avoid unnecessarily problematic language and cultural expressions that might reduce the accuracy of the interpreter's work (González et al. 1991, pp. 179–180). A proper understanding of the interpreter's role and ethical obligations should also help courtroom personnel avoid inadvertently placing interpreters in situations that might harm the appearance of their impartiality (Mikkelson 2000, pp. 55–56; Edwards 1995, pp. 68–69).

2.4 Revised Judicial Control Over Problematic Actions

The increased awareness of interpreters in the courtroom might also improve interpreter accuracy through the more efficient exercise of judicial control over interpreted proceedings. On the one hand, certain aspects of the interpretation process can be enhanced by stricter judicial control over the courtroom participants. For instance, before interpreted proceedings, the judge might instruct both parties to rigorously adhere to particular rules on speech involving volume, clarity, and the elimination of extraneous noise (Kahaner 2008–2009, pp. 228–229; Grabau 1996, p. 10; Davis and Hewitt 1994, pp. 133–135). Likewise, a detailed instruction on the proper role of the interpreter might make up for any deficiencies in knowledge that exist for witnesses and attorneys (Kahaner 2008–2009, p. 228; Grabau 1996, p. 10; Davis and Hewitt 1994, pp. 133–134). The judge might also reinforce the importance of linguistic simplicity when working with an interpreter (such as eliminating double negatives and idioms, avoiding needlessly complex questions, and not using cultural references) (Edwards 1995, p. 93; González et al. 1991, p. 175). The strict enforcement of these rules during the proceedings themselves will likewise assist the interpreter in her work. On the other hand, some aspects of the proceedings may be better served with a more relaxed approach. For example, allowing the interpreter herself to regulate the volume and speed of speech might be more appropriate, since the interpreter will be more aware of her specific necessities than the judge will be (Kahaner 2008–2009, p. 229). The same holds true for monitoring the length of speech and the placement of the interpreter in the courtroom (Grabau 1996, p. 10; González et al. 1991, p. 175).

Altering the current levels of judicial control over proceedings is not without its negatives, however. Even with increased training, some judges may inadvertently impact the interpreter's work in a negative manner by altering the rules of speech too much. For instance, by strictly enforcing the length of speech segments, a judge might cut off a witness at a moment that makes interpretation of their statement more difficult, not less. Furthermore, requiring attorneys to change their normal manner of speech to accommodate an interpreter is effectively diminishing their level of performance and increasing the complexity of the attorney's job. In addition to the myriad other factual and procedural issues on which they must concentrate, attorneys will also be forced to focus on an issue that is normally automatic. Finally, simplifying the language used in court, and changing the rules by which that language may be employed, produces a proceeding that is fundamentally different in its nature to that of a monolingual proceeding. In other words, accommodating the interpreter to improve accuracy, may, if carried too far, alter the proceedings to an extent that places the equality of the trial at risk.

2.5 Combating Fatigue

Currently, interpreters generally work beyond their fatigue threshold, much to the detriment of their performance (Stern 2011, p. 332; Mason 2008, p. 8; González et al. 1991, p. 509). Better informed courtroom actors should help eliminate this practice, as judges and attorneys will be more aware of the harmful effects such fatigue can have on the accuracy of the interpreter's work. The increased provision of courtroom breaks is one possible outcome, as is the safeguarding of the interpreter's "free" time from extra work assignments delegated by the court or attorneys (González et al. 1991, p. 177). Supplying court interpreters with a break every 30 minutes would preserve their cognitive alertness and protect the accuracy of the interpretation. However, it would also substantially increase the amount of time needed for normal court proceedings.

Another potential option is the expansion of team interpreting in courtrooms, whereby two interpreters alternate every 30 minutes, as is the standard practice in conference interpreting and the international tribunals (Stern 2011, p. 332; Edwards 1995, p. 74; González et al. 1991, pp. 509, 510). Adding an extra interpreter would also increase the possibility that any interpretation error would be discovered during the proceeding itself, since one interpreter would always be in a position to provide oversight (Heller 1994–1995, pp. 381–382; Shulman 1993, p. 193). Another advantage is that having two interpreters would minimize the necessity for breaks, and thereby reduce the overall length of the proceedings. The disadvantages to team interpreting, though, are fairly substantial. First, adding an extra court interpreter would significantly increase interpreting costs (Shulman 1993, p. 193; Steele 1991–1992, pp. 243–244). Second, since court interpreters rarely work in teams, they may be unfamiliar with the process, which may lead to an increase in concentration-related errors (Mason 2008, p. 8). Third, given that many courts are unable to find a single qualified court interpreter, locating two such individuals is perhaps unrealistic in many circumstances (Shulman 1993, p. 193).

2.6 Better Appointment Procedures

Finally, the increased training of judges with respect to the difficulty of interpreting and the importance of a court interpreter's skill and experience, should lead to an increased emphasis on employing qualified interpreters (thus marginalizing the unqualified and *ad hoc* interpreters who are most likely to make mistakes and produce inaccurate interpretations). In addition, a heightened understanding of the process on the part of judges and attorneys should end the false incentive that currently exists for court interpreters to improve a speaker's output in an attempt to look better themselves.

2.7 Conclusion

In these various ways, fostering a better awareness of the court interpreter's task and role in the courtroom can fundamentally decrease the potential for errors and inaccuracies in the interpreter's work. Better informed courtroom actors can exercise their decision-making powers with the knowledge of how their decisions will affect the work of the interpreter and the eventual accuracy of the proceedings. The end result would ideally be a courtroom proceeding tailored, where possible, to the specific necessities of a qualified court interpreter.

3 Better Court Interpreters

The most obvious way to improve the accuracy of court interpretations is to employ better trained and more experienced court interpreters. In fact, it could be argued that taking this one simple step would alleviate the vast majority of the specific issues discussed in previous Chapters. Yet, although the solution may appear obvious, it is far from easy to achieve. The reality of the situation is that demand for highly trained interpreters far outstrips the available supply. Given the increased level of globalization in the world, the demand for such interpreters seems more likely to grow than to diminish. Thus, if the gap between supply and demand is to be eliminated, it must come from an increase in the supply of qualified interpreters willing and available to work in court proceedings. There are several different ways to attack this problem.

3.1 Increased Quantity and Quality of Court Interpreter Training

One solution to the shortage of untrained court interpreters is to simply train more individuals to be court interpreters. However, as simple as this may sound in theory, in practice it proves rather difficult. Adequately training individuals to act as court interpreters would likely involve making significant changes to the existing practices in some countries.

In many instances, the currently available training options for interpreters are either inadequate or not specific enough to court interpreting (Stern 2011, pp. 339–341). In the United States, for example, there are very few educational programs dedicated specifically to teaching general interpreting skills (de Jongh 1992, p. 121). Normally, those interpreting programs or classes that have been created survive in the greater context of a literature or language department and not as a stand-alone program (Benmaman 1992, p. 448). A similar situation exists in Australia, where legal interpretation is not recognized as a specialization and most training is generalist in nature (Stern 2011, p. 340; Laster and Taylor 1994, p. 33). Even in Europe, where dedicated interpreting programs have long flourished, the emphasis is on training conference interpreters: an EU-wide proposal to teach court interpretation at the university level has gained little traction (Stern 2011, p. 340; see also Moeketsi 1999, p. 139). Thus, in order to increase the number of trained court interpreters, one must effectively create the educational programs that will provide such training. This would be a fairly significant, and costly, endeavor. Nor is it always even possible: with respect to rare languages, it can be extremely difficult to find one qualified court interpreter capable of teaching in such a program, let alone enough students with the requisite language skills to make the program economically feasible (Mikkelson 2000, p. 8; Mikkelson 1998a, p. 7).

In addition, even where specialty training programs exist, court interpreters generally display a lack of interest in participating in those programs; the low level of pay and the inability of court personnel to distinguish between good and bad interpreters provide little incentive for interpreters to invest their own time and resources in specialized training programs (Aliverti and Seoighe 2017, p. 141; Choolun 2009, p. 30; Hale 2007, p. 201). Finally, those interpreters that do partake in specialized training and thereby become highly-skilled in court interpretation are likely to be in such high demand in the private sector that the criminal justice system can no longer afford their services. In this manner, although improved training opportunities may lead to an increase in the number of interpreters trained in courtroom interpretation, it does not necessarily mean that those interpreters will invariably work in criminal courtrooms.

3.2 Increase in the Remuneration of Court Interpreters

Put bluntly, the level of pay afforded court interpreters in many jurisdictions is shockingly low given the level of expertise required to perform the job adequately (Stern 2011, p. 332 [generally]; see also for example Aliverti and Seoighe 2017, pp. 140–141 [with respect to the United Kingdom]; Ciorciari and Heindel 2014, p. 419 [with respect to the Extraordinary Chambers in the Courts of Cambodia]; Apostolou 2012, pp. 216–217 [with respect to Greece]; Phelan 2011, p. 79 [with respect to Ireland]; Sandrelli 2009 [with respect to Italy]; Ibrahim and Bell 2003, p. 216 [with respect to Malaysia] *Court Interpreter's Job Is No Easy Task* 2002 [with respect to Japan]; Miguélez 1999, p. 2 [with respect to Spain]). As detailed in Chap. 6, highly qualified, experienced interpreters generally do not work as court interpreters because they are more adequately compensated for their unique skillset elsewhere in the free market. This will likely also hold true for those interpreters who have undergone specific training with relation to courtroom interpretation. Yet, given the difficulty and importance of court interpreting, such highly skilled interpreters are the very individuals that the court system needs to more readily employ in order to improve standards. This can be done, quite simply, by increasing the levels of pay afforded to court interpreters to the extent that their remuneration is competitive with that given to "similarly qualified people in the private sector" (Shulman 1993, pp. 194–195; see also Hale 2004, p. 244; Laster and Taylor 1994, p. 22; de Jongh 1992, p. 121). Such a pay increase would have several positive effects on the availability of competent court interpreters.

First, increasing compensation to competitive levels would draw more qualified interpreters into the court interpreting market, thus improving overall quality in the market. Second, in addition to attracting more highly-qualified individuals back into the courtroom, better pay would likely help keep skilled courtroom interpreters working in that capacity (as opposed to transitioning into other, more lucrative professions). Third, improved remuneration for court interpreters would elevate the prestige and status for such interpreters within the interpreting profession and the judicial system (and perhaps even society generally) (see generally de Jongh 1992, p. 118). This, in turn, would make court interpretation a more attractive career prospect for beginning interpreters. In these ways, increasing the pay of court interpreters would contribute to an increase in the supply of competent interpreters willing to take such assignments; thereby making it more likely that a qualified interpreter would be appointed and overall quality improved.

Increasing the remuneration of court actors in order to raise the general level of competence exhibited by those employed is a solution that has been indirectly supported by the HRC as well. In its Concluding Observations on the State Report of Jamaica, the HRC expressed concern over the "state of current legal aid representation" and emphasized "that adequate remuneration of lawyers … would greatly assist in providing a proper defence of clients in a proper manner" (HRC Concluding Observations: Jamaica [1997] §14). While the HRC's comment arose in the context of the right to counsel, and they stopped short of requiring increased pay as a solution to poor representation, their statement, at a minimum, may be taken as an endorsement of the logic behind the proposal.

Unfortunately, although raising the level of pay for court interpreters has obvious merits, it also presents significant problems as well. At the outset, given the tight governmental budgets normally associated with the criminal justice system (Stern 2011, pp. 328, 339; de Mas 2001, p. 5; Scherr 1999, p. 2; Schweda-Nicholson 1989, p. 711), it is questionable whether sufficient money could (or would) be allocated by governments for this purpose. Furthermore, while increasing the pay of court interpreters would make it more likely that highly-qualified interpreters would take an interest in such assignments, the increased pay would in no way guarantee that courts would actually appoint those highly-skilled interpreters. As previously noted, courtroom personnel are often incapable of distinguishing between good and bad interpreters; as such, the increased compensation might simply funnel more money to the same incompetent interpreters the solution was meant to marginalize.

3.3 Mandatory Certification Standards

Another possible solution to improve the quality of courtroom interpreters involves mandatory certification procedures, wherein courts may only employ interpreters who have been judged competent using objective performance exams (Mikkelson 2000, p. 20). Requiring interpreters to pass such exams before accepting courtroom assignments not only ensures the competence of the interpreter, but it simultaneously relieves courtroom personnel of the impossible task of having to make such a determination. In this manner, highly qualified interpreters could be paid market value for their services, since the court would be objectively guaranteed that the quality of the interpreter merits such increased compensation. Likewise, interpreters without specialized courtroom skills would have a powerful incentive to participate in advanced training in order to achieve certification and the resulting increase in remuneration. Thus, in conjunction with increased training opportunities and improved pay, certification and other quality-control systems can result in a guaranteed higher standard of courtroom interpretation for criminal defendants.

Such certification procedures, however, have not always proved effective in practice. For instance, Australia maintains a nationwide accreditation system for interpreters and translators, but since accreditation is not mandatory, court interpreters are often employed without reference to their certification status (Hale 2011, p. xi; Hayes and Hale 2010, p. 123;

Laster and Taylor 1994, pp. 34–36). Even in jurisdictions where the court is technically required to appoint certified interpreters, the end result is often not dissimilar to the Australian experience. In the United States, for example, which maintains a mandatory certification system for its federal courts, only a very small percentage of court interpreters achieve certification (approximately 8% of exam takers) (de Jongh 2008, p. 25). Thus, the certification procedures serve to drastically reduce the number of qualified court interpreters available to the judiciary. The result is that judicial demand for certified interpreters far outstrips the available supply, leading to the eventual appointment of non-certified interpreters to make up the deficit (de Jongh 2008, p. 25; Kahaner 2008–2009, p. 228; Davis et al. 2004, pp. 14–15). Naturally, the employment of such interpreters defeats the purpose of having certification standards in the first place.

Moreover, maintaining the certification process itself is highly expensive and largely impractical in many instances (Stern 2011, p. 339; Mikkelson 2000, p. 18). Specific language exams (both oral and written) must be created and administered, and specialized interpreting skills somehow tested by independent (trained) assessors in an environment comparable to a courtroom setting. Given the attendant costs and the existence of over 7000 living languages throughout the world, providing certification exams in the rarer languages has proven cost-prohibitive in many instances (Stern 2011; p. 339; Romero 2008–2009, p. 29; Messier 1999, p. 1410). As such, even where certification procedures exist, they are often limited to only the most frequently employed languages (de Jongh 2008, p. 25; Kahaner 2008–2009, p. 228). The end result is that, while promising, the implementation of certification standards alongside increased pay and training is far from an assured solution to the scarcity of qualified courtroom interpreters.

3.4 Remote Video Interpreting

If the foremost reason for poor quality court interpretation is the overall lack of qualified and experienced court interpreters working in the market, then remote interpreting may prove a substantial aid in addressing these quality concerns. Unlike the other potential solutions mentioned previously, remote interpreting does not seek to increase the quantity or quality of court interpreters, rather it aims to more efficiently allocate those trained court interpreters that already exist. In remote interpreting, the court interpreter need not actually be present in the courtroom, rather they participate in the proceeding from a remote site, normally through a specialized videoconferencing system (Mikkelson 1998a, p. 7).

Remote video interpreting helps increase the overall quality of interpretation in several different ways. First, since the court interpreter can work from a different geographical location, courts are not restricted to finding an interpreter who resides in the immediate vicinity. This opens up a much larger pool of potential candidates, which is essential when dealing with rare language combinations, and allows courts to be more selective in their appointments. Second, eliminating geographical restrictions also reduces the burden of travel, and allows qualified interpreters to be more efficiently utilized (Mikkelson 1998a, p. 7). For instance, through remote interpreting, a court interpreter might handle several interpreting assignments in different jurisdictions all in one day. Remote interpreting thus gives courts access to the best interpreters, and provides those interpreters with the ability to work more often and more efficiently to meet judicial demand. Third, by handling more assignments in the same amount of time, the most qualified court interpreters can potentially earn a higher income, thereby providing a further incentive for other interpreters to obtain specialized training (Mikkelson 1998a, p. 7).[1] As such, remote interpreting can improve the overall quality of court interpretation by ensuring that the best court interpreters are more often available for appointment, and therefore more likely to be employed.

However, as promising as remote interpreting may sound, it too possesses considerable limitations. Since the interpreter is not in the same room with the speaker and the audience, their ability to notice and respond to visual clues is significantly limited, which can result in a less accurate translation (Braun and Taylor 2012, pp. 115–117; Kahaner 2008–2009, p. 231). In fact, a recent study has shown that remote video interpreting magnifies those problems that are already known to exist in legal interpreting, such as those errors associated with cognitive overload (Braun and Taylor 2012, pp. 115–117). The end result is that "the number of serious interpreting problems (e.g. omissions, additions, distortions, lexical/terminological problems, paralinguistic problems, turn-taking problems) was higher in remote interpreting compared to face-to-face interpreting" (Braun and Taylor 2012, pp. 115–117). Thus, any quality improvement gained by the employment of a more qualified court interpreter may actually be offset by the reduction in accuracy associated with video interpretation.

Furthermore, the regular usage of video interpreting requires that both court interpreters and judicial personnel undergo extra technological training, which can be both time-consuming and expensive. Moreover, the video technology must be installed in the courtrooms themselves, producing a substantial start-up cost that may be too onerous for smaller jurisdictions. There is also always the possibility that technological problems with respect to the audio or video will occur, significantly degrading the interpreters' ability to effectively interpret (Ogawa 2007, p. 31). Finally, there have been no significant studies done concerning the impact of video interpretation on the fact-finder's reception of interpreted testimony. Given the potential impact, as previously discussed, of the stylistic mannerisms of the interpreter on the believability of such testimony, complete removal of the interpreter from the courtroom is no small consideration.

3.5 Conclusion

While none of the suggestions presented above clearly and definitively improves the overall quality of court interpreters, each in their own way can serve as a single step in that direction. Requiring mandatory certification in the most frequently-used language combinations can guarantee a minimum standard of competence in the courtroom, thus allowing higher standards of pay to be given to those with the highest competence. Increased pay should expand the pool of qualified interpreters willing to work in a judicial setting, while simultaneously providing an incentive for untrained interpreters to develop their skills through specialized training. The use of video interpreting where a qualified face-to-face interpreter is not available should allow courts to substantially reduce the usage of *ad hoc* and unqualified interpreters. As such, a combination of each of these solutions can serve to incrementally improve the quality of court interpretation.

4 Better Oversight

Another possibility for increasing the accuracy of court interpretation involves the development of proper oversight mechanisms. Currently, most courts, even in highly developed and comparatively well-financed legal systems such as those on the European continent, lack adequate quality control systems to ensure the competency of work provided by court interpreters (eds. Hertog and van Gucht 2008, p. 197). Frequently, the court interpreter is the only individual capable of understanding both languages, and certainly the only participant likely to be educated in interpreting techniques and ethics (Hale 2004, p. 163). Moreover, there is rarely a verbatim record kept of any language other than that employed by the court (Stern 2011, p. 336; Kahaner 2008–2009, p. 226; de Mas 2001, p. 4; Messier 1999, p. 1408). Thus, little qualitative oversight is provided at any stage of the proceedings. There are, however, several ways in which acceptable oversight might be instituted.

4.1 Team Interpreting

One possible way to introduce quality control into interpreted proceedings is the employment of an extra interpreter. Team interpreting, whereby the two interpreters alternate turns every 30 minutes, is standard practice in conference settings and helps to alleviate the harmful effects arising from interpreter fatigue (Edwards 1995, p. 74; González et al. 1991, p. 510). The existence of a second interpreter, however, can also provide a practical method of oversight, since the inactive court interpreter could monitor the output of their active colleague (LaVigne and Vernon 2003, p. 921; Heller 1994–1995, pp. 381–382). In this manner, any mistakes or unclear interpretations would be immediately corrected, thus ensuring the ultimate accuracy of the evidence and the record. Furthermore, in addition to correcting errors as they occur, the existence of a second interpreter can also help to prevent errors before they occur: it is logical to assume that court interpreters subjected to contemporaneous oversight will interpret more carefully than those left on their own. Trechsel (2005) has made this very argument in relation to the preventative effect of the overall right to appeal (p. 362).

Unfortunately, the employment of a second interpreter is not without its drawbacks. The same concerns discussed above in the context of interpreting teams and fatigue apply equally with respect to oversight: adding a second interpreter increases courtroom expenses (Shulman 1993, p. 193; Steele 1991–1992, pp. 243–244); courtroom interpreters are not familiar with team interpreting techniques (Mason 2008, p. 8); and there can be substantial difficulty finding a second qualified interpreter in many instances (assuming it is even possible) (Shulman 1993, p. 193). An additional concern with interpreting teams particular to oversight situations involves the actual correction of errors themselves. Specifically, it is possible that the frequent correction of errors by the inactive interpreter may work to undermine the credibility and authority of the active interpreter, while also further adding to the length of the proceeding. As such, while the introduction of a second interpreter might help to improve the accuracy of the proceedings, such an action might also produce negative side effects that render its usage impractical.

4.2 Foreign Language Record

As previously mentioned, there exists little possibility to review the performance of court interpreters after the proceedings have been completed, since the standard practice in domestic courtrooms throughout the world is to only preserve a record of the proceedings in the language of the court (Kahaner 2008–2009, p. 226; de Mas 2001, p. 4; Messier 1999, p. 1408).[2] Thus, any appellate consideration of the interpreter's competence during the trial must rely exclusively on only one language or one side of the interpretation (eds. Hertog and van Gucht 2008, p. 198). This is akin to judging the accuracy of an answer without knowing the question asked. In short, it makes effective appellate scrutiny of interpreter performance virtually impossible.

One possible way in which to resolve this deficiency would be to record the proceedings in their entirety. This could be accomplished either through an audio record of both languages, or through a video record of the entire process (Kahaner 2008–2009, p. 229; LaVigne and Vernon 2003, p. 923; Davis and Hewitt 1994, p. 136; Heller 1994–1995, pp. 381–382; Hammond 1993; Shulman 1993, p. 194; Safford 1977, p. 27). Both methods have their proponents and opponents, but what is essential regardless of the exact manner employed is that there be some recorded evidence for appellate consideration of every utterance in every language used during the criminal proceedings. The existence of such a record could then form the basis of a substantive appeal concerning the actual demonstrated accuracy of the interpreter's performance. Even if the appellate judges themselves lack the competence to objectively analyze the record for interpreter error, they would at least be able to entertain arguments from experts, presumably put forward by appellate counsel, who are qualified to do so. The existence of such a multilingual record would at a minimum create the possibility of appellate oversight where none has heretofore existed. This, as noted above, is likely on its own to increase the accuracy of an interpreter's work (Trechsel 2005, p. 362).

Naturally, there are negative aspects related to the recording of trial proceedings as well. First, the practical difficulty of recording (audio or video) trial proceedings is fairly substantial. Not only can the equipment malfunction, but courtroom participants often move throughout the proceeding and vary their level of volume without reference to the recording devices (Berk-Seligson 1990, p. 49). As such, either the courtroom actors each must have individual microphones (which might prove immensely expensive), they must be confined to areas where a microphone exists (which might affect the comfort level of the participants), or someone must sit in the courtroom and operate a directional microphone (which might also add to the expense of the interpreted trial) (Berk-Seligson 1990, p. 49). Second, the introduction of recording devices or video cameras into the courtroom requires that such technology be purchased, and that someone be employed to coordinate and operate them, both of which place an added financial burden on the legal system (eds. Hertog and van Gucht 2008, p. 199). Finally, there is the real risk that the existence of a foreign language record, and the possibility of an appeal as to interpreter competence, would produce a flood of language-related appeals (both with and without merit) (Shulman 1993, p. 194). Not only would this increase the workload of appellate courts, but it also "is likely to reveal the huge risk involved in engaging unqualified interpreters in preparing evidential matters" (eds. Hertog and van Gucht 2008, p. 199). In other words, given the influence that interpreters can have on the fairness of a criminal proceeding and the prevalence of interpreter error as detailed in the previous Chapters, it is possible that effective appellate oversight of interpreting issues might ultimately undermine judicial confidence in the fairness of interpreted criminal proceedings. While such a result might help bring about the reform necessary to improve the accuracy of court interpreter performance, its short-term consequences would be very real and highly disruptive.

4.3 Conclusion

The development of more effective oversight procedures is an important aspect in decreasing the impact of court interpreters on the right to a fair trial. While the employment of interpreting teams may help eliminate interpreting errors during the course of an actual proceeding, better oversight overall can generate a dynamic that improves the level of interpreting throughout the entire criminal justice system. For example, the development of effective oversight will invariably lead to the occasional finding that an interpreter's performance was insufficient for the purposes of a fair trial. Such judgments will necessarily force trial courts to pay more attention to the quality of their interpreters, since real consequences can flow from the failure to do so. This in turn should lead to the overall improvement in the skill level of court interpreters who are employed within the system. Likewise, as the work of court interpreters is subjected to greater scrutiny, it is likely that these interpreters will be more cautious in their work, producing better interpretations. In this manner, the simple provision of better oversight can lead to a systemic improvement in the level of interpretation provided.

5 Final Thoughts

None of the proposals detailed above is a silver bullet that will solve all of the problems identified in this study. Some complications and errors are simply inherent in the complexity and absolute difficulty of the interpreting process: "*Der Himmel*" (German) will always mean either the sky or heaven, depending on the context. Increased rates of pay likely will lead to the employment of a better interpreter who has superior training. More informed court personnel will be more attuned to the needs of that interpreter, and she will therefore have more time to prepare and suffer from less fatigue. Improved oversight will ensure that many errors are subject to appellate review and correction. In short, conditions can be optimized for greater interpreter success. But, at the end of the day, the interpreter still must use her professional judgment based on the context of the word and choose between either the sky or heaven. Such an exercise of judgment may result in an incorrect choice, because humans make mistakes. Thus, some problems will inevitably remain, in spite of any changes to the system.

However, that some complications are inevitable is an unacceptable excuse for not eliminating those complications that are not. Where the State asserts its power to deprive an individual of his freedom, it must do so through the mechanism of a fair trial. This study has shown that court interpreters, as currently employed at the domestic level, jeopardize the fairness of such proceedings through the sheer magnitude and frequency of interpreter-created distortions. The options discussed above, while admittedly expensive and non-comprehensive, serve to diminish both the prevalence and significance of these distortions. As such, they lessen the negative impact that court interpreters can have on the right to a fair trial under international law. Given the findings of this study, this is an outcome that is well worth pursuing.

Notes

1. It is important in this context to understand that often court interpreters, though ostensibly paid by the hour, are generally not paid for the time they spend travelling, but rather only for the actual time they spend interpreting (see for example National Consultative Committee on Racism and Interculturalism 2007, p. 12).
2. Note also that many nations do not even preserve a verbatim record in the language of the court (eds. Hertog and van Gucht 2008, p. 197).

Bibliography

Aliverti, A., & Seoighe, R. (2017). Lost in Translation? Examining the Role of Court Interpreters in Cases Involving Foreign National Defendants in England and Wales. *New Criminal Law Review, 20*(1), 130–156.

Apostolou, F. (2012). Interpreting Services for Immigrants: A New Reality in Greece. *The Interpreters' Newsletter, 17*, 213–222.

Benmaman, V. (1992). Legal Interpreting: An Emerging Profession. *Modern Language Journal, 76*, 445–454.

Berk-Seligson, S. (1990). *The Bilingual Courtroom: Court Interpreters in the Judicial Process*. Chicago: University of Chicago Press.

Braun, S., & Taylor, J. L. (2012). AVIDICUS Comparative Studies – Part I: Traditional Interpreting and Remote Interpreting in Police Interviews. In S. Braun & J. L. Taylor (Eds.), *Videoconference and Remote Interpreting in Criminal Proceedings* (pp. 85–100). Cambridge: Intersentia.

Choolun, N. (2009). Lost in Translation? An Examination of Court Interpreting in Australia. *Queensland Law Student Review, 2*(1), 20–31.

Ciorciari, J., & Heindel, A. (2014). Experiments in International Criminal Justice: Lessons from the Khmer Rouge Tribunal. *Michigan Journal of International Law, 35*, 369–442.

Court Interpreter's Job Is No Easy Task. (2002, August 26). Japan Policy & Politics.

Davis, L. W., & Hewitt, W. E. (1994). Lessons in Administering Justice: What Judges Need to Know About the Requirements, Role, and Professional Responsibilities of the Court Interpreter. *Harvard Latino Law Review, 1*, 121–176.

Davis, L. W., McKell, M. N., Oldroyd, J. R., & Steed, B. C. (2004). The Changing Face of Justice: A Survey of Recent Cases Involving Courtroom Interpretation. *Harvard Latino Law Review, 7*, 1–25.

de Jongh, E. (1991). Foreign Language Interpreters in the Courtroom: The Case for Linguistic and Cultural Proficiency. *Modern Language Journal, 75*, 285–295.

de Jongh, E. (1992). *An Introduction to Court Interpreting: Theory & Practice*. Lanham: University Press of America.

de Jongh, E. (2008). Linguistic Presence v. Linguistic Absence. *Florida Bar Journal, 82*, 20–32.

de Mas, S. (2001). Translation, Interpreting & Legal Rights Within the European Union: The Law & Reality. In *Critical Link 3 – Interpreting in the Community: The Complexity of the Profession – Montreal* [online]. Available at: https://static1.squarespace.com/static/52d566cbe4b0002632d34367/t/5347f5f0e4b0bccee306dac1/1397224944878/CL3_deMas.pdf. Accessed 21 Nov 2017.

Edwards, A. B. (1995). *The Practice of Court Interpreting*. Amsterdam: John Benjamins.

Fowler, Y. (1995). The Courtroom Interpreter: Paragon and Intruder? In S. E. Carr, R. P. Roberts, A. Dufour, & D. Steyn (Eds.), *The Critical Link: Interpreters in the Community* (pp. 191–200). Amsterdam: John Benjamins.

González, R., Vásquez, V. F., & Mikkelson, H. (1991). *Fundamentals of Court Interpretation: Theory, Policy, and Practice*. Durham: Carolina Academic Press.

Grabau, C. M. (1996). Court Interpreting: View from the Bench. *State Court Journal, 20*(1), 6–11.

Hale, S. (2004). *The Discourse of Court Interpreting: Discourse Practices of the Law, the Witness and the Interpreter*. Amsterdam: John Benjamins.

Hale, S. (2007). Challenges of Court Interpreting: Intricacies, Responsibilities and Ramifications. *Alternative Law Journal, 32*, 198–202.

Hale, S. (2011). *Interpreter Policies, Practices and Protocols in Australian Courts and Tribunals: A National Survey*. Melbourne: AIJA.

Hammond, R. (1993, October 24). Lost in Translation; for Immigrants in Court, Bad Interpreters Rig the Jury. *Washington Post*, p. C3.

Hayes, A., & Hale, S. (2010). Appeals on Incompetent Interpreting. *Journal of Judicial Administration, 20*(2), 119–130.

Heller, D. J. (1994–95). The Language Bias in the Criminal Justice System. *Criminal Law Quarterly, 37*, 344–383.

Hertog, E., & van Gucht, J. (Eds.). (2008). *Status Quaestionis: Questionnaire on the Provision of Legal Interpreting and Translation in the E.U.* Antwerpen: Intersentia.

Ibrahim, Z., & Bell, R. T. (2003). Court Interpreting: Malaysian Perspectives. In L. Brunette, G. L. Bastin, I. Hemlin, & H. Clarke (Eds.), *The Critical Link 3: Interpreters in the Community* (pp. 211–222). Amsterdam: John Benjamins.

Kahaner, S. M. (2008–09). The Administration of Justice in a Multilingual Society – Open to Interpretation or Lost in Translation? *Judicature, 92*, 224–231.

Laster, K., & Taylor, V. L. (1994). *Interpreters and the Legal System*. Sydney: The Federation Press.

LaVigne, M., & Vernon, M. (2003). An Interpreter Isn't Enough: Deafness, Language, and Due Process. *Wisconsin Law Review, 2003*, 843–936.

Lindie, B. (1993). Inadequate Interpreting Services in Courts and the Rules of Admissibility of Testimony on Extrajudicial Interpretations. *University of Miami Law Review, 48*, 399–433.

Mason, M. (2008). *Courtroom Interpreting*. Lanham: University Press of America.

Messier, F. (1999). Alien Defendants in Criminal Proceedings: Justice Shrugs. *American Criminal Law Review, 36*, 1395–1419.
Miguélez, C. (1999). Current Issues in Court Interpreting: Spain, a Case Study. *Proteus, 8*(2), 1–4.
Mikkelson, H. (1998a). The Court Interpreter as Guarantor of Defendant Rights. In *First European Congress on Court Interpreting and Legal Translation – Graz* [online]. Available at: http://works.bepress.com/holly_mikkelson/8/. Accessed 21 Nov 2017.
Mikkelson, H. (1998b). Towards a Redefinition of the Role of the Court Interpreter. *Interpreting, 3*(1), 21 [online]. Available at: https://works.bepress.com/holly_mikkelson/17/. Accessed 21 Nov 2017.
Mikkelson, H. (2000). *Introduction to Court Interpreting*. Manchester: St. Jerome Publishing.
Moeketsi, R. H. (1999). *Discourse in a Multilingual and Multicultural Courtroom: A Court Interpreter's Guide*. Pretoria: van Schaik.
National Consultative Committee on Racism and Interculturalism. (2007). *Interpreting, Translation and Public Bodies in Ireland: The Need for Policy and Training* [online]. NCCRI. Available at: http://doras.dcu.ie/16924/1/Interpreting_Translation_and_Public_Bodies_in_Ireland_the_need_for_policy_and_training.pdf. Accessed 21 Nov 2017.
Ogawa, M. (2007). A Second Language Speaker in Court: Linguistic Phenomena Threatening Justice. *Alternative Law Journal, 32*(1), 28–31.
Phelan, M. (2011). Legal Interpreters in the News in Ireland. *Translation & Interpreting, 3*(1), 76–105.
Romero, B. G. (2008–09). Here Are Your Right Hands: Exploring Interpreter Qualifications. *University of Dayton Law Review, 34*, 15–33.
Safford, J. B. (1977). No Comprendo: The Non-English-Speaking Defendant and the Criminal Process. *Journal of Criminal Law & Criminology, 68*, 15–30.
Sandrelli, A. (2009). Interpreters in the Legal Process in Italy: A Survey. In *EULITA Conference – Antwerp* [online]. Available at: http://www.eulita.eu/sites/default/files/Interpreters%20in%20the%20legal%20process%20in%20Italy.pdf. Accessed 21 Nov 2017.
Scherr, D. (1999). Interpreting in Spain and Colombia: Two Perspectives – NAJIT Organizes International Round Table. *Proteus, 8*(3–4), 1.
Schweda-Nicholson, N. (1989). *Ad Hoc* Court Interpreters in the United States: Equality, Inequality, Quality. *Meta, 34*(4), 711–723.
Shulman, M. B. (1993). No Hablo Ingles: Court Interpretation as a Major Obstacle to Fairness for Non-English Speaking Defendants. *Vanderbilt Law Review, 46*, 175–196.

Steele, G. J. (1991–92). Court Interpreters in Canadian Criminal Law. *Criminal Law Quarterly, 34*, 218–251.
Stern, L. (2011). Courtroom Interpreting. In K. Malmkjær & K. Windle (Eds.), *The Oxford Handbook of Translation Studies* (pp. 325–342). Oxford: Oxford University Press.
Trechsel, S. (2005). *Human Rights in Criminal Proceedings*. Oxford: Oxford University Press.

Other Documents

Human Rights Committee. (1997, November 19). Concluding Observations of the Human Rights Committee. Jamaica. U.N. Doc. CCPR/C/79/Add.83.

Index[1]

A

Accent, 2, 80, 91, 263
Accreditation, *see* Certification
Accuracy, 26, 27, 40, 41, 59, 62, 71–74, 76, 81, 111, 131, 132, 159–161, 169, 173, 178, 179, 184, 188–191, 195–197, 212, 215, 218, 219, 226, 227, 234, 241, 251, 252, 255, 262, 263, 267, 268, 276, 277, 286, 291, 300, 302, 303, 311–315, 322–326
Actors, courtroom, 64, 97, 169, 311–315, 325
Adaptation, 86, 167–175, 179, 262, 264, 277, 286, 290, 300
Additions, *see* Content
Adversarial proceedings, right to, 104, 112–114, 134, 140, 151, 152, 173, 175, 235, 276, 285, 301
Advocacy, *see* Adaptation
Appeal, right to, 103, 104, 145–148, 289, 297–299, 301, 302, 323
Argot, 193–195, 197

B

Bias, *see* Impartiality

C

Capacity, cognitive, 77–82, 85, 88–98, 183, 251, 254, 255
Certification, 22–24, 40, 195, 260, 261, 319–320, 322
Charge
  autonomous, 17, 107

[1] Note: Page number followed by 'n' refer to notes.

J. H. Dingfelder Stone, *Court Interpreters and Fair Trials*,
https://doi.org/10.1007/978-3-319-75355-3

Charge (*cont.*)
criminal, 14, 16, 17, 36, 105, 107, 123, 125
right to be informed of, 104, 116–118, 174, 285
Communication
with counsel, right to, 119, 121, 134, 136–137
facilitator of, 68–69
non-verbal, 73, 91, 236–239
Conditions, working, 77, 252–255, 268, 311–312
Content
adding, 59, 203, 214, 279, 300, 314, 324
editing, 175–177
omitting, 94, 97, 186, 234
Control, issues of, 180–184
Coping strategies, 85, 90, 92–98, 175, 184–190, 196, 207, 208, 234, 241, 252, 255, 278
Counsel, right to, 104, 119, 121, 133–138, 151, 182, 289, 292, 294–295, 298, 299, 301, 318
Cultural, issues of, 24, 68, 193

D

Decalage, 56–58, 82, 84, 93–96, 96n5
Dialects, *see* Language
Discourse markers, 230–232, 240, 254, 279, 300

E

Editing, *see* Content
Effort Model, 54, 76–97
Efforts
coordination, 84–87
listening, 79–80, 82, 84, 88–90, 93
memory, 82–84, 88, 92, 93, 96
note-taking, 82–83
production, 80–82, 84, 87–89, 96
Elevation, *see* Style, speech
Equality, right to
equal access, right to, 108, 110, 111, 289
equality of arms, right to, 12, 108–112, 140, 174
Equivalence
legal, 199–200
linguistic, 197–199, 205
Ethics, 65, 75, 167, 169, 171, 253, 323

F

Facilities, right to adequate, 104, 118–123, 136, 143, 151, 152, 276
Fact-finders, 61, 144, 162, 163, 165, 166, 172, 173, 177, 179, 181–184, 193, 195–197, 202, 205, 210, 212–218, 220–222, 226–229, 234, 235, 237–240, 256, 262, 263, 267, 268, 276–280, 282–288, 295, 300, 301, 309, 322
Fairness, right to overall, 107, 149–151, 302–303
Fatigue, 4, 26, 95, 247–249, 253, 268, 314, 323, 324, 327
Fillers, 216, 232–235, 240, 279, 300
Friends, false, 5, 200–201, 203, 278, 300

H

Hedges, 71, 216, 232–235, 240, 279, 300
Hesitations, 71, 209, 215n4, 216, 217, 232–235, 239, 279, 300

I

Idioms, *see* Language, non-literal
Impartiality, 23n6, 178, 179, 254, 264–268, 312
Interpreter
  ad hoc, 259, 260, 265, 315, 322
  appointment of, 1, 2, 4, 10, 14–21, 25, 26, 260, 262, 265, 266, 296, 297, 320
  competence of, 20–25, 43, 122, 138, 148, 217, 260, 297, 319
  cost of, 32, 77
  defense, 62–63
  document, 63, 174
  multiple, 25–27, 29
  proceedings, 2, 4, 5, 9, 18, 26, 28, 34, 41, 59, 61–63, 113–114, 130, 151, 166, 167, 169, 241, 261, 265, 269, 311, 324
  remuneration, 317–319
  right to, 4, 9–44, 60, 68, 104, 105, 122, 138, 152, 289, 296–297, 299, 309
  role, 4, 62, 65–70, 76, 175–179, 205, 253, 256, 264, 266, 311–313, 315
  training, 21, 40, 77, 260, 286, 316–317
  witness, 60–61, 63
Interpreting
  consecutive, 56–58, 60, 64, 82, 85–87, 92, 93, 98, 180
  market, 257–261, 318
  remote, 320–322
  simultaneous, 56–57, 84–88, 93, 95
  summarization, 56
  team, Interpreter, multiple
  video, 320–322
Interruptions, 67, 93, 180, 182–184, 249, 312

J

Jargon, 193–197, 199, 201
Jurors, *see* Fact-finders

L

Language
  barrier, 1, 15, 26, 54n1, 69–70, 98, 122, 165, 169, 178, 203
  dialects, 91, 194–197, 250, 252, 263
  geographical variations, 194–195
  legal, 19, 20, 55, 58, 63, 168, 192–194, 199, 200, 209, 249, 253
  non-literal, 201–203, 206
  source, 55, 56, 59, 70, 73, 81, 82, 91, 94–98, 148, 187, 197, 199, 212, 256, 262, 264
  structure, 81, 95, 96, 185, 192, 211, 225
  target, 55, 58, 59, 70, 73, 81–83, 85, 87–89, 91, 94, 95, 98, 159, 187, 193, 196–199, 202, 203, 205, 209, 211, 225, 227, 231, 234, 236, 240, 249, 256, 261, 262, 267

M

Metaphors, *see* Language, non-literal

O

Omissions, *see* Content
Oral hearing, right to, 114–115, 276
Oversight, 1, 33–43, 145, 148, 164, 282, 297, 298, 301, 302, 310, 314, 323–327

P

Politeness, 216, 227–229, 238, 240, 279, 300
Pragmatic standard, 74, 161, 163, 165–167, 190, 191, 202, 205, 217, 237, 277
Preparation, lack of, 249–250, 252, 268
Presence, linguistic, 12, 133
Present, right to be, 11, 104, 112n2, 131–133, 173, 284, 288, 301

Q

Question, form of, 224–226

R

Record, trial, 39, 40, 42, 43, 163, 298, 299
Register, 73, 83, 219–221, 223, 229, 240, 256, 260, 267
Resources, mental, *see* Capacity, cognitive

S

Slang, 193–194, 196, 217, 263
Style, speech
  correction of, 168, 170–171, 175
  elevation of, 168, 170–171, 179
  generally, 2, 6, 283, 300
  impact of, 73, 97
  powerful, 216, 218–220, 223
  powerless, 216, 218, 219, 223, 234

T

Tightrope, theory of, 77–78
Time, right to adequate, 104, 136, 151, 276
Translation
  documents, 29–32, 30n7, 58, 63, 122, 250, 251
  right to, 30, 31
  sight, 56, 58–59, 63, 81, 84, 88, 250, 251, 256
Treatment, equal, *see* Equality, right to

U

Undue delay, right to be tried without, 104, 123–130, 289, 292–293

V

Verbatim standard, 73, 161–166, 237, 277, 285
Voice
  active, 221–223
  passive, 216, 221–223

W

Witnesses
- anonymous, 281, 283, 287, 288
- credibility, 114, 143, 173, 182, 215–219, 221, 226, 234, 235, 238, 240, 262, 263, 268, 278–280, 283, 286, 287, 324
- right to access related evidence, 143
- right to call, 10, 140–141, 145, 284, 298
- right to confront, 112n2, 141–143, 173, 226
- right to examine, 10, 104, 114, 115, 139–145, 152, 178, 181, 188, 197, 206, 214, 229, 232, 235, 239, 276, 281, 282, 284, 285, 288, 298

The manufacturer's authorised representative in the EU is Springer Nature Customer Service Centre GmbH, Europaplatz 3, 69115 Heidelberg, Germany. If you have any concerns regarding our products, please contact ProductSafety@springernature.com

Printed and bound by CPI Group (UK) Ltd, Croydon, CR0 4YY

25/09/2026

02222849-0011